Reading Hemingway's *The Sun Also Rises*

READING HEMINGWAY SERIES

ROBERT W. LEWIS, EDITOR

Reading Hemingway's *The Sun Also Rises*
   H. R. Stoneback

Reading Hemingway's *The Sun Also Rises*

GLOSSARY AND COMMENTARY

H. R. Stoneback

The Kent State University Press

KENT, OHIO

This book is for Sparrow
And for my students

Library of Congress Catalog Card Number 2006037406
ISBN: 978-0-87338-867-2
Manufactured in the United States of America

11 10 09 08 07   5 4 3 2 1

Library of Congress Cataloging-in-Publication Data
Stoneback, H. R. (Harry Robert), 1941–
    Reading Hemingway's The sun also rises : glossary and commentary / H.R. Stoneback.
        p.   cm. — (Reading Hemingway series ; 1)
    Includes bibliographical references (p.   ) and index.
    ISBN: 978-0-87338-867-2 (pbk. : alk. paper) ∞
    1. Hemingway, Ernest, 1899–1961. Sun also rises.   I. Title.
    PS3515.E37S9286 2007
    813'.52—dc22   2006037406

British Library Cataloging-in-Publication data are available.

CONTENTS

FOREWORD

Robert W. Lewis, Series Editor

The *Reading Hemingway* series of guides to Ernest Hemingway's (1899–1961) major works of fiction, short stories and novels, are written by scholar-teachers for students, fellow teachers, and other readers who also share an interest in the works of one of America's, and indeed the world's, outstanding writers. Just naming Hemingway's titles invokes recognition of his genius: "Big Two-Hearted River," *The Sun Also Rises, A Farewell to Arms,* "A Clean Well-Lighted Place," *The Old Man and the Sea,* "Hills Like White Elephants," *For Whom the Bell Tolls,* "The Snows of Kilimanjaro." His Nobel Prize in 1954 confirmed international recognition of his distinction, but it has been exceeded by the early, avid readership of each work that continues unabated and is likely to endure and to confirm an often-invoked maxim of Hemingway's: "*Il faut (d'abord) durer*" ("First of all one must endure"). Like some of the famed authors he learned from and sought to emulate or surpass, Hemingway endures, speaking to his readers through both his wisdom of worldly ways and his artistry in presenting them.

Our purpose is not to pursue a topic or theme such as "Hemingway's Pastoralism," "Hemingway and War," "The American Expatriates in Paris," "Hemingway As Existentialist," or any of the many rewarding approaches that have been and will continue to be taken to these works. Instead, the books in this series will gloss or annotate, page by page, word by word, if necessary, like a good guidebook to a city or country. These books will not tell Hemingway readers what to think and feel about an action, a character, or a place. Rather, the guides point out features and details possibly overlooked or misunderstood by the "visitors." As the good travel guide may enlarge one's experience of a place, its art, buildings, or neighborhoods, so these books, side by side with Hemingway's books, may enrich one's reading "tours."

Our plan and hope is to provide a reading or gloss of each detail that may be unfamiliar or obscure. Readers come to Hemingway's works with differing degrees of prior knowledge. The glosses may be glossed over by the cognizants or read carefully by the newcomers. The former users, however, knowing that Hemingway's plain style can mask subtleties, know to be alert to nuances and to attend to Hemingway's famous iceberg aesthetic. About seven-eighths of actual icebergs are submerged beneath the water's surface. Not knowing that hidden presence can be dangerous for sailors, as it infamously was for the passengers and crew of the *Titanic*. Hemingway drew an analogy to a writing style in which, similarly, concealment or omission implied a knowing presence, not omissions because of ignorance or, at the opposite end of such a range, overwriting or inflated prose.

In writing of the art of bullfighting in particular and of Spanish culture in general, in *Death in the Afternoon* (1932) Hemingway included two remarkable passages linking tauromachy to the art of writing. Writers, like bullfighters, may substitute fakery for "straight statement . . . to cover lack of knowledge or the inability to state clearly" (54), the bullfighters so doing in an analogous way. Then Hemingway famously and clearly stated his aesthetic in another—the "ice-berg"—analogy:

> If a writer of prose knows enough about what he is writing . . . he may omit things that he knows and the reader, if the writer is writing truly enough, will have a feeling of those things as strongly as though the writer had stated them. The dignity of movement of an ice-berg is due to only one-eighth of it being above water. A writer who omits things because he does not know them only makes hollow places in his writing. A writer who appreciates the seriousness of writing so little that he is anxious to make people see he is formally educated, cultured or well-bred is merely a popinjay. And this too remember; a serious writer is not to be confounded with a solemn writer. A serious writer may be a hawk or a buzzard or even a popinjay, but a solemn writer is always a bloody owl. (192)

Thus, these guides may help us note, navigate, and comprehend the "straight statement," but they may also help us see, feel, and understand the depth and success of Hemingway's art and craft, often "straight," often below the surface, subtle, and lovely, as both modern and ancient philosophers perceived existence as twisted, ambiguous, and paradoxical, yet sometimes present in honorable, dignified, and courageous ways.

Hemingway was a realist yet hopeful. "Reality cannot digest ideas," Jean Paul Sartre had thought. Hemingway witnessed and wrote about the stupidities and cruelties of the twentieth century. Studying his witness in his writings, beyond their aesthetic dimensions, may convince others of their continued importance. However much humanity has developed technologically, it is still often and largely bound by hypocrisy, ignorance, and mendacity, which Hemingway, with his heightened moral awareness, opposed often and well.

The Nobel Prize citation noted that "heroic pathos" centered Hemingway's elemental "awareness of life" and his "admiration for every individual who fights the good fight in a world of reality overshadowed by violence and death" (as quoted in Carlos Baker, *Ernest Hemingway: A Life Story,* 528).

Hemingway, the poet in prose, could not so pontificate. His *characters in action,* his stories could.

IN MEMORIAM

Years ago James C. Hinkle of the University of San Diego conceived of a series of books glossing and commenting on Ernest Hemingway's major novels and short stories. He recruited Hemingway scholar-teachers from around the country and began approaching potential university press publishers. He was something of a legend in Hemingway studies and could allegedly recite *The Sun Also Rises* from memory.

Hinkle's project was cut short by his premature death in 1990. (His parallel William Faulkner project was undertaken by Noel Polk as series editor for the *Reading Faulkner* series at the University Press of Mississippi, and Jim co-authored with Robert McCoy the first volume on *The Unvanquished* before his untimely death.) Jim himself was to have written the series book on *The Sun Also Rises,* but the co-editors-in-chief who succeeded him, Michael Reynolds and Paul Smith (also eminent Hemingway scholars), in turn died before launching the series.

Now at last the often-delayed series has begun with H. R. Stoneback's *Reading Hemingway's* The Sun Also Rises, and it is a study that richly rewards our patience. It is dedicated to the memories of James Hinkle, Michael Reynolds, and Paul Smith.

ROBERT W. LEWIS

PREFACE AND ACKNOWLEDGMENTS

Since its publication eight decades ago, *The Sun Also Rises* has come to be universally regarded as one of the most important twentieth-century American novels. It endures not just as a masterpiece of modernism and a vivid compelling study of expatriate life in the 1920s but also as a benchmark by which the reader may measure Hemingway's art and craft, his values and vision. *The Sun Also Rises* stands at the center of Hemingway's artistic achievement, one of the three or four enduring glories of his art. If I did not believe that, and if I had not found that view confirmed in my teaching of this novel to more than 4,000 students—from freshmen to graduate students—over the last four decades, if I had not discovered, in lecturing on Jake Barnes's narrative from the University of Paris to Peking University, from the Rotary Club of Bangkok to small-town American audiences at local libraries, that students, scholars, and readers of every description find this novel perpetually fascinating, compelling, and forever fresh and new, then I would not have spent decades learning to read truly and deeply one of the modern masterworks of fiction. Nor would I have spent years writing this book, in which the results, the lessons of all that study are recorded. This book is intended to serve all readers—students and teachers at every level, literary scholars and Hemingway specialists, and that perhaps mythical creature, the general reader—as they have served so well in contributing to my understanding, my *reading* of Hemingway.

In his foreword to this, the first volume of the *Reading Hemingway* series, Robert W. Lewis stresses Hemingway's famous iceberg aesthetic and the necessity for the reader to be alert to nuances and allusions, the seven-eighths of the story that is beneath the surface. Hemingway often noted that for every part of his writing that shows there is seven-eighths of it submerged, and whatever the reader gets from his writing will be the measure of what is brought to the reading. This book is designed as an exercise in close reading, grounded in narrative and aesthetic concerns as well as history, local knowledge, actual and symbolic landscape and inscape, and every aspect of what might be regarded as part of the submerged iceberg of the fiction. My purpose is to equip the reader to sound the depths, to take the full measure of the novel's allusiveness, obliquity, indirection, and understatement. When Hemingway went to Chartres and changed the title of his novel from *The Lost Generation* to *The Sun Also Rises,* he may have seen there an iconic depiction of the Cathedral of Chartres with a vast sun rising over it. Upon close examination, it can be noted that the sun is depicted as a circular labyrinth. Labyrinths, of course, suggest wrong turns and dead ends but they also convey the certain knowledge that there is a way through the maze, a path that must be followed to reach the center. *The Sun Also Rises* is a labyrinthine work, intricate, complicated, with interconnected passages leading ultimately to the center of Hemingway's vision.

Since I began my serious study of *The Sun Also Rises* in the 1970s, many people have contributed to my understanding of the novel and Hemingway matters in general. It would be impossible to acknowledge all the writers and critics whose work has been important to me over half a lifetime of study. Here I can only acknowledge those whose contributions have been personal, such as Carlos Baker, Mary Hemingway, Michael Reynolds, and William Walton, for encouraging my earliest ventures in Hemingway criticism. And then there was James Hinkle, who, as Robert Lewis notes, first conceived this series of Hemingway commentaries. When I first met Jim at a Faulkner Conference in the early 1980s, he was introduced to me as the legendary figure who could recite *The Sun Also Rises* from memory. I had only known Jim a few days when I challenged him to recite the novel, more in a spirit of fun than exactitude, and not because I had committed it to memory, although I did think I would recognize any passages where he missed a word or a line. He sailed flawlessly through the first two chapters but then I caught him when he fumbled a few lines from the third chapter. From that night on, Jim and I were friends, a friendship sealed in our love for *The Sun Also Rises*. When he began working on his commentary, the prototype for this study, he asked me to serve as his advisory reader, a task I cheerfully accepted. We had intensive conversations and exchanged long letters about details in the novel; before his death in 1990 I had provided commentary on the first draft of Hinkle's gloss of the first three chapters. After Jim's death, his project was taken over by William Balassi. Again, I agreed to serve as reader and exchanged letters with Balassi on his unfinished draft. Although I differed with Hinkle and Balassi on many points, their early work on a glossary of the novel paved the way for this book; thus I salute James Hinkle and William Balassi.

By the time I contracted to do this book the series editor was Robert W. Lewis. No writer could ask for a better editor—for his perspicacious commentary on details and larger matters of design, for his patience and steady encouragement when unforeseeable multiple surgeries and extensive hospitalization made it seem impossible to conclude this book, I salute Bob Lewis. Likewise, I am grateful to Larry Grimes and Allen Josephs, who served admirably as readers for this volume, providing valuable suggestions (sometimes under tight deadlines) and support. I especially want to express my gratitude to everyone at the Kent State University Press who worked on this volume, from editor-in-chief Joanna Hildebrand Craig, who offered much encouragement and guidance along the way, to Sonia Fülöp, whose fine copyediting improved the book.

I also wish to thank the State University of New York for sabbatical and research support over the years, which facilitated my work on this project. And my colleagues in the SUNY–New Paltz English department who encouraged this undertaking, especially my colleague Daniel Kempton, always willing to listen to my divagations regarding a novel and a writer far removed from his specialty and to drive across the county to reform my Luddite grasp of computer mysteries.

I am grateful to the Hemingway Society and Foundation for its support, especially to all my Hemingway Society colleagues who have listened to and commented on my papers on *The Sun Also Rises* since that first memorable conference on Thompson Island in 1980, when the Society was founded; and before that, at Don Noble's landmark Hemingway Conference at the University of Alabama in 1976. Thanks are due also to the librarians and archivists who facilitated my research, particularly to the Hemingway Collection staff at the John F. Kennedy Library in Boston, and the Firestone Library at Princeton.

I wish to thank the photographers who have contributed to this volume, most notably Kimmy Ruth and Brad McDuffie, who followed me around France and Spain on a Hemingway Pilgrimage in 2006, taking pictures of sites I deemed important to *The Sun Also Rises*. The fact that most of these places remain fundamentally unchanged since 1926 underlines the ways in which Hemingway chose to write about the real old things, the good places that do not change. Above all, I want to thank my graduate students, especially William Boyle and Matthew Nickel, for fetching research materials from places otherwise inaccessible and for much else besides; and all the friends and students who have accompanied me on *Sun Also Rises* pilgrimages, in classes *and* in France and Spain, those who have in many ways helped to keep the wheel(chair) turning and supported and contributed to the writing of this book—Larry Beemer, Michael Beilfuss, Mark Bellomo, Ed Butler, Nicole Camastra, Damian Carpenter, Jane Dionne, Steven Florczyk, Radmila Genyuk, Edward Meisel, Adam Romano, Jenica Shapiro, James Stamant, and Goretti Vianney-Benca. And Ann Gregory, coach, friend, and physical therapist who made me believe I could climb again to my third-floor study and library and finish this book.

Finally, I want to thank Jane Arden Stoneback—Sparrow—who has made all the pilgrimages with me and understood them, who has been fellow pilgrim and navigator from Paris to Roncevaux to all the other places, who has put up with the aftermath clutter from these pilgrimages, the scholarly detritus and debris on four floors of our house, who has been the first and best reader of everything I have written, who believed this book would someday be finished and—through it all—kept on singing.

SERIES NOTE

The following commentaries are keyed to the page and line numbers of the Scribner Library, Scribner Classics, and Simon and Schuster editions of the novel in which chapter 1 begins on page 3 and pages run to the last chapter, 19, ending on page 247. Line numbers begin with the first line of each page.

The commentaries can be read in tandem with the novel, chapter by chapter, or all together after a complete reading of the novel. The guide is like other reference works that may be consulted variously by different readers. We believe this *Reading Hemingway* book will greatly increase one's pleasure and understanding of *The Sun Also Rises,* one of Hemingway's finest works.

Reading *The Sun Also Rises*

FRONT MATTER

Title: At various stages of its writing and revision, Hemingway considered different titles for his first novel: *Fiesta, Rivers to the Sea, Two Lie Together, The Old Leaven, Perdu, Lost,* and *The Lost Generation.* In late September 1925, he went to spend a few days alone in Chartres, the great cathedral city of France, eighty-three kilometers from Paris. He took with him the manuscript of his novel; it had been called *Fiesta,* but Hemingway rejected the use of "a foreign word" for his title and then considered *The Lost Generation.* While he was in Chartres he wrote in his notebook a foreword to "The Lost Generation: A Novel," in which he told his first version of an anecdote about Gertrude Stein and a garage owner's proclamation that the World War I generation was a "lost generation." During his time in Chartres, in the shadow of the cathedral, with its multiple reverberations in sculpted stone and stained-glass iconography of Hemingway's subtextual subject matter in his novel—resonances of Roland and Roncevaux, motifs of pilgrimage, biblical allusions, Catholic historicity, art, ritual, tradition, and authority—Hemingway decided to change his title. "The chief result of his trip to Chartres," Carlos Baker notes, "was the decision to change the name of his first novel to *The Sun Also Rises*" (*Life Story* 155). It is a change of crucial import, accomplished in a symbolic landscape, sacred terrain that signifies—in the ancient and numinous Catholic Pilgrimage city of Chartres. Readers who are inclined to view the novel as pessimistic or despairing should pay close attention to Hemingway's process of title selection: if the title had been "The Sun Also Sets" or "The Sun Also Goes Down" or "The Lost Generation," it might seem a very different novel (see also Svoboda, *Crafting of a Style* 106–10).

In his Chartres notebook foreword, Hemingway pondered what redemption was available to his generation: "There will be many new salvations brought forward. My generation in France for example in two years sought salvation in First the Catholic Church, 2nd DaDaism"—here he had first written "Communism" before crossing it out—"third The Movies Fourth Royalism Fifth The Catholic Church again" (*Facsimile* 2:628). After his foreword he wrote a list of titles, with *The Sun Also Rises* at the top of the list, and *The Old Leaven* (the only other title underlined) at the end of the list. He must have known, with his superb eye and ear for titles, that *The Old*

Leaven was not a good title, even if it did point toward his novel's submerged thesis, the "salvations" it "brought forward": the *old* rituals and traditions, such as those of the bullfight and the Catholic Church, the *old* values that had been neglected and must be relearned, the *old* joys and delights, such as fishing and wine, that had been forgotten or prohibited. These old things would be the leaven, the agents that would lighten or enliven life and cause it to "rise." Hemingway's ear, already well attuned to French, may have heard in *leaven* the French *levain* (yeast), or *lever* and *se lever* (to raise, to rise), and maybe he already envisioned what would be his novel's title in French: *Le soleil se lève aussi.* Fortunately, his excellent ear selected the best biblical title—*The Sun Also Rises*—and his time in Chartres would have confirmed the wisdom of that choice, given the cathedral's traditional orientation to the rising sun, symbol of the risen Christ. Any guidebook he might have consulted regarding the cathedral would have drawn Hemingway's attention to the many depictions in stone and glass of the conflict between the Virtues and the Vices, to the famous maze on the floor of the nave, which symbolized the penitential path of the pilgrim, to the *Vierge au Pilier* (the Virgin of the Pillar, iconographical cognate to the *Virgen del Pilar* in Zaragoza, Spain), and to many other subjects that would become recurrent motifs in his work. And if he bought, as any curious traveler or even the casual tourist would, the standard guidebook then available at Chartres, *The Tourist's Practical Guide Book* (1924) by Étienne Houvet, Hemingway would have learned many things about the cathedral—ranging from structural matters ("without heaviness," "perfect in its proportions"), to religious mysteries everywhere depicted in the "mystic city" of the cathedral, to the importance of "two of the most beautiful windows in the church . . . that of Charlemagne and Roland," and, next to it, "that of Saint James the Great" (Houvet 3, 23). These matters would all be important in the months after Hemingway's stay at Chartres, when he faced months of difficult revision, tightening (and lightening) the structure, perfecting the proportions, crafting the iconography, and intensifying the Catholic themes and subtexts of his first and—for many readers—his best novel. In an unpublished essay entitled "On Cathedrals," in which Hemingway discussed cathedrals and different kinds of literary and Catholic conversions, he noted that certain places were not good for writing but were very good for *rewriting,* for "seeing what is not true and *seeing the true that you have not put in* and it is always much clearer and easier to re-write something in one of these places than where it was first written" (emphasis added; as quoted in Reynolds, *Paris Years* 326). And for seeing the "not true" in *The Sun Also Rises*, for "seeing the true" not yet put in, and beginning the process of rewriting—Chartres was the place.

Epigraphs: Just as Hemingway's titles are crucial clues to theme and emphases, so too are his epigraphs. It has not always been obvious to readers and commentators that Hemingway does not present Gertrude Stein's "lost generation" proclamation as a slogan to be endorsed, but as fatuous grandiloquence to be undercut, not only by the wisdom reflected in the second epigraph, from Ecclesiastes, but also by the action and design of the novel. Hemingway was pleased when reviewers recognized that he did not take "the Gertrude Stein thing very seriously," that he intended to "play off against that splendid bombast" (*Selected Letters* 229). Stein's "assumption of prophetic roles" is mocked just as much by the juxtaposed epigraph as it is by the larger motions of the novel: "Nobody," Hemingway said, "knows about the generation that follows them and certainly has no right to judge" (229). All generations were "lost," Hemingway would maintain, but at least his generation was conscious of how they were lost and how they might be "found." After the first printing of the novel, which carried a longer version of the epigraph from Ecclesiastes, Hemingway urged his editor, Maxwell Perkins, to "lop off the Vanity of vanities, saith the preacher, vanity of vanities; all is vanity—What profit hath a man of all his labour which he taketh under the sun?—delete all that" (229). Such precision regarding the content of the epigraph should lead the reader to recognize both Hemingway's exactitude and his skill as homilist, pointing to his actual message even before the novel begins. He does not presume to be the "Preacher" of Ecclesiastes, but he preaches obliquely nevertheless. The revised epigraph, he tells Perkins, "makes it much clearer. The point of the book to me was that the earth abideth forever—having a great deal of fondness and admiration for the earth and not a hell of a lot for my generation and caring little about Vanities." His novel, he insists, is not "a hollow or bitter satire but a damn tragedy with the earth abiding for ever as the hero" (229). The second epigraph, as printed in the shorter version since the second printing of the novel, consists of Ecclesiastes 1.4–7. (It should be noted that the ellipses do not indicate omitted words, but verse breaks.) Hemingway is astute in his insistence on the deletion of the "vanity," for that might seem to diminish the cyclical sense of renewal that he wishes to emphasize—the sun *rising* on the abiding earth. Nevertheless, it is useful for all readers to consult the entire book of Ecclesiastes as a kind of submerged subtext for *The Sun Also Rises.* In the manuscript pages where he lists tentative titles for the novel, Hemingway writes: "For in much wisdom is much grief; and he that increases [i.e., increaseth] knowledge increaseth sorrow" (*Facsimile* 2:629). This slight misquotation of Ecclesiastes 1.18 is a telling signpost for the progress of Jake's pilgrimage, his movement over the "abiding earth," his wisdom and grief, his knowledge and sorrow.

Years later in his memoir of Paris in the 1920s, *A Moveable Feast,* Hemingway tells another version of Stein's declaration that all the young men who served in the war were a lost generation: "'Don't argue with me, Hemingway,' Miss Stein said. 'It does no good at all. You're all a lost generation, exactly as the garage keeper said.'" Hemingway then notes how he tried to balance Stein's quotation with the Ecclesiastes epigraph, and he implicitly charges her with "egotism and mental laziness versus discipline," and he thinks: "Who is calling who a lost generation?" He concludes: "But the hell with her lost-generation talk and all the dirty, easy labels"

(*Moveable Feast* 29–31). Readers of *The Sun Also Rises* would do well to exercise caution with regard to the "easy labels" that have been affixed to the novel in the course of eight decades of literary criticism.

CHAPTER 1

3:1 **Robert Cohn:** Cohn is a common variant spelling of Cohen (census records indicate a total of 39,772 occurrences, 3,730 in the 1920 census), a surname said to be of Hebrew origin, signifying rabbi, bishop, or priest. In general practice the name Cohn is *not* pronounced "con," but in the same manner as Cohen, or "cone." Thus there is no hint of the "con man" in Robert's character; nor would there seem to be any rabbinical or priestly wisdom or authority. It is well known that Robert Cohn was based, to some degree, on Harold Loeb, Hemingway's friend who accompanied him to the 1925 fiesta at Pamplona. Loeb was of distinguished lineage—his mother was a Guggenheim, his father a member of Kuhn, Loeb and Company. Hemingway may have echoed the latter fact in the roughly homophonic naming (Cohn/Kuhn) of his character. It is interesting to note that the Loebs had strong, and far longer, associations with Harvard than with Princeton; they were major Harvard alumni benefactors from the 1880s to the 1930s (Synnott 11–12). Loeb certainly served as a partial model in the early stages of the novel's composition, but given Hemingway's axiom, embraced years before *The Sun Also Rises,* that the writer must invent from what he knows, that "writing about anything actual was bad," and that "everything good he'd ever written he'd made up," Loeb's role as initial character-model tells us nothing substantial about the *created* character of Cohn ("On Writing" 237). Long after *The Sun Also Rises* appeared, Loeb published his memoir *The Way It Was* (1959) and, after Hemingway's death, an article entitled "Hemingway's Bitterness" that was included (with memoirs by other presumed prototypes for Hemingway's characters) in Bertram Sarason's *Hemingway and "The Sun" Set* (1972), a study of the novel as roman à clef. All such reminiscences belong to the terrain of memoir, a very different country from the *terroir* of fiction.

It is far more important to give careful consideration to Hemingway's last-minute revisions that made "Robert Cohn" the first words of the novel and the primary subject of character presentation and analysis in the opening chapters. As late as the galleys, the novel began: "This is a novel about a lady. Her name is Lady Ashley and when the story begins she is living in Paris and it is Spring. That should be a good setting for a romantic but highly moral story" (Svoboda, *Crafting of a Style* 99). The radical changes suggested in Scott Fitzgerald's critique (*after* publication-ready copy had been sent to Scribners) convinced Hemingway to cut his first chapter, with its focus on Brett Ashley as the central subject of the novel, and much of his second chapter. Fitzgerald was surely right in urging Hemingway to get rid of the "careless + ineffectual" prose, the "condescending *casualness*" of the tone (Svoboda, *Crafting of a Style* 137–40). Rather than revision, Hemingway chose radical excision, and in the process he sacrificed some valuable background information about Brett and Jake. More important, by delaying Brett's appearance in the novel until more than midway through chapter 3, and beginning instead with Robert, he risked altering the focus, the deep structure, and the very rhythms of his "novel about a lady." Put another way, it could be argued that this revision radically and unduly foregrounds Robert Cohn as the principal subject of the novel. Indeed, after the opening chapters, and especially after chapter 6, Cohn is increasingly absent from the narrative, from the *rendered* action of the novel. He remains present, primarily as a touchstone of bad behavior, as it becomes clear that this is Jake's story "about a lady," and thus ultimately a story about himself. The revised beginning does have the effect of clarifying for the reader that this is, in one sense, a novel of manners, one concerned with conduct and character. And if Robert Cohn is a principal antiexemplar (as opposed to such exemplars as Count Mippipopolous, Montoya, and Pedro Romero), it may be a very effective strategy to begin with a definition of antiexemplary behavior before attempting to articulate, or codify, the "values" (see the crucial scene with the count, 57–61) that are the foundation of exemplary behavior.

3:1–6 **boxing . . . Princeton:** Since Robert Cohn is thirty-four years old in 1925 (see 9:9), it is likely that he entered Princeton in 1909 and graduated in 1913 (as did Harold Loeb, who was a wrestler, not a boxer, at Princeton). One reason that Jake is not impressed by Robert's championship title is that there was no intercollegiate boxing—only student boxing clubs—at Princeton from 1880 to 1919. At best, Robert's "title" would have been *intramural.* Another reason Jake is not impressed is implicit in Robert's dislike of the very sport at which he excels; his lack of passion suggests for Jake (and Hemingway) a certain inauthenticity, a betrayal of the spirit of sportsmanship. If boxers figure importantly in the novel as adumbration of the role of bullfighters, Cohn may be seen as a precursor to the bullfighter gone bad, the bullfighter without passion (e.g., the later out-of-retirement Belmonte, as compared to Romero, 213–15).

In fact, the reason given for Robert's pursuit of excellence in boxing—"to counteract the feeling of inferiority" he experienced as "a Jew at Princeton"—sheds historically precise light on anti-Semitism at Princeton in the early 1900s, and athleticism as the primary path to undergraduate success. In Robert's freshman year, 1909, Princeton admitted the largest number of Jewish students in its history—thirteen—a number not surpassed until the 1920s. (In comparison, Harvard admitted seventy-one Jewish students in 1909.) Princeton long had the lowest Jewish student enrollment of any Ivy League institution—in 1918, for example, Princeton's total was 30, Harvard's 385, Penn's 596, and Columbia's 1,475 (Synnott 16, 96, 181). Edwin Slosson's 1910 volume, *Great American Universities,* reported that anti-Semitism was "more dominant at Princeton than at any of the other" major universities he studied; it was commonly said that "if the Jews once got in," they would "ruin Princeton as they have Columbia and Pennsylvania" (105–6). Clearly, Jake is aware of Princeton's reputation for anti-Semitism. The important question to ask is what does Jake feel about Robert's experience as outsider, as the despised "other," at Princeton? Since Jake is Catholic, he surely knows that Princeton also had a reputation for anti-Catholicism; indeed, in 1909, when thirteen Jewish students matriculated, only fifteen Catholic students matriculated at Princeton, and both groups were treated with equal scorn (Synnott 179).

Thus Jake's meditation on Robert's experience of anti-Semitism at Princeton may indicate one important reason that Jake is, at the beginning of the novel, Robert's friend. Jake is empathetic because he knows that as a Catholic he, too, would have experienced Robert's sense of "outsiderness" at Princeton. In this Cohn-at-Princeton sketch that opens the book, then, it can be seen that Jake identifies with Robert, not with Princeton. He likes Robert at the outset; he thinks they share a love of sports, and they *are* tennis friends. At Princeton, undergraduate "success was measured principally by athletic accomplishment." Even if you were Catholic (but not if you were Jewish), "athletic honor" might well result in an invitation to join one of the prestigious, otherwise-closed, all-WASP eating clubs, such as the Tiger Inn, "which prided itself on the athletic prowess of its members" (Synnott 178). Given all these historical facts, one wonders why Robert went to Princeton. In the characteristic early twentieth-century view of the typical student at the "Big Three" American Universities, the Yale man, known for "conformity," had to be "athletic, hearty, extroverted," and the Harvardian, known for "individualism," was associated with "intellectualism" and "eccentricity"; but the Princetonian had to be "neither a strong individualist . . . nor a conformist," and what mattered most was to be "'smooth'—that is, socially adroit and graceful" (Synnott 4). Why indeed did Robert go to Princeton? He is anything but smooth, socially adroit, and graceful, and the progress of Jake's disenchantment with Robert is more an index of his social clumsiness and gracelessness than it is a mark of anti-Semitism. The fabric of the novel has threads of the widespread cultural anti-Semitism of its time woven throughout, yet Jake's focus remains fixed on Robert's conduct, the particularity of his behavior as an individual human being, not as a member of a prejudicially excluded or derided group. To dismiss the anti-Semitism clearly represented in the novel, to treat it as merely reflective of its time and place, as many commentators have, may risk evasion of a problematic matter; but to fail to see the rigorous focus on individual conduct is to miss one of the novel's primary themes entirely (see, e.g., Traber 169–72).

3:9–10 **Spider Kelly:** There have been many boxers named Spider Kelly, more than twenty of them, and five who were in the ring during the 1888–1915 era. It has been widely and apparently erroneously reported that Hemingway's Spider Kelly was an undefeated flyweight who fought from 1887 to 1901. Detailed boxing records from as far back as 1880 indicate only one flyweight Spider Kelly, with a record of 0-1 in his one fight in 1924. In fact, since almost all the Spider Kellys (and dozens of other Kellys) who fought in the pertinent years had dismal records, with more losses than wins, it could be that Hemingway, who was familiar with boxing history, chose the name "Spider Kelly" as a kind of marker for those familiar with boxing history, to indicate that supposed star-pupil Robert Cohn had a less than admirable trainer and thus was not much of a boxer, thereby underlining Cohn's other antiexemplary traits. This assumption does not ring wholly true, since Jake seems to admire Spider Kelly, and he seems to see Spider's training skills reflected in Robert's performance in the ring—"very fast" and "good." The historical subject files of the Seeley G. Mudd Manuscript Library at Princeton contain materials indicating that John H. "Spider" Kelly was head of Princeton's boxing programs from 1902 or 1903 until his death in 1937. I can find no record of a John *H.* Kelly among boxers active from 1880 to 1903, or at any other time. Of the twenty-six John Kellys with listed fights in boxing archives, all but two began their boxing careers after 1910. According to Princeton archivist Daniel Santamaria, "The establishment of a boxing program, at either the intramural or intercollegiate level, was a matter of some debate" at Princeton during the years of John H. Kelly's presence there (letter to author, 2 March 2005).

The Princeton archives also contain a 1940 article entitled "The Manly Art of Self-Defense" (no author given) with information about John H. Kelly. A hard-hitting iron foundry worker from Trenton, New Jersey, he is said to have received his "Spider" sobriquet from Gentleman Jim Corbett because he was so fast and moved in the ring like a "nervous insect." He turned professional in 1887, and he "easily became champion of the Paperweight class (less than 100 lbs)"—how many boxers were there *under* 100 pounds? Eventually, it is reported, he won the flyweight and bantamweight titles "and then courageously fought George Dixon for the Featherweight crown[,] receiving a draw decision." Another fighter he is reported to have fought is one Jack Hagen, with whom he toured the country during the war, "giving exhibition bouts for the Liberty Loan drives," and raising millions of dollars. It is reported that he had been "unbeaten in the professional ring" from 1887 to 1902, before he came to Princeton in 1903 "as boxing instructor, on a private fee basis." This 1940 article indicates that he gave private lessons to boxing club members, or to whoever sought instruction. There are several problems to be noted here: (1) If he was a champion, an undefeated professional for fifteen years, why is there no mention of him in detailed boxing archives that list even the fights of winless boxers who had career records of 0-1 (including at least two Spider Kellys)? (2) If he fought George Dixon, who was featherweight champion (record: sixty-three won, twenty-nine lost, forty-seven draw), why is there no record of it in the detailed list of Dixon's fights? (3) Dixon did fight a draw with the Bantamweight Tommy Spider Kelly ("The Harlem Spider") in 1888 but it was not a title fight and this Spider Kelly's dismal career record was five won, eight lost, four draw. (4) Dixon fought a certain Paddy Kelly twice in 1888–1889; this Kelly fought him to a draw in 1888 and lost in 1889, and that was his total fight career: 0-1-1. (5) If Princeton's Spider Kelly fought one Jack Hagen, why is there no listing of such a fight, no record of any boxer named Jack Hagen? The answer may lie between the lines of an article that celebrates Spider Kelly as synonymous with Princeton boxing and equally trumpets his Irish wit and gift for storytelling (*The Nassau Sovereign*). An obituary article from the Princeton archives notes that Spider Kelly was "a figure surrounded by legend, brimming with color . . . ready Irish wit . . . countless stories" ("Obituary" 729). Clearly a beloved figure at Princeton, this Spider Kelly (who claimed he didn't know how old he was) also seems to have been a man well acquainted with the Blarney Stone and other magical sources of talk and storytelling.

3:11 **featherweights:** Boxers weighing between 118 and 127 pounds are known as featherweights. It would be a forced reading to detect here the secondary sense of featherweight, meaning an insignificant or unimportant person or thing. Neither Jake nor Hemingway would base approval or disapproval of boxers on their weight class. Indeed both Jake and Hemingway admired Charles Ledoux, the bantamweight (i.e., 112–118 pounds, thus lighter than a featherweight) who was regarded as one of the hardest punchers, pound for pound, in boxing history (see 80:8–9).

3:17–18 **read too much:** This is the first of numerous references to Robert's reading, which is an important motif in chapters 2, 3, and 6. The reference to Robert's "spectacles" is echoed in later allusions to his nearsightedness and introduces a significant pattern of eye and vision imagery that recurs throughout the novel.

4:3–10 **mistrust:** By the second paragraph of the novel, Jake has mentioned three times Cohn's supposed title—"middleweight boxing champion." He is naturally suspicious of this claim both because it probably comes off as undergraduate boastfulness and because he knows there was, strictly speaking, no boxing championship, or nothing but club boxing and private instruction, at Princeton. Whatever Cohn's "title" was, if any, his classmates do not remember him—and this was Princeton at a time when athletic skill was the key to undergraduate popularity. Moreover, Jake is a precise observer and a kind of investigative reporter who likes to see truly and get the facts right. Finally, given his experience of the world, Jake mistrusts the very notions of frankness and simplicity. But he does get Robert's boxing "story" verified indirectly from Spider Kelly, whose reputation for storytelling, for blarney, may also have some bearing on the reports of Robert's championship. And maybe Robert learned more than just boxing from Spider Kelly, especially if we see Robert as a romantic storyteller given to fantasy and daydreams, with a deficient sense of fact.

4:18–19 **nice boy:** The repetition of the word "boy" stresses Jake's view—later confirmed —of Robert's immaturity for a man of thirty-four, his perpetual "undergraduate" demeanor. At the same time, Jake sees Robert as "nice," "friendly," and "shy," endearing qualities that help to explain Jake's friendship with him. Jake's addition of "bitter" to his list of Robert's personality traits suggests the complexity of Jake's understanding of his friend's character.

4:20 **painful self-consciousness:** Again, Jake may empathize (as a Catholic) with Robert's experience of being an outsider at Princeton; also, given his war wound, Jake knows a good deal about "painful self-consciousness," and where it crosses the line into self-absorption and self-pity.

4:21 **married by:** Robert's passivity and inability to act decisively—in matters of the heart and art—are stressed by the passive grammatical structure here and the carefully ironic constructions in the next three paragraphs: "fell among literary people," "taken in hand by a lady," "the lady who had him."

4:32 **fell among:** Jake echoes the biblical and proverbial expression "fell among thieves," ironically associating with thieves the "literary people" who lead Robert to spend his money on a literary magazine that he funds as an "angel" (a patron, or financial backer, especially in the arts). Biblical echoes pervade *The Sun Also Rises*, although they are often submerged as they are here. See the story of the Good Samaritan in the Gospel of Luke (10.27–36). Given Hemingway's subtle mastery of the art of deep allusion, the reader might be expected to sense here an ironic or straightforward reference to Jake's efforts, especially in the opening chapters, to have compassion, to alleviate Robert's suffering, to be his friend, and to love his "neighbor."

5:2 **review:** The so-called little magazines of the period played a crucial role in the development of modernism in all the arts, and in particular in the international literary renaissance that developed shortly before and peaked not long after World War I. Although Jake is ironic about Robert's editorial role in this review, noting that he began as a financial backer ("purely as an angel") but then grew to like the exercise of editorial authority, he does not criticize—indeed, he reveals nothing about—the content of Robert's review. Hemingway probably had in mind here *Broom,* the little magazine established by Cohn's prototype, Harold Loeb. For a number of years Loeb had owned and operated the well-known avant-garde Sunwise Turn Bookshop in New York City at 53 East Forty-fourth Street, an important bookstore but also a center of the arts where important new artists had their first solo exhibits (e.g., Charles Burchfield in 1916), and where the art celebrity Peggy Guggenheim (Loeb's cousin) worked and first met the great photographer Alfred Stieglitz. Loeb sold his interest in the Sunwise Turn (a name echoed in the title of Hemingway's novel) to establish in 1921 *Broom: An International Magazine of the Arts.* The first issues listed Harold Loeb and Alfred Kreymborg as editors until the latter was dropped and Loeb became the sole editor. Expensively and handsomely produced, and printed on fine paper with color prints by noted artists such as Wassily Kandinsky, Paul Klee, Henri Matisse, and Pablo Picasso; original woodcut covers by Natalia Goncharova and Fernand Léger; and photography by Man Ray, *Broom* in its brief existence (1921–1924) published a list of writers that constitutes a veritable roster of modernism: Jean Cocteau, Malcolm Cowley, Hart Crane, e. e. cummings, John Dos Passos, T. S. Eliot, Luigi Pirandello, Ezra Pound, Gertrude Stein, Wallace Stevens, William Carlos Williams, and many others. The magazine began in Rome, and at various times Berlin, London, and New York were listed as its place of publication. It was one of the most important arts magazines of its time.

5:3 **Carmel . . . Provincetown:** Both towns were known for much of the twentieth century as rather elite artsy retreats, or what some might call "bicoastal bobo" (bourgeois bohemian) centers, to distinguish them from, say, Greenwich Village, the more authentic or gritty bohemian quarter of New York. Although in the later twentieth century both towns were associated with elite vacation or seasonal retreat patterns, the origins of their reputations may be found in the early concentration of artists and writers for reasons centered in low-priced picturesque landscape. When the so-called Great Gale of 1898 destroyed much of Provincetown's fishing industry, for example, many of the abandoned buildings were taken over by painters and writers. And when Carmel's most famous writer, Robinson Jeffers, went to Carmel just before World War I, he went for reasons of landscape and cheap real estate. By 1925, when Jake associates Robert with Carmel ("Garden of God" country) and Provincetown ("Land of First Light"), both places, though still evocative of the arts, had taken on an identity that had more to do with wealth than art. The best days of the Provincetown Players (Eugene O' Neill, Djuna Barnes, Edna St. Vincent Millay et al.) were in the past. This fact probably plays a part in Jake's place fixing for Robert's review, which, in its shifting of locations both echoes and diminishes the locations among which Harold Loeb's *Broom* moved: Rome, London, and Berlin. That is, Robert's magazine is provincial, not part of the international scene, in Jake's eyes.

5:21 **Braddocks:** This is a transparent naming of a character based on Ford Madox Ford (1873–1939), the English novelist and an important editor-publisher in the Paris expatriate community. In 1924 Hemingway became a deputy editor for Ford's *transatlantic review,* which during its brief existence (1924–1925) published work by

Joseph Conrad, H. D. (Hilda Doolittle), and James Joyce as well as cummings, Dos Passos, Hemingway, Pound, and Stein. Hemingway may well have been influenced by Ford's work, especially *The Good Soldier* (1915) and the second volume—*No More Parades*—of the World War I tetralogy *Parade's End*. Hemingway owned the typescript of *No More Parades* and probably read it carefully in 1924, when he was Ford's editorial assistant. The role of Braddocks was more substantial in *The Sun Also Rises* before Hemingway cut several pages that dealt with him from the opening—material that Hemingway later used in the ninth chapter ("Ford Madox Ford and the Devil's Disciple") of his Paris memoir, *A Moveable Feast*. Although this passage identifies Braddocks as one of Cohn's two friends ("his literary friend"), the deleted material makes it clear that Braddocks doesn't think much of Cohn's work.

5:23 **Frances:** The character of Frances is based on Kitty Cannell, Harold Loeb's companion. Kitty and Harold socialized with Ernest and Hadley Hemingway and, in March 1925, introduced them to Pauline Pfeiffer (who would become Hemingway's second wife in 1927).

5:27–28 **allowance:** Three hundred dollars a month was a considerable sum of money in the 1920s, especially given the exchange rate at twenty or more francs to the dollar. With apartment rentals available at the equivalent of ten dollars per month, and breakfasts, drinks, and restaurant meals averaging from five to twenty-five cents, one could live comfortably for a dollar a day. Some American expatriate memoirists have cited the exchange rate as the main reason there were so many writers and artists in 1920s Paris.

6:1–2 **novel:** Jake seems to take away from Robert's novel with one hand as he gives with the other: it's not as bad as the critics would say it is, but it is a "very poor novel." But this amounts to a double condemnation of Robert's writing, which is here linked, as in the recurrent pattern, with Robert's reading. He reads a great deal, but what kind of books does he read, and what effect does their quality have on his writing? (See 8–9.) Harold Loeb's first novel, *Doodab*, was published in 1925 and was neither a popular nor a critical success. Reviewers cited its propensity for daydreams and fantasy.

6:6 **l'Avenue's:** The restaurant Lavenue (the correct spelling) was at 1–3, rue du Départ, near the Gare Montparnasse (the train station for points west), a part of the Hôtel Lavenue. After dinner, Jake and Robert follow the Parisian custom of going somewhere for coffee and drinks. The Café de Versailles was across the place de Rennes from Lavenue, at 171, rue de Rennes. It was a *restaurant de nuit* (open late) with dancing. (The reader who wishes to trace exactly Jake's movements around Paris should consult a Baedeker or Blue Guide from the 1920s.)

6:7 **fines:** *Fine* (rhymes with seen) is a type of brandy familiar to readers of Hemingway's work, yet not as easy to find in France now as it was in the 1920s. Some readers have confused it with cognac, the most celebrated of French brandies, produced in the region of Cognac. The confusion may stem from the fact that certain expensive cognacs are identified as *fine champagne.* It is linguistically and economically incorrect to assume that Jake, given his exactitude when it comes to details, would drink the much more expensive drink without specifying that he was drinking a cognac—*fine champagne.* The *fines* ordered in *The Sun Also Rises* may be *fine d'Alsace, fine de Bordeaux, fine de Bourgogne,* or whatever brandy of whatever region the café had as its house *fine*—but they are not cognacs.

6:10 **Strasbourg:** The capital of the Alsatian region in eastern France, Strasbourg is a large historic city on the French-German border. Jake seems to have a fascination with frontiers, with border crossings. (See his later multiple French-Spanish border crossings.) In 1922–1923, Hemingway wrote three *Toronto Daily Star* articles dealing with Strasbourg, one about a hair-raising Paris-Strasbourg flight he made in 1922, and two others dealing with inflation and French-German border crossings ("A Paris-to-Strasbourg Flight," "German Inflation," and "Getting into Germany," in Hemingway, *By-Line*). Exemplary Hemingway characters always know exactly where they are and where they are planning to go and why. Seasoned travelers and well-informed pilgrims have a lively sense of place, a strong devotion to the *deus loci* (the spirit of place). Unlike Robert, who has drifted or has been led by someone else ("taken in hand," as if on a leash) from Carmel to Provincetown to Paris, Jake knows why and where he wants to go. In this scene, Jake proposes all the destinations, four of them in addition to Strasbourg. Strasbourg, the ancient *Strataburgum* ("fortified town on the roads"), interests Jake not only because it is a borderland that has been both French and German but also because it has one of the most celebrated cathedrals of Europe, the cathedral of Notre-Dame. Such features as the red sandstone west front (by Master Erwin Steinbach) and the sculpture of the south transept doorway featuring the Coronation and Death of the Virgin, and allegorical figures of the Church and the Synagogue (Jake and Robert?) place the Cathedral of Strasbourg, considered one of the great achievements of medieval art and architecture, very high on the list of European cultural and religious routes and pilgrimages. This is the kind of place knowledge that compels Jake's travels.

6:10–11 **Saint Odile:** In French, this is Sainte Odile, or, if referring to the place, mont Sainte-Odile. When Jake proposes a "walk" from Strasbourg "up to Saint Odile," he is not talking about a little stroll in the woods; it is forty-one kilometers, one way, and the last six kilometers are steeply uphill. Why does he propose Sainte-Odile? Although it is one of the most visited sites in Alsace, it is, for the casual tourist, a rather obscure place. Yet mont Sainte-Odile, obscure only for nonpilgrims, has long been one of the important sites of Christendom and a famous place of pilgrimage. As Catholics living in France, Hemingway and Jake would have known this, or they could have read it in any good guidebook, where they would have learned that Sainte Odile was the patron saint of Alsace; born blind, she recovered her sight when she was baptized. Her father, the Duke of Alsace, rejected her because of her disability and because he wanted a son. At last, he recognized her vocation and gave her the Hohenberg mountain (renamed the Odilienberg) as a sacred place to establish her famous convent, where, after a legendary lifetime of wonder working, of healing and miracles, she died in 720. The pilgrimage to Sainte-Odile was immensely popular in the Middle Ages, went through a long period of neglect, and once again became popular by the early 1900s. During five pilgrimages each year, pilgrims stop on their climb up the mountain to bathe their eyes in the *source Sainte-Odile,* the miraculous spring of the patron saint of the blind, believed to heal all eye ailments, all vision problems (in the physical *and* the spiritual senses of the term). At the top of the mountain, pilgrims visit the saint's sarcophagus in her chapel, after which many take the long walk around the so-called Pagan Wall, the Celtic and Roman ruins that surround Sainte-Odile's ridge. It is thus an adumbration of the Pagan-Christian nexus, the sacred-profane landscape pattern that informs other settings in *The Sun Also Rises,* such as Roncevaux, Pamplona, even Paris.

It is instructive to see that the first place Jake suggests as a walking destination is a well-known place of pilgrimage. Yet the significance, the reach of this allusion, does not stop there, for we are dealing, as always in Hemingway's works, with precisely coded signals. A survey of the novel reveals an extraordinary number of references to eyes, vision, nearsightedness, and blindness, especially in the sense of "blind drunk." In fact, however, the most extensive and explicit variation on the blindness motif occurred in the deleted opening chapter, just before the Sainte Odile allusion. In some respects, Fitzgerald may have been right to urge Hemingway to cut that chapter, yet many important matters are, shall we say, *seen* much more clearly with the help of the deleted material. This is what Jake says about blindness in the discarded chapter 1: "But when [Brett] had been drunk she always spoke of it as having been blind. 'Weren't we blind last night, though?' It was short for blind drunk, and the curious part was that she really became, in a way, blind. . . . Brett first lost her power of speech and just sat and listened, then she lost her sight" (Svoboda, *Crafting of a Style* 133). Eye-blindness-vision image clusters recur throughout the novel (see especially 224, 235). From the beginning of the novel, when Jake is contemplating a pilgrimage to the numinous place of Sainte Odile, whose blindness was healed by baptism, Jake's primary need is to see clearly his situation with Brett, to deal with his version of blindness. Hemingway's buried landscape clue, his allusion to Sainte Odile, might have been clear to readers before now if the initial "blindness" passage that precedes the Sainte Odile allusion had not been cut. And given that this novel, this *book,* is centrally concerned with vision, we should not be surprised to learn that the standard iconographic representation of Sainte Odile shows her holding an open *book,* with the open pages turned outward, facing the viewer: one large piercing eye gazes from each open page. It is a powerful and haunting image of vision, of eyes that—as Jake says in another context—"look on and on after every one else's eyes in the world would have stopped looking" (26). And here, as Jake the writer invites Robert the writer to walk up to Sainte-Odile, he may be hoping for a miracle, thinking of his own book, and thinking of Robert's nearsightedness, his problem with books, with reading and writing them, with seeing clearly. (See also Stoneback, "From the Rue Saint-Jacques.")

It should be stressed that Hemingway's Sainte Odile allusion is anything but *obscure,* or accessible only to a limited group of French or Alsatian Catholic pilgrims; indeed, he might have expected most of his readers to recognize it, given the fact that the American National Shrine of Saint Odilia, from which location prayer cards and "Saint Odilia Blessed Water" (from her spring in France) are distributed throughout North America, is in the Midwest (Minnesota). The Prayer to Saint Odilia implores, "through the intercession" of Saint Odilia, that the "Patroness of the eyes and afflicted" will protect the petitioner "from the darkness of ignorance and sin" and cure "the blindness of the eyes and other bodily infirmities."

6:13 **kicked:** Robert, fearful of Frances's reaction when Jake mentions the girl in Strasbourg, kicks Jake under the table to get him to change the subject. Jake continues, and Robert kicks him again. This is a perfect example of how Hemingway renders character in concrete details—the particularity of Robert's action reveals, with no authorial commentary necessary, the uxorious, insecure, immature "taken in hand" and leash-led aspect of Robert's personality. For decades, I have asked students to comment on one *rendered* action in each chapter that reveals character, and what it reveals; hundreds—no, after thirty-some years, thousands—of students have stated that the key piece of behavior in chapter 1 is this kick, that it shows Robert is some kind of a "wimp," a guy they would not like to have as a friend; and if they feel negative toward Robert already after chapter 1 (and most do), it is not because of what Jake says *about* Robert in his biographical summary, but because of his surreptitious kicking.

6:18 **Bruges:** Changing the location subject after he is kicked, Jake proposes Bruges, the "Venice of the North," across the French border in West Flanders, Belgium, a picturesque and historic city, a place of pilgrimage famous since the Middle Ages for its Procession of the Holy Blood. In 1150 the count of Flanders returned home to Bruges from the Crusades with a few drops of the blood of Christ given to him by the patriarch of Jerusalem. The sacred relic is conserved in a gold and silver reliquary that is carried in the Procession of the Holy Blood. The Bruges allusion may do more than reinforce the novel's overarching pilgrimage theme, for the focus in

Bruges is the blood, just as the focus in the novel is those arenas of blood ritual that emphasize that much knowledge worth having is bought with blood: the bullfight, the church, hunting, fishing, and war (as in the baptism of fire, the "blooding" of Jake). It should be noted, too, that Bruges was an important staging area for pilgrims to Santiago de Compostela, in western Spain, from northern Europe, and there is a thirteenth-century Church of Saint-Jacques (see 78:6–7).

6:19 **Ardennes:** The Ardennes Forest stretches over parts of France, Luxembourg, Belgium, and Germany; again, Jake's fascination with borders, frontiers, is suggested. Especially around the village of Saint-Hubert, Belgium, the woods are—or were, in the 1920s—regarded as among the most beautiful in Europe. It might be that Jake, as a war veteran, has some interest in seeing the sites of the Battle of the Ardennes (also known, interestingly enough, as "the battle of the two blind men"). But since Jake seems more interested in hiking in the woods than visiting battlefields, we must assume it is the Saint Hubert–hunting resonances that lead him to suggest the Ardennes. Saint Hubert, known as the Apostle of the Ardennes, is the patron saint of hunters, and he is particularly venerated in the village of Saint-Hubert, in the heart of the Ardennes. The abbey contains the shrine of Saint Hubert, and there is an annual pilgrimage. The Mass of Saint Hubert is celebrated there (as it is in many forest villages in Belgium and France) to the accompaniment of hunting horns. The legend of Saint Hubert, frequently depicted in sculpture, stained glass, and painting, tells how Hubert, a very worldly man and an avid hunter, met a great stag in the forest on Good Friday, bearing between its antlers a crucifix surrounded by rays of light. Then he heard a voice saying: "Hubert, unless thou turnest to the Lord, and leadest an holy life, thou shalt quickly go down into hell." This event, of course, marked his conversion and his turn to an exemplary Christian life. Had Jake and Robert gone to the Ardennes, they might have witnessed one of the splendid huntsmen's Masses of Saint Hubert, with horns reverberating from the church into the surrounding forest; or they might have participated in the pilgrimage to Saint-Hubert, with hunters and animals gathered inside and outside the basilica for the *bénédiction des animaux,* the blessing of the beasts. The only Hubert specifically mentioned in the novel is the Montana boy with his parents on the train full of pilgrims in chapter 9; Hubert's parents are ironically presented, in part, as anti-pilgrims, and even though they're from Montana, they don't care for fishing or, presumably, hunting. All that we know about Hubert is that he desperately longs to "get in the water," to swim; there may be a hint that he plays a part in the novel's pattern of bathing and immersion, the cleansing and baptismal imagery, and thus the *named* Hubert may hearken back to the implicit but *unnamed* presence of Saint Hubert in the opening chapter (see 85–88).

6:31 **Senlis:** Jake's final place proposal is much closer to home, forty-four kilometers north of Paris. He seems to have given up on the more complicated, longer-distance pilgrimage locations and settled for nearby Senlis. Jake may also feel that Robert will be bored by the pilgrimage places, as he later says he might be bored by the bullfights. In any case, Senlis is one of the oldest French towns and has a very rich history. It was a royal residence for the first two dynasties. Sights one can assume Jake would want to see are the Gallo-Roman arena (where bullfights may have been held, as they once were in Paris), the magnificent cathedral of Notre-Dame (which contains sculpted pilgrim figures, including Saint Jacques/Santiago), and the *cabinet de travail* of Saint Louis in the old Château royal. (Saint Louis, the crusader, was one of Hemingway's favorite saints—see, e.g., *Selected Letters* 683, 824.) Given the walk-in-the-woods theme of the overall conversation, we can assume Jake's "hike in the woods" around Senlis might be in the *bois* or Forest of Saint-Hubert, long a center of *la chasse,* of hunting, as well as the French center of the cult of Saint Hubert (as the village of Saint-Hubert in the Ardennes is the cultic center of Belgian hunting). And their "hike in the woods" from Senlis would likely take them through the Forest of Chantilly, and a few kilometers down the way to the tiny forest village and Church of Saint Firmin (San Fermín), that native of Pamplona who became the bishop of Amiens and has at least seven French towns named after him. Thus this proposed walk is a kind of submerged foreshadowing of the journey to the Fiesta of San Fermín (chapters 15–18).

7:2 **Grand Cerf:** The Hôtel du Grand Cerf was in the heart of Senlis, at 47, rue de la République. *Grand Cerf* means Great Stag, and popular lore associates the many hotels and cafés in rural France that are called the Grand Cerf with the mystical stag of Saint Hubert. I have confirmed this connection in conversations with hunters in rural France, in cafés and restaurants and hotels named the Grand Cerf, and once, long ago, in a café (called the Grand Cerf) in rural Brittany somewhere near the magical Forest of Paimpont, I saw a fine wood carving of Saint Hubert meeting the great stag with the crucifix in its antlers occupying the entire front of a rustic bar. Jake knows what the voice from the Grand Cerf says: "Change your life or go to Hell." In less than a page, then, Jake proposes to Robert five particular (not random) pilgrimages involving borders, frontiers, medieval history, cathedrals, and the Christian iconography of hunting, with place adumbrations of the possibility of healing, miracles, and transformed lives. Place and symbolic landscape are always touchstones in Hemingway's work.

7:12–13 **she led him:** As chapter 1 closes, Jake reiterates that he rather likes Robert, feels compassion or empathy over his situation with Frances, and underlines again how Robert's passive life is "led."

CHAPTER 2

8:1–11 **his novel:** Praise for his first novel spoils Robert, who is no longer as "simple" or as "nice" as he was, although he now gets more attention from women. Harold Loeb's first novel, *Doodab*, published by Boni and Liveright in 1925, was centered in fantasy and daydreaming; his second novel, *The Professors Like Vodka*, about an innocent American in Paris who falls for a mysterious, sophisticated woman, followed a year after the publication of *The Sun Also Rises*. Loeb's final novel was *Tumbling Mustard*. Was there ever another novelist with such a terrible ear for titles?

8:12 **never been in love:** Robert suffers from a lack of "love"—or passion, endearment, and engagement with persons and things that would take him outside himself—in every area of his life. This is why he feels he is not really living his life (10). Compare Robert, who has "never been in love," with the count, who is "always in love" (61). The count's all-encompassing love of life, as the crucial secret-of-the-values scene makes clear (59–61), is rooted in a life authentically lived, in the values he has learned through suffering, wounding, and vast experience. Put simply, the person who is selfish, self-centered, locked in the trap of self-absorption, cannot possibly love anything beyond the self.

8:18 **divine miracle:** The use of religious language (sometimes referred to as "churched vocabulary") occurs throughout the novel. Jake's occasionally ironic use of religious terminology, as here, does not indicate an antireligious or blasphemous sensibility. To the contrary, it indicates how religious language comes naturally to a person steeped in his faith, as Jake is. (See also, e.g., the ironic use of "promised land," 22.) Moreover, Jake is attuned to such use of religious terminology in the speech of others. (See Bill's humorous "Pilgrims . . . Puritans" confusion, 86.)

9:7–8 **W. H. Hudson:** Novelist and naturalist William Henry Hudson (1841–1922) was born in Argentina of American parentage, settled in England in his twenties, and later became a British citizen. Several of his books, including *Far Away and Long Ago*, *Green Mansions*, and *The Purple Land*, deal with his experience in South America in a rather romantic fashion. Hemingway alludes to Hudson in "A Natural History of the Dead" and *The Garden of Eden,* when David Bourne, a writer with far more credibility (and better taste) than Robert Cohn, praises *Far Away and Long Ago* and also mentions Hudson's *Nature in Downland.* It would be misleading to suggest that Jake's association of Cohn with Hudson in the following sentences functions simplistically as a marker to associate one bad writer with another. Hemingway's literary allusions are always more complex than such a reading allows.

9:9 **The Purple Land:** After *Green Mansions,* Hudson's best-known work, *The Purple Land,* is one of Hudson's better-known works, at least in America. (These two works were the only two by Hudson in my father's substantial library, assembled largely between 1920 and 1940; as a preteenager, I read *Green Mansions* twice but could not finish *The Purple Land* once.) First published in 1885 under the title *The Purple Land that England Lost,* Hudson's first novel, after being neglected for two decades, was brought out in a new 1904 edition after the success of *Green Mansions,* under the shortened title *The Purple Land.* In his preface to the new edition, Hudson refers to his novel's neglect and notes the changes he has made. The 1916 edition, printed in New York by E. P. Dutton and Company—which could very well be the edition that Robert and Jake (and Hemingway) read—prints the title as *The Purple Land: Being the Narrative of One Richard Lamb's Adventures in the Banda Orientál, in South America, as Told by Himself.* The dust jacket of this edition (front and back) carries the subtitle *Adventures in South America.* This stress on "adventure" points to why Robert has read and reread the book, with its "splendid imaginary amorous adventures . . . in an intensely romantic land," and it is very "sinister" reading indeed for a thirty-four-year-old writer trying to be a literary success in the avant-garde context of the 1920s, of Paris, and of modernism. It is also sinister for Robert to take it as a "guide-book" to experience. To be always longing for romantic adventure in some faraway place is to risk not living one's life where one is (see 11:31–32). The extended allusion to *The Purple Land* is the setup for the primary subject matter of chapter 2—how to live life fully and authentically.

There may be yet another connotation carried by the title of Robert's beloved book, that is, "purple" writing, ornate, lush, elaborate *purple prose.* Although this sense of purple may have been intended by writers who have, at least since Coleridge, referred to "purple patches" of writing, the current sense of purple prose as lush, overly romantic writing seems to have developed since the 1920s. When he chose the Hudson book as Robert's favorite, Hemingway may well have had in mind this emerging sense of purple prose, since he was, after all, on the cutting edge of evolving usage (see "hard-boiled," 34:24). It is also interesting to note that the 1916 edition of *The Purple Land* that Jake and Robert (and Hemingway) are likely to have known has a gaudy purple cover with gold lettering, an image of a golden sunset (or, possibly, sunrise), and a dust jacket that stresses adventure and romance, as well as a blurb by John Galsworthy about how the book leads "into a rare, free, natural world" (a world Robert avoids, as in fishing and the bullfight), and a large advertisement for the "sombre but splendid" book by one Samuel Gordon entitled *God's Remnants,* which notes that "the Jewish Race has long needed a real Interpreter." The depth of Hemingway's iceberg, his submerged and deeply layered allusiveness, should never be underestimated.

9:16 **Alger:** Horatio Alger Jr. (1832–1899) was the prolific author of more than 130 books, most of them juvenile fiction "dime novels" that employed a formulaic rags-to-riches motif depicting the way—through hard work and determination, pluck and luck—to realize the "American Dream" of wealth and success. Although immensely popular for many decades (as late as 1920), Alger's books are generally considered to be poorly written, unrealistic, and sentimental reading for boys. Jake's ironic sense of humor is on display throughout this passage—as he sees it, there is nothing "practical" about the Alger books, and W. H. Hudson is just as dangerous for a man of thirty-four. Jake may also know that Alger studied at Harvard under Longfellow and lived in Paris for a while before he returned to America to be, briefly, a Unitarian minister, and then a successful writer. Jake (and Hemingway) may or may not have known the story, in circulation after his death, that Alger was dismissed from his ministerial post for having sexual relations with boys in his parish. They would not have known that one chapter of NAMBLA (North American Man/Boy Love Association) is named after Alger.

9:18 **R. G. Dun:** Robert Graham Dun (1826–1900) established his credit-rating firm in 1861 and published the weekly *Dun's Review* of business. With offices in major cities nationwide, R. G. Dun and Company (later known as Dun and Bradstreet) was the best-known credit-rating firm in the United States. Again, Jake's irony, his sense of humor, is in evidence as he assesses just how much "credit" we can give to Robert's reading and to his character.

9:21 **my office:** Readers of the novel—and this includes some Hemingway critics—have all too often thought of the characters as a set of feckless expatriates, aimlessly drifting around Paris and Spain. Such readers would do well to note carefully Jake's emphasis on his work. Here, Jake refers to his office for the first time, thinking—as Robert invites him on a trip, an "adventure" in South America—about his writing obligations, the articles he has to write and get dispatched on deadline. In the material that was deleted at the last minute from the novel's typescript, Jake talks about his job, his career as newspaperman and European director of the Continental Press Association, a job he works hard at and likes very much. And in another deleted segment from an early draft, Jake thinks (in Spain) how good it would be to get back to Paris and "get to work again. . . . It was always fun to get back to Paris" (Svoboda, *Crafting of a Style* 83,134). In short, Jake *works* in Paris, *lives* in

Paris, and is very happy with his working life in the city he loves. If readers keep Jake's work-and-place identity straight from the beginning, they will be less likely to be lured into the many false place contrasts that have plagued interpretations of the novel for decades, procrustean patterns that force readings (e.g., of Paris as wasteland). Jake's job and office—and its location—are modeled on those of Hemingway's friend Bill Bird, whose work and office, even down to the office location (rue d'Antin, near the Opéra), resemble Jake's. Bird was a journalist and the European director of the Consolidated Press Association from 1920 to 1933. He was also the publisher whose Three Mountains Press printed, at Ezra Pound's instigation, Hemingway's second slim volume, *in our time* (1923). Hemingway met Bird in Paris in 1922, and they were together on various trips, including a trip to Germany in 1922, Hemingway's first trip to Spain in 1923, and his second Pamplona fiesta in 1924 (Reynolds, *Chronology* 28–35; Baker, *Life Story* 88–89, 118).

9:28–29 **real:** Robert's difficulty in knowing what's "real" is underlined here by Jake, who doesn't want to go to South America with Robert, and who knows that Robert wants to go to the "unreal" South America of his fantasies derived from his reading of *The Purple Land*. Almost all of chapter 2 is driven by this travel/adventure/reality motif through repetition (a device Hemingway had learned to deploy skillfully for emphasis from Gertrude Stein), with ten references to South America in less than three pages, following the keystone passage about *The Purple Land*.

9:32 **dirt:** "Dirt" here signifies gossip. Again, *The Sun Also Rises* operates at the cutting edge of evolving word usage. Among its many citations of Hemingway in its date-specific usage or currency notes, the *Oxford English Dictionary* cites this exact passage as the *first* recorded occurrence of "dirt" in the sense of gossip or scandal. (See also 14:5, 34:24, 59:29, 64:4, 84:1, and 122:30.)

10:4 **Why me?** Quite naturally, Jake expects Robert to give some persuasive reason why Jake would want to go to South America. But Robert, self-centered as usual, talks only in terms of why Jake's presence would be useful to him and essentially offers to buy Jake's services as translator.

10:7 **this town:** Jake doesn't want to go to South America, not only because he's not interested in Robert's fantasies of romantic "adventure" but also because he has a carefully ordered life that suits him fine: a job that he likes in a town that he likes, in perfect combination with an annual summer pilgrimage to Spain during his time off from work. He doesn't say he's excited that he's going to have an adventure in Spain on his vacation: he says, "I go"—he goes every summer on the same pilgrimage to Spain, a journey he values deeply and wishes to share with his friends. In a fundamental sense it is Jake's well-ordered and ritualized life that gives the novel its basic pattern, its deep structure. It seems hardly likely that any of the other characters would go to Spain for the bullfights or the fishing if Jake had not invited them and wanted them to share his cherished rituals. At the most obvious level, in the contextual flow of the conversation, Jake is saying he doesn't need to go to South America to speak Spanish: Spain will do just fine.

10:9 **like that:** As usual, Robert doesn't listen to what somebody's just said and remains wrapped up in his own fantasies. The grammatical referent of his "trip like that" should be Jake's trip to Spain, but Robert is going to South America—in his mind—and won't hear what Jake is saying in this entire conversation.

10:14 **started:** This statement refers to more than just Robert's fantasy trip to South America. He can't get "started" on anything very effectively; he can't even "start living" his life where he is, in Paris, as Jake says, echoing Robert's word choice toward the end of this crucial conversation (see 11:32). This is a very sad commentary, indeed, for a man of thirty-four.

10:19–31 **life all the way up:** This is the central question posed by the novel: given our mortality, the evanescent transience of life, how do we live our lives authentically and passionately every day of the short time we have? One answer, for Jake, is epitomized and symbolized by the bullfighter, who looks death in the face in the arena, who confronts mortality—if he does his job well—with dignity, poise, passion, discipline, and highly formalized grace under pressure and achieves a ritual and communal sense of immortality. Jake's firm pronouncement in this sentence tells the reader not only why Jake goes to "Spain in the summertime" but also what Jake's personal "story" is about: how to live his life all the way up in spite of his war injury. It is one of the axiomatic assertions of the novel, performing a homiletic and scriptural function in its implicit response to the "lost generation" assertion of the first epigraph. It also responds directly to Robert's existential anguish expressed in the preceding sentence: he feels his life going very fast, and he's "not really living it." Jake does not condescend to Robert in this sequence, as has sometimes been maintained. In fact, he feels empathy, compassion; he feels "sorry" for Robert, who has "it badly." The "it" is the existential nausea created by a sense of the rapid erosion of time in combination with a sense of not getting "started" on a life lived fully, "all the way up," the anguish of a fear of death compounded by a sense of "not really living." Jake is very well acquainted with this "it," and he has made a good "start" on dealing with "it," so he suggests here one answer: the mortality-immortality paradigm, the passionate engagement that he finds in the bullfight. Robert understands the problem, perhaps, but he is not "interested" in Jake's answer to "it"; he thinks bullfighting is "an abnormal life." In this response, Robert shows again that he is not really listening to Jake and asserts again that he wants his adventure in South America. Then Jake suggests hunting—another life-death ritual where knowledge is underlined by blood—in Africa and says he'll go there with Robert. But Robert isn't interested in hunting either, because he's determined to have his romantic adventure in the purple land of his fantasy. Jake grows impatient with him and tells him to read some romantic book about Africa, since Robert seems to get all his ideas from books. But Robert can only reply, for all the world like a stubborn little boy, a thirty-four-year-old adolescent, "I want to go to South America."

10:32 **stubborn:** The entire dialogue that constitutes most of chapter 2 illustrates Robert's "stubborn streak," but, as exemplified in conversation and conduct, his stubbornness has everything to do with his adolescent fantasies and his boyish insistence, nothing to do with his Jewishness. Hemingway added this gratuitous slur when he revised this scene, perhaps to illustrate the unfortunately common human tendency to resort to group-identity slurs when one is impatient or angry—as Jake does again when he characterizes the homosexuals with Brett in chapter 3 (see 20). Or perhaps Hemingway added this to suggest that Jake—even though he is sympathetic to Robert's sense of "outsiderness" at Princeton and would have experienced a similar bigotry (as a Catholic) had he gone to Princeton (see 3:1–6)—is not immune to the casual anti-Semitism of his time and place. Compare the scene in chapter 8 where Bill and Jake discuss the black boxer in Vienna—Bill clearly admires him and discussed his admirable character yet calls him a "Wonderful nigger" (71–72).

11:2 **café:** Although this café is not named, the description fits the Caves Mura at 19, rue d'Antin, which was on the ground floor of Bill Bird's Consolidated Press office, on which Jake's office is modeled (see 9:21). In the novel's first draft, Hemingway had written: "we went downstairs to the Cave Mura" (*Facsimile* 1:80).

11:6 **graceful exits:** As always, Jake stresses a code of conduct, ritualized behavior: the newspaperman's code says that he should seem to be not working, even when he is, and Robert has interrupted him by coming to his office to talk about South America. So, in a ritual based on Bill Bird's actual method of getting rid of unwanted visitors, Jake takes Robert down for a drink as a way of getting rid of him so he can get back to work and meet his deadlines. Ironically, as the scene unfolds, the "graceful exit" doesn't work, since Robert follows Jake back upstairs when he says he has to get back to work. It is worth noting, too, given the tendency among readers to overstate the amount of drinking that occurs in the novel, that—as Jake emphasizes twice in this paragraph ("a drink," "a whiskey and soda")—this occasion involves *one* drink, and it functions as a device, even if it doesn't work, to get rid of Robert so Jake can get to work. Codified behavior doesn't work with Robert because he doesn't get the code.

11:14 **half the time:** Robert reiterates the theme expressed on the previous page (see 10:20–31): he has, given a normal life span, lived half his life already, and it hasn't really "started." But "taking advantage" of it is not exactly the same thing as living it "all the way up." Jake grows impatient with the line of talk ("What the hell, Robert"), not because he hasn't thought long and hard about the question Robert raises—that they're halfway to death—but because Jake has long since confronted his fear of dying when he was wounded in World War I. When Robert tells Jake, somewhat bizarrely, that he "ought to" worry about death, Jake replies that he's "through worrying"—and he probably is through worrying about death, although he worries plenty about how to live throughout the course of the novel.

11:26–32 **Listen, Robert:** This is another reminder that Robert does not listen. He has just repeated again, in his juvenile monotone insistence: "Well, I want to go to South America"—as if that will answer all the life-death questions they've been discussing. Mere motion, mobility, traveling aimlessly from place to place, going just to be going, to be "on the road," drifting pointlessly or in pursuit of some fantasy, some adventure, will not cure what's wrong with anyone. Hemingway here evokes (and rejects) the great American theme of restless mobility—Huck Finn's lighting out for the territory or Jack Burden's fleeing west to California to escape his problems (in Robert Penn Warren's *All the King's Men*)—flight, relocation, change of scene, as a solution to all problems. Jake has "tried all that"; although we don't know much about Jake's earlier travels before his move to Paris, where he has been settled and at home for several years, we do know that he now travels deliberately, to carefully selected destinations for specific reasons, not in some vague hope of changing himself by changing place. Robert has "tried all that"—in drifting from coast to coast, from Provincetown to Carmel, and in coming to Paris because it's the fashionable thing to do, even though he doesn't like Paris and doesn't want to live his life there, to connect with place—and he wants to keep on trying the romance of the road, travel, and motion, as the answer to his problems. But in that kind of travel, Jake tells Robert, in an analysis that is more subtle than it appears at first glance, the perpetual tourist takes his problems with him and thus never really sees the place to which he flees. With characteristic understatement, Jake tells Robert that Paris is a "good town" and he should "start living" his life there. Paris, of course, was and is a magnificent city, the most beautiful *and* comfortable urban place in the world in the view of many, and the place where in the 1920s a great renaissance of the arts was happening. As Gertrude Stein often asserted, Paris was where the twentieth century was; and as Hemingway put it in *A Moveable Feast,* "If you are lucky enough to have lived in Paris as a young man, then wherever you go for the rest of your life, it stays with you, for Paris is a moveable feast. . . . There is never any ending to Paris" (epigraph, 211). In this scene, early in *The Sun Also Rises,* the nature of one's response to Paris is established as a benchmark of character:

Jake, Bill, Count Mippipopolous, and even Brett love Paris. Robert Cohn, Georgette the prostitute, and Robert Prentiss the phony novelist do not like Paris.

12:1–2 **Quarter:** Often mistakenly confused, by literary tourists and Hemingway commentators, with the Latin Quarter (the ancient university quarter south of the Seine, surrounding the Sorbonne) in the fifth arrondissement, the "Quarter" of *The Sun Also Rises* is the quartier Montparnasse in the fourteenth arrondissement. Paris has twenty arrondissements, or administrative divisions, each with its own *quartiers*, or neighborhoods. Three years before he wrote *The Sun Also Rises*, Hemingway himself was confused about the boundaries of the various quarters; in his 1922 article for the *Toronto Star Weekly*, "American Bohemians in Paris," he calls the Café Rotonde "the leading Latin Quarter show place for tourists in search of atmosphere" (*By-Line* 21). The Rotonde is in the heart of the Montparnasse Quarter, a good distance from the Latin Quarter. When Hemingway refers to the "Quarter" in *The Sun Also Rises*, he means Montparnasse. Before the nineteenth century, Montparnasse was on the outskirts of Paris; it acquired its name from the students of the Latin Quarter, who derisively named the exurban area (with "mountains" of quarry rubble) after the home of the Greek Muses—Mount Parnassus. But by the end of the nineteenth century, the center of artistic life—and with it the fashionable cafés and cabarets—had begun to shift from Montmartre on the Right Bank to Montparnasse on the Left Bank. The 1927 Blue Guide, for example, listed among the fashionable restaurants of the Left Bank the Closerie des Lilas (one of Hemingway's favorite places)—with the annotation "frequented by artists"—and the Café de la Rotonde, "frequented by foreign students" (Muirhead and Monmarché, *Paris* xl). Jake tells Robert to "stay away" from the Quarter because it is not the *real* Paris that Jake loves: it is not where he works, where he lives. This point is made much more directly in the deleted galley proofs of the opening chapters, where Jake says he "never hung about the Quarter . . . until Brett and Mike showed up"; he visits occasionally to "sort of see the animals," but he finds it "awfully dull." It is such a "sad and dull place to write about" that he wouldn't include it, "except that Robert Cohn had spent two years in it," a fact that "accounts for a great many things" (Svoboda, *Crafting of a Style* 135). Hemingway put it even more forcefully in his 1922 article, published under the headline "American Bohemians in Paris a Weird Lot," which begins: "The scum of Greenwich Village, New York, has been skimmed off and deposited in large ladlesful on that section of Paris adjacent to the Café Rotonde." This "strange-acting and strange-looking breed" makes the Quarter the main "show place for tourists in search of atmosphere." You can find anything there "except serious artists"; "the real artists of Paris . . . loathe the Rotonde crowd" (*By-Line* 21–22). In the early stages of composition of *The Sun Also Rises*, Hemingway had written in his first manuscript notebook: "To understand what happened in Pamplona you must understand the Quarter in Paris. There is nothing romantic about the Quarter and very little that is beautiful. . . . It is really more a state of mind than a geographical area. . . . This state of mind is principally contempt" (*Facsimile* 1:56–57). In this entire sequence, which immediately precedes what became the opening chapter of the novel, Jake makes it clear that the Quarter is not *his* Paris, but he has to "put it in because Gerald [the character whose name is later changed to Robert] had spent two years in it" (*Facsimile* 1:57). All these descriptions of the Quarter, "sad and dull" home of pseudoartists and weird bohemians, where Robert has actually lived for *two years,* provide important place background that helps to explain Robert's character and the conduct of *some* of the expatriates who follow Jake to Pamplona.

12:2 **Cruise around:** Jake deploys a word—"cruise"—in its developing sense: to get away from the phoniness of the Quarter, see the rest of Paris, do some reconnaissance, go looking for some real action (solidified and in daily usage by the 1950s).

12:4 **Nothing happens:** Again Jake notes Robert's passivity, his waiting for something to happen to him. He walks alone all night—no doubt in some fanciful notion that an adventure will happen to him—but nothing happens except that a cop stops him to confirm his identity, such as it is. (Foreigners had to carry a *carte d'identité,* an identity card.)

12:8 **Paris:** Jake, who knows that Paris is "nice at night," thinks Robert should have seen and enjoyed this nightscape, even if nothing happened to him. But Robert sees nothing and doesn't like Paris. Again, one's response to Paris as an index to character, to aliveness, is underlined.

12:11 **two stubbornnesses:** Robert can't get "started" on living his life "all the way up" because all his ideas come from books, here, South America as cure-all, Paris (his *unreal* Paris, the Quarter) as wasteland.

12:19–20 **Editor and Publisher:** Again Jake tries to get away to do his work, but Robert follows him. Jake works hard for two hours, but he is not working with his editor and publisher. There is no editor, no publisher, present in Jake's foreign press service office—they would be in the home office in the United States. This confusing passage was improperly punctuated by Hemingway, and then again by Scribners. With the comma removed after "papers," and a comma inserted after "Publisher," it would be clear that Robert reads the newspapers and the trade magazine *Editor and Publisher* while Jake works. This passage is a perfect example of why students and readers of Hemingway should be urged to use with extreme caution the many Hemingway commentaries and "resources" found on the Internet, which, more often than not, get the facts of Hemingway's text wrong. And a lack of exactitude when it comes to *fact,* to the precise significance of allusions, generally leads to larger misreadings—especially in Hemingway's fiction. Interpretive "openness" and other variations on the validity of "reader response" reactions to a literary text may sometimes be appropriately urged; but accurate construal of fact must precede and provide the foundation for creative openness in interpretation. What is important here is that Robert, a writer, gets sleepy while reading the trade journal of his ostensible profession.

12:23 **Gare St. Lazare:** Jake is as precise about his work as he is about everything else: after he writes for two hours, he then sorts carbons, stamps bylines, puts the articles in envelopes, and sends for the messenger service to deliver his work to the nearby train station, gare Saint-Lazare, whence it will be taken via either Le Havre or Dieppe on the boat train across the English Channel to Southampton or Newhaven.

12:24 **asleep:** While Jake works, Robert falls asleep. It is ironic that Robert, a writer, is put to sleep by the sound of the typewriter. Notice other references to Robert sleeping, for example, 93:28, where Robert sleeps while Bill and Jake quietly share their delight in the Spanish landscape.

12:27–28 **can't do it:** Although the reader is not told directly what Robert is dreaming about here, and it is not immediately clear what he refers to when he repeats, talking in his sleep, that he "can't do it," this scene serves as foreshadowing for, and is clarified by, Jake's conversation with Frances on 46–47. There, Frances tells Jake that Robert has changed his mind about marrying her, and "he says he just can't do it" (47:13). She also talks about the "dreadful scenes" she and Robert have, which seems to refer in a clarifying sense to this passage, where Jake pictures the "bedroom scenes" of Robert and Frances, after Robert says he was up all night "talking." Frances is not mentioned in this passage, although Jake is aware that she's the subject of Robert's dream and the all-night talking, so the reader might not immediately grasp the frame of reference for Robert's "rotten dream." Typically, Jake does not tell the reader everything that he knows. This is an essential aspect of Hemingway's art of understatement, revealing only gradually, through allusions and reiterative echoes, the true substance of various scenes.

13:5–6 **bedroom scenes:** This has sometimes been taken as a reference to Jake's "picturing" the sexual activities of his friends, presumably with a kind of envy or self-pity, since his war wound has put an end to his conventional sexual experience. For some readers, this will not ring true and will not seem in accord with Jake's character. It is, no doubt, a "rotten habit" to picture the "bedroom scenes" of friends, and even more rotten and dull to envision not sexual activities but arguments— the specific referent in this passage. In the notebook first draft, immediately after the bedroom scenes reference, Hemingway had written and then crossed out, "No wonder he wanted to go to South America" (*Facsimile* 1:84).

13:6 **Napolitain:** The Glacier Napolitain, or the Café-Glacier Napolitain, at 1, boulevard des Capucines (place de l'Opéra), is near Jake's office. Guidebooks of the 1920s list it as one of the best-known and most popular cafés on the boulevard, with a sidewalk *terrasse* "where the customer may spend a pleasant hour in watching the passersby" (Muirhead and Monmarché, *Paris* xli). We note that Jake and Robert each have *one* drink—"an apéritif" (a broad term to cover a wide range of predinner drinks intended to enliven the palate and stimulate appetite)—and watch the fashionable evening strollers on "the Boulevard." Though it is part of the Right Bank neighborhood known generally as les Grands Boulevards, "the Boulevard" refers precisely to the most elegant stretch of the boulevards Madeleine, Capucines, and Italiens (the same street, but the name changes every few blocks), running from the Church of la Madeleine to just beyond the place de l'Opéra. Readers, especially American readers with puritanical or prohibitionist inclinations, should not confuse this civilized evening ritual hour of the aperitif with American drinking habits and happy hour behavior. And students and aficionados of the novel should not allow themselves to be misled by intemperate critical views that consider *The Sun Also Rises* one long drunken party, or "a remarkable portrait of the pathology of the disease of alcoholism" (Djos 139). For Hemingway's disdain for disgusting and excessive American drinking habits (especially as contrasted with French drinking rituals), see his unjustly neglected short story "Wine of Wyoming" (*Complete Short Stories* 342–54).

CHAPTER 3

14:2 **watching:** The precision of Jake's observation—his attention, his *watching* every-thing that goes on—is underlined in this paragraph, from this initial "watching it get dark" reference through three repetitions of "watched," "lost sight," "saw . . . again," and "caught her eye." The pleasure of watching the lights come on—in the City of Light (as Paris is often called)—on a warm spring Parisian night is very real for Jake and for the attuned reader. Watching the traffic light changing, the passing crowd, the horse-cabs clip-clopping, and the *poules* strolling by seems far more serene than some commentators have suggested in trying to force Jake's Paris to fit some rigid wasteland thesis. Hemingway did evoke a largely "nocturnal city" (although there are very pleasant daytime scenes, too), but it is hardly "a nightmarish whirl of bars, cafés, taxis, restaurants, and dance halls" (Kennedy 97). Exactly how do taxis, cafés, and res-taurants constitute a nightmare? And why should bars and dance halls—with a pro-prietor playing "pleasant" folk-inflected accordion music accompanied by a banjo, while everyone dances and Jake feels "happy" (see 19–23)—be considered the stuff of bad dreams? There is, to be sure, nighttime anguish in the Paris scenes (as well as in other settings), but it is *not* a function of place. Jake knows, and Hemingway knows, what millions of travelers know: Parisian nights are beautiful.

14:3–4 **traffic signal:** Contemporary readers should be aware, before concocting some elaborate red light–green light symbolism or suggesting that Jake's watching the light change indicates his boredom, that this traffic light is a great novelty since very few were first introduced in Paris in the mid-1920s; in fact this one at the cha-otic place de l'Opéra intersection may well have been the very first traffic light in Paris. Traffic lights were a curiosity everywhere in the 1920s. Still, given the fact that Hemingway inserted the traffic light during his revision process, the careful reader may detect a recurrent pattern of traffic signal imagery beginning here and ending with the traffic policeman's signal in the novel's concluding lines (247).

14:5 **poules:** Literally meaning "hen," *poule* (pronounced "pool" whether singular or plural) here means prostitute. The *OED* includes it as an anglicized word mean-ing a "young woman, esp. one regarded as being promiscuous. Also *poule-de-luxe,* a prostitute." Again recording Hemingway's role in evolving word usage, the *OED* gives as the earliest source quotation for *poule* this passage from *The Sun Also Rises*. However, Hemingway's usage here is French, and he clearly knows that Georgette, a streetwalker, is something more than just "promiscuous," just as he knows that she is not a *poule-de-luxe,* a call girl available by appointment. The primary point for the purposes of the narrative is that she is instantly recognizable—not just to Jake but also to the people to whom he introduces her—as a prostitute. She is not actually looking for "the evening meal," but for a customer, thus the irony of her time spent with Jake, actually eating an "evening meal" and not practicing her profession. Jake, however, always precise and honorable, pays her for her time (see 23:23).

14:13 **Pernod:** Properly, all occurrences of Pernod (pronounced pear-no) over the next page should be capitalized, since it is a brand name, used, for circa two hundred years, for the popular licorice-flavored, anise-based *apéritif* (as well as for the original absinthe). Jake may be jokingly referring to its reputed aphrodisiac properties when he tells Georgette it's bad for "little girls"; she doesn't think the joke's very funny and calls the waiter to order her own Pernod ("Dites garçon"). When Jake orders a Pernod too, she assumes they're going to "party."

15:3 **like Paris:** Throughout the opening chapters, the attitude of various characters toward Paris functions as an index to taste and character—Georgette, like Robert Cohn and Robert Prentiss (and Mencken), does not like Paris.

15:9 **absinthe:** Invented in Switzerland in 1797 by a Frenchman, Dr. Pierre Ordinaire (who sold his secret recipe to Henri-Louis Pernod), absinthe was produced in quantity at Pernod's distillery in Pontarlier, France, from 1805 on. By the mid-nineteenth century, it had become the preferred aperitif of the upper classes, and its popularity had spread throughout Europe (and North America). When the blight in the French vineyards in the 1870s forced distillers to produce absinthe from a grain alcohol base, rather than the original wine-based formula, it could be produced more economically and was thus less expensive, and it came to be viewed as the de rigeur drink of artists, writers, and bohemians. Writers from Poe to Baudelaire, Rimbaud to Oscar Wilde, helped to spread the reputation of absinthe. Its popular name—*la fée verte* ("the green fairy"; also referred to as the green goddess)—led to the identification of the aperitif hour before dinner as *l'heure verte* ("the green hour"). Even bartenders were known to quote Wilde's pronouncement on the effects of absinthe: "After the first glass you see things as you wish they were. After the second, you see things as they are not. Finally you see things as they really are, and that is the most horrible thing in the world." Vincent van Gogh's madness (and his art) was sometimes attributed to excessive absinthe drinking; by the turn of the century, several sensational murders had been attributed to absinthe, and a new disease—"absinthism"—had been identified. Thus the extremely potent light-green liquor of spirits infused with anise and wormwood and many other herbs became a prime target of the Prohibition movement. It was banned in the United States in 1912. Other countries banned it, including France in 1915. Ironically, for a drink sometimes viewed as an aphrodisiac, absinthe was associated with declining fertility rates and harmful effects on male sperm. Thus Pernod, from 1915 on, produced its namesake absinthe substitute from its still-secret formula, ostensibly unchanged except for the exclusion of wormwood, the most harmful of the original ingredients. Absinthe was never banned in Spain, and the Pernod distillery there produced a version of its original-formula absinthe throughout the twentieth century.

Absinthe remained available, albeit illegally, in certain establishments in France and, for example, New Orleans. See Hemingway's "The Strange Country" for his most detailed treatment of absinthe. In a hotel bar in New Orleans (in the 1930s) Roger asks for "real absinthe . . . real Couvet Pontarlier sixty-eighth-degree" (*Complete Short Stories* 640). The waiter says he will bring it "in an ordinary Pernod bottle" with the "dripping saucers," and Roger is very happy to have found the "good old poison" (640–41). After the dripping ritual is performed, Roger warns Helena that it's "pretty strong medicine" as he feels "the warmth of the alchemist's furnace starting at the pit of his stomach" (642). As it begins to take effect, Roger wishes they had "never taken it although it was the drink he loved best of almost any in the world. But almost everything bad that had ever happened to him had happened when he was drinking absinthe; those bad things which were his own fault"; and he notes that the "second one always tastes better than the first because certain taste buds are numbed against the bitterness of the wormwood." They both agree that it is "strange and wonderful," even as it takes them to the "edge of misunderstanding" (643–44). Hemingway's complex analysis of absinthe in "The Strange Country" sheds some light, then, on the "medicine" of the "imitation absinthe" consumed in Jake's "green hour" aperitif with Georgette. By the beginning of the twenty-first century, absinthe was once again legal in France.

15:14 **grinned:** Because Georgette is sullen, probably brought to the edge of misunderstanding by drinking Pernod, Jake makes a joke—inverting their roles and asking if she's going to buy him dinner. This makes her smile, and he sees her bad teeth (in the manuscript, her "fantastic dental wreckage").

15:16 **saucers:** Café bills in France were traditionally tabulated on the basis of accumulated *soucoupes,* or saucers. Each drink was brought on a fresh saucer, stacked on top of others from preceding rounds of drinks.

15:19 **fiacre:** As he often does with foreign-language terms, Hemingway has twice in fewer than two pages employed the English term—"horse-cab"—before he introduces the French term. Given Hemingway's knowledge of and frequent allusions to saints throughout his work, he probably wants his informed reader to hear a reference to Saint Fiacre, the patron saint of cabdrivers, especially the cabdrivers of Paris. Fiacre is also the patron saint of gardeners, and here he is invoked indirectly, as Jake and Georgette are about to enter the Tuileries gardens. The object of numerous French pilgrimages, Saint Fiacre was known as a healer skilled in the use of the healing properties of herbs (cf. Pernod, and its herbal ingredients), and he was invoked against sterility, venereal disease, and syphilis. Thus, in the opening passage of chapter 3, Hemingway typically constructs a rich congeries of associations in his prostitute/Pernod/absinthe/*fiacre* textual under-song, or subtext, as Jake watches the red and green traffic signal and in the green hour buys a prostitute an imitation absinthe before he rides through the garden with her in a *fiacre,* revealing that he is "sick" or wounded, as he moves toward the crucial moment of Brett Ashley's first appearance in the novel. The manifold resonances—ironic and otherwise—of these details deserve close attention. The details of this taxi scene should be compared with those of the two taxi rides with Brett, at the beginning of the next chapter, and in the novel's closing scene.

15:22 **clocks:** The office of the *Herald* at 49, avenue de l'Opéra is the official address of the *Herald Tribune—European Edition,* which is still the American newspaper of record in Europe. The clocks show the time in Paris and in all the American time zones. Georgette, who has always lived in one time zone (literally, Belgium and France, and perhaps symbolically, the eternal present or "now"), thinks Jake must be kidding about the clocks. Jake, who has a vivid and urgent sense of time—and history—notes that they turn onto the street of the Pyramids.

15:28 **Tuileries:** The cabdriver takes the romantic route into the jardin des Tuileries, turning off the rue de Rivoli at the arched gateway into the place du Carrousel, past the Arc de Triomphe du Carrousel, with its resonances of war (and wounds), and here, in the garden that was a traditional place for lovers, the place where the guillotine was set up in 1793, the place where by tradition the early kings of France on certain occasions tried to heal the sick by the laying on of hands, Georgette cuddles and Jake pushes her hand away, thus providing the first clue that Jake has been wounded, and where he has been wounded. This entire scene is a perfect instance, in miniature, of how Hemingway constructs his symbolic landscapes.

15:29 **kissed:** In the manuscript, Hemingway wrote: "and I kissed her, teeth and all" (*Facsimile* 1:88). In the final version, it is not clear whether he kisses her. Such details, including Jake's deleted observation that Georgette is "well built," suggest that Hemingway is uncertain about the attraction that Jake feels for Georgette, and this has some bearing on his statement that he picked her up only for dinner company

(16). In his first draft, Hemingway may not have fully decided to what degree Jake, in spite of his wound, would feel sexual desire.

15:32–16:1 **sick:** Georgette makes the move a prostitute would be expected to make, putting her hand where she assumes Jake wants it—the *poule*'s version of healing, of laying on of hands—and Jake removes her hand, telling her he's "sick." What the reader understands from this first clue regarding Jake's wound, and what Georgette understands, is open to question. Does she think he's just not in the mood, has a headache, feels momentarily ill, wants to wait until after dinner? Or does she understand immediately—"Everybody's sick. I'm sick, too"—what she clearly understands after dinner, one page later (17:4)?

16:2–3 **Saints Pères:** They leave the dark garden, come into the light, cross over the river on the pont du Carrousel, and head south on the rue des Saints-Pères—the Street of the Holy Fathers, with its Catholic overtones that foreshadow what we later learn about Jake's Catholicism. Hemingway's street references, indeed all his place references, are never merely incidental or accidental. On any possible route that the *fiacre* could follow to get to Lavigne's, where they eat dinner, they must follow a minimum of three streets (or as many as six), but Hemingway only *names* the Street of the Holy Fathers. Cartography is always part of Hemingway's aesthetic iceberg. As they talk about being sick, and Jake tells Georgette his name is Jacob, they are passing the major landmark on the rue des Saints-Pères, the Hôpital de la Charité, the Charity Hospital, at the corner of rue Jacob. "Sickness" notwithstanding, Jake charitably buys her dinner.

16:6 **difference:** The role of absinthe/Pernod as tonic or medicine continues to figure in the conversation. What does Georgette mean when she says it makes no difference to women, only to men? Is she thinking of its reputed aphrodisiac properties and why, if Jake is "sick," he should not drink it? Why would he drink an aphrodisiac if he doesn't want her to touch him? Or is she thinking of its harmful effect on male fertility? Though this wouldn't matter to her, she may be thinking of both reputed effects of the drink.

16:11 **Flemish:** Jake's name would be Jacob in Flanders, the Dutch-speaking region of Belgium; in Wallonia, or French-speaking Belgium, it would be Jacques. Georgette is pleased that Jake is not "Flamand" because as a Walloon, a Francophone Belgian, she participates in the Flemish-Walloon tension that existed since the creation of the artificial country of Belgium in 1830, yoking together by nation-making legislative fiat two peoples with two distinct languages and cultures. (Belgium is roughly 60 percent Flemish and 40 percent Walloon, with a very small German minority.) Jake indicates his knowledge of Belgian history and culture when he says that the food at Lavigne's is better than what she would eat in Liège, the capital of Wallonie, Belgium. Georgette corrects him, saying she is from Brussels, which is—geographically at least—in the Flemish section of Belgium. This does not mean, however, as has sometimes been suggested, that Georgette is a self-hating "Flamand." Brussels has been a Francophone city since the foundation of Belgium in 1830, and the Walloons, politically and culturally, long dominated the city (and the country). Hemingway, from early childhood, was probably well aware of Walloon identity, since he spent many summers at the family cottage on Walloon Lake in northern Michigan. His mother wrote a song called "Lovely Walloona."

16:19 **Foyot's:** Accurately, Foyot, a famous and expensive restaurant, established in 1848 by Emperor Louis-Philippe's chef Foyot, was located at 33, rue de Tournon, not far from where Jake and Georgette dine at Lavigne's. Jake's suggestion that Georgette keep the cab and go to Foyot's alone is ironic on several accounts: (1) It was a very expensive restaurant, frequented by senators and politicians from the nearby Palais du Luxembourg; (2) Georgette could not afford it, nor would she be admitted. The building that housed Foyot was torn down in 1938.

16:24 **Lavigne:** Lavigne's restaurant, Le Nègre de Toulouse (later named Cahors), was at 159, boulevard du Montparnasse. The restaurant was one of Hemingway's favorites when he was with Hadley (his first wife); as he indicates in *A Moveable Feast,* they were regulars there, and—in the old French custom—their own napkins, in their designated napkin rings, always awaited their arrival. Many other expatriates were regulars at Lavigne's, including Harold Loeb and Kitty Cannell, and Ford Madox Ford and his companion Stella Bowen (models for Mr. and Mrs. Braddocks, who are in the restaurant when Jake arrives with Georgette). Stella Bowen, however, was Australian, not Canadian (see 17:23). One of her best-known and most ambitious paintings, *Le Restaurant Lavigne,* was a triptych with the proprietors, Monsieur and Madame Lavigne, in the middle, flanked on both sides by the restaurant staff, who are depicted as a chorus of angels.

16:31 **wine:** In the first draft, Hemingway was more specific about the wine and food consumed by Jake and Georgette at Lavigne's. The wine was specified as Chablis—the famous flinty dry white wine of the Burgundian region around the town of Chablis, celebrated for two thousand years as one of the greatest white wines, cultivated for one thousand years by monks of the Cistercian order. The wine accompanies—appropriately, as always in Hemingway's work—*coquilles Saint-Jacques,* a traditional preparation of scallops. Along with the civilized delight in good food and wine, for Hemingway, wine and food often function symbolically as thematic signposts, a kind of road marker indicating direction. Chablis became famous not just because of the monastic discipline that produced it, but because such great wine came from vines grown on thin-soiled, infertile hillsides in difficult conditions. The wines Jake drinks and the food he eats are objective correlatives for his situation, the *terroir* of his experience. *Coquilles Saint-Jacques* are named specifically after the pilgrimage of Saint-Jacques-de-Compostelle (or Santiago de Compostela), the pilgrimage route that Jake follows in the novel, which provides the deep structure of the narrative. The *coquille*, or cockleshell, is the symbol of the Compostelan pilgrim and of Saint James (or Saint Jacques or Santiago) in his avatar as the pilgrim saint. The shells are commonly referred to in France as *pèlerines*, or pilgrim shells. Hemingway probably deleted his reference to *coquilles Saint-Jacques* because, by the aesthetic imperatives of his iceberg theory and his stylistic economy of understatement, it gave too much away. The pilgrimage allusions in chapter 1 (Sainte-Odile, etc.) are less obvious. But here, after they have just passed rue Jacob and discussed Jake's name—Jacob is the same name as Jacques, James, and Iago; the first pilgrim guide to Compostela was the celebrated twelfth-century *Liber Sancti Jacobi*; and *jacquet* is the common French term for a Compostelan pilgrim—the reference to *coquilles Saint-Jacques* must have seemed a pilgrimage allusion that was too obvious, and too early in the novel (see also 78:6–7 and passim).

17:4 **dirty war:** This entire key passage (lines 2–7) centered on Georgette's succinct characterization of the war was added after Hemingway's first draft. It is a crucial revision because (1) this is the first direct statement that Jake was wounded in the war, with the clear implication that the wound has resulted in sexual incapacitation (see also 30:26); (2) Georgette seems to understand immediately, if she has not already understood when she declared on the preceding page that everybody is "sick," and she shares Jake's sense of the war as a great wound to their generation; and (3) Jake's ensuing ironic commentary and protestation of boredom with the subject of the war do not signify that he is indifferent to the subject—he just doesn't want to talk about it. The fact that Jake shares with Hemingway an almost superstitious reluctance to talk about certain things does not mean that he is not profoundly aware—personally and generally—of the pervasive effects of the "dirty war." The war is the backdrop, the subtext, the ground of being of the novel. The major characters—especially Jake and Brett—are who they are and do what they do in large part because of the war. Other novelists more given to documentation, historical saturation, and digression would probably devote many tedious expository chapters to the war background if they were dealing with similar characters and situations. Consider what is gained by Hemingway's extreme economy in letting a prostitute's four-word characterization of the war serve as the novel's primary pronouncement on the subject.

17:11 **big table:** Having just noted he was bored enough, Jake's boredom is not relieved by encountering Braddocks (see 5:21 and 16:24) and his wife, Cohn, Frances, and others. Notice Cohn's conspicuous lack of *presence* in this entire scene. It is remarkable, given the focus on Robert in chapters 1 and 2, that for almost five pages of this sequence of scenes, it is as if he is not there—he says and does nothing.

17:18 **had a smile:** Before he returns to the other room to finish his meal and wine with Georgette, Jake makes the curious observation that Frances (who is presumably sitting down) is tall and "had a smile." This odd characterization of a smile echoes Jake's earlier observation that Frances is the "lady who had [Cohn]" (5:23). Frances, then, seems to embody the inauthenticity of *having* as opposed to *being*, a metaphysical (and existential) distinction of which Jake is acutely aware.

17:26 **writers and artists:** Georgette is not the simple dim-witted prostitute that some commentators have made her out to be. She agrees with Jake that there are too many pseudowriters and artists on the Left Bank. In the first draft of the manuscript, Georgette's background is given in more detail—for example, she has lived with an artist, a painter who abused her, in Brussels. Given the abuse in Brett's background, the variations on the theme of prostitution and promiscuity that the novel explores, and even the partially homophonic (Georgette-Brett) naming, it seems clear that Georgette's rendezvous with Jake was intended to prefigure the imminent arrival of Brett on the scene. Paired scenes and situations that resonate without intrusive narrative commentary are a familiar device in Hemingway's work. However, this is not to say, as some commentators have suggested, that we *must* see prostitution as a major theme or some kind of master key to the action of the novel. Georgette is a prostitute; Brett is sexually promiscuous, but she is *not* a prostitute—she even turns down the ten thousand dollars (an extraordinary sum in the 1920s) that the count offers her (33). A careful reading of the novel's transactions, of balance sheets—financial, behavioral, moral, and spiritual (not to mention the basic facts of place and character)—will not permit the kind of interpretation that maintains that Jake's (or Hemingway's) Paris is the "City of Brothelly Love" (Caswell, passim). "Georgette" may partially *rhyme* with "Brett," but suggestion is not identity, analogy is not perfect equivalence, and sound is not always sense. If such imperfect rhymes were indeed a key to anything, then we would have to consider carefully that Georgette and Brett are both central actors in the *bal musette* scene that follows, and we might be required (under such a system of misinterpretation) to ask whether Georgette or Brett is the "Little Muse" that a misreading of *musette* might suggest. Since a synonym for *musette* is *cabrette* (the latter actually containing Brett's name), and they both mean a goatskin bagpipe (see 19:16), then we might have to consider the entire history of lascivious associations with goats, not to mention the appearance later in the novel of the wineskin (made from goatskin) drinking scene, and who knows what feverish Georgette-Brett-*musette*-*cabrette* (throw in Lett, the homosexual at the *bal musette*) misreadings might arise from criticism based on contorted wordplay and half-rhymes forced to serve a thesis? Speaking of tone-deaf wordplay, what does Paris (which is not a city of only "brothelly love") have to do with Philadelphia (the "City of Brotherly Love")?

18:7 **Georgette Leblanc:** Jake's complicated sense of humor is richly evident here. When Jake and Georgette join the others, the men at the table—in the proper rite of good manners—stand up in a lady's presence, even though it is clearly a prostitute whom Jake introduces as his fiancée. Making a joke that would not be lost on this group of Montparnasse Quarterites—or indeed on almost anyone in Paris in the 1920s—Jake introduces her as Georgette Leblanc, one of the best-known Parisian personages of the period. Leblanc was an opera singer (with the Paris Opéra-Comique), an actress (stage and film), a writer, and the longtime mistress of the Nobel Prize–winning (1911) poet and playwright Maurice Maeterlinck. She starred in his most popular play, *L'Oiseau bleu* (1909), or *The Blue Bird,* a kind of "fairy play" in the *Peter Pan* mode. They lived together from 1895 until 1918, when Maeterlinck left her to marry a younger woman. By the time Hemingway arrived in Paris, Leblanc was a well-known eccentric sometimes seen bicycling through the streets in operatic costumes and flowing medieval robes. By 1923 she was living in an openly lesbian relationship with Margaret Anderson, the publisher of the *Little Review,* one of the leading little magazines at the center of the modernist movement, in which Joyce's *Ulysses* was first published—as well as the work of many other modernist writers, including Hemingway. Leblanc's Paris studio was the headquarters of a so-called Gurdjieff Circle, where acolytes (including a number of well-known lesbians in the Paris community) of the Turkish "mystic" (or philosopher or "spiritual master") George I. Gurdjieff conducted their studies at the intersection of the mystical and the avant-garde, where pseudomysticism, "freakishness, aestheticism, sex, went hand in hand" (Putnam 82). In 1924 Leblanc starred in (and partially financed) Marcel L'Herbier's avant-garde film *L'Inhumaine,* the story of a young scientist who falls in love with and is rejected by a world-famous singer (played by Leblanc); after she is poisoned, he resurrects her from the dead to win her love. The slight murky plot was of little interest to filmgoers, but the aggressively avant-garde staging of the story, with extravagant Cubist settings by the painter Fernand Léger, score by Darius Milhaud, and other aspects of the film, caused it to be both praised as an innovative celebration of the art forms of the 1920s avant-garde and denounced as an insistently chic exercise in aesthetic dilettantism. Leblanc's film career was short lived. She lived with Margaret Anderson until her death in 1941. Hemingway knew Leblanc and Anderson, would have seen them around Paris, and would certainly have been familiar with the arc of Leblanc's life and career. In a 1924 letter to Ezra Pound in Italy, Hemingway brings Pound up to date on the latest Paris gossip, including the fact that "Margaret Anderson is in town with Georgette Mangeuse le Blanc" (*Selected Letters* 115). Lest the wrong conclusion be drawn from the crudity of Hemingway's sexual reference (*mangeuse* means "big eater"), it should be added that, years later, when Leblanc was dying of cancer and being cared for by Anderson, who was struggling with poverty, Hemingway sent Anderson four hundred dollars (not a paltry sum at the time). He sent it via Solita Solano, another member of that remarkable lesbian community of the Left Bank, and he sent it to "Dearest Solita," with "Much love" and admonitions not to worry "because as long as any of us have any money we all have money" (*Selected Letters* 522; see also Benstock, passim).

Why then does Jake introduce his *poule* as Georgette Leblanc to these denizens of Montparnasse who, he has every reason to assume, will get the joke because they know all about the real Leblanc? First of all, at the most obvious level, because Georgette is from Belgium, and Leblanc is the cast-off lover of the most famous Belgian writer, Maeterlinck, the association comes naturally to Jake's mind. This associative link, as it were, is even clearer in the first manuscript version, in which we learn that Georgette Hobin has also been mistreated by a Belgian artist. If the reader assumes that the friends to whom Jake introduces Georgette know about his love for Brett, the Leblanc allusion could be read as a way of saying, yes, I've picked up a prostitute but I've only done it for amusement, for company, just as I might pick up a famous lesbian. If the reader assumes that Jake's friends know about his hopeless love for Brett (i.e., about his sexually incapacitating war wound), there is another layer to the joke. This is a key question—who *does* know about Jake's wound?—that has rarely, if ever, been asked or answered in the extensive commentary on the novel. There is no evidence anywhere in the text that would lead the reader to believe that anybody but Brett, and probably Bill, knows the specifics of Jake's wound; and he is certainly not the kind of confessional, self-pitying character who would talk about it. If Jake's friends have seen Leblanc's recent film *L'Inhumaine,* they might divine Jake's private joke about the cruel beauty who rejects her lover, as well as the suggestion of some kind of resuscitation or transformation. If they know Jake is a fairly serious Catholic, they might see some humor in his announcement that the prostitute he's with is Georgette Leblanc, the well-known acolyte of the pseudo-mystic Gurdjieff. In any case, the more the reader knows—about Leblanc—the more the allusive resonance reveals the depths of the iceberg of meaning. The entire Georgette scene is more carefully structured than it might at first seem; most important, Jake's arrival on the scene at Lavigne's with a prostitute whom he introduces as a famous lesbian directly prefigures Brett's first appearance in the novel, two pages later, with a "crowd" of homosexuals.

18:15 **Hobin:** This may be one of Hemingway's buried language jokes (more visual than auditory): *ho* in French is "oh," *bine* is "hoe," and *biner* means "to hoe." If Georgette's name stands for "Oh, hoe," Hemingway's cross-language pun is obvious.

18:31 **love Paris:** Again, the nature of one's response to place—specifically, to Paris—figures importantly in the conversation. Here, however, Frances Clyne's touristic superficialities about Paris are ironically played off against the views of a Parisian "working girl" who knows the streets of Paris in a very different way. Georgette, taking Frances for a phony character, turns to Jake and asks if she has to talk to Frances. Clearly, in the interaction between Georgette and Frances, Georgette comes off better in Jake's eyes. He respects the honest working girl at the same time that he disdains the phoniness of Frances and the ostensibly higher-class mode of prostitution that might be discerned in her relationship with Robert.

19:16 **bal musette:** Although *bal musette* is often construed, in Hemingway studies and certain tourist guidebooks, as the common "French term for any popular dancing hall" (Oliver 17), the term in fact has a much more particularized meaning. And with that precise signification comes a set of connotations (for the 1920s especially) that Hemingway was likely well aware of, since his first apartment in Paris (1922–23) was above the *bal musette* at 74, rue du Cardinal Lemoine. (Hemingway referred to this *bal musette* repeatedly in his work, from his early journalism to "The Snows of Kilimanjaro" and *A Moveable Feast.*) By the 1920s, *bal musette* was generally defined as a popular dance-hall with an accordion band; the term was also sometimes used to refer both to the kind of music played and to the old-fashioned dance (the *bourrée*) that sometimes went with the music until newer dances like the java began to predominate. Until 1900, these *bals* in Paris still featured the *musette* (also called the *cabrette*), a small goatskin bagpipe that was very popular in the Auvergne region of France. In the nineteenth century, immigrants from the Auvergne brought their *musette* or *cabrette* folk music and dances to Paris with them and opened the first *bals musette* in Paris, usually very small dance-hall cafés or bars. Auvergnat *bals musette* particularly thrived in the fifth arrondissement, which is where Hemingway lived above one *bal musette* and where his characters in *The Sun Also Rises* dance at another *bal.* With the increasing presence of Italian immigrants in Paris at the turn of the century, the accordion was introduced into the *bal musette.* Purists continued to insist that a true *bal musette* must have music provided only by the *musette* or *cabrette* and the *grelottière,* the ankle bracelet of little bells that the proprietor of the *bal musette* wears in this scene (19). One Eugène Guitard, president of the association La Cabrette, summed up the problem in January 1896 in this fashion: "Where the accordion and violin have replaced the musette, where uproar has replaced the bourrée . . . is also where open laughter has been replaced by the knife" (Tchamouroff 3). By 1918 there were three distinct kinds of establishments that were called *bals musette:* the *bal des familles* (or family dance-hall, usually run by Auvergnats and often still featuring the music of the *musette* or *cabrette,* especially in the fifth arrondissement); the *bal musette populaire* (where the Italian influence prevailed, the accordion reigned, and newer dance styles were the fashion); and the *guinche* (really not a *bal musette* at all, just a dance-hall hangout for low-life crooks and other seedy characters). In the 1920s the style of *music* that was called *bal musette* evolved significantly, first through the introduction of the banjo and guitar by Gypsy musicians, and eventually the introduction of drums (and sometimes horns) and elements of jazz. By the mid-1920s, the time frame of *The Sun Also Rises,* some *bals musette* had become fashionable places for the middle and upper classes, for writers and artists, for lesbians and homosexuals, for tourists, and for anyone looking for the thrill of some imagined folk authenticity to indulge their fantasies of mingling with the "masses," the working class, and the criminal and tough-guy class. Some *bals musette* even staged fake police raids, complete with fake criminals and gunfire, to entertain the tourists and others who went slumming at *bals musette.*

The *bal* that Hemingway knew best was undoubtedly the one beneath his apartment; he and his wife Hadley often went downstairs to dance in the tiny dance hall that had the atmosphere of the "real old workmen's France," although there was occasionally a "scattering of sailors and *poules*" among the regular customers (Baker, *Life Story* 95). Hadley and some of her friends found the place somewhat rough, but "Ernest seemed to revel in the smoky atmosphere"; wearing his "striped Breton fisherman's shirt, he might have been mistaken for a native of the place" (95). During special fetes such as Bastille Day, the accordionist, accompanied by drummers and a bagpiper, moved the music out into the street, where they played and locals danced for several days (95). What do these details really tell us about the *bal musette* that Hemingway knew best? Because of its location in the fifth arrondissement, and because on special occasions the bagpipe—the *musette* or *cabrette*—was still played, it seems clear that this was a traditional Auvergnat *bal musette* still retaining some folk or traditional elements but clearly (cf. the additional musical instruments and the identity of the customers) undergoing its 1920s transformation into a more modern *bal musette.* Also, we note another instance of Hemingway's quest for authenticity, his desire to blend in with the true locals (as he generally did throughout his life, going so far, e.g., as to stain his skin with berry juice and wear appropriate clothes when he participated in the Gypsy pilgrimage in Provence in 1927, or his various efforts to "go native," as in Africa—see *Under Kilimanjaro*).

How does the *bal musette* described in *The Sun Also Rises* resemble Hemingway's local *bal?* We are told that the location is on the rue de la Montagne Sainte-Geneviève, a few blocks away from Hemingway's *bal.* Local "working people" make up the crowd five nights a week, but one night a week, Braddocks makes some sort of arrangement to reserve it as a "dancing-club" for his expatriate friends. (Apparently, Ford Madox Ford, the model for Braddocks, rented Hemingway's home *bal musette* on the rue du Cardinal Lemoine for his dance parties.) The "pleasant" music is provided by the proprietor's accordion and *grelottière* and supplemented by banjo, introduced into *bals musette* by Gypsies in the early 1920s (see 23:7). Again, the fifth arrondissement location, the presence of traditional folk elements (the *grelottière*), and the fact that for five nights a week the place is frequented by local working people all suggest that this is another Auvergnat *bal musette* evolving or devolving into its 1920s avatar.

At least one commentator on the novel has argued that the "real Bal de la Montagne Sainte-Genevieve was no ordinary working-class dance hall" and suggested that Hemingway chooses this *bal* because it was a notorious hangout for homosexuals and lesbians, and it thus prefigures the "sexual ambivalence" at the heart of the *bal musette* scene (Kennedy 104–6). First of all, it is necessary to point out that Hemingway does not call the *bal* by this name, and then it should be noted that there were several *bals* on the rue de la Montagne Sainte-Geneviève. Indeed, Jake walks "down the street" to the next *bal* for a few minutes. Moreover, since Braddocks and his expatriate friends, as heterosexuals, would not be likely to hire on a regular basis a famous homosexual hangout (or *bal des invertis*) for their dance night, and since Hemingway specifically states that five nights a week the *bal* was the terrain of the local working people, it seems misleading at best to suggest that the *bal musette* rendered in this scene is a notorious "Left Bank conclave of Sodom and Lesbos" and then use that forced reading to reach the highly suspect conclusion that the *bal musette* scene "provides a revealing first glimpse of the sexual confusion at the crux of Jake's agony" (Kennedy 107). This is, in various ways, a curious reading of the *bal musette* setting and sequence of events. Just how does this scene represent a *conclave,* a secret meeting, as if this *bal musette* were some pseudo-demimonde-Vatican conclave of "Sodom and Lesbos"? And just what "sexual confusion," the reader should ask, is at the core of Jake's anguish? The fact that Brett enters the *bal musette* with homosexuals signifies nothing more than a familiar fact of nightlife in all times and places—that an attractive heterosexual woman might choose to barhop with male homosexuals for the freedom from sexual harassment that such company offers— with such a crowd, as Brett says, "one can drink in such safety" (22). Clearly, it is a sexual *wound* that is the cause of Jake's agony, not any kind of sexual *confusion.*

The precision with which Hemingway constructs this superbly rendered *bal musette* scene is typical of the historical and local knowledge, the exactitude of detail, that Hemingway brings to the settings of his fiction. His genius of selection in choosing the *bal musette* as the setting for this crucial scene is evident when readers know something about the history of the *bal musette* and are able to recognize such a place as an exemplary urban symbolic landscape that incarnates themes centered in the clash of tradition and modernity, authenticity and inauthenticity, folk and sophisticated sensibilities, country and city contrasts—themes that inform the novel throughout. Hemingway has created a kind of composite *bal musette* based on his intimate knowledge of his "home *bal*," an Auvergnat folk *bal musette,* crossed with one of the more *louche* and *outré bals* in 1920s Paris. The days of the *musette* or *cabrette,* the folk pipers of the Auvergne with their traditional *grelottière* around their ankles, are clearly numbered, as are the old traditional dances, in all the *bals* of

Paris in the 1920s. Some such sense, which is much more than mere nostalgia, is at the heart of Hemingway's (and Jake's) perennial quest for the last authentic things, what he calls the "real old stuff" (*Selected Letters* 131), that remain in a radically desacralized world—the world after that "dirty" war, after all the physical and moral and aesthetic and spiritual bankruptcies and betrayals of the nineteenth century (cf. Ezra Pound's *Hugh Selwyn Mauberley* and T. S. Eliot's *The Waste Land*). Those authentic things, "intact from the old days," as Hemingway put it (*Selected Letters* 237), include, in *The Sun Also Rises,* not only the world of *toreo* (the bullfight), the Catholic Church and the notion of pilgrimage, the last good country and unspoiled fishing, but also the last good city and the unspoiled *bal musette.* The reader who wants to find aural entry to that *bal musette* world, where Jake feels "happy" dancing to the "pleasant" accordion music, might start by listening to certain songs of the legendary Edith Piaf, who (like her mother before her) began her singing career on the streets and in the *bals* of Paris (circa 1930). For example, one of her most famous songs, "L'Accordéoniste," tells the story of a prostitute who falls in love with an accordionist—Piaf's tribute to the *bal musette,* its traditions, and its musicians.

19:17 **Sainte Geneviève:** Geneviève (422–509) is the patron saint of Paris. An early type of the warrior saint, she is said to have led an armed band when the Franks besieged Paris and to have been instrumental in turning Attila and the Huns away from Paris. Subject of a long-thriving cult with attendant pilgrimages and processions, she was credited with many miracles; her shrine was in the Church of Saints Peter and Paul (later renamed after her), which stood where the Panthéon (still regarded as her burial place) now stands. Her shrine and her relics were desecrated and mostly destroyed during the French Revolution. Although her bones were burned by a revolutionary mob, a fragment of her sarcophagus is enshrined in the church of Saint-Étienne-du-Mont, adjacent to the Panthéon on the place Sainte-Geneviève. The *montagne,* the mountain named after her, is the highest point on the Left Bank of Paris, sometimes referred to as the Mont de Paris. Along with Montmartre and Montparnasse, it is one of the three mountains of Paris. Hemingway refers, of course, to all three in *The Sun Also Rises.* He sometimes signed his letters with variations on "Mountain Man," accompanied by a sketch of three mountain peaks. Some observers have explained this logo merely as a reference to the Three Mountains Press, the small Parisian press that printed Hemingway's second book, *in our time* (1924); but real knowledge of the three mountains of Paris will suggest a deeper private symbolism behind Hemingway's logo.

19:18 **Pantheon:** An imposing building with a majestic dome, dating from 1764, the Panthéon was originally the Church of Sainte-Geneviève. With the Revolution, the church was deconsecrated and made a secular temple and burial place dedicated to distinguished French citizens and writers such as Rousseau and Voltaire, as well as

Mirabeau and Marat, although the remains of the latter two revolutionary leaders "were soon cast out with ignominy" (Muirhead and Monmarché, *Paris* 120). For much of the nineteenth century after the Panthéon was reconsecrated with the Restoration in 1814, it was again a place of Christian worship until its final deconsecration in 1885, when, with Victor Hugo's interment there, it again became a temple of secular fame. Nevertheless, extensive signs—exterior sculpture and interior murals and frescoes—remind the observer that this was the Church of Sainte-Geneviève, and the iconography of her representations (e.g., miracles, processions, homage paid to her by rulers of France such as Charlemagne and Saint Louis), mingled with the memorials to famous writers and military figures, still declares her role as the patron saint and protector of Paris. Opposite the Panthéon, on the north side of the *place* is the Bibliothèque Sainte-Geneviève, one of the famous libraries of France. Among the other famous buildings of what Jake calls "the Pantheon quarter" is the Collège Sainte-Barbe, the oldest public educational institution in France, where Saint Ignatius Loyola was a student in the 1520s. Saint Barbara (Sainte Barbe) is the patron saint of artillerymen and those in danger of sudden death. Saint Ignatius was a soldier who received a serious groin wound from a cannonball in the siege of Pamplona in 1521, what Hemingway calls in *Death in the Afternoon* "the wound that made him think" (274)—the wound that led to his conversion. Like Loyola, both Jake and Hemingway are wounded soldiers *and* Catholic converts. After his serious wounding in Pamplona, Loyola's conversion found issue in his famous book of *Spiritual Exercises* and his meditative technique of "composition of place." Hemingway knows all this, and given *his* serious wounding by artillery, he later considered giving his Nobel Prize medal to Saint Barbara (Stoneback, "From the Rue Saint-Jacques" 3). Jake, who is preparing to make his annual pilgrimage to Pamplona, invites the reader of his narrative to participate in his "spiritual exercises," his version of composition of place, a compelling necessity initiated by his war wound. These, then, are just some of the resonances evoked by *place,* by the actual facts of "the Pantheon quarter," the deepest layers of Hemingway's unstated iceberg. Only the most obvious fact of this quarter is rendered in this scene—the desecration of the traditional *bal musette,* an echo in a minor key of the far greater desecrations of tradition, secular and spiritual, that occurred on Sainte Geneviève's mountain and in the desacralized Panthéon.

20:8 **young men:** Hemingway's indirection, his technique of obliquity, should be noted here. Many authors would introduce a group of homosexuals into a scene by immediate naming, through labeling at their first appearance. Hemingway does so through rendered details in a sequence of increasing clarification. In quizzes on this scene, I have asked thousands of students (over a thirty-year period) when they *first* realized that Brett's young men were homosexuals. Approximately 10 percent of readers said they understood from these first details (hands, newly washed, wavy hair), 10 percent saw it from the policeman's smile in the next sentence, 20 percent saw it when the young men first speak, 50 percent saw it only when Jake expresses his anger—and 10 percent never saw it at all. These tabulated results from surveys of college students conducted over some three decades may suggest nothing more than the fact that there is a wide divergence of attention to detail among readers; or they may suggest that early in the novel, Hemingway's style has not yet imposed its hermeneutic necessities (the essential strategies and tactics of attention and interpretation) on the reader. All great stylists teach readers, as they go along, how their work is to be read and understood.

20:13 **policeman:** Why is this policeman standing by the door of the *bal*? Is he a real policeman on duty or one of those fake policemen hired by the clubs to provide phony thrills and excitement for the bohemian clientele? In any case, what matters here is the smile of recognition that he shares with Jake when they both watch the young men arrive at the *bal*.

20:13–19 **With them:** By having Brett arrive on the scene with a "crowd" of homosexuals, Hemingway dramatically foregrounds Brett's first appearance in the novel and underlines the intensity of the moment for Jake through prose rhythms and repetitions. In a triadic sequence of incremental repetition, Hemingway writes three times in seven lines that Brett is "with them," forcing the attentive reader to hear the rhythmic variations and emphases: Brett is *with* them, and with *them*. As is often the case with such carefully wrought passages in Hemingway's prose, his revisions intensified both the meaning and the rhythm of the sequence, since he added the third repetition (the sentence that ends "she was very much with them") after the first draft of the manuscript.

20:21 **tolerant:** Some twenty-first-century readers will no doubt find Jake intolerant and homophobic in his attitude toward these homosexuals. Whatever strains of homophobia (and heterophobia) may be discernible in this scene, Hemingway seems to suggest that Jake's reaction is conduct centered (i.e., more a response to individual behavior than to group identity), and his main point is that Jake's anger is perfectly natural (and directed at least in part toward Brett), since "they" presumably could perform heterosexually with Brett but choose not to, while Jake physically desires and loves her but cannot consummate that love sexually. In any case, Jake controls his anger, goes down the street to the next *bal*, and drinks a bad beer and a "worse cognac," trying to get the taste of the entire scene out of his mouth. But when he returns, his distaste lingers as he watches "them" taking up Georgette and dancing with her. Throughout the scene, his intense distaste is indicated by his noun aversion, his use of "they" and "them."

21:1 **Prentiss:** In what amounts to a brief cameo appearance in the novel, lasting half a page, Prentiss (another bad novelist, it seems, named Robert—certainly an "apprentice" novelist, since he's a "new novelist," "only a child") functions as an index of inauthenticity and a focus for the extension of Jake's distaste for homosexuals. Some commentators have noted that his affected speech patterns and his "superior, simpering composure" (20:23) indicate his sexual kinship with and possible inclusion in the crowd of homosexuals that arrives with Brett. To judge from the name changes this character underwent in the novel's revisions, Hemingway intended to make clear Prentiss's homosexuality. In the manuscript he was called Ralph Severn, which was changed to Roger Prescott in the typescript, and finally, after Hemingway's editor, Maxwell Perkins, objected that Prescott was too close to Wescott, he became Robert Prentiss. Glenway Wescott (1901–1987) was a Midwesterner who had early success with such books as *The Grandmothers* and *Goodbye, Wisconsin.* He was a well-known homosexual, a central figure in the gay communities of Paris and New York. When I met Wescott at a literary event in Kentucky in the early 1980s, he was still talking in the speech patterns and strange accent that Hemingway attributed to Prentiss/Wescott in the 1920s. He asked me: "Do you find Kentucky amusing?" And three times in the course of one evening, I heard him say to others "oh, how charmingly" they did this or that—further evidence of the deadly accuracy of Hemingway's ear and his precision of observation. (Or was Wescott, by then largely forgotten, deliberately echoing the speech patterns attributed to him in his most famous appearance in literature?) Prentiss is yet another antiexemplary character who does not like Paris. Jake, with his impeccable radar for the phony, and his existential nausea when confronted with the inauthentic, walks away from Prentiss (thinking he might "throw up") and—establishing a straight-line connection between two mediocre novelists named Robert who dislike Paris—talks with Cohn.

21:32 **whole show:** It is not just the homosexuals who make Jake "sick" but the "whole show": the phoniness of people like Prentiss and the Braddocks crowd, the corruption of the *bal musette* atmosphere, the tediousness of the talk of whether Paris is "amusing" or not—and earlier whether Paris is "clean" or "dirty"—and, most of all, the central presence of Brett in all this sickness. Hemingway here deploys his characteristic device of juxtapositional sentence sequence in which one sentence seems at first to have no apparent relation to the preceding sentence but, when examined closely, the odd sequence brings the question at hand into sharp focus. Jake's statement that the whole show makes him sick, followed by the succinct action sentence—"Brett came up to the bar"—sums up the events and feelings of the entire chapter and takes the reader back to Jake's discussion of sickness and that "dirty war" with Georgette. Jake is sick, and what makes his sickness unbearable at this point in the story is Brett, who arrives at the bar and speaks her first words in the novel.

22:2 **tight:** "Tight" is a common slang term for drunk. Some readers may find it curious, or impolite (or even mean), that the first thing Jake says to Brett is to ask her why she isn't drunk. Other readers may see this as the kind of gentle banter that very good friends use with each other. If it's the former, then Jake's question will be construed as an indication of how upset he is by her arrival with the homosexuals. If it's the latter, his banter might be seen as a sign of how happy he is to see her, and to see her sober though it's late in the evening and he himself is a "little drunk." Maybe it's both or neither. The abruptness of this first dialogue between Jake and Brett would lose its edge if Hemingway's last-minute galley deletions regarding Brett's background had not been made. In the deleted chapter 1, Jake discusses in great detail the way Brett drinks and how it affects her; there is "nothing of the alcoholic about her," she never drinks alone, and she is never "dissolved" by drinking—she is always "clear run, generous, and her lines were always as clear." When Brett does get "blind" it happens in "three successive stages"; if, for example, she drinks "whiskey and sodas from four o'clock in the afternoon until two o'clock in the morning," Brett first stops talking and just sits and listens, then she sees nothing that is going on around her, and finally she ceases "to hear"—but observers of her in this condition "would never know she had been drinking" (Svoboda, *Crafting of a Style* 132–33; see 6:10–11). This is one of several instances where Hemingway's late decision to discard entirely chapter 1 (and much of chapter 2)—although Fitzgerald had only urged him to *revise*—created problematic passages later in the text. If Jake's careful analysis of Brett's drinking had remained in chapter 1, this passage, and Jake's first words to Brett, would follow naturally, and the reader would better understand that Brett has not been drinking much—perhaps because she knows she's going to see Jake at the *bal musette*—and has not yet even reached her first stage of being blind, because she still speaks, still responding with witty repartee as she says she's never "going to get tight any more" and orders a brandy.

22:7 **promised land:** Cohn's "compatriot," Moses, saw but never entered the "promised land." Biblical allusions abound in the novel, and Hemingway often trimmed them in revision to make them less obvious. Here, he had originally written, "his compatriot Moses," but deleted the obvious naming and retained the witty observation that Cohn was much younger than Moses. And, no doubt, more eager, and less deserving, since for him the "promised land" of Brett is just another romantic "Purple Land."

22:9 **damned good-looking:** Again, war wound notwithstanding, Jake responds to a woman's physical presence (as he did—more clearly in the manuscript—to Georgette). Some of Hemingway's best descriptions of Brett's looks were in the deleted opening chapter: she has "a certain grand vitality," she's "not supposed to be beautiful" but when she's in a room with other women "who were supposed to be beautiful she killed their looks entirely," and painters were always wanting her to pose for them (Svoboda, *Crafting of a Style* 133). Jake, always a careful observer of detail, comments on Brett's fashion sense, her *style:* she "started all that," meaning both her hairstyle and her way of dressing. It was widely reported in the 1920s that within a year after the publication of *The Sun Also Rises,* many American women, college students and others, were modeling their dress, speech, and hairstyle after Brett. Short hair for women, of course, was fashionable before Brett, but the bobbed hair of the typical Jazz Age flapper (cf. Fitzgerald) is not the same thing as Brett's "brushed back" Eton-crop hairstyle. Nor is Brett a flapper in any other way—since flapper style generally aimed for an androgynous adolescent look, with bound breasts and undefined waists under curve-concealing sack dresses, the exact opposite of Brett's appearance, as Jake points out: "you missed none of it." There is no gender ambiguity or sexual confusion in Brett's appearance—she is very much, boldly and independently so, a woman. Brett was based on Duff Twysden, a well-known British aristocrat and expatriate resident of Paris. In the original manuscript version of the novel, Brett's name was Duff. If, as seems to be the case, Hemingway was attracted to Duff in Paris and when she was at the fiesta in Pamplona with Hemingway and his wife Hadley, and if, as also seems to be the case, he was faithful to Hadley, this would help to explain Fitzgerald's comment to Hemingway in a letter that Jake isn't "*like an impotent man. He's like a man in a sort of moral chastity belt*" (Svoboda, *Crafting of a Style* 140; Fitzgerald's emphasis).

22:21 **in restraint of trade:** The repartee between Jake and Brett centers on the company they keep—Brett arriving at the *bal musette* with a "fine crowd" of homosexuals, Jake with a prostitute. Brett, laughing, says that by bringing "it" (Georgette), Jake has insulted the other women, and wittily employs the legal term for an action preventing free competition in business, the limiting of a market, the creation of a monopoly. Obviously, however, Georgette's professional presence does not create unfair competition (or restrain trade) for Brett.

22:28 **biblical name:** The second biblical reference on this page, this reference to Jacob is probably intended to remind the reader that in the Old Testament Jacob wrestled with the angel (i.e., in the exegetical tradition, with God) all night; that Jacob received a wound, a "touch" in the hollow of his thigh (or groin); and that Jacob prevails and thus has "power with God and with men," for he has "seen God face to face," his "life is preserved," and "*the sun rose* upon him" (Genesis 32.24–31; emphasis added). Brett probably knows, too, that the biblical Jacob's wound was temporary and he went on to father many children. This biblical naming should also be recalled later when it becomes clear that Jake is a *jacquet* (i.e., a pilgrim on the road to Santiago de Compostela), and his New Testament biblical kinship is with his namesake, Sancti Jacobi/Saint Jacques/Saint James/Santiago, all one and the same pilgrim saint (see 78:6–7 and Stoneback "From the Rue Saint-Jacques," passim). Thus he has a doubly biblical name.

22:30 **Montmartre:** Brett's reference to one of the three "mountains" of Paris resonates in various ways, for in Montmartre's diverse neighborhood(s) there are strong associations with the sacred and the secular, the high country (at the top of the *mont*) of the spirit (art and religion), and the low country of nightclubs and brothels, of sin and sexual entertainments at the base of the mountain. Brett does not say exactly where she and Jake have a "date" (they don't), just "*up* at Montmartre" (emphasis added). Given the direction indicated, and the fact that it follows immediately the biblical reference, the matter should be considered closely. Montmartre, *Mons Martyrum,* or the Mount of the Martyrs, also known as the *butte sacrée,* rises high above Paris on the Right Bank and is crowned by the massive basilica of Sacré-Coeur, begun in 1876 as a kind of war memorial (the Franco-Prussian War of 1870–1871) decreed by the government as votive token of humiliation and repentance. Saint Denis, the patron saint of France, was said to have been martyred here in the third century, and later Sainte Geneviève built a chapel on the site of the martyrdom (where Saint Ignatius Loyola and his companions founded the Society of Jesus in 1534). Thus the "up" direction proposed here by Brett would take them from Sainte Geneviève's mountain, across the river and up the hill to another sacred mountain with strong associations with Sainte Geneviève and Saint Ignatius Loyola, with a history of pilgrimages and processions. There is an echo of all this, of *Mons Martyrum* and Jake's "martyrdom" or war wound, a few pages later in Brett's reference to Mons (27:1).

Also at the top of the hill is the neighborhood known as Old Montmartre, which became in the late 1800s "a real center of artistic endeavour, where poor living and high thinking were combined with unconventional gaiety"; by the end of the nineteenth century, as a 1927 guidebook put it, "a tide of pseudo-bohemians, foreign tourists, and less desirable hangers-on" began to flood the area, the artists moved away, and Montparnasse became the "successor of the old Montmartre" (Muirhead and Monmarché, *Paris* 58).

At the base of the sacred mount is the other Montmartre, the nightlife world of place Blanche, place Clichy, and place Pigalle (christened "Pig Alley" by American and British soldiers during World War I), where now, as in the 1920s, "*les innombrables établissements de plaisir*" range from the floor show of the Moulin Rouge to seedy bars and brothels; by the 1920s the nightlife of Montmartre had lost its traditional local Parisian character, and the establishments, as the 1931 Baedeker guide to Paris indicated, had numerous foreign clientele and were more or less Americanized (Baedeker, *Paris* 26; emphasis added). The 1927 Blue Guide to Paris cautioned visitors that the "motley crowds to be seen in the cafés and 'cabarets artistiques' of the Place Pigalle, etc., have now but a shadowy connection with art or letters, and are apt to include elements against which the tourist should be on his guard" (Muirhead and Monmarché, *Paris* 58). At the surface level of Hemingway's iceberg, then, his composition of place proposes a movement from a desecrated traditional *bal musette* to another locale of modern desecration. At the deepest level of the iceberg, the proposed movement would be from one sacred mount to another sacred mount—and if Jake and Brett were truly to ascend, to go *up* to the real Montmartre, they could not take a taxi up the treacherously steep road: they would either have to walk up (and Brett refuses to walk "across the street") the steep flights of steps that link lower and upper Montmartre or ascend by the funicular railway. Later, in chapter 7, when Brett and Jake do go up to Montmartre with the count, they go to a nightclub at the base of the mount.

23:7 **banjo:** This would be a banjo-guitar, which has six strings and is tuned like a guitar, an instrument that was particularly popular with the *Manouches,* the French Gypsies who lived around Paris. The presence of the banjo is further evidence of the distance this particular *bal* has traveled from its traditional musical roots in the *musette.* Indeed, throughout the 1920s, Gypsies, with their banjos and guitars, were an increasing presence in *musette* bands. The legendary Gypsy guitarist Django Reinhardt (1910–1953) began by playing banjo in just such a *bal musette.* He grew up in Gypsy encampments at the edge of Paris; before he was thirteen he had mastered the banjo-guitar and was playing in the *bals musette,* especially in the fifth arrondissement. Historical records indicate that by 1923 he was playing banjo-guitar in a *bal* on the rue Monge, a few short blocks from the *bal musette* in this scene. Hemingway was always fascinated by Gypsies, first as a boy in Oak Park, where "the gypsy wagons used to camp" at the edge of town (*By-Line* 162), then in the south of France, where he participated in the pilgrimage of les Saintes-Maries-de-la-Mer—the famous so-called Gypsy pilgrimage—in 1927, and later in Spain. So perhaps Jake feels "happy" here not just because he is dancing with Brett but also because the music is very good, the proprietor's *grelottière* and pleasant accordion here enhanced by a Gypsy banjo-guitar—possibly played by a young Django Reinhardt, who, though he would remain relatively unknown until the late twenties, was astounding Parisian *bal musette* audiences with his picking from 1923 on.

23:26 **entendu:** Agreed, understood, okay, the *patronne* (the proprietor's wife) says. Jake, always exact and generous when it comes to conduct, acknowledges his obligation to Georgette, that he owes her for occupying her evening; he gives her more than the usual amount, which in Paris at the time would have been fifty francs for the entire night. He is exact about the code of obligation, specifying that if she leaves with one of Brett's "crowd," the money should be held for him. Brett tells him he'll lose his money because she knows that Georgette will not leave with one of the homosexuals. Jake trusts the *patronne,* with good reason if this is, as it seems to be, an Auvergnat *bal musette.*

24:2 **walk up:** Jake loves walking; Brett can't stand it. To walk up the hill to the Panthéon, the temple of all the gods (*pan* + *theos*), would not only be to approach the sacred mountain appropriately; it would also improve their chances of flagging down a cab at a major intersection (since you could not order a taxi by telephone in 1920s Paris).

24:14 **Parc Montsouris:** The parc de Montsouris, completed in 1878, is the second-largest park in Paris. From the park's higher elevations, there are good views of le Val-de-Grâce (see 78) and the montagne Sainte-Geneviève. There are streams, waterfalls, and a lake, and a famous restaurant, the Pavillon du Lac (now called the Pavillon Montsouris). As usual, Jake knows exactly where he wants to go, and even though Brett just wants to "drive around" aimlessly, Jake tells the driver to go to Montsouris. *Souris* means "mouse," but Mount Mouse hardly seems to indicate significant symbolic landscape; *souris* also means "smile," in archaic or poetic usage, but since their ascent to Montsouris is anything but cheerful or smiling, that signification could only be ironic. The role of Montsouris in Hemingway's symbolic landscape is clarified three pages later (27:20–21).

24:17 **miserable:** The final words of the chapter leave no doubt as to the intensity of Brett's feelings for Jake—no matter what we learn later—just as the entire *bal musette* scene, in spite of the ironic banter in Jake's conversation with Brett, leaves no doubt about Jake's feelings for her.

CHAPTER 4

25:2 **still climbing:** The taxi goes *up* the hill into the light of the place Sainte-Gen-eviève then, "still climbing," turns alongside Saint-Étienne-du-Mont, a thirteenth-century church rebuilt in the sixteenth century. Claimed briefly by the Revolution as the Temple of Filial Piety, it was reconsecrated after the Restoration, when it reclaimed its identity as one of the holiest places of pilgrimage in Paris because of the relics of Sainte Geneviève it contains. At the back of the church the taxi turns south on a "dark street," the rue Descartes, with its smooth modern asphalt pavement, then continues *down* to the place de la Contrescarpe and *down* the rue Mouffetard before going *up* again to Montsouris. All this up-and-down motion in Paris, Hemingway's exact denotation of the hills, or "mountains," of Paris, sug-gests another kind of symbolic landscape, or *paysage moralisé,* which shapes *The Sun Also Rises.* This type of landscape, which does not depend primarily on allu-sion, on specific topographical and historical knowledge brought to the text by the reader, proceeds through organic metaphor, through exoteric symbolism that pervades the linguistic and poetic texture of the novel. Given the pattern of in-sistent verticality, the up-and-down, ascending-descending, rising-falling motion throughout the book—and especially in Paris—readers would be well advised to approach with caution the many critical studies that posit Paris as a kind of hellish, low country wasteland set in opposition to the good high country of Spain. The notion of Paris—and in the more extreme versions of the argument, all France—as a wasteland (or *the* Waste Land, in T. S. Eliot's sense) has been all too common in Hemingway studies, at least since Philip Young's 1952 assertion that "Eliot's London is Hemingway's Paris" (59) and Carlos Baker's 1952 treatment of "The Wasteland-ers" of *The Sun Also Rises* (*Writer as Artist* 75–93). While Baker and Young, among the earliest and most influential Hemingway critics, treat this matter somewhat moderately, later writers take the argument to such extremes that the Paris/France/wasteland equation may be said to be one of the most insidious truisms, one of the regnant gaucheries and most blatant misreadings in Hemingway studies. Consider Wirt Williams, who belabors his false formula of France as the "low country," the "anti-idealistic" and "lower reality" that is contrasted with the "exaltation" of the higher "reality" of Spain (60–62), or Frederic Svoboda, with his insistence (even while his cited evidence argues to the contrary) on "the novel's France/Spain split in values" (*Crafting of a Style* 82), or Edward Stanton, whose egregious treatment of the matter (through the lens of an equally sentimental Hispanophilia and Francophobia) professes to discover in the novel Hemingway's "withering view" of a Parisian (and French) wasteland, where "Jake's existence in Paris [is] a kind of living death" (49, 87). Almost all such studies are rooted (explicitly or implicitly) in false assumptions regarding Paris (or all France) as the dark, low wasteland country contrasted with Spain as the bright, high, redemptive country. These matters are further addressed where appropriate in passage entries below; what matters in the immediate passage (and related ascending-descending movements in Paris) is that, if we read the geography accurately, there are many "ups" and "downs" in Paris and throughout the novel; and there are more symbolic hills, more sacred mounts, evoked in Jake's Parisian landscape than anywhere else in the novel (see also Stoneback, "Very Cheerful," passim).

25:4 **Contrescarpe:** This small *place,* or square, in a neighborhood Hemingway knew well (where he first lived in Paris), is poised on a counterscarp that was part of the ancient city walls; the scarp was a "cliff," or a steep slope at the outer portion of the fortification. When the taxi turns off the smooth modern blacktop, where Jake and Brett are "sitting apart," onto the cobblestones of the "old street," the rue Mouffetard, they are "jolted close together." The rue Mouffetard, running steeply downhill, was the beginning of the ancient Roman road to Italy, thus suggesting the direction, or place, where Jake was wounded in the war, the wound that is the core subject of the rest of this chapter and the source of the anguish Jake and Brett feel in this scene.

25:12 **acetylene flares:** After the taxi descends the ancient rue Mouffetard, it emerges onto the broad, modern avenue des Gobelins and heads south toward the place d'Italie. The avenue is under construction—"torn up"—and the men are working on the streetcar or trolley tracks (in French, *tramway*); in contrast to the streets just traveled, Gobelins (in 1925) was a busy, modern avenue served by no fewer than five *tramway* lines (numbers 47 and 82–85). In the modern light of the "acetylene flares," Jake observes closely Brett's face and neck. When the street is dark again, he kisses her. Acetylene is a highly flammable and explosive gas; what follows for two pages, after the mention of the flares, is a highly flammable and explosive scene of frustrated sexuality. No further details specify the route that the taxi takes to Montsouris, but the fact that the vast, imposing buildings of the Gobelins tapestry factory, famous for centuries, are not mentioned suggests that the taxi turns west on boulevard Arago (also, in 1925, the best route to Montsouris), and thus, while the sexually charged ride continues, they pass the Hôpital Broca, for women suffering from venereal disease, occupying since 1836 part of a thirteenth-century Franciscan nunnery established by Margaret of Provence, sister of one of Hemingway's favorite saints—Saint Louis. Again, symbolic landscape numinously renders—defines—action and theme and foreshadows both Brett's sexual promiscuity and Jake's monastic discipline dictated by his war wound.

25:18 **What's the matter:** In another paired scene, Brett moves away from Jake after the kiss and asks not to be touched. Jake asks, "What's the matter?"—directly echoing Georgette in the taxi scene at the beginning of chapter 3, when he moves her hand away. Importantly, it is a *contrasting* scene in every sense, including the opposed implications of the Georgette-Brett linkage (for the first taxi ride, see 15:19 and 15:28; and for the last taxi ride, the culmination of Hemingway's pattern of echoic scenes, see 247:8).

26:11 **whether she really saw:** The extraordinary eye imagery of this paragraph (and later), the textual interrogation of the act of *seeing,* echoes both the deleted passage regarding Brett's version of blindness (22:2) and the passage in the first chapter alluding to Sainte Odile, whose pilgrimage is centrally concerned with eyes, seeing, and blindness healed (6:10–11).

26:20 **isn't all that:** Love isn't all sex, Brett says, and Jake agrees. (To avoid possible confusion, there probably should be a comma separating "that" and "you know.") Yet they both agree that being "in love" always gets to be about sex, the sexual consummation that is impossible because of Jake's wound. This taxi scene defines the basic problem of their relationship that will be worked out throughout the novel, but the scene also establishes the larger theme of love, including the love that is beyond sex, without sex, the transcendent kind of spiritual, all-embracing love that Count Mippopopolous refers to when he says he is "always in love" (61:4), the love that determines how we live in the world, and whether we live our lives "all the way up" (10:19). This is the kind of love Robert Penn Warren evokes when he writes: "We must try / To love so well the world that we may believe, in the end, in God" (*Collected Poems* 233). And, as Robert Lewis has it, the primary "subject of Hemingway's novels" is chosen in his first novel, "and that subject is love . . . the love themes can be divided into three: eros, agape, and romantic love" (19–20). Agape is the kind of love for which Jake quests but apparently has not yet attained, at this point in the novel, because of his intense and frustrated physical desire for Brett, a mode of love thwarted by the impossibility of incarnation.

26:30 **funny:** Jake doesn't want to talk about his wound and tries to pretend it's a funny joke. Note the remarkably intense and repetitive use of the word "funny" in connection with his wound throughout this chapter (27, 30–31) and the way "funny" reverberates later in the novel (see, e.g., 97:15).

27:1 **Mons:** Mons, which means "mount" or "mound," is a city in Belgium known for its religious processions (e.g., Saint George slaying the dragon), but above all, especially in the 1920s, for the Battle of Mons, the first battle fought by the British army against the advancing German army. Brett's brother's friend received a groin wound (like Jake's) in the Battle of Mons (1914). The reason it "seemed like a hell of a joke" is because *mons* also signifies the mons veneris (in Latin, the "mound of Venus" or the female pubic mound). To say that a soldier received a sexually incapacitating wound at Mons, then, might sound like a joke, but it isn't to Brett and Jake. The "joke" may be extended by the implicit reference to the most famous battlefield "miracle" of World War I—the so-called Angels of Mons, who appeared to save British soldiers at a decisive moment in the battle. In popular song, in artists' renderings, in popular lore, and in literature, many versions of the miraculous intervention of the Angels of Mons circulated. Sometimes they were angelic warriors assisted by Saint George in the slaying of the German dragon of evil. In other versions, angels intervened to save wounded soldiers. Brett was a nurse's assistant with the VAD (Voluntary Aid Detachment) during the war and met Jake in a hospital after he was wounded (see 38:28). As a wartime volunteer taking care of soldiers, she might be seen as a kind of angel, but there was not much she could do for Jake when she met him in the hospital; and even if she is some kind of angel of *mons,* there is not much she can do for Jake in this taxi in Paris years after the war has ended. Finally, we note that Mons, as a symbolic location on the border of Belgium and France, is an important part of the novel's sex-suffused Belgian subtext (cf. Georgette).

27:10 **lot of fun:** In three lines of dialogue in this scene, Jake says the words "funny" and "fun" five times. "Funny" functions in several usual senses—amusing (straightforwardly and ironically), and strange or odd. Jake, who is happy to be with Brett, is less ironic than he is sincere when he says it's fun "to be in love"—"it's an enjoyable feeling" even if they can't make love. Brett says it's "hell on earth," and Jake says it's good just "to see each other"—but since her eyes "looked flat," how much is she *seeing* here—is she "blind" again? Although for Brett it's hell being together, and for Jake it's fun being together, they do agree here that they "have to" *see* each other. Since commentators have made much of the hell imagery and often associated it with *geography,* with Paris as "hell on earth"—usually associated with the Paris-as-wasteland notion discussed above (25:2)—it seems necessary to insist that Brett's "hell" refrain ("hell of a joke," "hell on earth") concerns a personal hell that has nothing to do with *place* (cf. *Paradise Lost:* "Me miserable! . . . Which way I fly is Hell; myself am Hell"). As the novel demonstrates, Jake knows this; Brett does not, or if she does, she remains "miserable," "flying" from the arms of one lover to another.

27:20–21 **pool of live trout:** They have arrived at the Pavillon du Lac (see 24:14), but the restaurant with the live trout is "closed and dark." This trout allusion foreshadows the crucial trout-fishing interlude at the heart of the novel (chapter 12). By that point in the novel, readers familiar with *the* watershed work of literary modernism, T. S. Eliot's *The Waste Land* (1922), will have recognized that Jake is, in Eliot's terms, a Fisher King figure. Although there are many versions and variants of the Fisher King in myth and in Grail legend and literature, the most familiar version involves the ruler who has received a wound in the thigh or groin and is thereby rendered impotent, and as a result his country has turned into a barren wasteland. To redeem his lands, he must participate in a transformational quest. In Eliot's deployment of the Fisher King myth, he is depicted, for example, speaking these words: "I sat upon the shore / Fishing, with the arid plain behind me / Shall I at least set my lands in order?" (lines 424–26). The act of fishing was often associated with the quest for Christ, frequently symbolized as the fish and identified through the Greek-derived acrostic Ichthus (or Ichthos), or "fish." Jake, then, like so many Hemingway characters, is the fisherman on a redemptive quest, a specifically Christian quest. Before the novel is over, Jake will be positioned as is the Fisher King at the end of *The Waste Land*, spiritual aridity behind him, determined to set his lands in order, in possession of Eliot's codified values ("Give. Sympathise. Control."), renewed and made whole by what Eliot renders in his final line as "Shantih"—"the peace which passeth understanding."

The influence of *The Waste Land* on *The Sun Also Rises* (and much of Hemingway's work) is pervasive, but readers should be cautious about simplistic applications of the Fisher King matter, the Grail legend, vegetation rites (ceremonies of death and rebirth), and the like, to both works. A good place to start would be with two of Eliot's primary influences: Jessie L. Weston's study of the Grail legend, *From Ritual to Romance*, and Sir James Frazer's monumental study of myth and religion, *The Golden Bough*. Frazer, as Eliot put it in his notes to *The Waste Land*, "influenced our generation profoundly," and anyone familiar with Frazer's volumes dealing with Adonis, Attis, and Osiris, Eliot notes (50), "will immediately recognize" his poem's "references to vegetation ceremonies"—and, we should add, Hemingway's references to similar patterns of death and rebirth (e.g., the bullfight). Since Hemingway generally covered the tracks of his deepest influences rather thoroughly, and the printed record shows little evidence of his debt to Frazer, I offer the following testimony on that matter. In the 1990s I went marlin fishing in Cuba with Hemingway's son, Gregory; there was no action, so we discussed literature. As we passed the harbor of Havana and the cliffs of El Morro, Gregory said: "It was right here that Papa handed me a copy of Frazer's *Golden Bough* and said, read this, it's *all* in here." All of this sheds important light on what Hemingway had in mind when he insisted that *The Sun Also Rises* was really about "the earth abiding for ever" (*Selected Letters* 229).

In sum, while reverberations of the Fisher King have been pointed out by commentators—sometimes misleadingly, to suggest that Jake and other characters are wounded and irredeemably lost in a wasteland, a notion rooted in a misreading of both the novel and Eliot's *The Waste Land*—it has rarely if ever been noticed that the first submerged Fisher King allusion occurs here in the parc Montsouris, with the living trout in the dark lake, in the one chapter that is centrally concerned with Jake's wound, the chapter that presents the most extended dramatization of Jake's hell, his wound and its consequences. Hemingway's text is every bit as allusive, as layered with coded signification, as Eliot's *The Waste Land* (see 27:28).

27:26 **Café Select:** One of the three principal cafés of the Montparnasse Quarter clustered at (or near) the junction of the boulevards Montparnasse and Raspail, Le Sélect was (and is still) located at 99, boulevard du Montparnasse. The other two at this intersection are La Rotonde at 103, boulevard du Montparnasse, and across the street, the Café du Dôme at 108, boulevard du Montparnasse. A fourth favorite café (actually brasserie) of the Quarterites was (and is) La Coupole, which does not figure in the novel because it did not open until December 1927. The establishment that Hemingway called his "home café," La Closerie des Lilas, is set off somewhat from this cluster of cafés, several blocks down the street at 171, boulevard du Montparnasse. It is misleading to suggest (as Hemingway criticism and biography have often done), however, that the Lilas was just a neighborhood café, chosen by Hemingway as his favorite because artists did not go there. In fact, even the 1927 Blue Guide to Paris listed the Lilas as one of the most popular cafés of Paris, with this annotation: "frequented by artists" (Muirhead and Monmarché, *Paris* xl). And the reason that the Rotonde, once the most fashionable cafés among French writers and artists, is avoided by Jake and others is suggested by this description of the Rotonde in the same Blue Guide: "frequented by foreign students" (xl).

27:28 **Montrouge:** Montrouge is a community at the edge of Paris, just beyond the parc Montsouris. Readers inclined to read the Parisian landscape as a "low country" wasteland that is contrasted in some grand scheme with the high redemptive country of the Spanish landscape (see 25:2) should note that on this one page alone there are five references to *monts*, or mountains: Montparnasse (twice), Montrouge, Mons, and Montsouris. All these *monts* seem to echo images and themes of central concern in *The Waste Land*. Montparnasse (or Mount Parnassus) evokes the mountain sacred to Apollo and the Muses and, more particularly, the literary associations and echoes that are at the heart of Eliot's design, the touchstones and "fragments" that the persona of *The Waste Land* shores against his ruins (line 430). Montrouge ("Red Mountain") echoes Eliot's "red rock," as in the reiterated invitation—"Come in under the shadow of this red rock" (lines 25–26, a reference from Isaiah 32.1–2 to the coming of the Messiah). Mons may be linked with all the sexual wounds, impotence, and sterility that pervade *The Waste Land*. Montsouris ("Mouse Mountain") may echo the recurrent rat imagery used by Eliot, especially in association with the Fisher King (e.g., lines 187–89). If that is not enough symbolic landscape for one page, consider the destination, the Café Select (the select, the chosen), as Jake and Brett ride *down* from Montsouris into the place Denfert-Rochereau, a large square named after a nineteenth-century military leader whose name, Hemingway would have noticed, sounds suspiciously like inferno-rock-water, thus evocative of all the water and rock imagery, the longed-for deliverance from hell, in *The Waste Land*. If that seems a stretch, consider that until 1871 the place Denfert-Rochereau was in fact called the place d'Enfer ("Place of Hell")—Hemingway would have read this in any good guidebook of the period—and it was and is the location of the entrance to the vast rat-infested catacombs and charnel house of bones and skulls (cf. Eliot: "I think we are in rats' alley / Where the dead men lost their bones," lines 115–16). But before we read this symbolic landscape as an image of a dead-end wasteland, as hell without hope, as a diagram of despair, we should read the street signs carefully. As they circle the place d'Enfer, Jake notes that the Lion of Belfort *guards* it (and the "passing Montrouge trams"). The Lion of Belfort, a magnificent sculpture by Bartholdi (the original is at Belfort), and one of the "finest lions in the world" (as my neighbor used to say almost daily when I lived in this lion's neighborhood), literally commemorates Colonel Denfert-Rochereau's victory at Belfort. But the lion, of course, is also a Christ symbol; see, for example, Hemingway's use of Mary's lion as a Christ symbol, at the center of an Ichthus ceremony and quasi-eucharistic meal, in *True at First Light*, or Aslan in C. S. Lewis's *The Lion, the Witch, and the Wardrobe*. (Lewis, like his contemporary Hemingway, was a wounded World War I veteran who underwent a religious conversion after the war.) The shorthand translation of this landscape, then, reads like this: the Christic Lion "guards" Jake and Brett as they circle past the gates of hell and also "guards" the trams coming from Montrouge, from the "Red Rock," from the prophesied Messiah.

28:9 **Zizi:** In his first manuscript appearance, he was called Izzy. The model for Zizi, according to James "Jimmie the Barman" Charters, was one Mitzy, the "best-known person in Montparnasse . . . the Duke of Mitzicus of Greece—who acted as guide and interpreter for all newly arrived English and Americans" (Charters with Cody 82). In French, *zizi* is the term used for penis when one is talking to little boys. Apparently, it was also a term sometimes used in the 1920s to refer to homosexuals.

28:13 **Count Mippipopolous:** Seemingly an insignificant minor character when he makes his first appearance in the novel, the count grew in importance as Hemingway constructed the following chapters until, by the all-important "values" scene in chapter 7, he has assumed the role of one of the novel's most important exemplary characters. (In this, he bears some resemblance to the exemplary Count Greffi in *A Farewell to Arms*.) According to Hemingway's plot outline in one of his manuscript notebooks, he intended to have the count appear in the Pamplona scenes. Extensive searching has unearthed no particular significance for the name Mippipopolous, and no occurrence of the actual name in Greek or Greek-diaspora name archives.

Most Greek names, of course, are patronymic in origin, and *polous* means "son of." Names that may sound similar to the English-speaking ear, such as Pappadopoulos, were often shortened to Pappas, indicating descent from a priest. H. L. Mencken, in what some regard as his major work, *The American Language*, observed in 1921: "A Greek named Papademetracopoulos . . . would find it practically impossible to carry on amicable business with Americans; his name would arouse their mirth, if not their downright ire"; thus, if he were to do business in America, he would probably shorten it to Pappas or some other brief form. Since Count Mippipopolous, we learn, does conduct "amicable business with Americans," perhaps his unabbreviated name represents yet another anti-Mencken gesture from Hemingway, and from Jake, who mocks Cohn's probable reliance on Mencken for his opinions regarding Paris (42).

28:16 **elk's tooth:** What does this elk's tooth signify? Jewelry (e.g., cuff links, watch chains) with elk-tooth design was popular in the Victorian period and the early twentieth century. In Lakota Sioux animal symbolism, the elk is the ultimate exemplar of gallantry and protection; the mythical elk was said to control the power of love and to be a teacher of man, of male Lakotas. Long after an elk carcass has rotted away, two teeth remain intact; these are said to last longer than human life and are thus a symbol of longevity. In the 1920s, elk's tooth jewelry was particularly associated with members of the namesake fraternal organization, the Benevolent and Protective Order of Elks. (See Sinclair Lewis, for example, where Babbitt belongs to the BPOE and carefully dresses every morning and wears his elk's tooth jewelry.) Perhaps the count is an Elk—he does after all own "a chain of sweetshops in the States" (32:26); thus he lives and runs a business in the States and would be likely to belong to a fraternal organization. On both levels—Lakota Sioux and BPOE symbolism—the count embodies the key attributes of gallantry, benevolence, and protectiveness.

28:19 **Paris:** By asserting in his first conversation in the novel, "Paris is a fine town all right," the count has passed the test—response to Paris as an index of character—that Hemingway has carefully constructed in the opening chapters. The count's speech patterns, which some observers have found problematic, range from formal to colloquial ("your Ladyship," "big doings") and probably reflect nothing more than a natural mix of politeness and informality appropriate to a person of his station, and one who is also probably not a native speaker of English, although he lives at least part of the time in the United States (see 56:27–28).

28:26 **yellow card:** Prostitutes in Paris were required to carry a health card with a record of regular inspections by a doctor. At the *bal musette*, Georgette has had some kind of argument with the *patronne*'s daughter. According to Braddocks, Jake's "girl" was "rather splendid" in her witty demand to see the other woman's health card, thus, probably more ironically than seriously, calling the *patronne*'s daughter a prostitute. We also learn that Georgette did go home with "some one," probably not one of "them" or "those gentlemen" (see the *bal musette* scene, 20–23).

29:14 **Crillon:** Long known as one of the great deluxe establishments of Paris, the Hôtel de Crillon is situated majestically on the place de la Concorde. There are certain ironic reverberations in Brett's selection of the Crillon as a place to meet: (1) It is very expensive, a place she (living on bad credit) cannot afford and Jake cannot really afford, but a good place for Brett to be "seen"; (2) She may be aware, and Jake certainly is, that after the war the American Peace Delegation occupied the Crillon in 1919; and, after the American Revolution, Benjamin Franklin signed a Friendship Treaty with Louis XVI here; (3) Since the Crillon dominates (architecturally) the place de la *Concorde,* the symbolic landscape of the planned but aborted (by Brett's failure to show up) rendezvous calls attention to the *discord* in the relationship of Brett and Jake. He tells her to *be there* at five, knowing from experience that she will either be late or not show. When she asks if she's ever let him down, he seems to change the subject but really answers obliquely by mentioning the man she plans to marry: "Heard from Mike?" There will be no concord at the Crillon the next day (41:1–7).

29:22 **Rotonde:** Jake's lonesome walk down the "deserted" boulevard Montparnasse takes him from the Sélect, past the other major cafés frequented by writers and artists and expatriates (the Rotonde, the Dôme), past one of his favorite restaurants, Lavigne's—"closed tight"—where he had dined with Georgette, past the shutting-down Closerie (meaning enclosure or "walled garden") des Lilas. The doubleness of this "deserted" walk is emphasized by the fact that Jake wants to "get home," and though he chooses, he has little choice but to be alone, since his safe havens are "closed tight." Someone waves to him across the street from the Dôme, but he doesn't know who it is, and he walks on alone until, in a sense, Marshal Ney waves to him.

29:28 **Ney's statue:** The statue, by François Rude, of Michel Ney (1769–1815), famous soldier made "Marshal of France" by Napoleon, who called him "le Brave des Braves" (the bravest of the brave), stands on the west side of the carrefour de l'Observatoire at the southern end of the boulevard Saint-Michel, very near the spot on which he was executed for treason. Ney almost seems to "wave" at Jake, "gesturing with his sword." Celebrated for being the last French soldier on Russian soil when he bravely commanded the rear guard during Napoleon's retreat from Moscow, Ney survived the fall of Napoleon and pledged allegiance to the restored Bourbon monarchy; however, when he was supposed to arrest Napoleon on his return from exile, he chose to fight for him again and led part of Napoleon's forces against Wellington in the Battle of Waterloo. After Waterloo, and Napoleon's final defeat and exile, Ney—refusing to wear a blindfold, and giving the command to fire—was executed by firing squad. If Marshal Ney is "waving" to Jake in this scene, it is a gesture that evokes a complex image of bravery and folly, loyalty and betrayal, similar in some ways to that associated with another more celebrated commander of a French rearguard army—Roland at Roncevaux, leading Charlemagne's rear guard back to France after the siege of Pamplona, betrayed, ambushed, fighting bravely to the end on the terrain where Jake has chosen to go fishing (see 108:26). Jake may also be aware of the legend that has Ney surviving his supposed execution and, with the help of Masonic conspirators, escaping to the United States to live out his days. And Jake probably also knows that Marshal Ney in 1809, during the Napoleonic campaigns in Spain, plundered the pilgrim's treasury at the Cathedral of Santiago de Compostela. Decades after *The Sun Also Rises,* Hemingway is still thinking of Ney as emblematic of loyalty and betrayal. In *A Moveable Feast* he writes about his "old friend, the statue of Marshal Ney with his sword out," and "what a fiasco he'd made of Waterloo," which leads him to think: "All generations were lost by something and always had been and always would be." So he stops at the Closerie des Lilas—"to keep the statue company"—and drinks a cold beer. Over that beer, "watching the statue," Hemingway meditates on Ney's *personal* bravery on the rearguard retreat from Moscow and invokes "God and Mike Ney" to help him "serve" Gertrude Stein well in spite of all "her lost-generation talk and all the dirty, easy labels" (30–31). Thus Hemingway provides, years later, his explication of at least part of the iceberg, the significance of the Marshal Ney allusion left unstated in Jake's apparently casual survey of his Parisian symbolic landscape.

29:34 **Boulevard St. Michel:** Popularly referred to as the Boul' Mich', the boulevard Saint-Michel is the "main street" of the Latin Quarter, running just under a mile from the carrefour de l'Observatoire, past the Luxembourg Gardens, and down to place Saint-Michel on the Seine. It is *not* named after Michel Ney, who occupies Jake's thoughts in this paragraph, but after Saint Michael the Archangel, whose intercession was believed to be so powerful that souls could be retrieved from hell. In religious iconography and medieval art he was depicted with scales, weighing souls, and also as a slayer of the dragon of evil. His widespread cult proclaimed him the patron saint of the sick and the wounded. His principal place of pilgrimage is Mont-Saint-Michel, one of the medieval wonders of the world, where Hemingway was with the U.S. troops that liberated the sacred site from the German occupiers during the Normandy campaign in 1944. Jake's Saint-Michel address, then, may be more than incidental. At the very least, it separates him from the crowd of pseudo-writers and artists and bohemians who inhabit the adjacent Montparnasse Quarter. Since, in this scene, he walks "a little way down" (toward the Seine) the Boul' Mich', and the next morning he walks "down" to the rue Soufflot, and later, "down" to the "juncture of the Rue Denfert-Rochereau" (35, 72), he must live near the juncture of the rue du Val de Grâce with the Boul' Mich' (around #137).

30:1 **concierge:** In this context, the concierge is the caretaker of the flats, the apartment building where Jake lives. The concierge not only observes all the comings and goings of the persons in her building but also distributes mail and manages all details concerning apartments.

30:6 **balance:** In 1920s Paris, where Hemingway rented an apartment for about ten dollars a month and dinner in a decent restaurant cost about a quarter, Jake's bank balance ($2,432.60) indicates that he has plenty of money to live very comfortably—unlike Brett or Mike. Of course, Jake has a good job and works for a living. To put Jake's bank balance in perspective, readers who know the current cost of apartments in various locations might calculate whether they have anything like Jake's amount of about 240 times a monthly rental figure (or the cost of 9,728 decent meals) in their *checking* accounts.

30:14 **good Catholic name:** The two references to Catholicism in this scene (see also 31:20–21) are the first clear indications in the text of Jake's Catholicism. Later, the fact that he is Catholic becomes obvious when he prays in cathedrals, goes to confession and Mass, and discusses his Catholicism. Before Hemingway lopped off his opening chapters from the galleys, it would have been clear to the reader from the outset that Jake was Catholic: "So my name is Jacob Barnes and I am writing the story, not as I believe is usual in these cases, from a desire for confession, because being a Roman Catholic I am spared that Protestant urge to literary production" (Svoboda, *Crafting of a Style* 134). Once again, it is arguable that the radical last-minute surgery Hemingway performed on his novel, largely due to Fitzgerald's suggestions, cost the narrative some clarity of identity and focus. If the reader knew, for example, from the very beginning that Jake is a self-conscious Catholic, the religiously charged subtext of the symbolic landscape of Paris would likely be more discernible in the opening chapters. The "good Catholic name" in this passage—Aloysius Kirby—may be taken as a reference to Saint Aloysius Gonzaga (1568–1591), scion of a noble Italian family destined for a military career, who became a Jesuit renowned for nursing the sick. He was declared the patron saint of youth in 1729. Since Jake is so name conscious, he is probably aware too that Aloysius Kirby is doubly a "good Catholic name": the surname Kirby has its origins in *kirk,* or "church." Why is Aloysius "a funny name"? Because Jake associates it with Saint Aloysius, known for his precocious piety and extreme physical austerity? Because Jake consistently associates the word "funny" with his war wound–enforced celibacy? That's another way Aloysius is "a good Catholic name." Note Jake's sequence of associations here: from a "funny" name (echoing a Catholic saint) that is ironically associated with a marriage announcement, to a passing thought of Zizi, who is probably a homosexual (his real-life model was—see 28:9), to the count—"the count was funny"—in whose company he has just left Brett. By a curious chain of associations involving titles (duke, count, lady, and perhaps saint) *and* sexuality, Jake is back to thinking about Brett, with whom he wants to live in a quasi-celibate relationship; and since he knows he cannot marry her, he thinks "to hell" with her, taking the reader back to his "hell on earth" dialogue with her a few pages earlier when they discuss his "funny" wound (27:10).

30:26 **wounded:** Naked, Jake looks at himself in the *armoire à glace* (the mirrored wardrobe that typically serves as a closet) and considers his wound: "Of all the ways to be wounded," he has to have such a wound. It may be that Hemingway, in this key scene, would have preferred to be precisely specific about Jake's wound, more specific than publishing etiquette (and censorship) would have allowed in the 1920s. Had this been possible, a great deal of misleading and egregious critical commentary would have been avoided—for example, all the arguments based on the false notion that Jake is a *castrat,* or eunuch, a man without testicles. In extratextual commentary, Hemingway was very specific regarding this matter. In an important interview, George Plimpton referred to a reading of the novel based on the notion that Jake is "emasculated precisely as is a steer." Hemingway finds this "a little bit screwy" and asks: "Who ever said Jake was 'emasculated precisely as a steer'? Actually he had been wounded in quite a different way and his testicles were intact and not damaged. Thus he was capable of all normal feelings as a man but incapable of consummating them. The important distinction is that his wound was physical and not psychological and that he was not emasculated" (Bruccoli 120). In a humorous mode, writing to Scott Fitzgerald in 1926, Hemingway declared: "I am asking Scribners to insert as a subtitle in everything after the eighth printing THE SUN ALSO RISES (LIKE YOUR COCK IF YOU HAVE ONE)" (*Selected Letters* 231). In a 1951 letter to the editor at Rinehart, the publishing house that was preparing to release Philip Young's *Ernest Hemingway*—a book Hemingway regarded as grievously flawed—Hemingway expressed his discontent with Young's thesis "that I am all my heroes" and clarified Jake's wound: "I could have told Mr. Young the whole genesis of The Sun Also Rises for example. It came from a personal experience in that when I had been wounded at one time there had been an infection from pieces of wool cloth being driven into the scrotum. Because of this I got to know other kids who had genito urinary wounds and I wondered what a man's life would have been like after that if his penis had been lost and his testicles and spermatic cord remained intact. I had known a boy that had happened to. So I took him and made him into a foreign correspondent in Paris and, inventing, tried to find out what his problems would be when he was in love with someone who was in love with him and there was nothing they could do about it. . . . But I was not Jake Barnes" (*Selected Letters* 744–45). Hemingway's commentary, then, clarifies the exact nature of Jake's wound, and, in stressing that he still feels the "normal feelings" of a man, he underlines the problem of Jake's physical desire for Brett. Some critical commentary has suggested that there are other possibilities of sexual consummation for Jake—some form of oral or manual sex—but it should be noted that Hemingway says he was "incapable of consummating" his sexual desires; there was "nothing" that could be done about it.

30:30 **Le Toril:** Jake has two *French* bullfight papers from the Midi (the south of France), where bullfighting was (and still is) very popular—both the Spanish-style corrida (or *mise à mort*) and the *Course Camarguaise* (where the bull does not die, but the bullfighters, or *razeteurs,* sometimes do). Jake may be contemplating a visit (like those Hemingway made)—before or after his trip to Pamplona—to the famous bullrings and fiestas of Arles or Nîmes. But the point here is that he reads *Le Toril* from cover to cover, trying to keep from thinking about his wound, about Brett, trying to get to sleep to no avail since his "head" starts to work, and the "old grievance" of thinking overcomes his daytime discipline of not thinking about his wound.

31:2 **joke front:** Jake gets his "rotten" wound on the Italian front, in unspecified circumstances that seem to be of little military consequence. The reader is never told who Jake was flying for—American, British, or Italian forces—or even if Jake was a pilot, although his later joking with Bill about joysticks (115–16) suggests he was. Genital wounds from ground fire were fairly common among pilots before airplane seats were made of armor plate. (I am indebted to Robert W. Lewis for this information.) The "joke front" continues, in another sense, as Jake repeats "funny" six times in less than a page here—"funny name" (twice), "funny thing," "funny" (three times). Thus, through this sequence, and the preceding "funny" and "joke" sequence (see 26:30), more than a dozen repetitions of "funny" and related variants in a few pages establish "funny" as a keyword inseparably linked to Jake's wound (and his way of dealing with it).

31:5 **Ospedale Maggiore:** The main hospital in Milan, Italy, where Jake was treated first after his wounding before going to a British hospital is also the hospital where Hemingway had been a patient in 1918 after his wounding on the Italian front. Again, Jake seems unusually attentive to statues (see 29:28, 41:12, and 72:15), although he cannot remember if the statue is of Ponte or Zonda (benefactors of the two hospital wings Jake mentions). All the statues may be for Jake an associational link to "bridge" his military and hospital experience—from Marshal Ney to Ponte (*ponte,* Italian for bridge) or Zonda, even if Jake is not the "prisoner" of Zonda, or the Zonda wing of the hospital (cf. Anthony Hope's immensely popular 1894 novel *The Prisoner of Zenda,* of which no fewer than three movies were made in Hollywood in the decade preceding *The Sun Also Rises*). The semiology of Jake's procession of statues is rounded out in the following chapters, where he acknowledges "the inventor of the semaphore engaged in doing same" (41:12) and the "Gentlemen who invented pharmacy" (72:15).

What treatment, surgical or pharmaceutical or otherwise, was Jake likely to have received at the Ospedale Maggiore (or before, at a battlefield medical station, or after, in the British hospital where he met Brett)? Historical research and my conversations with genitourinary specialists suggest that there was little recourse in the early twentieth century for someone who suffered a wound like Jake's. It is not clear what the battlefield protocol would have been for such a wound, or what follow-up procedures might have been possible at the Italian and British hospitals in which Jake recuperates. The answers may be seen to reside just around the corner from Jake's apartment, if we remember that he lives on the boulevard Saint-Michel at or near its juncture with the rue du Val de Grâce, a short street leading to the Val-de-Grâce, the famous church and military hospital. Every time Jake walks up and down the Boul' Mich', he would see the famous dome of Val-de-Grâce, and this wound-meditation scene follows after his taxi ride with Brett to the parc Montsouris, celebrated for its view of Val-de-Grâce—where their discussion of his wound takes place. Eventually Jake will walk by Val-de-Grâce and name it specifically, thus clarifying his Parisian symbolic landscape (78:7). Along with the church and the hospital for wounded soldiers, the Val-de-Grâce contained museums that illustrated (in the words of a source contemporaneous with *The Sun Also Rises*) "military hygiene . . . with pictures and documents illustrating the treatment of the wounded from the 16th cent. to the present day," including the "apparatus used in 1914–1918" (Muirhead and Monmarché, *Paris* 160). Jake, then, not only has to live *with* his wound but he lives *near* the principal museums featuring graphic reminders of his wound and its inadequate treatment. In any case, it is clear that penile reconstructive surgery and phalloplasty, as practiced in the twenty-first century, were not available for Jake.

Before leaving the wound-centered chapter 4, the novel's most specific evocation of Jake's *physical* state of being, there are certain questions that should be asked, certain observations that should be made. Who else knows about Jake's wound? As the late James Hinkle (the Hemingway scholar who studied this novel for decades and initiated this series of close-reading, line-by-line glossaries) used to say to me, "Is Jake known around Paris and Pamplona as the guy without a joystick?" We discussed this repeatedly over the years, and I think we finally agreed, given the textual evidence, that *only* Brett and Bill know—and Bill may just be guessing. Robert, Jake's "tennis friend," surely does not know. The aficionados in Pamplona cannot know. Georgette knows only that Jake is "sick" from the war—and that may be, at most, all that others beside Brett know. All the evidence argues that maudlin confession or talky therapy is beyond the realm of possibility for Jake. Would he even specify his condition to a priest in the sacrament of confession? (He does go to confession; as he tells Brett, who wants to go with him, it wouldn't be very "interesting" to her. See 150–51.) Another related question is this: how is it that generations of readers, millions of men and women, have admired Jake; have found him a strong, exemplary character who truly understands and possesses passion and joie de vivre, the joy of living; and have not *felt sorry for him*? This is the overwhelming consensus among the approximately 3,300 college students to whom I have taught this novel in the past thirty-three years. Quizzes and discussions and essays again and again point to Jake as the favorite character, the person they'd like to "hang out" with, dine with, travel with, fish with, be with. I have never detected gender-based difference in the responses. Women and men seem to respond in the same fashion to Jake; and the women tend to be much harder on Brett than are the men. When I pose exactly the question—"What do you think about Jake's wound?"—the answers I get are remarkably uniform and generally run pretty close to this: "There's more to life than sex" (a favorite answer for men and women), and, from men specifically, "If I had to be wounded like Jake, I'd want to handle it like him, be like him, and discover other more important things." Does all of this signify some deep pattern of meaning in the novel that rarely finds its way directly into literary criticism? Even student readers and writers who at first, misled by standard critical and Internet sources, think that Jake is emasculated, castrated, point out that eunuchs were often a priestly class in many societies, and celibacy may be one valid path to God. And they all seem to recognize what Brett might mean when she says: "You've a hell of a biblical name, Jake" (22:28). When I assigned members of one class to comment specifically on that passage in an out-of-class quiz, a music major said she had heard a performance of Gian Carlo Menotti's cantata on the theme of Jacob and the angel, and the theme of "spiritual struggle" reminded her of *The Sun Also Rises.* She attached a clipping from the *New York Times* in which Menotti is quoted: "You know the story . . . Jacob dreams he's fighting with the angel, and they fight all night until he wakes up in the morning with a wound that gives him his vision of God" (White 26). Thus, early in classroom discussions, long before I introduce Fisher King motifs or sketch out the pilgrimage motif and structure of the novel or quote Hemingway on Saint Ignatius of Loyola and his "wound that made him think" or even mention matters of religion in the novel, many students seem to recognize the "spiritual struggle," even the "vision of God," that is at the heart of the story. It seems, then, that Hemingway's literary iceberg is more mysterious than we have guessed and operates in ways that literary criticism cannot measure. (On the question of "impotence," see 115:27.)

31:14 **Che mala fortuna:** Translated as "What bad luck" (Italian), or the reiterated sense of "rotten" luck (e.g., 31:1–2, 47:14–15), *fortuna mala* carries the strong sense of "evil" fortune or luck.

31:20–21 **The Catholic Church:** Jake has been advised, probably in confession and more generally in homilies, not to think about "all that"—sex and, in his case, his wound. Clearly, Jake doesn't want to "make trouble for people," whine, or worry about his wound and proclaim his rotten luck, and if he hadn't met Brett in that hospital, he might have been all right. But he met her, and "she only wanted what she couldn't have." And Jake, too, at this point in his struggle, wants what he cannot have.

32:8 **Half asleep:** After crying, after thinking about Brett and his wound, Jake finally gets to sleep. At 4:30 AM, Brett rouses the concierge to wake Jake up. Half-awake, Jake momentarily confuses Brett's voice with Georgette's, thus connecting them again, bringing full circle the entire Georgette-Brett sequence of chapters 3 and 4. Brett, we note, is "quite drunk" and doesn't care if Jake's asleep or has to go work in the morning or has a "rotten headache"—the reason he told her goodnight hours before.

32:22 **one of us:** Hemingway commentators often assume that there is a code of conduct—or style—that governs the novel, that determines which characters, to put it simply, are "insiders" and which characters are "outsiders." Most simplistic lists of insiders would include Brett, Jake, Count Mippipopolous, Bill, Montoya, Pedro Romero, and possibly Mike Campbell, while the outsiders list would be headed by Robert, then Frances, and a number of minor characters from Braddocks to Woolsey and Krum, and from the Americans on the train to, possibly, Mike Campbell. Yet, since one of the main thrusts of the novel is to differentiate, for example, between Jake's character and behavior and Brett's, to draw distinctions, to scrutinize and finally to discard the "one of us" rubric, it is important to note that it is Brett who makes the pronouncements on who is "one of us" (here, twice in nine lines) and to try to discern what she means by this. The evidence here suggests that the count is an insider, in Brett's perception, because (1) he knows a lot "about people," (2) he has money ("owns a chain of sweetshops," has a uniformed chauffeur and limousine, buys the best champagne a dozen bottles at a time, etc.), (3) he has a title (when Jake is suspicious about the title, Brett says he "deserves" it, presumably based on his money and style), and (4) he's generous with his money (his $10,000 offer to Brett, etc.). Jake clearly reserves judgment in this scene; later, when he is getting to know the count, he finds him admirable—but for very different reasons than those Brett offers here. And Jake does not make the self-privileging and presumptuous pronouncement that he is "one of us" (see especially 57–61). In fact, that very statement might disqualify anyone from membership in a genuine insiders' circle where real values (e.g., *afición*, passion) determine "insiderness" and "outsiderness," and only the touch of confirmation is necessary (see 131–32). Much of the critical confusion over this matter could be avoided if Brett's pronouncements were rigorously inspected; and if readers examined carefully the scenes where Brett promulgates membership in *her* secret order of style, it would be obvious that there is usually something built into the scene that disbars her from the true inner circle—based on values, passion, spirituality, living life "all the way up"—that is defined by the novel's deepest designs, patterns, and actions (see

57–61, 245). Brett, for all her facile assumption of a shared insiders' code of values or style, is really quite alone and quite without the values that sustain such characters as Jake, the count, Montoya, and Romero. All of this is not to say that she is not attractive, engaging, and compelling, or that I would not buy her a drink in Paris or Pamplona: that is precisely the central problem presented by the book. (But I would not take her fishing. Or on a pilgrimage.)

32:32 **buck on:** "Buck on," also "bukh," from the Hindi *buk buk*, a slang carryover from the British raj, chiefly used by the upper class, means to talk, especially boastfully. Thus, Lady Brett Ashley, having deigned to confer "one of us" status on the count, acknowledges the implicit boastfulness of her designation, her seal of approval.

33:6 **Biarritz:** From the mid-nineteenth century on, Biarritz was the most fashionable French seaside resort on the Atlantic Ocean, located eight kilometers southwest of Bayonne, twenty-four kilometers north of the Spanish frontier. In the 1850s Napoleon III and Empress Eugénie built their sumptuous seaside palace there, and Biarritz became a favored resort of European royalty; after Queen Victoria vacationed there in 1889, increasing numbers of British travelers visited. A 1920s guidebook attributes "the fashionable success and prosperity" of Biarritz to the "beauty and diversity of its shores," the pure air and the proximity of the mountains, and its geographical situation as the gateway to the Basque country; moreover, "the city is lively, gay, coquettish, with generally clean and airy streets" (Monmarché 101–2). The count has just offered Brett an extraordinary amount of money (several years' wages, for example; also more than four times the amount in Jake's bank account) to go to Biarritz with him; if she were the gold-digging, upper-class quasi prostitute that some readers insist she is, citing as evidence the Georgette linkage, she certainly would have gone. Her given reason for not going—that she knows "too many people" there—is not convincing. For one thing, it's June, and thus preseason in Biarritz; the high season is July and August. In addition, she *does* go with Robert to San Sebastián, a seaside resort just down the road that has much in common with Biarritz, both the low and high seasons, and the fashionable status of its visitors. One conclusion that may be drawn, especially if we bear in mind the "something funny" that Brett later tells Jake about the count (97:15), is that Brett is more interested in sex than money and that the count's offer was for companionship alone. The novel has a brief scene in Biarritz lasting less than two pages, when Jake, Bill, and Mike drive into Biarritz after the fiesta for drinks at "a very Ritz place" (229–30).

33:15 **Cannes:** A fashionable resort town on the Mediterranean Côte d'Azur, twenty-six kilometers west of Nice, Cannes is described in a leading 1926 guidebook as "one of the oldest and still perhaps the most aristocratic of the Riviera *winter* resorts"

(Muirhead and Monmarché, *Southern France* 164; emphasis added). Again, Brett's stated reason for not going (she knows "too many people there") does not ring true, since it's June and Cannes was then a winter resort, where most of the best hotels closed for the summer.

33:16 **Monte Carlo:** Another fashionable resort town on the Côte d'Azur, Monte Carlo is twenty kilometers east of Nice, in the miniature principality of Monaco, an enclave surrounded by France, and French in everything but formal political identity. Like Cannes, Monte Carlo was in the 1920s a winter resort town, where the best hotels closed in the summer, so once again Brett's stated reason for not going rings false. Finally, she gives the count another reason for not going—that she's in love with Jake. Why, then, does she go to San Sebastián with Robert?

33:30 **breakfast in the Bois:** Jake seems surprised to hear that the count is waiting outside (in his limousine with his liveried chauffeur), and disappointed because he probably hoped Brett would stay the rest of the night—on the next page he says: "You don't have to go." "The Bois" refers to the bois de Boulogne, at the western edge of Paris. The larger bois de Vincennes at the eastern edge of Paris is far less fashionable and never referred to simply as "the Bois." Apparently, the count has at least two hampers—large covered baskets, sometimes called picnic baskets—well stocked for an elegant breakfast picnic in the Bois. The notion that they would be going to breakfast at one of the elegant restaurants in the Bois, as has sometimes been suggested, is highly unlikely and a somewhat absurd image to entertain: arriving, say, at the elegant Restaurant du Pré-Catelan (*if* it had opened for its summer-only schedule and *if* it was serving breakfast) with multiple hampers filled with champagne. A picnic with champagne and caviar is far more likely. The count got it "all"—all the different items?—at Zelli's, the Montmartre cabaret (16 *bis,* rue Fontaine) where Jake, Brett, and the count go the following evening. The American proprietor, Joe Zelli, was known as a man who could get anything for his customers. The count also gets a dozen bottles of Mumm (the proper designation for the famous champagne), one of the *Grandes Marques,* a major champagne *négociant* (dealer) since the 1820s. As usual, the count spares no expense, buying the best. Jake refuses the invitation to breakfast in the Bois because he has to go to work in a few hours and because he doesn't want to be with Brett *and* the count.

34:12 **cordon:** Jake calls for the concierge, who controls all access to and exit from her building, to pull the *cordon de la porte,* the door pull, to let Brett out. Possibly also an ironic allusion to the famous *cordon rouge,* the red cord or ribbon emblazoned across the labels of Mumm champagne.

34:17 **empty glass:** As usual, Brett's glass is empty first (see also, e.g., 59:16).

34:24 **hard-boiled:** In the original manuscript version, this key final sentence of chapter 4 does not appear. There, after Jake watches from his window Brett walking up the street, and then, after the limousine is gone, he *thinks* about how she looked walking up the street—another engaging example of Hemingway's stylistic deployment of repetition—he feels "like crying again" (see 31:28). In the final version, Hemingway deletes "crying," inserts "hell" ("felt like hell again"), and adds the entire last sentence. It is a telling instance of the precision of Hemingway's revision process, and the introduction of the striking (especially in 1926) word "hard-boiled" provides a key characterization of Jake.

Hemingway's use of the term "hard-boiled" is another good example of his role on the cutting edge of evolving linguistic usage, as a creator or refiner of the emerging sense of words (see also 9:9). According to the *OED*, the word "hard-boiled" (in its various nuances of hardened, callous, hard headed, shrewd, practical) is of American origin, and the first recorded occurrence (in a sense only vaguely related to Hemingway's usage) was by Mark Twain in 1886 when he wrote of "hard-boiled, hide-bound grammar." Beyond Twain's apparent intended connotation of rigid narrow-mindedness, "hard-boiled" evolved through avatars of hardness and toughness until, after the mid-1920s, it had acquired its current edge of implication regarding a cynical protective stance adopted by someone toughened by experience—especially as employed in hard-boiled detective fiction and related modes of "tough guy" writing that developed after the 1920s. Oddly enough, the first *OED* citation of "hard-boiled" occurring in a sense close to the latter is from the *Ladies' Home Journal,* 26 August 1926 (less than two months before *The Sun Also Rises* was published and *after* Hemingway had written it in his manuscript): "The hard-boiled cynic has a shell [satire] can never penetrate." Hemingway's use of the term to characterize Jake's complex day-night sensibility adds a richness and ambiguity to "hard-boiled" that it has retained. Hard-boiled detective fiction and its most famous practitioner, Dashiell Hammett, are certainly indebted to Hemingway's variations on the "hard-boiled" motif. Readers of *Black Mask* magazine (where the hard-boiled genre developed in the 1920s), for example, could follow a Hammett detective "into a sitting-room on the second floor where Mrs. Gungen put down a copy of *The Sun Also Rises* and waved a cigarette at a nearby chair." This Hammett salute to Hemingway, this acknowledgment by allusion (in a story called "The Main Death"), appeared in the June 1927 issue of *Black Mask.* Another practitioner of hard-boiled fiction, Mickey Spillane, repeatedly asserted—in my conversations with him in the 1980s—that Hemingway had been a major influence on his work.

Further evidence of Hemingway's crucial role in the evolution of the word "hard-boiled" and in the development of hard-boiled fiction may be found in Allen Tate's 15 December 1926 review of *The Sun Also Rises* entitled "Hard-Boiled." Indeed, Tate's boldly titled review in the *Nation* could well be responsible for the christening of the hard-boiled genre. In the review itself—one of three reviews of Hemingway that Tate published in the *Nation* in 1926 (the others dealing with *In Our Time* and *The Torrents of Spring*)—Tate expresses disappointment with *The Sun Also Rises,* especially as compared to *In Our Time,* where, Tate maintains, Hemingway's "sentimentality was submerged" (642). Tate's view of *The Sun Also Rises* pivots on what he sees as Hemingway's betrayal of his earlier sufficient and efficacious hard-boiledness: "It is not that Mr. Hemingway is, in the term which he uses in fine contempt for the big word, hard-boiled; it is that he is not hard-boiled enough" (642). It is difficult to say precisely what Tate means by this, although he clearly wants less "sentimentality" and more character development. The main point of Tate's essay on the "Hard-Boiled" Hemingway is that *The Sun Also Rises* "actually betrays the interior machinery of his hard-boiled attitude"; after this observation, Tate quotes Jake's comment on how easy it is to be hard-boiled in the daytime, "but at night it is another thing" (643). Tate thinks this demonstrates Hemingway's "sentimentality." (Has he missed Jake's admonition to Brett in their parting words here: "Don't be sentimental"?) By 1929, when Hemingway and Tate met in Paris and became friends—they often went to Mass together (both were Catholic converts) and to the bicycle races—Tate seems to have changed his mind about Hemingway's supposed "sentimentality" and betrayal of the "hard-boiled attitude." Tate had been writing to his Vanderbilt Fugitive-Agrarian colleagues about the ways in which Hemingway was the ideal modern novelist because, for example, he "sticks to concrete experience" and he has "that sense of a stable world, of a total sufficiency of character, which we miss in modern life" (Fain and Young 245). And in 1968, when as a graduate student at Vanderbilt I sat in on Tate's lectures and had conversations with him about Hemingway, his views of *The Sun Also Rises* were not those expressed in his 1926 "Hard-Boiled" review.

What did Hemingway have to say on this question? On 21 December 1926, less than a week after Tate's review of *The Sun Also Rises* announced that Hemingway was not sufficiently hard-boiled, Hemingway wrote to his editor, Maxwell Perkins, that it would be a good idea to publish three of his stories, including "The Killers" (Hemingway's most celebrated example of so-called hard-boiled fiction), "In Another Country" (with its perspicacious distinctions of degrees of hard-boiledness), and "A Canary for One," in *Scribner's Magazine.* The publication of these stories, Hemingway told Perkins, might "cheer up" critics like "Allen Tate, and the other boys who fear I'm on the toboggan." Hemingway elaborated: "Critics, this is still Mr. [Allen] Tate—have a habit of hanging attributes on you themselves—and then when they find you're not that way accusing you of sailing under false colours—Mr. Tate feels so badly that I'm not as hard-boiled as he had publicly announced. As a matter of fact I have not been at all hard boiled since July 8 1918—on the night of which I discovered that that also was Vanity" (*Selected Letters* 239–40). Hemingway refers here to the night of his grievous wounding in World War I. He also alludes to the "Vanity of vanities" passage from Ecclesiastes that had been included in the novel's epigraph as first published, although Hemingway urged Perkins (19

November 1926) to cut the "Vanity" verses from further printings because it was misleading (see entry for epigraphs). In any case, Hemingway's emphasis in this letter on the vanity of mere superficial hard-boiledness—or, in Tate's terms, avoidance of sentimentality—illuminates a crucial aspect of Jake's character and how his wounding informs his vision of life and death, and his conduct. After such knowledge, Jake and Hemingway know, a mere cynical or callous or hardened or "awfully easy" hard-boiled "daytime" attitude will not suffice. The physical—and spiritual—anguish of the night demands a different response.

What then do Jake and Hemingway mean when they say "hard-boiled"? Generations of readers have had an immediate and intuitive (if sometimes radically misleading) sense of Jake's hard-boiledness. When the book came out, as many witnesses attest, it attracted a "cult following"; Thornton Wilder described Yale undergraduates "mimicking Jake," and Malcolm Cowley recalled "bright young men from the Middle West trying to be Hemingway heroes, talking in tough understatements from the sides of their mouths" (Carpenter 191). Although we would be hard-pressed to find Jake talking tough from the side of his mouth, understatement—or saying nothing at all—is certainly his preferred mode of dialogue. Indeed, the novel is driven by a tough stance *against* talking too much—note the recurrent motif that talking is "all bilge" (55), or "you'll lose it if you talk about it" (245)—a recognition shared by key characters that things are always more complicated than one can *say*. And it is clear that antiexemplary characters like Robert Cohn talk too much. (Even in the age of talk, our talk-show and talk-therapy American culture of recent decades, these points are immediately clear to most readers.) It also seems reasonably clear to the vast majority of readers that Jake's hard-boiled "daytime" code of conduct forbids whining and self-pity *and*—Tate's view notwithstanding—sentimentality. Robert is, of course, the chief antiexemplar on all these scores.

Jake's comment in these closing lines of chapter 4, after the reader has acquired all the knowledge the text makes available about his wound, may be among the most misapprehended passages in the novel. It is not at all the case, as some commentators have maintained (especially in the 1960s and 1970s, when a hard-boiled attitude was deemed *dépassé*, old-fashioned), that Hemingway's (or Jake's) supposed toughness precludes tenderness, that hard-boiledness precludes that cherished mantra of the American age of talk—"sensitivity." Indeed, Hemingway's fiction (at least since "The Battler" in early 1925) had been articulating how tenderness and toughness were opposite sides of the same coin, how true tenderness required toughness, and vice versa (see the characters Bugs and Ad, and Nick's lessons learned from them). It is precisely the most sensitive characters who possess exact and profound recognition of the need for understatement, hard-boiledness. In sum, on the Hemingway stock exchange, the daytime hard-boiled index is the clearest indicator of nighttime sensitivity.

CHAPTER 5

35:1 **rue Soufflot:** The rue Soufflot is a broad, majestic street running a few blocks from the boulevard Saint-Michel to the place du Panthéon. Up the rue Soufflot from the Boul' Mich', there is a splendid view, framed against the sunrise sky on its hilltop, of the Panthéon, previously evoked in the night scene and anguished taxi ride with Brett. If Jake looks the other way, across the Boul' Mich' he sees the magical Luxembourg Gardens, chestnuts in blossom. Sidewalk flower-vendors, as always arranging their displays, add to Jake's sense of morning joy. In spite of the fact that Brett has kept him up past five in the morning and he has had very little sleep, it is a "fine morning" with a "pleasant early-morning feeling." Indeed, the sun also *rises* in Jake's Paris, which is anything but a wasteland. It is good to watch students walking, as they have for centuries, down to the Sorbonne, seat of the first university of Europe, or uphill to the law school, past the place of the chapel that had been dedicated to Saint Jacques (Santiago) and had been a hostel for pilgrims on their way to Compostela before the Dominicans took it over and Saint Thomas Aquinas studied and taught there in the thirteenth century, and past the rue Saint-Jacques, the ancient pilgrimage road. Jake is happy to be watching people go to work and to study, and happy to be going to work: "It felt pleasant" (36:1). This entire chapter-opening paragraph evokes one of Jake's happiest scenes, one that recurs for him every morning in Paris. It is reminiscent of what Hemingway's first Parisian mentor, Gertrude Stein, meant when she wrote, "Paris, France is exciting and peaceful" (1), and it is so because Parisians have a firm daily awareness that "Life is tradition and human nature" (8); and thus "Paris was where the twentieth century was" (11). It also reminds us of what Hemingway meant when he praised "always beautiful" Paris—"the city I love best in all the world" (*By-Line* 337).

35:9 **S bus:** Letter-designated Paris buses in the 1920s carried route markings from A to Z, AB to AZ, and BA to BL. (*Tramway*, or trolley, routes were designated numbers 1–128.) The S bus that Jake takes to work comes down the rue Soufflot to the Boul' Mich', where Jake boards. Standing on the open back platform, Jake passes the Luxembourg Gardens and Palace, comes alongside the Cathedral of Saint-Sulpice, turns down the boulevard Raspail to the boulevard Saint-Germain, crosses the

Seine on the pont de la Concorde, and goes through the place de la Concorde (and past the Crillon, where he will be stood up by Brett later in the day) and up the rue Royale to place de la Madeleine, where he *chooses* to get off and walk several blocks to his office—he could have stayed on the S bus and gotten off at his office.

35:10 **Madeleine:** Jake gets off the bus at the Madeleine, the Church of Saint Mary Magdalene, thus making yet another church part of his Parisian *paysage moralisè* (symbolic landscape). The Madeleine, considered the most fashionable church in Paris, is in the style of a classical temple, surrounded by a Corinthian colonnade. Begun in the eighteenth century, with the Revolution it was deconsecrated and by Napoleonic decree made into a Temple of Glory, a military landmark dedicated to Napoleon's Grand Army. It was reconsecrated as a place of Catholic worship in 1816, and construction was completed in 1842. During World War I, when Paris was bombarded by the German Big Bertha at a range of about 125 kilometers, the Madeleine was hit by several Big Bertha shells, and the signs of that long-range artillery attack are still visible. The exterior statue of Saint Luke was decapitated by one of the shells. Thus, the Madeleine provides a dual reminder (both Napoleonic and German) of the "glory" of war about which Jake has every reason to be cynical—that is, *not* about Mary Magdalene but about her ravaged and finally restored temple.

35:14 **manipulated the boxers:** In his early-morning happiness (*without* Brett present), Jake doesn't seem bothered by the street merchant selling toy boxers manipulated by a "girl assistant" pulling a thread; but the reader may discern the only shadow in this morning scene, foreshadowing indeed Brett's manipulations of all the "boxers," the men who fight over her later in the novel.

35:18 **CINZANO:** One of the best-known producers of Italian aperitifs, especially vermouth, Cinzano has been operating out of Turin, Italy, since 1757. The roller described paints, or stencils, sidewalk advertisements.

36:6 **Quai d'Orsay:** The longest *quai* in Paris, on the left bank of the Seine, extending (in the 1920s) from the pont Royal to the pont de Passy, the Quai d'Orsay is the center of foreign and diplomatic affairs of the French government. Jake is probably attending a briefing at the Ministère des Affaires Étrangères, next to the Esplanade des Invalides (the Invalides itself, as a home for disabled soldiers, and, under the dome, Napoleon's Tomb, would constitute yet another reminder to Jake of his war wound and invalid status).

36:8–9 **Nouvelle Revue Française:** *La Nouvelle Revue française* (commonly referred to as the *NRF*), since its founding in 1909 by a group of writers including André Gide and Jean Schlumberger, has generally been regarded as one of the most prestigious

French reviews, or magazines, concerned with literature and the arts. It is *not* concerned with foreign affairs or diplomacy. Why then does Jake refer to the *NRF* "diplomat"? Because a number of important French writers associated with the *NRF* also had diplomatic careers in the foreign service, including most notably Paul Claudel and Saint-John Perse. Claudel was not "young" and not in Paris at the time Jake attends this briefing (he was the French ambassador to Japan from 1921 to 1927), but Saint-John Perse (under the name Alexis Léger) was; he was publishing in the *NRF,* and he was a rising star in the foreign ministry, where Jake attends the briefing. Was Jake briefed by Saint-John Perse, the French poet who won the Nobel Prize in 1960? Perhaps. Hemingway, it seems, met Perse several times in Paris in the 1920s; that is what Perse's widow, Madame Léger, told me in 1983 when I was studying her husband's manuscripts in Aix-en-Provence. Hemingway and Perse had a mutual friend: Allen Tate (see Stoneback, *Hemingway's Paris* 13–14).

36:11 **Lyons:** In French, Lyon, this is the largest city of France after Paris (in 1926). Incorrect critical conclusions have been drawn based on a misunderstanding of Jake's (Hemingway's) spelling of "Lyon" with a terminal *s.* James Hinkle, in an important and detailed essay that is essentially a brief for a new edition of *The Sun Also Rises* that would, for example, remove all the incorrect spellings and insert omitted accent marks, states that Hemingway has made a serious error here with his spelling of "Lyons." For Hinkle, it is far more than what he regards as a spelling mistake; he correctly notes Jake's insistence on accuracy and precision and concludes that for "someone who knows French and France," this is more than just a spelling error since it "torpedoes Hemingway's whole sequence about Jake's expertise and exactness" ("Dear Mr. Scribner" 49). Hinkle gets it wrong on several counts here. First, in 1926 (and in 2006) "Lyons" is not just what he admits is an "acceptable British spelling" for Lyon—it is in fact the *only,* the *standard,* spelling in English, and the sole stated spelling in the *OED;* and if you look up Lyon in any good French-English dictionary (such as the 1999 edition of Larousse) the *only* English form given for Lyon is "Lyons." Moreover, all the standard guidebooks (the German Baedekers as well as the British Blue Guides, throughout the twentieth century) spell Lyon with the final *s.* And, finally, since Jake is a newspaperman, we should note that newspaper style sheets, certainly for the European and international (and Canadian) press, require the *s* form of Lyons. Thus the exact opposite of Hinkle's argument is true: it would "torpedo" Jake's reportorial correctness to print the French spelling for "Lyon." On the larger point of Hinkle's textual argument, I certainly agree that it would be desirable to have an edition with all the French place names spelled in the French manner, including, for example, proper capitalization, hyphenation, and accent marks. This is the practice followed here (e.g., Notre-Dame, not Notre Dame; l'île Saint-Louis, not Ile St. Louis; quai d'Orléans, not Quai d'Orleans; rue Saint-Jacques, not Rue St. Jacques; le Val-de-Grâce, not Val de Grace); would that it were the practice not just in any new editions of Hemingway's works but in the blizzard of incorrect forms found in Hemingway criticism. If the French standardization were clear, then erroneous critical arguments leading to larger questions (such as Hinkle's point regarding Jake's use of "Lyons" and its purported effect on his credibility) could be avoided. Finally, Hinkle's overall textual argument and *some* of his cited instances are well taken, yet some of his own examples blur the very case he attempts to make (e.g., his misspelling, or use of the British terminal *s* form of "Marseille," his incorrect capitalization of place terms such as *quai, rue,* and *pont,* etc.—see 49–50).

36:15 **Woolsey and Krum:** The brief appearance of these two characters, Jake's journalistic colleagues, serves to remind the reader that there is another side of expatriate life in Paris—the Right Bank side, the quiet (some would say dull) life of the married-with-children set who intend to get over to the Left Bank, to the Quarter, who intend to get out in the country but never do. Everything that Woolsey and Krum say—and the vague way they say it—suggests that they live in another world. Note, too, that Jake says very little, exercising his usual recourse to silence when he doesn't like the situation he's in, or what others are saying. (Also, the evocation of "normal" married life—a wife and kids and a place in the country—reminds Jake of a world from which he is excluded by his wound.) Woolsey and Krum may be memorable chiefly for their names—Woolsey suggesting linsey-woolsey, a coarse fabric, and a woolly texture (i.e., blurry, fuzzy); the implications of Krum are obvious, an inevitable result of such name typing.

36:19 **The Dingo:** Originally a small working-class bar at 10, rue Delambre, around the corner from the major cafés of Montparnasse, the Dingo (meaning, literally "wild dog," and by extension "crazy man" with these connotations in Australian slang: a cheat, scoundrel, coward), which became a popular expatriate hangout, was where Hemingway met Fitzgerald in 1925 and where Jake finds Brett and Mike when they are not, as expected, at the Sélect (81–83). James "Jimmie the Barman" Charters, celebrated bartender at the Dingo (and other Montparnasse establishments), wrote a good deal about the Dingo in his memoir, *This Must Be the Place* (1937), for which Hemingway wrote an introduction. The name was later changed to L'Auberge du Centre.

37:19 **Wetzel's:** When Jake gets to his office and finds Robert there waiting for him, he knows he won't get any work done, so he goes for lunch with Robert at a restaurant close to his office. Wetzel's, listed in the 1927 Paris Blue Guide as Vetzel's, was at 1, rue Auber.

37:25 **don't think so:** Robert's characteristic reply to Jake's pleasant small-talk question about having any fun reminds us that we are back in the presence of an antiexemplary character who kicks you under the table, who sleeps at your office, who is led around by women, and whom you can't get rid of—and all the other things we learn about in the novel's opening two chapters, incisively focused as they are on Robert Cohn. Jake specifically reminds the reader of those opening chapters when he mentions Robert's escapist fantasy about South America. And who else in this novel would reply to Jake's question about having fun as Robert does—"I don't think so"? That is to say, it's yet another way of showing that Robert is not *living* his life. Here, and for the remainder of this chapter, the ongoing characterization of Robert as an antiexemplar becomes the main focus of the narrative again. In fact, a regular pattern that shapes book I (actually the first eight chapters) may be discerned—two chapters focused on Robert, followed by two chapters focused on Brett, and so forth (it could be charted this way: 1–2, Robert; 3–4, Brett; 5–6, Robert; 7–8, Brett), until in chapter 9 the pattern is resolved when Jake learns Brett was in San Sebastián with Robert, and the narrative patterns and rhythms shift when Jake leaves for Spain with Bill. In this four-page scene, which takes up most of chapter 5, Robert, who has been largely absent from the last two chapters (even when ostensibly present in the background), returns, with devastating results, to center stage.

38:9 **Lady Ashley:** Typically, Jake's exactitude comes into play as he corrects Robert on the proper use of Brett's title. He will spend the rest of this conversation correcting Robert on the subject of Brett, who has become his new "South America," his latest romantic escapist fantasy; Jake informs Robert she's a drunk, she's married twice for reasons that have nothing to do with love, she's been around, she's thirty-four, and she's not "a kid," nor was she when Jake met her in the hospital in 1918, when she was a VAD (a volunteer with the Voluntary Aid Detachment of hospital assistants).

39:14–15 **face white . . . little plates:** After Robert, who has just met and is infatuated with Brett, outrageously and presumptuously (not to mention insensitively) tells Jake about the woman he has known and loved for more than six years, Jake finally loses his patience and tells Robert to go to hell. In a remarkably rendered scene Robert stands up and keeps standing there, his face "white and angry behind the little plates of hors d'oeuvres." When teaching this novel, I ask students at the beginning of our discussion which *concrete* images of Robert they find most immediately memorable and definitive; their responses almost always indicate Robert kicking Jake under the table in chapter 1, Robert punching people, and Robert's white face behind the little plates in this scene. When we discuss *why* this scene is so vividly memorable, some students talk about metaphor, how Robert's white face is like a little white plate, but that never seems to be a satisfactory explanation for most of the class. Other students with more background knowledge of the period try to relate this vignette to Ezra Pound's imagist principles. Still others discuss the little white plates of snacks as an *objective correlative* for Robert's juvenile rage, comparing this scene to the one in Hemingway's short story "Soldier's Home," where Krebs's distaste for his mother's piety as she serves him breakfast is vividly defined and indelibly fixed in the reader's mind by the rendering of Krebs staring "at the bacon fat hardening on his plate" (*Complete Short Stories* 115). Yet these critical terms and approaches to the passage never seem to satisfy the entire class; Robert's white face *behind* the little plates is the kind of image, or device, we all agree, that Hemingway uses to great effect—but there should be a critical term, a new name, my students usually insist, for this minimalist juxtapositional imagism that has the effect of foregrounding and freezing a scene, in much the same way that William Faulkner uses triads of frozen motion to fix and define an image.

In any case, Robert stands there, like the perpetual adolescent that he is, demanding that Jake take back not what he said about Brett but his telling Robert to go to hell. Is it possible to take Robert seriously after this, to think that he is a character capable of change or positive transformation, to regard him as anything other than an adolescent buffoon? Jake apologizes; Robert gladly sits down. When Jake wonders what Robert would have done "if he hadn't sat down," Hemingway's foreshadowing device of paired scenes is in full play, and the reader later gets the answer to Jake's question when Robert stands there at Jake's table, Jake tells him again to "go to hell," and Robert knocks him out cold (see 190:32–33).

40:3–4 **Café de la Paix:** At 12, boulevard des Capucines on the place de l'Opéra, the Café de la Paix was (and still is) one of the most elegant and fashionable cafés on the Right Bank. When Jake and Robert get "sore" at the Germanic (or Alsatian) Wetzel's, they make up and end the contentious conversation at the café of "peace" (*la paix*). Yet again, Hemingway employs symbolic landscape, the juxtapositional minimalism of *place*, to underline a point (as he will in the immediately following sentence that begins chapter 6, where Jake waits in *discord* for Brett, who does not show up for their date at the Crillon on the *Concorde*).

CHAPTER 6

41:5 **Jack Rose:** Jake waits patiently for Brett in the lobby of the Crillon (see 29:14), writing letters on the elegant hotel stationery. After forty-five minutes he goes to the famous bar (once said to be the longest bar in Europe) and has a Jack Rose with George the barman—typically, Jake knows by name and values the company of a bartender. The Jack Rose, largely forgotten now, was a popular drink in the 1920s. The classic recipe called for one-and-a-half ounces of applejack (or apple brandy, or Calvados), one-half to one ounce of lime juice, and half an ounce of grenadine, shaken with cracked ice and strained into a cocktail glass and garnished with a lime wedge. Popular between World Wars I and II, the drink was said to be "a favorite of Humphrey Bogart and Errol Flynn. . . . It was strong enough for a Real Man, yet smooth enough for a lady . . . despite its simplicity, it is commanding; despite its smoothness, it is self-assured. Its taste is equal parts crispness, sweetness and sour-ness" (Zaineddin and Gagosian 18). Some say it's named for its rosy color, others say it's named after applejack and Rose's Grenadine, and some say it's named for a nineteenth-century New York gangster. When Hemingway specifically *names* a drink, as when he names places, the reader may assume it has some telling significance. It does seem to be the right drink for Jake at this time and in this place. Indeed the *charged concreteness* of Hemingway's sense of exact detail is surely one of the factors that makes his work classic and that compels readers to retrace the paths and actions of *The Sun Also Rises*. For example, two writers for the *Washington Post* were recently compelled by their mutual memories of *The Sun Also Rises* to go on a quest to the best and oldest of Washington's bars to find a Jack Rose. They found a very few older bartenders who knew the formula but didn't have the proper ingredients. They went to sixty bars, looking for the real thing, the Hemingway thing (Zaineddin and Gagosian 18). If Hemingway had merely written, as many writers would have, that Jake had *a drink* at the Crillon, there could be no quest, no sense of how a Jack Rose colors the situation, how it is the exactly authentic drink for Jake to have at the Crillon as he waits for Brett. Whether Hemingway's readers search out the significance of a minor detail like a drink or are driven in their quests to the numinous places of his fiction—the streets of Paris, the symbolic landscape of Roncevaux, the fiesta at Pamplona—it is the authority of Hemingway's highly charged exactitude that propels the pilgrimage.

Some readers are always on the lookout for double entendres and sexual puns in *The Sun Also Rises;* one that seems to have been missed is suggested by Jake's Jack Rose, especially in this context. Jake, in French, is Jacques, which sounds like Jack; thus, Jake "rose" while anticipating Brett's arrival. But, of course, Jake has nothing to "rise," and Brett stands him up anyway. Like his friends and mentors Pound and Joyce, like most high-modernist writers, Hemingway plays intricate word games; in this case, I would not necessarily argue for authorial intentionality, but intention is not the sole and final determinant of literary effect. (For other instances of double entendre and sexual punning, see Hinkle, "What's Funny.")

41:8–11 **barges . . . river . . . bridges:** There is a curious notion, unfortunately recurrent in Hemingway criticism, that there is something depressing about this scene, that the empty barges somehow make a sad or melancholy image that reflects what some readers are pleased to call Jake's emptiness, his hollowness. With real attention to what's actually written in this passage, and with some common sense *and* local knowledge (a quality highly esteemed by Hemingway), we may dismiss this absurd reading for what it is—a misreading driven by a thesis that is determined to prove that Jake is empty, a lost and adrift member of a "lost generation." First, the reader might well say that there has been not one shred of evidence from page one of the novel that Jake is empty or lost. Wounded, yes, but these empty barges that are somehow supposed to constitute an objective correlative for Jake's inner state of being are not *wounded* barges. They are empty, *riding high,* moving swiftly "down the current." Common sense will suggest that there is something profoundly satisfying about an empty barge, indicating that a job has been done, a product has been delivered, and the barge now moves freely rather than struggling with its burden. And common visual sense will reveal that there is something powerful about an empty barge with its lines revealed—bow, stern, hull—its structural strength, aesthetic force, and functional dynamism plainly visible and riding high, rather than submerged almost to the waterline with a heavy load. The beauty of construction of the traditional wooden river barges of France—the kind of craft Jake is watching here—is far more obvious when they are moving empty. They may still be seen on the rivers and canals of France, and particularly in Paris, where many such barges have been converted to elegant homes, houseboats. A friend of mine, a writer and journalist and longtime expatriate in Paris, lives aboard his 1900-vintage barge, moored at the port on the quai des Tuileries, where barges have long been moored three or four deep, in the 1920s, as now. (This is where Jake is looking in this scene as he crosses the Seine on the pont de la Concorde.) My barge-residing and river-riding friend says there's something "exhilarating" about an empty barge in motion, riding high, and something "depressing" about a loaded barge, barely moving and submerged almost to the point of sinking, as it seems to the eye of the observer.

So much for common sense and visual sense—now the local knowledge. Jake, observing the barge (looking upstream) from the pont de la Concorde, and being a great possessor of local knowledge, knows that these empty barges are at the safe end of a notoriously dangerous passage through Paris. The stretch of the river that these barges have just traversed was known for centuries among the river people, the bargemen, as Misery Valley. Because of the buildup of the river walls and quais over the centuries, because of the many bridges with thick arches, a "damming effect" was created, so that "the water level upstream of the Ile de la Cité could be as much as five and a half feet higher than the downstream end," thus causing "a concomitant speed-up of water" (More and More 54). The worst part of this "urban gorge" was between pont Notre-Dame (rebuilt in 1913, it occupies the site of the main ancient Roman bridge) and pont au Change (built in 1859 to replace an earlier bridge lined with moneylenders' shops). The arches of these two bridges, separated by roughly two city blocks of fast-moving current, were not in line with each other, so the river pilots (some specially trained for this passage) had to shift course mid-rapid, but many crashed—with deadly results—into the so-called Devil's Arch of the pont au Change (Muirhead and Monmarché, *Paris* 93). Such facts provide the background explanation of the official motto (borrowed from the ancient Waterman's Guild) of Paris: *Fluctuat nec mergitur*—"she has a rough passage but stays afloat" (More and More 54). Jake, then, understands why the bargemen are "at the sweeps"—the long poles or oars used to steer (sweeps may also designate the curve of a boat's timbers)—as the barges approach the pont de la Concorde, a few bridges downstream from the worst of the dangerous passage. And if there is an analogy, an objective correlative, in this river vignette that suggests Jake's identity and inner state of being, it has nothing to do with empty barges and some presumed emptiness that he feels. It has everything to do with local knowledge of Paris and its river, with the fact that (to paraphrase the motto of Paris) Jake has a rough passage, but, riding high, he stays afloat. If the barge passage foreshadows the design of Jake's progress, it tells us that he moves through Misery Valley (see the "miserable" taxi ride with Brett, 24–27) from the bridge of Notre-Dame (and the next river scene is centered on the cathedral of Notre-Dame, 77), past the Devil's Arch at the bridge of *change,* to some final peace at the bridge of *concord.* Many writers employ sense of place, or the spirit of place, to suggest that character is a function of landscape or that landscape illuminates character, yet few have done so as subtly and rigorously, with such subtextual particularity, as Hemingway. Throughout the novel, as throughout Hemingway's work, symbols are never obvious and are always grounded in local knowledge and terrain—or *terroir,* the unique and specific properties, natural and historical, of *place.*

At the surface level of the narrative, in spite of the fact that he's just been stood up by Brett (which he expected), Jake still feels good in this scene: the river looks "nice," and it's "always pleasant crossing bridges in Paris." In 1925, thirty-two bridges spanned the Seine in Paris, many of them architecturally compelling and historically significant. For example, the Pont-Neuf—the "New Bridge"—just upstream from Jake's vantage point in this scene, is the oldest bridge (1578) and one of the most picturesque. The pont de la Concorde, which Jake is crossing in this scene, was completed in 1790, with stone from the Bastille, the notorious prison razed by the revolutionaries on 14 July 1789, used to build the upper sections. Many of the most famous views of Paris, the celebrated painterly cityscapes, are from the bridges. Parisian folklore and folk song and street lore evoke the bridges of Paris, and the way that Paris and the Seine "make love" with each other. In Paris, the river is always there.

The Seine is the principal river of this novel, which begins with an epigraph from Ecclesiastes about all the rivers running into the sea. There are allusions to other rivers—the Loire, the Adour (in Bayonne), the Arga (in Pamplona), the Irati—but none is as central to the rendered and foregrounded landscape as is the Seine. (Contrary to much critical commentary on the novel, the Irati, which rises in southern France in the forêt d'Iraty and flows into Spain, passing near Burguete, is *not* depicted in rendered action and is *not* where Bill and Jake are seen fishing—a pride of place that is accurately attributed to the Río de la Fábrica; see 118:8.) The Seine, which flows 792 kilometers from its source in Burgundy to the sea at Le Havre, flows 11 serpentine kilometers through Paris, shaping and defining the city's geographical and aesthetic identity. In 1925, it was a very busy river, the most important commercial harbor in France. At its source, 480 kilometers upstream at mont Tasselot, the river goddess Sequana (hence "sequoine," then contracted to Seine) presides at the spring, the birthplace of the river. The nymph was enshrined there by Baron Haussmann, who oversaw the reconstruction of Paris in the nineteenth century, designing many of the boulevards and monuments and parks—all with a sense of the strategic and aesthetic centrality of the Seine—that constitute Hemingway's Paris of the 1920s.

For Jake, then, who here finds, with characteristic understatement, the river "nice" and the bridges "pleasant" to cross, not just the sun but also the Seine and his spirits rise every morning when he crosses his river, the river he loves, to go to work. Far from being like an empty or hollow barge, Jake loves many things: he loves his work, he loves Paris, he loves food and wine, he loves travel, he loves fishing, he loves bullfighting, he loves churches (and the Church, that "grand religion"—see 97:18–20). And he loves Brett, the only impossible love in his life, the love with which he comes to terms in the course of the novel. As he crosses the bridges of Paris, with Brett and without Brett, stood up by Brett and betrayed by Brett, he begins a journey that, like his river, runs to the sea, to his final ritual cleansing after the fiesta, where another river runs into the sea at San Sebastián.

For a sense of how well Hemingway knew and how much he loved the Seine—its bridges, barges, quais, views, fishermen—the reader of *The Sun Also Rises* should see his other works, such as the memories of Paris sequence in *Islands in the Stream* and especially *A Moveable Feast*. These works, written toward the end of his life, remind us how local knowledge informs love, how the bright particularity of place, of Paris, creates the unending moveable feast that is the sacrament of life well lived, life lived—in Jake's words—"all the way up." Or, years before Hemingway imagined Jake on the bridges of Paris, we can read in his apprentice journalism: "It is wonderful in Paris to stand on a bridge across the Seine looking . . . up the river spanned by many bridges . . . to where Notre Dame squats in the dusk" (*By-Line* 112).

41:12 **statue:** Coming from the pont de la Concorde on the boulevard Saint-Germain, Jake calls the reader's attention to yet another statue, this one at the junction of the boulevards Raspail and Saint-Germain and the rue du Bac. As if to remind readers that signs and signals are indeed important in this novel, that barges and bridges, cafés and churches, and all the details of symbolic landscape are part of the system of coded telegraphy in this text, Jake tells us that this statue depicts the inventor of the semaphore. Actually, Claude Chappe (1763–1805), who is memorialized by the statue, was the inventor of the "aerial telegraph," a preelectronic form of rapid communication. The statue was taken down under the German occupation of Paris during World War II.

41:15 **dull riding:** Unlike the barges "riding high" on the Seine that give Jake a "pleasant" feeling in the preceding paragraph, the "dull riding" on the boulevard Raspail, one of the ugliest and newest (completed in 1907, having erased many historic buildings) main thoroughfares of Paris, makes Jake feel "bored and dead and dull." Although he wonders why he feels this way and considers some unconscious "association of ideas" as the possible source of his feeling, no explanation is needed other than the physical fact of the fast-moving traffic on the long, straight modern road flanked by architecturally boring modern buildings. The boulevard Raspail is not the historic and traditional Paris that Jake loves. (When, in 1974, I daily walked or rode down the boulevard Raspail to my office, I felt like Jake; I hated riding, but I didn't mind Raspail at all when I walked. Perhaps that was an "association of ideas" I had picked up from *The Sun Also Rises*, which, at the time, I had not read in ten years.)

41:16 **P.L.M.** One of the five principal railways of France, the PLM (*de Paris-Lyon-Méditerranée*) departs from the gare de Lyon. Jake probably finds this route dull because the railway line does not pass close enough to Fontainebleau (fifty-eight kilometers southeast of Paris) to afford a view of its famous palace or good views of the beautiful forest, although from the train he might get a glimpse of the École militaire and the large military garrison at Fontainebleau, which would serve as an unpleasant reminder of the war. It is more likely, however, and exactly parallel with the effect of the boulevard Raspail, that Jake is bored by the modern development (e.g., grain mills and large factories) along the banks of the Seine (the route followed by the railway) from Fontainebleau to Montereau (actually Montereau-faut-Yonne). At Champagne-sur-Seine, halfway between Fontainebleau and Montereau, the large factories of Schneider and Cie, one of the largest arms manufacturers in France, were between the railway and the river. The Schneider company developed, for example, a barbed-wire cutter and the first French tank used in the trench warfare of World War I. The Schneider CA1 (or *Char d'Assaut Schneider*) wasn't much of a tank, but the Schneider name and factory along this PLM railway route would be enough to remind Jake of the horrors of the war and make him feel "dead and dull" until this stretch of the ride was over.

42:5 **Mencken:** In chapter 2, Jake assumes that Robert Cohn got his dislike for Paris from a book (see 12:11). Here he attributes Cohn's "incapacity to enjoy Paris" to Mencken, who "hates Paris." Jake is unusually tentative in these attributions—"possibly," "I believe"—but Mencken is unmistakably a negative presence in his thoughts for the next two pages and later, in the fishing scene at Burguete (122). H. L. Mencken (1880–1956) was a journalist and essayist known as the "American Nietzsche" and the "Sage of Baltimore," a caustic critic of everything from Prohibition to Puritanism to religion—especially the fundamentalism that he mocked during his coverage of the Scopes trial in 1925, or, as he christened it, the "Monkey Trial." As a literary critic, first for the magazine the *Smart Set*, and then in his own journal, the *American Mercury*, he was one of the most influential voices of the World War I era. His literary tastes were more rearguard than avant-garde; he championed writers such as Theodore Dreiser and especially Sinclair Lewis and freely expressed his distaste for such modernists as Dos Passos, Faulkner, and Hemingway. Jake is correct in saying that many young readers "get their likes and dislikes from Mencken."

Hemingway had good reason to dislike Mencken, who had said in a review that Hemingway's *in our time* (1924) was the "sort of brave, bold stuff that all atheistic young newspaper reporters write. Jesus Christ in lower case" (Oliver 218). Hemingway, of course, was not an atheist, and *in our time* was experimental avant-garde writing, not journalism—but who could expect Mencken to appreciate that? In 1925, the manuscript of Hemingway's next book, *In Our Time,* was considered and rejected for publication by, as Hemingway put it, "Menken [sic] . . . that shit." Discussing that volume in a letter to John Dos Passos, in which he complained about how he had to leave his somewhat risqué (for the time) story "Up in Michigan" out of the volume, Hemingway said: "I suppose if it was called Way Out in Iowa, Mencken would have published it if the fucking would have been changed to a community corn roast" (*Selected Letters* 143, 157). Writing to Fitzgerald in December 1925 (while Hemingway was working on *The Sun Also Rises*), he sarcastically observed that "your boy friend Menken [sic]" only gets excited about books that "deal with the much abused Am. Scene" (*Selected Letters* 176; see 115). Clearly, Mencken was much on Hemingway's mind as he composed *The Sun Also Rises* (see 122:18). This novel's literary landscape, then, with numerous allusions to writers, is also a form of *paysage moralisé*, a symbolic landscape of taste and style.

42:13 **Harvey Stone:** Based on Harold Stearns (1891–1943), American writer and editor and a well-known expatriate fixture in the cafés of Montparnasse, Stone is an important if minor member of the cast of writers who make up the novel's literary landscape. In one sense, Stone serves in this entire three-page scene as a representative of the expatriate writer who wastes his time and talent, drinking his life away in the Quarter; when Jake meets him, he notes that Stone is unshaven and has already had a number of drinks ("a pile of saucers"). He says he hasn't eaten in five days, yet Jake remembers that three days before, Stone won two hundred francs from him—which would buy a lot of meals or a lot of drinks. Then Jake, always generous and concerned about a friend, gives him one hundred francs and suggests they go somewhere and eat. But Harvey would prefer to drink. In another sense, the function of this scene with Stone is to elaborate on the key Mencken allusion that immediately precedes the scene; since Stone knows Mencken, he can give Jake the inside information on him. (In the manuscript, there was even more literary gossip in this scene.) Stone also knows Cohn and defines him as precisely as Jake does, but with far less sympathy, and thus helps to set up the primary business of this chapter—the devastating portrait of Robert provided by Frances in the last five pages of the chapter.

The portrait of Harvey Stone is very close to the actual Harold Stearns. Stearns was the author of *America and the Young Intellectual* (1921) and other books, and editor of the important volume *Civilization in the United States: An Inquiry by Thirty Americans* (1922). Contributors to Stearns's *Civilization in the United States* included a number of important American writers such as Conrad Aiken on "Poetry," Van Wyck Brooks on "The Literary Life," Ring Lardner on "Sport and Play," and Mencken on "Politics." After Stearns moved to Paris in the 1920s and began drinking heavily, he had less to do with the American literary scene, although he continued to write for American newspapers, including a regular column devoted to horse racing for the *Chicago Tribune*. Just as Jake is "fond of" Stone (44:30), Hemingway liked Stearns, even using the same language in a letter written while he worked on *The Sun Also Rises*: "I'm sorry as hell for H[arold] S[tearns] but there's nothing anybody can do for him except give him money and be nice to him. . . . No solution. And again I'm fond of him" (letter to Scott Fitzgerald, 24 December 1925, *Selected Letters* 181). By the late twenties, things had gotten worse; Fitzgerald wrote to Hemingway, in December 1928: "I met old H. Stearns just before leaving Paris and feeling drunk and Christ-like suggested a title to him, 'Why I Go On Being Poor in Paris,' told him to write it as an informal letter to me and I'd sell it" (*Correspondence of Scott Fitzgerald* 330).

42:23–24 **through with them:** Stone probably means he's through with his literary colleagues in America, although he's pretty much "through with" the States, too.

42:31 **New York Bar:** Harry's New York Bar, at 5, rue Daunou on the Right Bank, is famous as the alleged birthplace of the Bloody Mary and a favorite gathering place for American expatriates. (An old sign on the front window—"Sank Roo Doe Noo"—still serves as a pronunciation aid for French-challenged Americans.) The proprietor, Harry MacElhone, was a friend of Hemingway's; pictures of Hemingway, along with many other American writers (who also used Harry's in their writing) and athletes, have long covered the walls. Very much an American saloon (rare in Paris), its college banners and sports memorabilia still make it a popular American hangout. The American college and sports decor, along with the fact that it was one of Fitzgerald's favorite bars, may have been the associative link in Hemingway's compositional process that suggested Cohn's football reference two pages later (44:9).

43:2 **like a cat:** This is clearly one of Stone's favorite phrases; see Bill Gorton's repeated echo of the phrase in his conversation with Jake about Harvey Stone (73).

43:15 **Hoffenheimer:** This is the novelist Joseph Hergesheimer (1880–1954), as Hemingway had written in the manuscript, whose name in the book was later changed because of editorial wariness regarding libel suits. Hergesheimer, a friend of Mencken's, was listed in a 1924 issue of Mencken's journal, the *American Mercury,* as the leading American novelist of the day. His best-known novels included *The Three Black Pennys* (1917) and *Java Head* (1919). In 1925 he published his autobiography, which Hemingway may have read while he was writing *The Sun Also Rises.* His later novels—*Balisand* (1924) and *Tampico* (1926)—might be associated with the kind of romantic escapism that Robert Cohn would find appealing. In any case, in Hemingway's avant-garde literary landscape, Hergesheimer (to whom Sinclair Lewis dedicated *Main Street* in 1922) would definitely be part of an outdated literary scene.

43:16 **garter snapper:** Both Stone and Jake approve of Mencken's phrasemaking, probably because it's a phrase they haven't heard before. Mencken, at his best, had a good ear for the American language and fresh idioms. Although "garter snapper" does not appear in any standard source, it probably signifies that Hergesheimer was a woman chaser.

43:18 **He's through now:** Although this is sometimes taken as a reference to Hoffenheimer/Hergesheimer, to whom it is applicable, the full context of the conversation makes it clear that Stone and Jake are talking about Mencken, who, in their view, has exhausted his best material and is now writing about "all the things he doesn't know" (e.g., avant-garde writers, Paris, the Scopes trial).

43:23 **Alexander Hamilton Institute:** A well-known international correspondence school of business, the Alexander Hamilton Institute was established in 1909 and is still in business. They also produced many publications dealing with all aspects of business and management, and (in 2005, according to their Web site) they specialize in "all aspects of employment law," and their "products are written in a practical and easy-to-read style that all levels of management can understand." Among my grandfather's papers, there were documents certifying his successful completion in 1913 of a series of small-business management courses shortly before he successfully managed a chain of small businesses. Thus, as Jake says, the Alexander Hamilton Institute had once been, like Mencken, "a good thing."

44:9 **football:** Remarkably, Robert Cohn, thirty-four years old and a struggling novelist, replies to Stone's question about what he would most like to do if he could by saying he'd "rather play football again with what I know about handling myself, now." While this might be just the kind of thing that some men in their thirties might say to each other while working out at a gym, it is incongruous in context, and Stone revises his assessment of Robert as "a moron," calling him instead a case of "arrested development." (In the manuscript he calls him a *retardataire,* someone who "never grew up." *Facsimile* 1:153.) Then Robert threatens him with getting his face pushed in, as he had Jake in the previous chapter (see 39:14–15), foreshadowing the faces Robert will push in (Jake's, Mike's, Romero's) at the fiesta in Pamplona. With the immediately preceding mention of one of Fitzgerald's favorite saloons, Harry's New York Bar, with its Ivy League pennants and sports memorabilia, this looks very much like an allusion to Tom Buchanan, one of the most unpleasant characters in Fitzgerald's *The Great Gatsby,* which came out in 1925 shortly before Hemingway met Fitzgerald. Hemingway read *Gatsby* closely as he was preparing to write *The Sun Also Rises,* and Robert Cohn sounds a good deal like Tom Buchanan, a former star football player at Yale, one of those men, Fitzgerald writes, "who reach such an acute limited excellence at twenty-one that everything afterwards savours of anti-climax" (*Gatsby* 10). In a way, Robert is even worse than Tom because he did not achieve that excellence at twenty-one but still craves it at thirty-four, like Tom, "seeking a little wistfully for the dramatic turbulence of some irrecoverable football game" (*Gatsby* 10). And like the physically aggressive Tom Buchanan (with his "cruel body"), Robert likes to threaten people physically (*Gatsby* 11).

Stone, however, leaves not because Cohn has threatened him physically but because he can't stand Robert. After Stone's gone, Cohn says he "can't stand" him, but Jake says he's fond of him and changes the subject by asking Robert if he did any writing that afternoon. Yet it's not really changing the subject, because Robert's response about his difficulty with his writing has been predicted by his juvenile behavior in the scene with Stone.

45:11 **undergraduate quality:** Note the timing and placement of this paragraph, in which Jake as narrator seems concerned that he hasn't clearly shown Robert's character, coming as it does just *before* Frances arrives to give the most thoroughgoing assessment of Robert anywhere in the novel and *after* Jake's clearly shown scenes of Robert's antiexemplary behavior from the first chapter on. Jake seems genuinely concerned that he hasn't shown Robert's "nice, boyish sort of cheerfulness," and Jake seems ambivalent about Robert's "funny sort of undergraduate quality," not sure if this is a good thing or a bad thing. Jake is sure, however, that Robert never says anything perceptive or original, anything that stands out—a very bad sign for someone who purports to be a writer. On what may seem the positive side of the balance sheet, Jake notes that Robert is "nice to watch on the tennis-court, he had a good body, and he kept it in shape." This sounds a good deal like the description of Francis Macomber in "The Short Happy Life of Francis Macomber": "he was thirty-five years old [Robert is thirty-four], kept himself very fit, was good at court games . . . and had just shown himself, very publicly, to be a coward" (*Complete Short Stories* 6). The descriptions are interchangeable, and Robert, who has just shown himself publicly to be a "moron" or a case of "arrested development," is about to show himself, very publicly, to be a coward as Frances berates him and Jake wonders why he just sits there and takes it. Jake's view of Robert has much in common with Wilson's view of Macomber; Wilson, the professional hunter whose judgment dictates the story's code of values, wonders how it is that American men "stay little boys so long. . . . Sometimes all their lives. . . . The great American boy-men" (25–26). Yet Robert, unlike Macomber, never does grow up; never has a life-changing epiphany; never discovers courage and the "wild unreasonable happiness" that comes with it; never learns how to love women, or the world; and seems more and more "boyish" and "undergraduate" as the novel progresses.

45:20 **Lenglen:** Suzanne Lenglen (1899–1938), the French tennis star known as the "diva" and "La Divine," was the first female tennis player to achieve international celebrity. An extraordinary athlete, hard driving and flamboyant, she won twenty-five Grand Slam titles in the 1920s and was also the first female tennis player to wear more revealing dress (i.e., bare forearms, tennis dress cut above the calf), and she was known for sipping brandy between sets. Cohn's desire to win may resemble Lenglen's competitiveness, but his style—in all things—does not.

46:4 **Are you here:** Frances ignores Robert, and she has every right to do so, since he has just broken off their engagement, probably because he has fallen for Brett and has already made plans to go to San Sebastián with her. Although Frances deliberately insults Robert by asking ironically, "Are you here?"—does her emphasis fall on *you* or *here*?—she points to one of Robert's defining characteristics: his lack of *presence*.

46:10 **Ritz:** The most expensive hotel in Paris in the 1920s, with one of the most expensive restaurants, the Ritz is located at 15, place Vendôme, on the Right Bank. The Ritz was one of Fitzgerald's favorite places in the 1920s (see his short story "Babylon Revisited," and his novel *Tender Is the Night*). Hemingway did not frequent the Ritz in his early years in Paris because it was too expensive; later, he often stayed there and famously "liberated" the Ritz when the Germans fled Paris in 1944. Ironically, given Fitzgerald's more extensive association with the Ritz, there is now a Hemingway Bar at the Ritz. The point of this scene would seem to be twofold: (1) to suggest that Robert doesn't "support" Frances well enough for her to be able to pay for her own lunch at the Ritz and (2) to echo the fact that Jake was stood up by Brett at the only slightly less expensive Crillon (not far geographically from the Ritz) at the beginning of this chapter.

46:25 **we crossed:** An interesting game of "musical cafés" that illustrates the style and daily mode of being in the Montparnasse Quarter is played in this entire scene (44–51). First, Harvey Stone and Jake are at the Sélect; shortly after Cohn arrives, Stone leaves and crosses the street to go to another café to eat. Jake suggests to Robert that they walk up the boulevard to the Lilas, but Robert has a date with Frances at the Sélect. She arrives, ignores Robert, asks Jake to cross the street with her to the Dôme, and tells Robert to stay at the Sélect. After they talk while waiting for a drink that never arrives, Frances and Jake cross the street again to the Sélect and rejoin Robert. As Frances berates Robert, Jake grows increasingly uncomfortable and finally invents a patently false reason to excuse himself—that he must go inside and see Harvey Stone, when both the reader and Robert know Harvey Stone is not inside, because Jake and Robert have watched him leave the Sélect shortly before. (Why does Jake give this obviously false reason to get away? To let Robert know he is uncomfortable with what's going on?) In any case, Jake watches Frances and Robert from the bar inside for a moment then leaves by the side door, thus ending this game of café crossings.

Yet there may be more to this scene—there *must* be more, given Hemingway's carefully constructed prose—than mere illumination of the café landscape of Montparnasse. Consider the extraordinary repetition of the action and language of crossing: *nine* times in less than five pages (43–48), Hemingway writes "across the street" or "crossing the street" or "crossed the street" or some close linguistic variant of these words. Even for Hemingway's repetition-saturated early style, in which he often deploys repetition to great effect (see, e.g., 20:16), the rhythmic drumbeat of all this crossing should alert the careful reader to some pattern of significance that might otherwise be overlooked, some key point that Hemingway wants to make obliquely. Hemingway had learned, as he put it, "many truths about rhythms and the uses of words in repetition" from Gertrude Stein, but this ninefold repetition demands to be read as more than Steinian emphasis or insistence, more than *insistance poétique* (*Moveable Feast* 17). Readers on a symbol-hunting excursion may be forgiven, and may ultimately be right, if they detect the presence of some Christian pattern of cross symbolism here. But that may be baldly (and prematurely) asserted, given the nature of Hemingway's typically charged wordplay. First, the repetition pattern might suggest the ways in which Harvey Stone, Robert Cohn, and Frances Clyne are *cross* with each other. Then Robert, in this entire scene, is essentially caught in the *cross fire* from Harvey and Frances. And the redoubled *crossing* may suggest the *crosscurrents* of *double-crossing* in this scene: Robert betrays Frances *and* Jake in his plan, just formulated, to go off with Brett. And the *crossover* in Robert's relationship from Frances to Brett prefigures her betrayal of Jake and the *cross-purposes* in their relationship caused by her deception. To cross the street may imply change, a shift in direction at some key intersection; all these characters are at a *crossroads* in their relationships, and the changes implied by all the crossing are implicit here: Jake will never quite feel the same about Robert after this scene, first because of the way he just sits there and takes the tongue-lashing Frances gives him, and second, in a deeper change, Jake will eventually realize the *double cross* that Robert and Brett have planned sometime between the scene at the *bal musette* and Jake's being stood up by Brett at the Crillon. And there is Frances, most deeply *double-crossed* by Robert, who has strung her along with the prospect of marriage for years only to discard her when he is suddenly infatuated with Brett. Frances, who ironically employs biblical and Christian language and metaphor throughout this scene ("live by the sword . . . perish by the sword," "make sacrifices," "vision," "mystic," "Lourdes"), certainly has her *cross* to bear and cannot be blamed for nailing Robert on the *cross* of his own conduct. All this crossing, then, may have Christian reverberations, under the rubric of the cross, the long shadow of human betrayal and suffering and the promise of redemption, under the sign of the cross that Jake will soon make in the Cathedral of Pamplona. And this, in turn, has much to do with what Robert Gajdusek calls "psychic and religious crossover," or the "crossover pursuit of human transcendence achieved through a possession of eternity in time" (*His Own Country* 36–37).

If all the crossing in this chapter is construed as symbolism, we may want to recall what Hemingway, who was always reluctant to answer questions about symbolism from interviewers, had to say on the subject: "I suppose there are symbols . . . [but] I dislike talking about them and being questioned about them. . . . Read anything I write for the pleasure of reading it. Whatever else you find will be the measure of what you brought to the reading" (Bruccoli 120). The first thing that should be brought to the reading of this scene is a good ear, a capacity to hear the intensification through repetition of the cross pattern that is ineluctably present here and inarguably intentional. Another insight that might be brought to the reading here by a student of Hemingway's career is the recognition of his unusual fondness (especially in titles), from his earliest to his later work, for "cross" variants: from "Crossroads—An Anthology" (early apprentice work) to "Cross-Country Snow" (published in 1923) to "Crossing the Mississippi" (a fragmentary story first published posthumously in *The Nick Adams Stories*), and from "Across from the Post Office" (early journalism) to "Across the Board" (a 1949 poem about a wounded soldier) to *Across the River and into the Trees* (his 1950 novel, where the title echo of General "Stonewall" Jackson's last words refers to the final crossing—death) to "Black Ass at the Cross Roads" (a late short story where the idiosyncratically spelled "Cross Roads" emphasizes change, transformation, conversion). And there is Hemingway's story of Christ on the Cross, *Today Is Friday* (1926). Far from being blasphemous, as has sometimes been suggested, this brief playlet was written by Hemingway, already an avowed Catholic convert, while he was revising *The Sun Also Rises* in the spring of 1926. It is centered on the conduct and courage of Christ on the Cross, as observed by three Roman soldiers. This three-page tale contains two extraordinary sequences of repetition: the phrase "come down off the cross" (with one variant "get down off the cross") occurs five times in eleven lines and is linked with the leitmotif phrase "He was pretty good in there today," which signifies Christ's grace under pressure and is repeated five times in one-and-a-half pages (*Complete Short Stories* 272). Perhaps this brief, neglected tale written in the midst of Hemingway's composition of *The Sun Also Rises* tells us far more than we have recognized about the novel and confirms and underlines far more than just Hemingway's stylistic experimentation with repetition (see 80:8–9, 122:24, and 222:30).

47:14 **rotten luck:** The reverb function, the echo chamber of Hemingway's style, is always in play. In the lead-in to Frances's lament that she may never have children, Jake utters the words that the Italian colonel said to Jake in the hospital when he knew he would never have children: "Che mala fortuna"—the bad luck, the evil fortune, of a "rotten way to be wounded" (31).

47:24 **children:** As always, it is necessary to follow Hemingway's dialogue transcription closely with the eye and the ear. Here Frances speaks lines 22–23, and after looking at Jake "very brightly," she continues speaking lines 24–26. The fact that Frances discusses having children with Jake is, most likely, further evidence that most of Jake's friends and acquaintances in Paris do not know how he was wounded (see 31:5). If she knew, even Frances would not be so indecorous or indelicate as to bring up with Jake the matter of having children.

48:13 **what he wants:** Frances thinks that Robert wants to get rid of her so he can be free to pursue all the young ladies ("little chickens") of New York, who will swoon over the successful writer. Jake disagrees, defending Robert and saying he's not really that way. But Frances may be right; it's certainly true that Jake (Cohn's "tennis friend") doesn't know Robert as Frances does. And Jake may be thinking only about Robert's infatuation with Brett. In any case, this may be Jake's last "defense" of Robert in the book. This moment marks a shift, a change in the focus and intensity of this scene, a change in the characterization of Robert as a naive romantic who may be capable of growth, redemption. Frances and Jake cross the street, and she begins her devastating indictment of Robert with Jake as silent witness.

48:23 **what are you smiling at:** Frances is ready to wipe the smile off his face. Here begins the longest sustained speech in the novel, a magnificent set piece, Frances's tour de force, and her reason for being in this novel: to provide the definitive portrait of Robert's antiexemplary behavior and character. The reader should pay close attention to her specific definition of his traits and to how her views resonate with what we already know, and will learn later, about Robert's character. Through it all, Cohn offers no defense but interrupts briefly, begging her to "shut up," and Jake, wondering why Cohn sits there and takes it, says nothing.

49:6 **generous:** Frances pronounces Robert "very generous" with withering sarcasm, and her evidence defines him as the opposite of generous in every respect: cheap and miserly, a self-centered tightwad who uses other people and discards them when he has used them up. He thought he could get rid of her, buy her off with a hundred pounds, but she's forced him to give her two hundred pounds. Clearly, she has no money to fall back on, no inheritance. (Her mother lost her money on French war bonds.) She could have had alimony from the husband she just divorced in order to marry Robert, as he had promised, but she gave up the alimony for the "quickest" divorce so they could be married. Robert had earlier discarded his "little secretary" who followed him from Carmel to Provincetown— "and he didn't even pay her fare back to the coast" (50:6).

50:15 **get material:** In a more subtle analysis than it might appear at first to be, Frances pokes fun at the kind of writer who thinks that *living* is about getting material to write about—a notion, not uncommon, that is reducible to romantic absurdity, escapism, since if a writer is taking notes on life as he lives it, he is not living it "all the way up" (see 10:19). The kind of self-absorbed writer who regards his life as "material," as Frances so clearly defines the matter, will always be cut off from life: "so busy all the time that we were living together, writing on this book, that he doesn't remember anything about us." This connects with Jake's earlier analysis of Robert as someone who gets all his ideas from books, and, especially if they are romantic books by second- and third-rate writers (like Robert's favorite writers), what kind of life can be lived at third hand, twice or thrice removed from any reality, doomed to the abstract romanticism of getting *material* for a fourth-rate book (see chapter 2)?

50:24 pity yourself: Self-pity is of course the besetting and defining sin of romantic egotists, self-absorbed third-rate writers, and solipsists of every description who are simply unable to connect with the world outside the self and are thus doomed to inauthentic lives. For the writer, as Frances astutely observes, self-pity is perilous because "you can't remember what the other person's said." Frances is a writer who can't get published, as she said earlier in this scene, and the evidence of her conversation (contrasted with his) suggests that she's probably a better writer than Robert. Certainly she is more exact, and exactitude of observation is where good writing begins. As Hemingway put it, echoing Frances a decade after he wrote this scene, the good writer must "listen completely. . . . Most people never listen. Nor do they observe"; writers must also "get in somebody else's head" and "feel for other people"—all these qualities are lacking in Cohn, as a man and a writer, because, as Frances sees it, he's so busy pitying himself (*By-Line* 190–91). However we define this novel's framework of values, or in a larger sense, Hemingway's code of values (see especially 59–61 and 131–32), it is clear that self-pity is a primary obstacle to knowing and living the values. And crying, it should be added, is not necessarily an index to self-pity; Robert seems to cry a great deal, and Jake also cries, but there is a radical difference in the sources and occasions of their tears (see 31–34).

50:32 Hardy . . . Anatole France: In the course of her ironic musing on "young writers" and Robert's place in that context, Frances demonstrates her literary sensibility and her grasp of historical exactitude. Thomas Hardy (1840–1928) published several neglected works before he was thirty-four, but his first critical and popular success, *Far from the Madding Crowd,* appeared in 1874 when Hardy was, like Robert Cohn, thirty-four years old. Anatole France (1844–1924) published his first books in his late twenties, but his first literary success and recognition came with *Le Crime de Sylvestre Bonnard* in 1881, when he was thirty-seven. In the World War I era, France was a leading French writer known for his ironic wit and urbane skepticism; he received the Nobel Prize in 1921 and died in October 1924—as Frances notes, "a little while ago." Robert doesn't like his work, Frances says, because his "French friends" told him he wasn't "any good"; as usual, Robert gets his ideas secondhand because he doesn't read French. France certainly never looked for writing "material" and never cried when he had scenes (if he had scenes) with his mistresses, as Robert does. Is it merely incidental that *Frances* likes and cites *France,* that both she and Jake probably know that his real first name was *Jacques*? Also, Anatole France is the most likely source of the unattributed quotation about irony and pity later in the novel (see 113:31).

51:8–9 mystic . . . Lourdes: In a novel that is centrally (if often subtextually) concerned with the mystic, with religious mysteries (the Catholic Church and the bullfight), and with the theme of pilgrimage, Frances makes the first direct, if ironic, reference to these matters. She has her "vision in the Café Sélect." Saint Bernadette (i.e., Bernadette Soubirous of Lourdes) received her visions, eighteen apparitions of the Virgin Mary, and the revelation of a miraculous spring of healing waters, in Lourdes, in the south of France, in 1858, which led to the establishment of the most famous modern Christian pilgrimage (see 86:2–3). "Bernadette" may rhyme with "Georgette" and "Brett," but there is little connection between them, except perhaps as echoed in the novel's many references to "bathing," such as Jake and Brett's talk of bathing two pages after this first reference to Lourdes (53). Bernadette was instructed by the Virgin Mary to bathe in the stream mysteriously revealed to her, and more than two hundred million pilgrims to Lourdes have since bathed there, seeking miraculous healing.

51:14–15 **end of all the romance:** The subtle analysis and demolition of Robert's romantic sensibility performed by Frances throughout this entire scene culminates with her proposition that the romantic abstractionist like Robert, who must remain detached from the particularity of a life authentically lived, can fulfill his *idea* of having a mistress by not marrying her.

51:20 **sit there:** Jake cannot believe that Robert just sits there and keeps on "taking it." The answer to Jake's question—"Why did he sit there?"—is this: Robert knows every word of it is true and thus has no reply, no comeback, no defense. This scene will be echoed at the fiesta when Robert just sits there and takes it from the others, who wish he would go away. Another question that is raised by this scene's structural placement in the novel is this: since Frances knows and here reveals what Brett will soon learn about Robert, the reader is compelled to ask why Brett (who is always so sure about who is "one of us") goes off with Robert. The one-word answer is sex. A more complicated answer has to do with promiscuity that is not merely sexual but covers all behavior—the promiscuity that Hemingway was talking about when he said this novel was "the most moral book he had ever written," and it was a "tract against promiscuity" (Bruccoli 94; see especially the "values" scene, 57–61).

CHAPTER 7

52:14–15 très gentille: As the presentation of Jake's conversation with his concierge makes clear, he is speaking French with her. Hemingway skillfully employs various devices to translate for the reader of English without losing the texture of a conversation in French, including syntax ("In the end . . .") and repetition in both languages ("very nice"—"très gentille"; "some one"—"quelqu'une"). We discover the reason for the concierge's reassessment of Brett as somebody, a very nice somebody, on the next page when we learn that Brett has tipped her two hundred francs.

53:5 pelouse . . . pesage: Although the concierge had been a racetrack concessionaire in the *pelouse*, the lawn enclosure area with the cheapest admission (three francs in the mid-twenties), she studied the ritzier area of the *pesage*, the paddock, where admission was thirty francs for gentlemen, twenty francs for ladies—thus her natural association of money with class.

53:18 France: Jake and Hemingway are correct in referring to the ship on which Bill Gorton is traveling as the *France*. It cannot be the *Île de France*, as some Hemingway commentators have said, perhaps with an intent to cast doubt on Jake's (or Hemingway's) accuracy. The *Île de France* was not yet built and did not make its maiden voyage, its first transatlantic crossing, until 22 June 1927, long after the novel was published, and more than two years after Bill's crossing. The *France* was the grandest ship of the Compagnie Générale Transatlantique—or the French Line—from her maiden voyage in 1912 until the *Île de France* entered service in mid-1927. Known as the Château of the Atlantic for its grand interiors, the *France* also served during World War I as a hospital ship and a troop transport that carried thousands of American soldiers to and from France (thus yet another reminder of the war). She left service in 1932 and was scrapped in 1935. (A later famous French Line ship named *France* began her transatlantic service in 1962, continuing until the rapid decline of ocean travel in the jet age when she was refitted as a cruise ship in 1979. Rechristened the *Norway*, she is still sailing.)

53:24 bathing: This ostensibly incidental and passing reference to bathing is part of an extensive recurrent image pattern that pervades the novel. Broadly construed, this bathing pattern includes everything from the specific references to Jake and Brett bathing to the wading and swimming in trout streams around Burguete to Jake's solitary sea bathing in San Sebastián to the allusions to the miraculous healing springwaters that are the goal of pilgrims to Sainte-Odile and Lourdes. All of the more than two dozen references, then, add up to a motif of ritual immersion, with cleansing, healing, and baptismal overtones. This pattern echoes the revivifying role of the waters of renewal in Eliot's *The Waste Land,* and the biblical redemptive "water of life," the Christological "river of water of life" that flows from the "throne of God" (Revelation 22.1). If Jake is, as noted earlier, a Fisher King figure seeking renewal in a spiritually barren wasteland, then Brett's reference here to Jake as a "fortunate man" because he's "bathing" harks back to the colonel in the Italian hospital who bemoaned the bad *fortune* of Jake's wound. Jake replies that he's only had "a shower," only a foreshadowing of the full immersion in cleansing waters that he longs for near the end of the fiesta, when the water will not run in the bathtub (195), and the baptismal immersion he finally attains at the Concha in San Sebastián (235–38).

54:1 **had a day:** This conversation reveals that Brett was with the count when she was supposed to be meeting Jake at the Crillon, that in fact she and the count have been together all day, since 4:30 AM when they left Jake's apartment with a dozen bottles of champagne to have breakfast in the Bois (33). Brett has been "quite drunk," but the count's been a "brick," a splendid fellow, which may or may not suggest that he has made no sexual advances while Brett is drunk. Also, since Brett has been with the count all day, and much of the night before, and since Brett is about to tell Jake that she's going off to San Sebastián, this must mean that Robert Cohn asked her to go to San Sebastián with him during their conversation at the *bal musette*—note the repetition and emphasis on Cohn "still talking to Brett" as Jake and Brett leave for their taxi ride (23). Moreover, later that night, between the end of Jake and Brett's taxi ride and her reappearance at Jake's apartment with the count, Brett has been offered $10,000 to go to Biarritz with the count. This means that during the scene in which Brett and Jake express their love and their anguish over their relationship (25–27), Brett is entertaining at least two offers of ostensibly romantic getaways (while she waits for Michael, the man she intends to marry, to arrive in town). In this scene, the reader may surmise that she has decided to go to San Sebastián with Robert, quite possibly because she has learned "something funny" about the count, as we learn later (97:15). But she does not tell Jake who's going to San Sebastián with her, so Jake may be wondering throughout this scene if it is the count.

55:9 **Then later:** This scene, beginning with "Then" on the preceding page (54:27), has been much discussed and in recent years widely taught—so my students inform me in their reports on other college and high school classes—as a sequence that involves some sort of sexual activity (oral, manual, and anal have all been suggested) between Jake and Brett. Because I do not think Hemingway wants to encourage in the reader the "rotten habit of picturing . . . bedroom scenes" that Jake alludes to earlier (13:5–6), and because it is somewhat difficult to imagine, given the specifics of Jake's wound, the orgasmic activity (such is the usual assumption) that Brett performs to make Jake feel "better," the notion that anything goes on here besides a head rub seems far-fetched. (Again, given the nature of Jake's wound, the sexual pun that such readers find in Brett's question—"Is the head any better?"—is not possible; it is simply not there.) Moreover, all the details of the scene support this view. Jake is dressed; given his usual attention to such details (e.g., 54:20–21), he would tell us if he undressed after Brett came in his room. He is dressed, lying "face down on the bed" with his face turned away from Brett as she "stroked" his head. And if there were some sort of sexual activity here, why would Jake say immediately afterward, "Couldn't we just live together?" If there were sex between them, wouldn't he say something like "See, we can be creative and at least we'd have that?" And Brett says no, they can't *just live* together, because she would "*tromper* [Jake] with everybody." (*Tromper*: to cheat, deceive, be unfaithful to; in the manuscript, Hemingway had originally written "betray.") They both know that even if they do love each other, they cannot "live quietly in the country," and there's no use in talking about it since talking is "all bilge" (stupid talk, nonsense). So Brett is going away to San Sebastián—for a sexual fling—which Jake knows (even if he does ask why she's going), and he does not want to know who's going with her.

Frederic Svoboda, in one of the best discussions of this scene, analyzes the extensive revisions Hemingway made to this passage. Svoboda concludes that Hemingway had to establish here "that Jake and Brett emotionally *are* lovers" and he finally decided "upon a restraint in the use of language which echoes and reinforces our perception of the inescapable restraints that fate has placed on the relationship between Brett and Jake" (*Crafting of a Style* 50). Thus the scholar who has examined the evolution of this scene more closely than anyone else has detects no sign of sexual activity here (a conclusion with which I concur).

56:7–9 **low . . . stood up:** In his examination of humor in the novel, James Hinkle notes that "words deliberately taken as words are the basis of much of the humor." This might involve a literal response to "words rather than to their intended meaning"—and here Hinkle cites Jake's response to Brett's "Don't look like that" with "How do you want me to look?" Immediately preceding these lines is another example of what Hinkle regards as typical humor when Jake says twice that he feels "low" and then "sat up" and "stood up." Hinkle thinks this "example tells us quite a bit about Jake. Only to a person with an enormous regard for words would it ever occur to think of standing up as a remedy for feeling low" ("What's Funny," 113, 116; for another approach to Hemingway's humor, see Scott Donaldson, "Humor in *The Sun Also Rises*".

57:1–2 **Veuve Cliquot ... Mumms:** This passage might be read as a straightforward conversation in a scene intended to indicate Brett and the count's familiarity with the finest champagnes, a natural outgrowth of the count's assertion that, given Prohibition, there's not much "chance to judge good wine in the States now" (but he got this champagne from his friend the proprietor, i.e., Baron Mumm). But at the deepest layer of Hemingway's iceberg there is an elaborate Joycean wordplay here that depends on knowledge of French and British vocabulary and slang and close attention to what is actually said. First, we note that Brett asks if *his* name is Veuve Cliquot; that's the first part of the joke, since *veuve* means "widow." If Cliquot (or in the correct French spelling, Clicquot), which is a family name, suggests the clinking of glasses (*cliqueter*), then we have a woman who is a glass-clinking widow to whom Brett refers as *him*. Since Brett is in some sense a mannish glass-clinking, hard-drinking widow (the one man she wanted to marry died during the war, as we learn from the discarded first chapter), then she *is* the Veuve Cliquot. Moreover, "the widow" (due to the popularity of Veuve Cliquot in England) was Victorian slang for champagne. *La Veuve,* of course, was French slang for the guillotine; and if we see a guillotine echo on this same page in the count's cigar cutter, used to "behead" his cigar, maybe that's why Jake says nothing in response to Brett's question that follows immediately after these lines. Mum's the word. In fact, Jake says nothing while the count and Brett exchange five lines of dialogue, then finally, always polite, he asks the count to sit down and offers to "take that stick." If all this adds up to a humorous linguistic mishmash evoking a cross-gendered, glass-clinking widow who lures men into her *clique,* who is wed to or synonymous with champagne and given to the performance of beheading (cigars, sticks, phalluses), then, for Jake, mum (not Mumm) *is* the word—and for Brett, too, who on the next page jokes that she must tell her "Mummy" about how much class the count says she has. Or, if sometimes a cigar is just a cigar, and a walking stick is just a walking stick, the reader can still enjoy the cross-language wordplay centered on two of the finest proprietary brands of champagne: Veuve Cliquot and Mumm.

57:13 **flicking the ashes:** As he often does, Jake (and Hemingway) defines character, conduct, and manners through sharply focused attention to a particular action. This brief ashes image provides a key lead-in to the important discussion of values in the following pages. This glimpse of Brett tells the reader that Brett is rude, inconsiderate, and careless—the kind of messy person who will flick ashes on your *rug* and only ask for an ashtray when she sees that you've noticed what she's done and then, incredibly, attempt to make you feel guilty that you didn't already have ashtrays set out. Again, this is an example of Hemingway's use of recurrent imagery in paired or linked scenes. When Pedro Romero honors her in Pamplona with the ceremonial bull's ear awarded to him "by popular acclamation," she wraps it in Jake's handkerchief along with cigarette ashes and stubs and shoves it (and leaves it) "far back in the drawer" of her bedside table (199:4–8). Any reader who wants to make a case that Brett knows "the values," that she is in the inner circle of those who know ("one of us"), will have to explain her rudeness and carelessness in this scene, as well as her messiness and the profound dishonor she does to Pedro (and Jake) in the later paired scene.

58:22 **joke him:** This concludes a sequence of nine repetitions in fifteen lines of this usage of "joking," apparently intended to mean kidding or teasing. Since the count repeats it seven times, one authorial point may be his uncertain grasp of English idiom as a non-native speaker. Certainly his grammar could use some improvement. But this is hardly a negative, or antiexemplary quality—how much Greek do Brett and Jake speak? The larger point would seem to be concerned with the count's wisdom regarding the cost of "joking" people, and his perception of how Brett relates to Jake. In fact, he is right—Brett may betray and deceive Jake, but she doesn't "joke" him.

59:14 **toast-drinking:** The way the count conducts the entire champagne ceremony warrants close attention, since it is emblematic of the novel's structure of "values," of how to live and have the *taste* of life exactly and authentically: (1) Although Brett tries to rush the ceremony, wanting a drink immediately (as she wants everything), the count will not be rushed, twirls the champagne in the ice bucket twice, and waits patiently for the right moment; (2) When he carefully prepares to open the bottle, holding it up, looking at it, Brett again urges him to open it; (3) When he opens it in silence and with Jake tastes it in silence—Jake *says* nothing but tells the reader it is "amazing champagne"—Brett, who is sometimes wary of words and talking, talks too much here, making an inane toast; (4) The count instructs her, telling her the wine is "too good" for empty words—you "lose the taste" if you mix categories and "mix emotions up" with such champagne. The appropriate response (like Jake's) is full possession, in silence, of the taste of the thing itself. This is a highly particularized instance of a code of conduct, a way of living, that embraces all matters, large and small, that signifies, as Jake puts it, "how to live in" (148:27) the world, how to live "all the way up" (10:19). As if to prove the count's point about losing "the taste," Brett has heard nothing that he said and has tasted nothing; her "glass was empty." Jake, who is very impressed with the count's taste, in every sense, and with the taste of the champagne, suggests he should write a book on wine, but true to his values, the count doesn't want to *talk* about wine; he wants to "enjoy" it. Brett pushes her empty glass toward him, and he pours "very carefully," urging her to "enjoy that slowly" before she gets drunk.

59:29 **been around:** Repeated three times in four lines, "been around" together with the synonymous phrase "seen a lot" (or "seen as much"), repeated three times in the next three lines, establishes that Brett, Jake, and the count have all "been around"—all have wide experience and knowledge of the world. While this sense of the phrase has been familiar for much of the twentieth century, it is instructive to note that Hemingway is yet again on the cutting edge of colloquial usage, since the *OED* gives "We've all been around" from this passage as the first literary occurrence of the phrase in this sense.

60:4 **seven wars:** The count is not boasting about his experience but is merely giving a matter-of-fact statement in response to Brett's "ragging," her teasing (or "joking") him about his inexperience. Four revolutions and seven wars are indeed an extraordinary record, and if the count were the boastful type, he might go on at length here about all that he has seen and done and in what capacity. We note that Brett asks him if he was "soldiering" in all those wars, and he says, "Sometimes." Was he a soldier in a regular army, or a mercenary, a soldier of fortune? And when he was not a soldier, what was his "business" in these wars—was he an arms merchant or a purveyor of necessary goods to one army or the other? Some readers—and one might assume Jake and Brett too—might like to have more details on the count's background; and maybe Hemingway would have provided them if, as he had originally intended, the count had reappeared in the Pamplona section of the novel. No convincing models for the count have been suggested in Hemingway biography and criticism; Hemingway did admire his friend Colonel Charles Sweeny (1882–1963), whose experience and skill as a soldier of fortune who fought in many wars may have contributed something to the portrait of the count.

60:7 **arrow wounds:** The count is *not* the sort of wounded warrior who goes around showing off his scars; Brett insists on seeing them, almost as if she were here playing the role of the doubting Thomas, the skeptical and incredulous apostle who refused to believe in the Resurrection until he had touched the wounds of the risen Christ. (This is not to say that the count is exactly a Christ figure.) Jake is also very interested in the arrow wounds and wants to know in which of the seven wars and four revolutions the count received these wounds. The answer, in Abyssinia, gives the reader the only definite clue—geographical if not specifically chronological—about the count's war experience. European military involvement in Ethiopia began in 1868 with a brief British incursion in retaliation for the detention of European missionaries and envoys. If the count was involved in that military action, at age twenty-one as he says, then he would be seventy-eight in 1925, and although we do not know how old the count is, we might conclude that this age seems rather advanced in the light of his characterization, a tentative conclusion that must bear in mind that another exemplary count in Hemingway's fiction, Count Greffi of *A Farewell to Arms,* is in his nineties. The next major Abyssinian or Ethiopian battle occurred at Gura in 1876, when some 20,000 well-armed Egyptians, led by European and American soldiers of fortune, were defeated by an Ethiopian army still largely wielding spears and arrows. If the count, serving as a mercenary with the Egyptian army, received his arrow wounds in that action, he would be seventy, an age that does not seem entirely improbable given his depiction in the novel. Other minor Abyssinian-European clashes occurred throughout the 1880s as Italy attempted to expand its Eritrean foothold in Africa and acquire a colonial empire. This led to the First Italo-Abyssinian War (1895–1896) and its culminating Battle of Adowa in 1896, when approximately 120,000 Ethiopian troops, many armed by then with modern weaponry (although some 20,000 still carried only spears and by some reports arrows), soundly defeated an Italian army some 20,000 strong. If the count received his arrow wounds in this battle, he would be only fifty years old. There is some manuscript and textual evidence that this is what Hemingway had in mind; first, in the original manuscript draft of this scene, the count says he was nineteen when he got the arrow wounds; Hemingway crossed that out and changed his age to twenty-one, probably because he thought it unseemly to have such a wise and exemplary figure still in his forties; revisions were also made before Hemingway wrote the final description of the count's *black* chest hair and *bulging* stomach *muscles*. All of this suggests that Hemingway's conception of the count required him to be neither too young nor too old, and thus his arrow wounds were received in some action of the Italian-Abyssinian conflicts between 1885 and 1896; in this scene, then, the count may be anywhere between fifty and sixty-one years old.

Since the count was in ten other wars and revolutions (and there were dozens of them from the 1880s to the 1920s), and he may well have been wounded in other ways, why the stress on the arrow wounds? The easy answer has to do with the dramatic value of the visible scars, and also the fact of his young age when he received, and survived, these wounds. But there is also a typological answer dictated by the novel's deep structure of religious patterns and allusions. For anyone familiar with Western art and painting, or with Christian iconography, it is inevitable that the image of a man transfixed by arrows will call to mind Saint Sebastian. One of the Roman martyrs, Sebastian was a third-century Roman soldier, a secret Christian who assisted other martyrs and was thus sentenced by Diocletian to be shot to death with arrows. He survived this execution attempt, recovered from his arrow wounds, and eventually became the patron saint of soldiers and archers. Jake, a wounded soldier whose penultimate destination in the novel is the saint's namesake city, San Sebastián, must entertain at least a passing thought of Saint Sebastian when the count shows his arrow wounds. The most apt image of Saint Sebastian is not the familiar depiction of the young and, in many versions, effeminate Sebastian transfixed with arrows, popular in Renaissance art, but the earlier (and later) representations of the saint as an older bearded man holding a crown. Sebastian was, after all, a captain of the *Roman* pretorian guards who *survived* his arrow wounds. The count, as we have seen, was most probably with the Italian army, and he *survived* his arrow wounds. And if there is no need for the count to be, like Sebastian, a secret Christian, it may be a secret to some readers of this novel that his good manners, his generosity, his highly ritualized (even sacramental) sense of experience, his joie de vivre, and above all the doctrine of love that he is about to espouse (61:1–6) in this key scene are exemplary Christian virtues and values.

One other detail in this scene should be noted: it is obvious that Brett has not seen these arrow scars before. If, as has sometimes been suggested, the reader is invited to wonder if Brett has slept with the count, why is she seeing the scars for the first time here? This detail, and all the other evidence, argues against any sexual encounter between Brett and the count.

60:24 **one of us:** Many commentators on the novel recognize here a familiar epiphanic moment that recurs in Hemingway's work: when the *wounded* characters recognize each other's woundedness and thus the bond that ties them together. We should note, however, that Brett says he's "one of us" not after she sees the wounds but after the count, as a matter of style, *underplays* the wounds, saying only that he "was on a business trip." If he was a soldier of fortune, that would be a "business trip," but many such mercenaries would *overplay* that experience and thus not be "one of us," as Brett sees it. Stylistic restraint, then, understatement, is as much a key to the insiders' circle as is the fact of being wounded. As Hemingway put it in *A Farewell to Arms,* "The world breaks every one and afterward many are strong at the broken places." And the necessary coda to that axiom is found in Catherine's response to Frederic's statement of the Shakespearean notion that "the coward dies a thousand deaths, the brave but one"—"The brave dies perhaps two thousand deaths if he's intelligent. He simply doesn't mention them" (249, 139–40).

We should note, too, that in the overall structure of this key values scene (57–61), although Brett claims her place in the inner circle of those who know the values, her conduct—flicking ashes on Jake's rug, disregarding ceremony in her will to drunkenness, and misunderstanding entirely what the count says about values and love—argues her exclusion from the company of Jake and the count. Her sense of "one of us," then, is based more on style than on substance.

60:31–32 **secret . . . values:** These lines are the absolute center of what is arguably the most important values scene in the novel. Each of the novel's three sections, or "books," has a key scene that assesses conduct in relation to values—in book II, Jake's first scene with Montoya (131–32), and in book III, Brett and Jake's final conversation in Madrid (243–47). This scene is the culmination of book I and poses all the essential questions that the rest of the book must answer regarding values, love, passion, and how to live life authentically and "all the way up." Close reading, close attention to the mot juste (the exactly right word), is essential. Jake agrees—"Absolutely" (a rarity in his idiom)—with the count that when you have "lived very much," been "around," "seen a lot," then you can "enjoy everything." That might seem obvious, yet why does the count call it "the secret"? Because the *secret* is that you must "get to know the values." The count does not say, as perhaps the majority of his twentieth-century contemporaries (and twenty-first-century readers) would say, that when you have been "around" and "lived" a great deal you can invent or discover your own values or make them up as you go along. In the count's vision of experience—as in Jake's (and Hemingway's)—ethics, morality, and behavior are not situational or transactional and cannot be founded on behavioral relativism or nihilism or solipsistic appropriation of the world. The values are *there, unchanging,* for you to *get to know.* Whether the fact in question is *having fully* the uncorrupted *taste* of great wine or *living fully* the life-and-death mysteries of the Church and the bullfight, those values, truths, verities, exist under the rubric of the authority of tradition accurately apprehended, the accumulated suffering and sacraments and wisdom of the human race, and cannot be reinvented by every generation, by any individual—but they can be learned or relearned. One of the great misunderstandings of much literature of the 1920s and after is that the writers are concerned with the bankruptcy of traditional values; in fact, what many masterpieces of high modernism—from the poetry of Eliot and Pound to the fiction of Faulkner and Hemingway—depict is the bankruptcy of twentieth-century civilization, the *betrayal* of eternal and universal values, the wrecked civilization caused by human infidelity to the values. As Faulkner put it in his Nobel Prize address, "the old verities and truths of the heart, the old universal truths"—love, honor, compassion, courage, hope, pride, pity, and sacrifice—had been largely cast aside, forgotten, and must be *relearned.* Passion, courage, honor, compassion, and love are the same in 1926 as in 1026 and 2026—that is the *secret* of the values that the count knows, Jake knows, and Hemingway knows.

In the original manuscript version, Brett responded to these lines by filling her glass and saying, "It's all so simple." The count replied: "It is very simple My Dear if you know the values" (*Facsimile* 1:198).

61:4 **always in love:** Like a typical twentieth-century relativist, a self-help talk show guest, a graduate of some sensitivity-training or therapeutic program that requires values to be ever flexible, always in evolution, always adapting to a situation, Brett challenges the fixity and certainty of the count's values. She also demands to know what being "in love" does to his values. The count's response, that he is "always in love," is the rest of the secret, which is revealed when one gets to know, to possess, and to live the unchanging values. The count, of course, is talking about something very close to agape, Christian love or the love feast accompanied by Eucharistic celebration, a love that covers all things and celebrates, in joy, the world as an incarnation of God. Brett seems to be talking about eros or sex. Given her typically modern confusion regarding being and becoming, the assumption that *change is life,* Brett declares the count "dead," and he says she's dead wrong. An interesting aside: when I give this passage on quizzes and ask students to identify who's really "dead" and why, the vast majority reply that the count is much more alive than Brett, although they often say they're not sure why. Close reading of everything leading up to this passage makes it very clear who is "dead" and why.

61:11 **excellent place:** Food and wine, both the end product of a process of passion and precision, both timeless, universal, and incarnational verities, have an "excellent place in the count's values." Hemingway carefully revised this paragraph after the original manuscript version, emphasizing (in keeping with the ritual wine-champagne ceremony that opens the values sequence) that the dailiness of food and wine can be part of a values scheme that one can "get to know." His revisions also stressed the count's "fine form" and deemphasized Brett's. Originally, Hemingway had written: "The Count was very fine. Duff was in good form too." At the beginning of *Death in the Afternoon,* Hemingway discussed the "value" of wine, comparing it to bullfighting and "all arts" in which "enjoyment increases with the knowledge of the art." "Wine," he asserts, "is one of the most civilized things in the world and one of the natural things of the world that has been brought to the greatest perfection, and it offers a greater range for enjoyment and appreciation than, possibly, any other purely sensory thing which may be purchased" (10). Here we might note, too, the truly shocking aspect of the American Puritanism that is part of the novel's subtext—a Puritanism that banned, outlawed, prohibited wine drinking, one of humankind's oldest sacraments.

62:2 **oldest brandy:** Both Brett and Jake are made uncomfortable by the count's innocent suggestion that they should get married. Sensing their discomfort, the count changes the subject and suggests another brandy. Hoping to change the subject and the scene, Brett suggests they go somewhere noisy, "up on the hill" (Montmartre). The count knows that he cannot get the best brandy in the nightclubs "on the hill," so he orders a bottle of the restaurant's "oldest brandy." In the manuscript, the waiter replied, "1815 Sir." For no apparent reason, perhaps, other than placing the vintage more firmly in the mythical terrain of "Napoleon brandy," Hemingway changes the date to "Eighteen eleven." It is sometimes true, as most pertinent authorities note, that such labels as "Napoleon brandy" are "meaningless or worse, as any brandy kept in barrel since the days of Napoleon would have evaporated, and any kept in bottle would be the same, or perhaps not so good as when it was placed in glass" (Lichine 124). Notwithstanding the fact that "age is considered the great virtue in Cognac," and age imparts great delicacy, it remains true that a brandy or cognac that was in the bottle in 1811, even if it went to Russia with Napoleon, "would be no older than the day" it was bottled (Lichine 181). This may explain, in part, Brett's response to the count's ordering a bottle of 1811: "Don't be ostentatious." But the count knows his wines, his champagnes, and surely his brandies too. To make full sense of this passage, the reader must first understand (as the count and Jake must know) that true vintage cognac is a great rarity since most brandies are a blend of various years. One exception would be British Bonded Cognac, shipped in cask to England and aged in cask before bottling (also known as "Old Landed" cognac). Barrel aging up to "the optimum of about forty years," depending on the housing and the quality of the cognac, will enhance the brandy's subtlety and complexity (Lichine 181). Since brandies in cask will eventually evaporate, they are usually bottled well before they have spent forty years in barrel. Thus, if the count has a true 1811 vintage cognac served here, it would have been bottled by about 1850 at the latest, and as science and all the authorities attest, its taste would not have improved since 1850. Yet to use such evidence in an argument against the count's knowledge, the secret values of brandy, is to miss the point entirely. With every year that passes, from 1811 or 1850, the brandy grows not just older but more rare, and the investment, both financial and spiritual, in the ritual of tasting such an "antiquity" grows more substantial. What signifies is both the gamble of what the taste might be when the ancient bottle is opened and the occasion, the sacrament or ritual of betting on the past, on age, on the weight of tradition. (A French friend of mine tastes once every ten years on 11 November an eau-de-vie—"water of life"—that was put in barrel by his grandfather on 11 November 1918 to mark the end of World War I and transferred to two Nebuchadnez-zars—very large sixteen-liter bottles—on 11 November 1948, and when I tasted that eau-de-vie with him on 11 November 1998 to salute the eightieth anniversary of the end of World War I, we were engaging in a ritual acknowledgment of history, values, and tradition and also a sacrament of *pietas,* of reverence for earth and place, family and community, a communion as well as a gamble, a gesture of chance that some-thing extraordinary in the realm of taste will occur. And it did. For now, the history and the taste are holding. And even if on 11 November 2008 the taste of the eau-de-vie is diminished, nevertheless its history and rarity will be enhanced.) Apparently, since *nothing* is said here about the ancient bottle of brandy they drink—compare the response to the "amazing champagne" a few pages before—it is either not very good or too good for mere words.

62:10 **Montmartre . . . Zelli's:** For Montmartre, see 22:30; for Zelli's, see 33:30.

62:13 **drummer:** Hemingway writes the word "drummer" six times in three pages; only in the first mention, introducing the character, does Jake use the phrase "nig-ger drummer." In the second mention, he is a "Damn good drummer," Brett's "great friend." In the next four occurrences, he is simply "the drummer" (64). In one of these instances, in the manuscript, Hemingway apparently started to write "nigger" ("ni") again but crossed it out (*Facsimile* 1:204). The point is that Hemingway is sensitive to the use of the racist epithet, but the *writer* must be even more sensitive to the accuracy of what his characters would actually say. In the 1920s the "n-word" was of course common in everyday use; and although many people in the twenties were racist—not just the members of the Ku Klux Klan—it was also a time of great respect for the achievements of the many popular black musicians and singers, and everyday use of the word did not always signify race-based contempt or hatred. (As a child in the 1940s, I knew very well—it was made quite clear to me by my father, who was of Hemingway's generation and had been a jazz musician in the 1920s—that the word "nigger" was high on the list of forbidden words that, if I uttered them, would result in getting my mouth washed out with soap.)

Note the way Hemingway handles Bill's use—ironic overuse—of the word in a scene where he is clearly depicting the "splendid" and "wonderful" conduct and character of the black boxer in Vienna (71–72). See also Hemingway's use of the word in his earlier short story "The Battler," where Bugs, the black character, is the clear exemplar of the tale, the tutor in values for Nick Adams (*Complete Short Stories* 97–104). As writers must be, Hemingway was true to his artistic ear, and he insisted on having characters say what they would say in their time and place; as a man he found racial epithets offensive (Reynolds, *Paris Years* 279). Much the same argument applies to the novel's deployment of anti-Semitic terms.

62:22–23 **looked at the count:** Why does Jake look at the count while he dances with Brett? Probably because the count, and the entire secret-of-the-values scene just enacted, is very much on Jake's mind as he dances with Brett. In the manuscript, Hemingway had originally written (after Jake "looked at the Count"): "He was sitting there like Buddah" (*Facsimile* 1:201–2). This was deleted, no doubt because under the rubric of Hemingway's iceberg and his understated style, it gave too much away, too obviously, to depict the count as Buddha, the Enlightened One, especially since the count's somewhat Buddhist doctrine of suffering and illumination, joy and love, has just been carefully articulated in the preceding scene. Moreover, it probably reveals more than Hemingway would permit of his pervasive indebtedness to T. S. Eliot's *The Waste Land*; see especially Eliot's "III. The Fire Sermon," which concludes with the juxtaposition of quotations from the Buddha's Fire Sermon and Saint Augustine's *Confessions*, two primary examples of Eastern and Western asceticism. Eliot quotes the line from the Fire Sermon—"Burning burning burning burning"—that evokes how the senses are on fire and how such desire must be purged before the "disciple" can be free and achieve rebirth. Juxtaposed with this line, without explanatory commentary, is the line from Saint Augustine's *Confessions*—"O Lord Thou pluckest me out" of the "burning"—that images the need of the would-be Christian convert to be delivered from the "burning," from what Saint Augustine called the "cauldron of unholy loves" that "*sang* all about mine ears" (emphasis added), so that the Christian pilgrim, "famished for love but not yet knowing the love of God," might be reborn (Perkins and Perkins 1057–58). Hemingway's echo of Eliot is obvious and clearly intentional, especially when we consider the crowded, smoky, noisy interior of Zelli's—a close enough rhyme with "hell" or "hellish"—and the "burning" bodies packed tightly together on the jammed dance floor, while the singer evokes the cauldron of two-timing "unholy" loves. Jake, caught in the burning ring with Brett in Zelli's dancing "jam," looks at the Buddha-like count and feels trapped in a familiar "nightmare" (64:10–11). He is delivered from Zelli's by the count's car and bids Brett goodnight with a kiss, a kiss that is, in fact (although it seems to have eluded the notice of commentators on the novel), the *last* time *he* kisses her (see 65:3). As book I ends, Jake looks "back" (64:27) at the count one last time (since the count, having performed his essential narrative mission of enunciating the secret of the values and love, disappears from the novel); and as Jake looks back at the count, he looks forward to attaining fully the count's condition of deliverance, the count's incarnational possession of values and love. After the last kiss with Brett, there will be no more inflammable ("burning") encounters—just brief, almost detached and noncombustible moments in the following two chapters, before Brett disappears from the novel for *fifty* pages (84–134)—and Jake is delivered, plucked out from the unholy "cauldron," until he is tested again in Pamplona.

64:4 **You can't two time:** The song that the drummer is singing has been identified (or, more likely, misidentified) in an otherwise-valuable article by Frederic Svoboda—"Who Was That Black Man? A Note on Eugene Bullard and *The Sun Also Rises*"—that is primarily concerned with establishing the identity of the model for the drummer. Svoboda convincingly demonstrates that the drummer's prototype was Eugene Bullard, a black musician from Georgia who was well known in Paris in the 1920s. Interestingly enough, Bullard was a soldier and a pilot (like Jake) who was wounded in World War I; he was also a boxer, proprietor of a Parisian nightclub as well as an athletic club, and the leader of the house band at Zelli's. All of this underlines Hemingway's knowledge of the jazz world of Paris and serves to reinforce the notion of the drummer as a minor exemplar whose role is to deliver an important truth—"You can't two time"—as Brett prepares to two-time both Jake and her prospective husband, Mike, by running off for a fling with Robert Cohn.

Svoboda identifies the song as "Aggravatin' Papa," basing his argument on a citation from an unpublished manuscript by James Hinkle. "Aggravatin' Papa," with words by the well-known Tin Pan Alley lyricist Roy Turk (1892–1934), was a song in the popular/blues vein that was familiar by the mid-twenties. It was recorded three times in 1923, first by Alberta Hunter with Henderson's Dance Orchestra, then by Rickett's Stars, and also by Bessie Smith. None of these versions contained the line "You can't two time," nor did any other mid-twenties versions or even Sophie Tucker's 1933 hit recording of "Aggravatin' Poppa," which I inherited in my father's collection of ten thousand jazz and blues records (1920–1940). Almost all the versions contain the line "don't you try to two-time me!"—although Bessie Smith omits the "you" in that line. The mere presence of the word "two-time," suddenly fashionable in the early twenties, does not suffice to identify the song—as should be clear from, for example, Al Jolson's 1924 hit "My Papa Doesn't Two-Time No Time," as well as other songs. (It is interesting to note that, yet again, the *OED* places Hemingway at the cutting edge of new coinage, citing the drummer's song as the second—the first being in 1924—literary usage of "two-time.") Another important signifier when it comes to the identity of the song is the dissimilarity of the musical phrase, the disparity of syllable-and-stress count between the phrases "don't you try to two-time me" and "you can't two-time [me]." When, decades ago, I pointed this out to James Hinkle, who had already made the "Aggravatin' Papa" identification, we discussed late into the night the ways one might sing these phrases, as well as the accuracy of Hemingway's ear—about the latter we agreed (see also 114:1). I suggested to Professor Hinkle that the drummer was here singing the repeated line "you can't two-time me" from the 1924 recording of "Cherry Picking Blues"; he was very interested, and I promised to send him whatever else I could learn about that song for his possible use in the manuscript he was working on (in fact, the urtext of this volume and this entire series of Hemingway glossaries). At that time, I only knew that title and that one line that the drummer accurately sings because my father—who played piano and sang jazz and blues in 1920s nightclubs and said that "Cherry Picking Blues" was a *real* blues song, not a pop tune like "Aggravatin' Papa"—suggested it.

Now, decades later, the matter can be clarified. "Cherry Picking Blues" was recorded by Ida Cox in 1924, and it *does* contain the line Hemingway quoted—"you can't two-time [me]." It also contains the reiterated line "I've got my trunk all packed and I'm going to leave this town"—maybe those are the words that are omitted, indicated by ellipses, since Brett is packed and ready to leave town—and the singer concludes with "Goodbye little papa, another man has cut your cherry tree down." Also, it is precisely true that Jake *can't* two-time Brett. It also matters that this *authentic* blues song (unlike the Tin Pan Alley pop song "Aggravatin' Papa") was written and recorded by the legendary early classic blues singer Ida Cox. (Repeat that name and wonder if Jake knows the song and the singer, and reflect on the sexual double entendre that may resonate for readers, like James Hinkle, who consider such wordplay central to Hemingway's style. Does Jake know Ida Cox? That's part of the iceberg.) Moreover, if the drummer is based on Eugene Bullard from Georgia, then he might well be singing an authentic blues song written by Ida Cox, who was born about the same time in Georgia. And since she made her reputation and her early recordings in Chicago, where she moved around the time of World War I, maybe an Oak Park teenager named Hemingway knew all about Ida Cox.

Finally, about those three sets of ellipses in the text, indicating omitted words of the song: the words of "Cherry Picking Blues" are somewhat more risqué than the pop lyrics of "Aggravatin' Papa." In the manuscript, Hemingway had originally left blank spaces where there are now double ellipses, possibly indicating that he intended to fill in some words later. Or maybe he knew all along that he could not include some of the words (or even the title) of "Cherry Picking Blues," and that's why in the original manuscript he crossed out "You can't two time" and wrote in

"Me and My Boy Friend." But by the time the novel reached print, that was scrapped, and "You can't two time—" was back in because "Cherry Picking Blues" by Ida Cox was the right song by the right singer, with a devastatingly resonant subtextual rightness for the scene and situation.

64:27 **three girls:** After Jake and Brett leave, three girls join the count at his table; this has no bearing, one way or another, on the discussion of his Buddha-like presence, discussed above (62:22–23). In a place like Zelli's, with an obviously affluent customer like the count, that is exactly what the *poules,* or prostitutes, would do. Or maybe, given Hemingway's precise indication of *three* women, they are also the "Three Graces," the sister goddesses Aglaia ("splendor"), Euphrosyne ("mirth"), and Thalia ("comedy"), dispensing charm and beauty, which even ancient wounded Buddha-like connoisseurs of the values and a higher love—like the count—might "enjoy." He's "too old" to dance, the count says, but as he tells Brett, "I enjoy to watch you dance" (63:18–19). Doesn't that cut to the thematic heart of the novel? And isn't that close to the same reason Jake picked up Georgette?

Even more to the point, and far more resonant with implications for the count's role in the novel and Jake's meditations on the count, is the possibility that the "girls" at the count's table are meant to suggest the *three* "Holy Women" of the Bible—Mary Magdalene, Mary Cleophas (or Jacobé), and Mary Salome—who stood by Jesus at the Crucifixion and discovered the empty tomb on Easter morning. Mary Magdalene, of course, is the "archetypal repentant woman sinner" (and sometimes a reformed prostitute) in Christian tradition (Metford 169); Mary Cleophas is, according to tradition, either the sister or step-sister of the Blessed Virgin Mary; and Mary Salome is the mother of Saint James (Santiago, Saint Jacques). Given the fact that the count is presented throughout this chapter as a Buddha-like enlightened one, and more directly as a kind of Christ figure (see the arrow-wound scene, 60:7) or exemplar of Christian virtues, of Christian love (see 61:9), it hardly seems far-fetched to conclude that Jake's final glimpse, his final vision of the count, as he *looks back* and sees him with *three* women, is intended to resonate with the three Holy Women of Christian tradition. Indeed, if we recall that Hemingway wrote his short story or playlet about the Crucifixion, *Today Is Friday,* in the spring of 1926, while he was in the process of revising *The Sun Also Rises,* and remember how in that work he stresses that it was only Mary Magdalene and the women (the three Holy Women) who "stuck by" Christ on the Cross (*Complete Short Stories* 273), then the association here seems ineluctable. Finally, when we realize that these three Marys, according to legend, came to the south of France and evangelized Provence and are celebrated there in the annual Pilgrimage of les Saintes-Maries-de-la-Mer (a pilgrimage in which Hemingway participated in May 1927, seven months after the publication of *The Sun Also Rises*), and when we understand the connection of the Pilgrimage of the Holy Marys in France with the Pilgrimage of Saint Jacques and

Santiago in France and Spain and its importance in the novel, then the association sketched here seems yet another image, an emblem—a well-forged link in the novel's great chain of Christian being and symbolism (see Stoneback, "Hemingway and the Camargue"). Nor is it incidental that this scene takes place in Montmartre, "up on the hill" (a symbolic location stressed three times in less than a page, 62–63), and that Montmartre, *Mons Martyrum,* the Mount of the Martyrs, has for many centuries been a sacred place of pilgrimage and devotion to the Blessed Virgin Mary and the Sacred Heart of Jesus, and in the twentieth century the base of the mount became a kind of inferno, a place of debased sex-centered inverted pilgrimage, a center of prostitution (see 22:30 and 97:13–15).

65:3 **We kissed:** In terms of the overall arc of one of the novel's principal dramatic concerns—how Jake deals with his Brett problem—there has been critical disagreement, with allegiance to two main views widely noted: (1) Jake, at the end of the novel, has progressed, has dealt with his Brett problem, and is over her; and (2) Jake is caught in an ongoing cycle, makes no progress, and at the end is just as miserable over Brett as he is at the beginning. Although I must say that the vast majority of readers immediately and intuitively feel Jake has dealt with it and is over Brett—they *sense* it even when they can't cite evidence for it—we should not jump to that conclusion without considering all the evidence. We should resist, for example, pronunciations of Jake's ultimate freedom from Brett based solely on the knowledge and equipoise reflected in his final words, the novel's famous concluding line: "Isn't it pretty to think so?" (247:17).

There is, in fact, plenty of evidence that Jake achieves resolution and reconciliation regarding his wound, regarding Brett and their impossible love. Utterly aside from his spiritual and intellectual reconciliation, consider only the pattern of their physical contact. In their first encounter in chapters 3 and 4, they are both burning with desire; Brett is "miserable," Jake initiates contact—"I kissed her"—and Brett turns away because she "can't stand it," but as the taxi ride ends she asks Jake to kiss her "once more" (25–27). As chapter 3 ends and Brett leaves Jake's apartment, Jake notes, "We kissed good night" and "we kissed again," and then he goes to bed and meditates on being "hard-boiled" (34). The next time they are alone, two chapters and twenty pages later, Brett gives Jake a detached kiss—"She kissed me coolly on the forehead" (54)—before she rubs his head then tells him she is going away to San Sebastián. This intimate scene does not end with a kiss but with Jake's breaking it off, saying: "Let's have a drink" (56). The count returns, the secret-of-the-values scene is played out, and book I ends with a somewhat formal double goodnight kiss—"We kissed standing at the door." This kissing scene is cut short by Brett's rebuff and abrupt departure—"She pushed me away.... She turned quickly" (65:3–5). The careful reader, reviewing the novel's osculatory details, might be somewhat amazed to discover that this is *their last kiss,* the last (barely) mutual kiss. In fact, there is only one more kiss in the entire book, in the closing scene in Madrid, where Hemingway writes twice, with definitive exactitude, "*she* kissed me" (emphasis added; see 241: 20–21).

The crucial secret-of-the-values scene conducted under the count's aegis, then, concludes book I, with Jake giving Brett his last kiss "at the door," the door to a new life, the door to a rebirth founded on the recognition that even if he were not wounded as he is, nothing would be different with Brett and him. (Of course, his rebirth is also rooted in the spiritual certainty of a deeper passion, a higher love.) In the following chapter, Jake sees Brett in two scenes bridging Jake and Bill's night walk—a walk centered on the view from the bridge of the cathedral of Notre-Dame—and there is no physical contact between Brett and Jake in either scene. In the next chapter, Jake sees Brett briefly, they shake hands publicly, and after Mike leaves and they are alone for the first time since that last kiss, they have *no* physical contact, and the scene ends abruptly (81–84). Then Brett disappears from the novel for fifty pages. When they meet again, in the group scenes rendered in chapter 13, there is no physical contact—not even a handshake—between Brett and Jake. The next time they are *alone* together they are *in church*, because Brett wants to tag along while Jake goes to confession (and Robert follows them, lurking outside the church)—and there is no physical contact (150–51). And the next time they are alone together, they walk "arm in arm"—performing the novel's consistent design of increasingly physically detached *friendship*—and sit, not touching, in the "shadow of the cathedral" (182:31). Remarkably enough, the next time Jake is alone with Brett, they are *in church* again, praying, and after, they leave the church, still discussing religion, and having no physical contact. The extraordinary fact is this: of the three times Jake is alone with Brett in Pamplona, two scenes are *in church* and the third is a detached formal landscape composition conducted in the *shadow of the cathedral;* this points directly to the heart of the novel's concerns of the flesh and the spirit. Thus, as book I ends and Jake leaves the burning physical hell of Zelli's, his last dance with Brett, and his last kiss with her, he is indeed "at the door" of the deliverance promised by the Buddha's Fire Sermon and Saint Augustine (see 62:22–23), sustained and fortified with the count's secret knowledge, and well along the way of his pilgrimage road of renewal.

Notre-Dame de Paris from the pont de la Tournelle; l'île Saint-Louis is on the far right (see 77:11–21). Photo by Kimmy Ruth

The intersection of the boulevards Montparnasse and Raspail—the Dôme (see 27:26, 29:22, and 46:25). Photo by Brad McDuffie

Marshal Ney, with Closerie des Lilas in background (see 29:28). Photo by Kimmy Ruth

74, rue de Cardinal Lemoine near place Contrescarpe, where Hemingway lived from 1922 to 1923 (see 77:22–31). Photo by Brad McDuffie

Pilgrimage marker on the rue Saint-Jacques (see 78:6–7). Photo by Brad McDuffie

Roncevaux—the monastery, with "Charlemagne's Silo" and the Chapel of Santiago in the foreground (see 108:26 and 128:16). Photo by Kimmy Ruth

The village of Fábrica, where Jake and Bill fish the Fábrica, by the ruined munitions factory (see 118:8). Photo by Kimmy Ruth

The Hostal Burguete, where Jake and Bill stayed (see 109:13). Photo by Goretti Vianney-Benca

The spring where Jake chills the wine near the village of Fábrica (see 118:8 and 119:1). Photo by Goretti Vianney-Benca

Pamplona—the Cathedral (see 96:30). Photo by Matthew Nickel

The Café Iruña on the Plaza in Pamplona (see 95:26–27). Photo by Kimmy Ruth

The Bullring in Pamplona (see 94:7). Photo by Brad McDuffie

BELGIUM

Senlis

Strasbourg

PARIS

Chartres

Mont Ste-Odile

Tours

Orléans

FRANCE

Bordeaux

The Landes

Bayonne
St-Jean-de-Luz
Biarritz
Hendaye
San Sebastián

Cannes

St-Jean-Pied-de-Port

Roncevaux

Lourdes

Pamplona

SPAIN

France in *The Sun Also Rises*—the train ride from Paris to Bayonne

Spain in *The Sun Also Rises*—the train ride from San Sebastían to Madrid

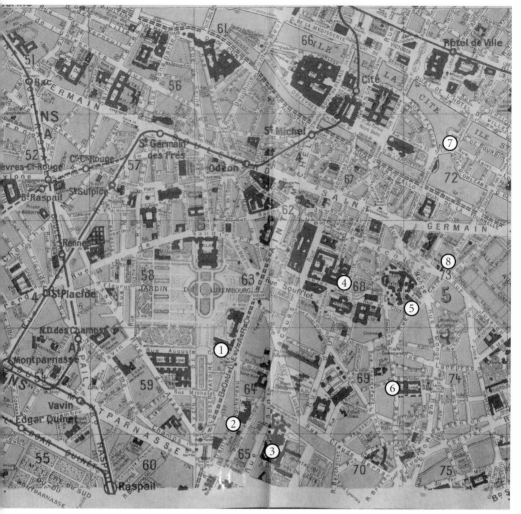

Paris in *The Sun Also Rises*. Map from Karl Baedeker, *Paris et ses Environs* (1921).

1. Jake's apartment on the boulevard Saint-Michel, south of juncture with rue Denfert-Rochereau (name changed late 1920s to rue Henri Barbusse)—site of statue of the "gentlemen who invented pharmacy"

2. The "rigid north and south " of the rue Saint-Jacques, with the first bend in the ancient pilgrimage route

3. Val-de-Grâce, Church and Hospital for wounded soldiers

4. The *Bal Musette*

5. Hemingway lived at 74, rue du Cardinal Lemoine from 1922 to 1923

6. Jake and Brett take a taxi from the bal musette to the Parc de Montsouris via the rue Mouffetard

7. "The island" where Jake and Bill dine before circling the island and looking down-river at Notre Dame

8. The route of the after-dinner walk to place de la Contrescarpe, the rue du Pot de Fer, and the rue Saint-Jacques

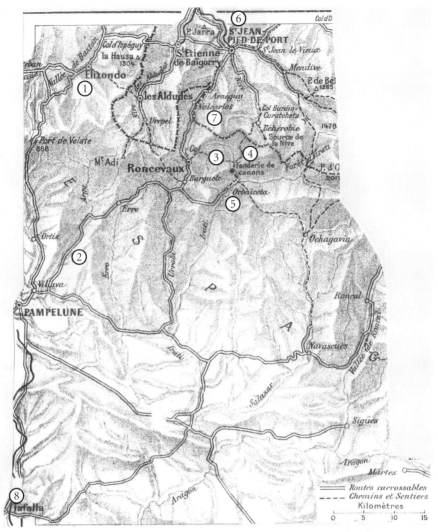

The Roncevaux Area in 1921. Map from Marcel Monmarche, ed., *Les Guides Bleus: Pyrenees*, *Paris* (1921).

1. Elizondo and the road Jake follows south from the French border into Pamplona

2. The road Jake follows north from Pamplona to Burguete and Roncevaux

3. The *chemin* or *sentier* (path or mule track) that Jake and Bill walk on their fishing excursion to the rio de la Fábrica

4. The ruined arms factory ("Fonderie de canons") in the village of Fábrica, where Jake and Bill fish

5. The end of the road at Orbaiceta, where Jake and Bill probably *drove* with Harris to fish the Irati

6. Important French pilgrimage town, staging area for pilgrims following the pilgrimage route across the mountains and the French-Spanish frontier to the celebrated Roland site at Roncevaux

7. Valcarlos ("Valley of Charlemagne"), where some of the fiesta dancers are from

8. Tafalla, where the man killed in the *encierro* is from

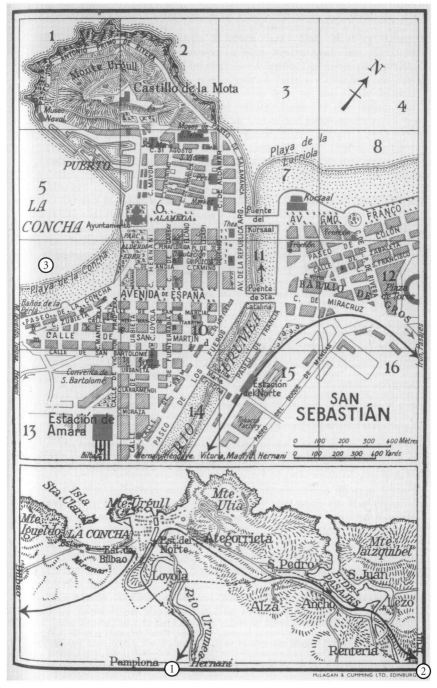

San Sebastián in the 1920s. Map from Findlay Muirhead, ed., *The Blue Guides: Northern Spain* (1930).

1. To Pamplona
2. To France
3. La Concha, where Jake swims

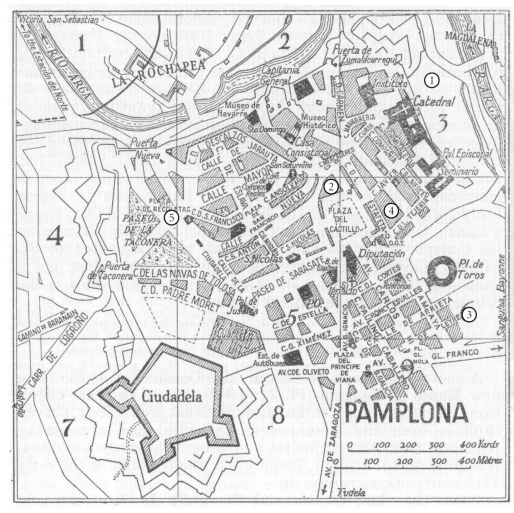

Pamplona in the 1920s. Map from Findlay Muirhead, ed., *The Blue Guides: Northern Spain* (1930).

    1. The Cathedral where Jake prays when he arrives

    2. The plaza del Castillo, where Jake stays at the Hotel Montoya (SE corner); Café Iruña (on the north side)

    3. The bullring

    4. The Route of the *Encierro*

    5. The Church of San Lorenzo (Chapel of San Fermín), where Jake prays with Brett

BOOK II

67: **Book II:** In the original manuscript version of the novel there is no division into "books." The formal timing or placement of the book divisions, inserted during the typescript phase of composition, raises at least two interesting questions: (1) Why here? (2) What effect is achieved by this particular location of a break or rest or shift in the narrative flow? At first glance, this may seem a curious place for the formal signal of separation or emphasis that the book division provides. Such divisions often coincide in novels with a change of setting or place, or with a forward or reverse time shift. In fact, the choice of the end of book II and the beginning of book III follows conventional narrative practice both in its indication of a shift in location (Pamplona to France) and in the way it serves as a time marker for the conclusion of a sequence of actions (the fiesta). In keeping with such conventional narrative principles, it would seem that Hemingway might better have chosen, for example, the passage two chapters later, when Bill and Jake leave Paris on the southbound train (84). Yet the powerful effect of his book I–book II division is to emphasize the importance of the action just concluded, the secret-of-the-values scene with Brett, Jake, and the count, and to provide the reader the meditative space to recognize that emphasis, as well as to prepare the reader for a distinct shift in the tonal modality of Jake's feelings regarding Brett after their last kiss, which concludes book I.

CHAPTER 8

69:1 **did not see Brett:** The information provided in the opening lines of book II—that Brett is in San Sebastián, that Robert is in some unspecified place for "a couple of weeks," and that Frances has gone to England—might suggest that Jake could (or should) suspect that Brett has gone off with Cohn. However, he apparently does not even consider this, since he seems surprised when he does learn that Brett has been with Robert in San Sebastián (see 83). All this may suggest several important things about Jake: He is not the suspicious type, for he cannot believe that a friend (and he does consider Robert a friend) would construct such an elaborate framework of lies and deception regarding his whereabouts, as indicated here by Robert's note and by the letter from Robert claiming to be in Hendaye (81:2–4). Most important, it seems that Jake is *relieved*, happy that Brett and Robert are gone.

69:3 **the Concha:** This is the famous beach in San Sebastián where Jake swims, toward the end of the novel (234–38). In the manuscript Hemingway had originally written "beach" before crossing it out for the more specific "Concha" (*Facsimile* 1:207); this revision is in keeping with Hemingway's stylistic exactitude, but it also adumbrates the importance of the Concha as symbolic landscape (see 235:28).

69:11 **not bothered:** In this paragraph, Jake again emphasizes his almost palpable sense of relief that Brett is gone, Robert's not around to bother him, and he can get more work done, go to the racetrack, dine with friends, and have the "very cheerful" company of his friend Bill Gorton.

In the original manuscript notebook, after the end of the novel's first draft, Hemingway had written three pages of revealing commentary that, after some revision in typescript, he had inserted here at the beginning of book II to explain Jake's sense of relief and happiness in the absence of Brett. This material also indicates Jake's (and Hemingway's) awareness of a shift in narrative tension at this point in the book, a formal transition in the tone, rhythm, and deep structure of *story and style* that is prepared for and predicted by the secret-of-the-values scene and the last kiss at the end of book I. This deleted manuscript material begins: "There is now a slackening [originally he wrote "break"] in the emotional tightness of the story.

That taughtness [sic] did not come again until we were all in Spain. There could not have been a worse business than the five of us being in Spain together. It was Cohn's fault. He had every chance to get out of it. So if he took so much punishment and there is no question but that he took plenty of punishment he had no one to blame but himself" (*Facsimile* 2:617). Since Hemingway wrote this in his manuscript notebook immediately after the conclusion of the novel's first draft, it would seem that this observation marks the beginning of his process of revision, which thus starts with his clear recognition of the intentional shift in narrative tension at the end of what became book I. The passage continues with Jake stressing that he wants his reader to believe "that such a passion and longing could exist in me for Brett Ashley that I would sometimes feel that it would tear me to pieces and yet in the intervals when I was not seeing Brett, and they were the greater part of the time, I lived a very happy life. The world was to me a very fine and pleasant place and"—here Hemingway crossed out the next seventeen words—"I believe that I got as much or more enjoyment from it than nearly anyone I know." (Jake does not mention the count here, but he is possibly thinking about him.) After the deletion of this last line, the passage read: "and if I felt alone in it being alone was a comfortable feeling." It is only when he has "just left" Brett that he feels "all of my world taken away. . . . Even the shapes of things were changed, the trees and the houses and the fountains" and then "life was just something to be gone through." He concludes by saying that he doesn't know what Brett felt and readers "will have to figure that out" for themselves (618–19). The entire passage functions more as literary criticism than as storytelling, and Hemingway clearly realized when he discarded this material that he was *explaining* too much, lapsing into *telling* what he had already *shown*. The attentive reader would surely recognize that Jake lived a "very happy life" when Brett was not around and would be able to "figure that out" without being told directly, just as it would be quite clear to any reader by the end of book I that Jake's main problem is to resolve how he felt when he was with Brett. Unnecessary as this explanatory passage might be, it is still instructive to see the author beginning his revision process with a recognition of the "slackening" of "emotional tightness" at the beginning of book II and stating clearly the absence and presence of Brett as the index to Jake's happiness and misery.

69:15 **Bill Gorton:** An important character, Bill Gorton is partially based on two persons who had accompanied Hemingway to Pamplona before he wrote the novel: (1) Donald Ogden Stewart, a highly successful writer and humorist, and (2) Bill Smith, who had been Hemingway's friend and fishing buddy since his boyhood in northern Michigan.

70:3 **Dempsey:** Jack Dempsey (1895–1983) was the heavyweight boxing champion of the world from 1919 until he lost his title to Gene Tunney in 1926. Bill and Jake share a passion for boxing; apparently neither Bill nor Jake cares for Dempsey, and they both look forward to his being trimmed, defeated. Dempsey was not one of Hemingway's favorite boxers.

70:7 **three weeks:** We note that more than three weeks "pass" in this paragraph; after Brett and Robert leave, Bill arrives, stays with Jake "a couple of days," then goes off to Budapest and Vienna for three weeks. During this time, Jake is happy, enjoying himself, getting ahead in his work to prepare for his vacation. And he continues to enjoy himself when Bill—cheerful and humorous and full of "travel stories"—returns from Hungary and Austria.

71:2 **Enormous Vienna prize-fight:** In Bill's account of this boxing match, although the word "nigger" occurs sixteen times in little more than one page, the emphasis is clearly on the admirable and exemplary traits of the black boxer—he is memorable, "wonderful," "awful noble looking," "splendid"; he is clearly the victim of "injustice everywhere," and Bill takes a considerable risk in rescuing the boxer when the riot ensues. Bill gets him away in his car, loans him his clothes, and gives him money to get back to his family in Germany. The insistent repetition of the "n-word," given Bill's writerly awareness of the power and effect of words, must be seen as something more than just the accurate daily usage of the time and place; it is in fact a writer's (i.e., Bill's) *ironic overuse* of a racist term to mock racism, to express contempt for the racism of the Viennese crowd. Nothing could be more obvious than the fact that Bill admires the boxer and despises the racist crowd and the injustice of the entire situation. Put another way, it could be said that the repetition of "nigger" in this sequence may in part reflect the novelist's concern for verisimilitude, but, more important, given Bill's admiration of the boxer's demeanor, Hemingway seems to be underlining the precise distinctions that must be made between conduct accurately observed and prejudices casually applied, linguistically or otherwise. In any case, from the novelist's perspective, to *articulate* is not to *advocate,* and the net effect of Bill's boxing story is to stress the injustice that results from race-based bigotry and how such prejudice can cause blindness to character, to performance with the "grace under pressure" that this boxer clearly exemplifies. In sum, there is ample evidence that Hemingway crafted this entire scene as part of a subtextual design regarding boxing, a thematic structure intended to call attention to a certain kind of boxer as exemplar, a pattern that would resonate with Pedro Romero's conduct both inside and outside the bullring and reflect negatively on Robert Cohn's conduct as a boxer and as a man. Yet certain narrative exigencies caused Hemingway to cut crucial aspects of his boxing motif (see especially 72:3 and 80:4; see also 62:13).

71:5 **Tiger Flowers:** Theodore "Tiger" Flowers, also known as the "Georgia Deacon," was the first black American since Jack Johnson to achieve a world championship, winning the middleweight crown from Harry Greb in February 1926. Sometimes ranked fifth on the all-time list of great middleweight boxers, Flowers was known as a friendly and quiet man who was very religious, a daily Bible reader, and a deacon in his church. These attributes must have been on Hemingway's mind when he added the reference to Tiger Flowers—which did not appear in the original manuscript—to underline the "noble" and "splendid" traits of the unnamed boxer in Vienna. Since Tiger Flowers was much in the news when he won the middleweight crown on 26 February 1926, Hemingway, in the revision process, probably inserted this allusion around that time.

72:1 **Cologne:** In the original manuscript, Bill's Vienna boxing story had a very different conclusion. This line and the following two-word sentence—"Lives there"— were the same, but they were followed by the information that the boxer *did* send Bill the money he loaned him—he *did* write Bill a letter. Bill adds yet another adjective to his inventory of the boxer's praiseworthy character attributes—"grand"—and asks Jake if he wants to see the boxer's letter: "He took out his passport, removed the rubber band and took out this letter." This was followed by the beginning of a letter, with the salutation "Dear Mr. Grundy" (Bill's manuscript surname before it was changed to Gorton), followed by a page and a half of blank space bordered by vertical marginal lines, and the closing signature of the letter: "Yours friendly, William Tate" (the capitalization of "yours" is unclear in the manuscript). Clearly, Hemingway intended to come back to and fill in this largest blank space in the manuscript, to *compose carefully* the boxer's letter, which for both Bill and Jake is meant to be very moving. After the blank space for the intended text of the letter and the boxer's sign-off, Jake says, "That's a letter," and Bill responds, "You're damn right that's a letter" (*Facsimile* 1:212–13). Here Hemingway's second manuscript notebook ends as Bill and Jake go out to eat.

There are a number of things, then, that should be noted about the differences between the manuscript and the published text: (1) The boxer has immediately written to Bill, repaying the loan; (2) The boxer has presumably thanked Bill for his Good Samaritan actions and rescue maneuvers in Vienna in very moving terms; (3) The boxer's letter has added another term to Bill's list of his admirable character traits— first "wonderful" and "noble," now "grand"; (4) Bill cherishes the letter, folding it in with his passport (any traveler will recognize what it means to keep something carefully secured with one's most important travel document, one's identity papers); (5) Finally, in the signature to the unwritten letter, the boxer is given a name—William Tate. If this letter was intended to play such an important role in the novel, why then did Hemingway not *write* it, why did he remove all mention of it?

One reason may have to do with the effect this scene would have on narrative thrust and balance, the danger of distraction from established motifs presented by the recounting of a compelling story involving a character who appears briefly, and at secondhand, in the novel. Also, given the fact that Hemingway originally wrote a detailed and powerful description of the Ledoux-Kid Francis fight at the end of this chapter, there was the risk that the double boxing motif might overpower the other important business of this chapter. Yet there is another reason, and it has to do with the difficulties of writing dialect or idiolect, or transcribing on the printed page the exact speech patterns of a given character without introducing unintended condescension into a narrative. It is one of the oldest and most widespread problems in American literature, plaguing writers—well before and long after (and including) Mark Twain—who wanted to depict "noble" or "grand" or "splendid" characters of another race or class or region, who wanted to render accurately the speech patterns of "local color" characters (especially mountaineers, poor southern whites, and blacks) and ended up with caricatures. Throughout the 1920s the problem persisted, in spite of the stylistic advances made by some American writers—especially Southern writers—in sophisticated techniques for depicting "folk speech," or dialectal voice (e.g., avoidance of eye dialect, textual clutter, and inadvertent condescension or caricature). Even William Faulkner, later acknowledged as a master of dialect writing, had not yet solved the problem in his early work, from *Soldier's Pay* (1926) through *Flags in the Dust* (1929).

The unusual signature to the boxer's letter that *is* in the manuscript—"Yours [or "yours"] friendly, William Tate"—shows that Hemingway intended to write the letter in the boxer's unique voice. And, in the manuscript, of the *thirty-one* words of the boxer's speech that are quoted, *eleven* words are hackneyed dialectal respellings meant to render the sound of the boxer's voice and his grammatical irregularities: "theyah" (there), "foh" (for), "fohty" (forty), "Ah" (I), "nevah" (never), "hisself" (himself). Fortunately, by the time the novel reached print, the boxer speaks *thirty-three* words (the same words except for the added "Mister Gorton"), and only *one* word remains that is a feeble attempt to represent dialect: "musta" (must have). This was a slight improvement over the manuscript's "mustah," but by all standards of the best dialect-flavored writing, Hemingway should have eliminated that, too, since it tells the reader *nothing* about the unique sound of a particular speaker's voice. Some readers might also wish that Hemingway had caught (and revised) the unfortunate effect of his flawed attempt at dialect writing in the brief spoken words of the drummer in the preceding chapter: "Hahre you" and "Thaats good" may try to evoke the voice of a Southern black drummer, but in combination with the description that "He was all teeth and lips," the effect is unintended caricature (62:15–18).

In sum, then, Hemingway must have recognized some of these difficulties and decided not to write and insert the boxer's actual letter, not to risk undercutting the "wonderful" and "noble" and "splendid" character that Bill describes. In *The Sun Also Rises*, Hemingway demonstrated that he had a superb ear, that he was a master of *dialogue*—and he could not afford to show that he had not mastered the writing of *dialect*.

The incomplete (i.e., unwritten) manuscript letter at least gives us another name to add to the catalog of boxers mentioned in the novel. The signature "William Tate" is probably an allusion to Bill Tate, a heavyweight boxer from Chicago who was active in the ring from 1912 to 1927 (although there is no record that he ever fought in Vienna). As Bill says, his boxer resembled Tiger Flowers, "only four times as big" (71:5–6). Tiger Flowers was five feet ten; Bill Tate was over six feet six. The choice of Tate's surname might also have been an oblique allusion to Allen Tate and Hemingway's disagreement with him over that category of conduct known as "hard-boiled" (see 34:24). Any inclusive definition of "hard-boiled" conduct in Hemingway's work should include careful consideration of his fascination with boxers and boxing.

Finally, we should note that in the manuscript before Hemingway followed the letter's closing "Yours friendly" with the name William Tate, he had written "Larry" and then heavily crossed it out. Clearly, the boxer (and the writer of the letter) was originally intended to be Larry Gains, a black boxer from Toronto with whom Hemingway had a friendly correspondence in 1923–1924. On 9 June 1924 Gains wrote to Hemingway on Cologne *Internationales Sport-Buro* letterhead with news of his performance in the ring and his coming to Paris soon, hoping that he could see Hemingway then. He includes a copy of his boxing record, with each fight listed, showing nine fights in Cologne, eight in Paris, and another dozen fights scattered among eleven European cities—but none in Vienna, not by 9 June 1924. His overall record is 20-7-2. He signs this letter: "yours Friendly—Larry." A year earlier, on 25 June 1923, Gains had written to Hemingway, telling him in detail about his progress in the ring and his improvement in strength, infighting, and hitting hard, and wishing that Hemingway could see him work now. He says that Jack Dempsey has been in Cologne, but he didn't get a chance to talk with him; but Gains's manager spoke with Dempsey's manager, who said Dempsey would not train with a colored man. (Yet another reason why Hemingway and Jake and Bill hope Dempsey will get beaten; see 70:3). Gains misspells "Dempsey" as well as other words, and the letter is sprinkled with other spelling and grammatical irregularities, but it is a very moving letter, and again it carries that unforgettable closing, "yours Friendly, Larry." It is clearly the letter that was intended to serve as the model for the letter in the manuscript, although it does *not* contain any of the awkward dialect spellings that Hemingway employed in writing the manuscript version of the boxer's dialogue (noted above) that, after revision, Hemingway included in the published novel. Since Hemingway wrote this manuscript scene—including the letter, but leaving it to be filled in—in Hendaye, in the south of France, did he remember only the emotional core of the letter and its "friendly" sign-off and intend to dig up the actual letter when he returned to Paris? Perhaps to reproduce more or less exactly the content of Gains's letter? Did he not find the letter? Or, more likely, did he decide not to use an actual model and, more important as stylistic choice, decide not to complicate and undercut his portrait of an exemplary black boxer with linguistic irregularities? (The unpublished Gains-Hemingway correspondence is in the Hemingway Collection at the John F. Kennedy Library.)

72:6 **travel stories:** Compare Cohn's escapist "adventure" yarns (*The Purple Land*) and desires with Bill's "travel stories" of human dignity and brotherhood, concrete acts of compassion exercised in the face of violent injustice.

72:12 **the island:** That is the "Ile Saint Louis," as Hemingway writes it; more generally (and correctly) in English, the Ile St-Louis or the Ile Saint-Louis; in French, l'île Saint-Louis. For detailed discussion of the island, see 76:9 and 77:8 and appendix. The particularly pointed choice of where to eat, and where they will take their Paris night walk through symbolic landscape, is further contextualized in the manuscript when Bill asks where they will eat, and Jake says, "anywhere but Montparnasse" (*Facsimile* 1:216).

72:15 **statue:** The bronze statue is a monument (1900) to the chemists J. B. Caventou (1795–1877) and Pierre Pelletier (1788–1842), famous as the "discoverers" of quinine, a primary antimalarial drug. Long known as "Jesuit's powder," because missionaries to South America had sent to Europe since the early 1600s the bark of the quinquina (or cinchona) tree as a febrifuge or fever-reducing drug, quinine was isolated (not exactly discovered) by Caventou and Pelletier in 1820. They are not precisely, as Bill calls them, the "Gentlemen who invented pharmacy," but they were distinguished chemists, cofounders of alkaloid chemistry, responsible for isolating many substances besides quinine (e.g., strychnine, caffeine) and for studying and naming chlorophyll. Thus another statue is added to Jake's inventory of the monuments of Paris—ranging from the Lion of Belfort at the ancient place d'Enfer to Marshal Ney gesturing, to the inventor of the semaphore (or "aerial telegraph"), to these chemist-pharmacists; and the careful reader may detect a pattern in these statues, from the war memorials and the Place of Hell, to Ney the bravest soldier, to the aerial telegraphy (Jake, a war-wounded pilot, would understand this), to (coming full circle to another Denfert—or d'Enfer—"juncture") the creators of the anodynes, the drugs that eased the pain (see 27:28, 29:28, and 41:12). The aficionado of Hemingway's Paris intent (as so many readers of Hemingway are) on retracing Jake's footsteps will want to note that the segment of the rue Denfert-Rochereau indicated here underwent a name change (sometime between 1926 and 1931) to rue Henri Barbusse, named after Barbusse the French novelist (1873–1935), author of *L'Enfer* (1908) and the most celebrated World War I French war (or antiwar) novel, *Le Feu* (*Under Fire*).

73:1 **road to hell:** Bill hilariously echoes and revises the old aphorism—"the road to hell is paved with good intentions"—in existence in various forms for centuries and used by luminaries ranging from Saint Bernard and Saint Francis of Assisi to Samuel

Johnson and George Bernard Shaw. In Bill's brand of wacky free-associational humor, his hilarious "stuffed dog" spiel is triggered when he passes the taxidermist's shop, near the rue Denfert-Rochereau, which in turn ignites the "road to hell" association with the rue d'Enfer ("Hell Street"). Since this entire "stuffed dog" sequence did not appear in the original manuscript, and Hemingway later added everything between the mention of the Caventou-Pelletier statue (72:15) and the appearance of Brett in the taxi (74:8)—one of the novel's longest later insertions—we should consider Hemingway's possible reasons for crafting and inserting the passage. Those reasons might include the fact that in 1924 Hemingway's landlady (at his apartment not far from Jake's flat) had her pet dog stuffed by a taxidermist and displayed it (Baker, *Life Story* 131); from that association Hemingway probably saw an opening for comic relief, the opportunity to allow Bill to display his inventive sense of humor. Bill's humor paves the way for the reappearance of Brett in a *taxi*, which resonates with the *taxi*dermy motif, especially since Bill says—before they know who the taxi passenger is—that he's going to have the horse-cab stuffed for Jake as a Christmas present (74:5–6). Bill's engaging hilarity also creates a powerful contrast for the cool detachment, the tense lack of interplay, the withheld attention, that characterizes the actions of Brett and Jake in the ensuing scene. Hemingway's acute writerly ear, always alert to humorous wordplay combined with deadly serious allusion, may also have detected echoes of his Ecclesiastes subtext (which goes far beyond the novel's title and epigraph). One of the best-known lines from Ecclesiastes—"a living dog is better than a dead lion"—may reverberate here both humorously and seriously, since the "living dog" of Ecclesiastes is a symbol of hope for "him that is joined to all the living" (Ecclesiastes 9.4). (Hemingway's fondness for the "living dog" passage is suggested by the fact that he considered "Than a Dead Lion" as a possible title for "The Short Happy Life of Francis Macomber.") Given the implied judgment of what it means to live authentically (and who is "dead"—*not* the count, but Brett) in the secret-of-the-values scene in the preceding chapter (the last appearance of Brett before she reappears in the horse-cab), maybe what Jake hears in Bill's humor runs something like this: A stuffed dog is better than a stuffed horse-cab with a stuffed (or dead) Brett in it (see 74:9). Or, a stuffed dog is better than a dead liar. Also, given Bill's penchant for literary quotation and association, he may be echoing T. S. Eliot's 1925 poem that begins: "We are the hollow men / We are the stuffed men" (*Complete Poems* 56). Eliot's "The Hollow Men" also contains eye imagery, vision and blindness and religious motifs that resonate significantly with *The Sun Also Rises. The Waste Land*, then, is not the only Eliot work that informs Hemingway's fiction and serves as nuanced modernist backdrop and sounding board for his allusive structure and wordplay. Indeed the "stuffed dog" sequence ends with an allusion to yet another Eliot work—"Portrait of a Lady" (see 75:24–25).

73:11 **daunted:** Bill's humor depends in part on the sound of words and their repetition until they sound even funnier; here he repeats "daunted" nine times in less than a page. Since Bill seems to be always looking for literary echoes, maybe the reader should do likewise. The only famous quotation listed in standard sources that contains the word "daunted" is the following passage from Thoreau's *Walden:* "A farmer, a hunter, a soldier, a reporter, even a philosopher, may be daunted; but nothing can deter a poet, for he is actuated by pure love." Given the fact that immediately after his ninefold repetition of "daunted," Bill humorously declares: "I'm a nature-writer" (74:7), this may well be a deliberate echo of Thoreau. Jake is, we know, a hunter, a soldier, and a reporter who may be daunted in those identities; but he is also a kind of poet—"actuated [necessarily] by pure love"—and in that respect he may be dauntless. Also since Jake and Bill are about to leave for Roland country, for fishing at Roncevaux, maybe they both hear in Bill's admonitions against being daunted an echo of Robert Browning's celebrated line from "Childe Roland to the Dark Tower Came": "Dauntless the slug-horn to my lips I set, / And blew" (Darwin 90; a slug-horn is a primitive trumpet, often made of animal horn like Roland's legendary horn, Oliphant; a slug-horn is also a flawed or ill-formed horn in cattle—especially bulls).

73:14–15 **Crillon . . . Jack Roses:** See 29:14 and 41:5.

73:19 **like a cat:** The repetition of this phrase seems to flow naturally from the conversation about dogs. However, note Jake's close attention, as always, to what another character says; here he immediately recognizes that Bill has been with Harvey Stone because Bill uses one of Stone's favorite expressions (see 42:13 and 43:2).

73:29 **hard-boiled eggs:** This is another joke, since being "hard-boiled" is one way to avoid being "daunted." Yet the joke, as always in the intricately woven tapestry of Hemingway's prose, resonates in various ways, looking back to Jake's very serious (and very precise) definition of "hard-boiled" at the end of chapter 4 (see 34:24), and looking forward to the "hard-boiled eggs" that appear in the serious/humorous discussion centered on the Scopes trial in chapter 12 (see 121:18–20). It should also be noted that hard-boiled eggs are not really very hard.

74:9 **In it was Brett:** This sentence directly echoes Brett's first appearance in the novel when she gets out of a taxi with a group of homosexuals and Hemingway writes: "With them was Brett" (20:13). The textual juxtaposition of the horse-cab and the taxi with Brett in it may be an ambiguous description of one cab or of two distinct taxis.

74:18 **must bathe:** The first three sentences Brett speaks are concerned with bathing— "must bathe," "must clean myself." Hemingway's ever-present symbolic landscape, sometimes requiring intensive depth analysis, is sometimes a straightforward matter of recognizing location and the meaning generated by spatial juxtaposition. When Brett appears and announces her need to bathe, from the taxi stopped on the boulevard Saint-Michel, it is quite likely that they are next to the Palais des Thermes, the ancient Roman baths that are the most strikingly visible feature of this part of the Boul' Mich'. Jake and Bill have walked a good ways down toward the river as they talk. Twice Jake says they "went on"; they stop for a drink and then walk "on again" until they see Brett in the cab. That Brett pronounces three times her need to bathe, in the proximity of the ancient ruins of the Roman baths, with sculpture of Saint Jacques (Saint James, Santiago) with figures of a bull, an eagle, and a lion (symbols of the Evangelists) on the steps leading to the *piscina* (pool), emphasizes her need to cleanse herself of the affair with Robert at the same time that it reinforces deeper patterns of the novel's symbolic landscape.

75:1 **Brett smiled at him:** The distance between Jake and Brett in this scene is emphasized by the repetition, *five* times in less than two pages, of Brett *smiling* at Bill, *turning* to Bill, "wrinkling the corners of her eyes" at Bill. In contrast, Jake notes, she only *looks* at him, and only *once* throughout the scene. As usual, Hemingway's revisions reveal his reiterative hermeneutics, his interpretive insistence through repetition, since he added all three instances of "Brett smiled at Bill" or "him." The progression, the change in Jake's feeling for Brett, from the last-kiss scene at the end of book I to this first post–San Sebastián encounter is remarkable, as well it should be when her actions are considered: just back from a two- or three-week sexual rendezvous with Robert, she informs Jake that she must "bathe," wash away that encounter to make ready for the imminent arrival of her next lover, Michael, and as she relays this information she cannot stop flirting with Bill while she barely looks at Jake, to whom she had been protesting her undying love a few weeks before. As Jake realizes clearly in a later passage (from the Pamplona section) that was deleted from the manuscript (and the typescript), he was "pretty well through with Duff [i.e., Brett]" after she got back from San Sebastián (*Facsimile* 2:397; also Svoboda, *Crafting of a Style* 21). As with many of his manuscript deletions, Hemingway must have felt they were too talky, explaining too much, and in most cases he was right to prefer that the reader *feel,* through unexplained but precisely rendered action, what his scenes were intended to convey. This scene is one small instance of many that illustrate what Hemingway meant when he said that as a writer he was after "the real thing, the sequence of motion and fact which made the emotion" (*Death in the Afternoon* 2). Brett's "motion" here and the "fact," noted five times in rapid succession, that she smiles at and flirts with Bill, makes the "emotion"; Jakes says nothing—no editorial commentary is necessary. My students often point to this scene as one of the places where Jake feels most intensely how he has been betrayed, by both Brett and Cohn. Discussing the sense that still lingers today (in a world without many other strongly felt values) of how "sick and twisted" it is felt to be when one friend betrays another by dating his "ex" ("the ultimate betrayal"), a recent *New York Times* article analyzes the "stigma" of such conduct, a violation of the "sacred bond" of friendship; and such "multiple infidelity," as sources for the *Times* article put it, is even more "icky" than adultery (Navarro 1–2).

75:10 **leave Paris:** Although she jokes about "this pestilential city," Brett knows "One's an ass to leave Paris"—especially to leave Paris with the Paris-hating Robert Cohn.

75:24 **in another country:** In the capstone to this inserted (post–original manuscript) "stuffed dog" sequence of literary allusions, Bill here humorously paraphrases lines from Christopher Marlowe's *The Jew of Malta* (circa 1589), apparently taken from T. S. Eliot's recasting of Marlowe's lines as the epigraph to his early poem "Portrait of a Lady": "Thou hast committed— / Fornication: but that was in another country, / And besides, the wench is dead." (Hemingway alluded to this passage again in his short-story title "In Another Country" and more directly in his later novel *Across the River and into the Trees.* There, Colonel Cantwell says, regarding his ex-wife: "But that was in another country and besides the wench is dead." "Is she really dead?" asks Renata. "Deader than Phoebus the Phoenician" [213]. Here Hemingway doubles his allusion to Eliot with references to "Portrait of a Lady" and *The Waste Land,* transforming Eliot's Phlebas (a merchant sailor) into Phoebus, or Apollo, the sun god; and he indicates directly that the "lady" under discussion is *dead* even if she doesn't know it.)

It may be perilous to try to wring all the nuances out of such literary allusions, but Hemingway comes close to forcing the reader to see it this way: although Bill does not know this, and Jake probably only suspects it, the Marlowe/Eliot quotation glosses Brett's recent experience in San Sebastián—she has committed "fornication" not with the "Jew of Malta" but with Robert Cohn, in another country. And given Jake's ironic identification of Bill as a "taxidermist"—who on the preceding page was going to have the horse-cab (juxtaposed with the taxi with Brett in it) "stuffed" as a present for Jake—Brett is the "wench" who is "dead." Since the "Portrait" is of a "Lady" (and in Eliot's poem the narrator is *leaving* the lady), Lady Brett Ashley cannot be a "wench" in the old dictionary sense of a peasant woman, but in the sense of a "wanton woman." Bill as taxidermist may want to stuff her, in another sense, since he finds her very attractive (76:2), but for Jake, from here on and increasingly as the novel progresses, she is over, dismissed, "dead," even as she continues her fornication "in another country." Hemingway's allusion to Eliot's "Portrait of a Lady" also foreshadows Bill and Jake's later discussion of Henry James and his mysterious wound and alludes, by extension, to James's classic novel *Portrait of a Lady* and his trouble with ladies (115–16).

If, as has been argued, the stuffed dogs (and the hard-boiled eggs) in this scene serve as "metaphors of life arrested in process" that yield "an ambiguous victory over time," and if these "facsimile effigies of frozen life are meant to amuse us as ironic commentaries on the strategies of art and the vanities of transcendence" (Gajdusek, *His Own Country* 324), then we should consider carefully Jake's humorous identification of Bill as a "taxidermist." Jake, the writer, jokingly calls Bill, the writer, a taxidermist, one who manipulates, orders, arranges the skin ("taxi-" indicates arrangement or order; "derm" indicates skin) of dead creatures to achieve a lifelike appearance for exhibition. But the writer as artist—Bill, Jake, and Hemingway—knows that the rendered life must be more than skin-deep, and the taxonomies of *The Sun Also Rises,* the principles of order and arrangement, must deal deeply, must get inside the "skin" of a character such as Brett, who is repeatedly imaged in a taxi (bringing disorder, disarrangement), if Jake, the writer as artist always dealing with death in life, life in death, is to achieve more than "an ambiguous victory over time," a "transcendence" that is more than mere "vanity." Taxidermy, concerned as it is with stuffing the skin, does not concern itself with questions of the spirit. Hemingway's art does.

76:9 **Ile Saint Louis:** Generally referred to simply as "l'île," an identification that suffices for all Parisians and experienced travelers, l'île Saint-Louis has been for centuries one of the most remarkable and compelling neighborhoods of Paris. The 1927 Blue Guide characterizes it as "the quietest and loneliest part of Paris" (Muirhead and Monmarché, *Paris* 110); the 1931 Baedeker describes it as "une oasis paisible," a peaceful oasis or haven in the hectic heart of Paris (*Paris* 306). The 1950 Blue Guide is more effusive, calling l'île "a kind of little land independent of Paris, a realm of the past, very peaceful, which many fine scholars claim as their own"; also noted was the "unique charm" of the quais, and, as travel writers have recommended for centuries, it was advised that it was "best to begin one's walk on the southern quays, to enjoy the superb views that they give of the back of Notre-Dame" (Martineau 104). Travel writing about l'île often waxes poetic and overstates the island's ancientness. Still, having stayed on l'île many times and *lived* there, I can attest that it richly deserves all the romantic or inflated prose that has been written about it over the centuries.

L'île is not really *ancient* (except maybe from an American perspective or sense of history), since the island did not even *exist* in its present form until the early 1600s, when two smaller islands, the île Notre-Dame and the île aux Vaches (Cow Island, a pastoral grazing ground), were joined to make l'île Saint-Louis. L'île assumed its present form and appearance in the seventeenth century, when the quais and most of the *hôtels particuliers,* or mansions, were built. But l'île is connected by a bridge to the île de la Cité, which *is* the truly ancient heart of Paris. Paris—then called Lutetia (or Lutèce)—began on the île de la Cité, where, by 53 BC under Julius Caesar, the deputies of conquered Gaul had their seat of government. Radically transformed by vast public buildings in the nineteenth century, the Cité lost much of its historical sense of place, although some marvels were spared (barely) by the Revolution, such as the thirteenth-century Sainte-Chapelle, the church built by Saint Louis to house Christ's Crown of Thorns and part of the True Cross. Still, the Cité retained its identity as the center of Paris, the center of France (and some would say Europe), due to the numinous presence of Notre-Dame, the magnificent twelfth-century Gothic cathedral that dominates the east end of the island, where the Cité is connected to l'île Saint-Louis by a bridge, the pont Saint-Louis. (The bridge that was there in the 1920s collapsed into the Seine in 1939 after being hit by a barge and was replaced by an ostensibly temporary and unattractive pedestrian bridge). It is the view of the cathedral of Notre-Dame from upstream, from *behind* the cathedral, from the pont de la Tournelle (joining l'île to the Left Bank) that centers Bill and Jake's walk around l'île and across the Seine, south to the rue Saint-Jacques, one of the most highly charged symbolic landscapes in the novel (see 77:8 and 78:6–7).

Although he never lived on l'île, Hemingway knew the island well. He worked there and, as associate editor in 1924 for Ford Madox Ford's *transatlantic review,* had an office there, located at 29, quai d'Anjou (on the north side of the island), which was also the office of the Three Mountains Press, publisher of his collection of vignettes, *in our time* (1924). Sometimes when Ford asked his deputy editor to read a batch of manuscripts, Hemingway would take them outside, descend the nearby steps down to the quai, and edit the work of others (including Gertrude Stein) down by the river (Baker, *Life Story* 123). He also socialized there, especially at Ford's Thursday afternoon teas, where Hemingway met many of his contemporaries and fellow writers, such as Harold Loeb, the prototype for Robert Cohn. And he relaxed there, walking along the quais after working, watching the fishermen, and talking to the fishermen he knew, who fished the "fruitful parts of the Seine between the Île St.-Louis and the Place du Verte Galente [sic]"—the Square du Vert-Galant—and he knew where to get "a very good *friture* on the Île St.-Louis" (*Moveable Feast* 44). He knew what some travel writers and tourists did not know, that the *goujon,* the little fried fish, fresh from the river, were delicious. He remembered decades later how the island looked with its "narrow streets and the old, tall, beautiful houses" and how you could "walk along the quais with the length of the Île St.-Louis and then Notre-Dame . . . opposite as you walked" (*Moveable Feast* 41). Hemingway knew the island very well, as he knew Notre-Dame.

In this scene, then, Bill and Jake are drawn inexorably to the island. As they walk down the boulevard Saint-Michel toward the river and the island—determined to eat there, to eat anywhere but in Montparnasse—they are sidetracked by meeting Brett, who insists that they drink at the Closerie, thus causing them to turn around and go back up the boulevard toward Montparnasse (74:23). But once they get rid of her, they resume their unswerving course to the island. And it's a good thing that she refuses the invitation to eat with them, because if she went to the island, there would be no walk—she won't walk across the street—and the history-infused, symbol-laden pilgrim's progress through the highly charged *paysage moralisé* of Paris that is about to transpire after the meal on the island would not take place (see 77:8 and appendix).

76:12 **Madame Lecomte's:** Lecomte's restaurant, Au Rendez-vous des Mariniers, was at 33, quai d'Anjou, two doors down from the Three Mountains Press and the *transatlantic review* office (see preceding entry); thus Hemingway probably knew this restaurant well. He would have heard about it, even before he worked next door in 1924, from his friend John Dos Passos, who lived above the restaurant in 1918; and it was here, in 1923, that he met Donald Ogden Stewart (a model for the character of Bill Gorton)—Stewart said that he was at the restaurant (Dos Passos had told him about it) and he happened to meet Hemingway, whom he liked immediately (Stewart 116). It was decidedly not a fancy restaurant; and standard guidebooks of the 1920s made no mention of it, unlike the other places Jake frequents. One 1920s Parisian dining guide found it a "shabby little eating place . . . a queer little place, *very French*" (Street 203; emphasis added). A recent book entitled *Found Meals of the Lost Generation* suggests that this meal at Lecomte's Rendez-vous "may well be the most famous meal of the decade" (Rodriguez-Hunter 180). Given such a claim, we should examine the menu carefully.

There seems to be some confusion (among Hemingway critics) regarding this restaurant and this meal. One source asserts that the roast chicken/new green beans/mashed potatoes/salad/apple pie/cheese menu is "probably meant as a swipe at the changes brought about to please the American Women's Club. This is a seafood restaurant, yet Jake and Bill are served an all-American non-seafood meal" (Balassi, "Glossary" 76:22–23). The confusion here is multiple: (1) The American Women's Club has recommended it, as such social and cultural clubs for expatriates the world over are still wont to do in their newsletters and on their Web sites, precisely because it is a "quaint," *authentically French* restaurant—and such places do not change their menus to satisfy the influx of expatriates, who are there precisely to eat a very French meal; (2) Madame Lecomte's is *not* a "seafood restaurant"; *Mariniers* does not indicate seafood and indeed has nothing to do with the sea! *Marin* means sailor or seaman, and *fruits de mer* means seafood, but *mariniers* means bargemen, watermen, the working people of the *river* whom this "shabby" and "quaint" rendezvous exists primarily to serve (there were also cheap hotel rooms for bargemen above the restaurant); (3) The menu, a quintessentially French meal, has nothing to do with "all-American" food; consider each item listed: (a) "a roast chicken," the classic French *poulet rôti*—and French roasting chickens are generally much smaller than American roasting chickens, thus the whole French roasting chicken would aptly serve two; (b) "new green beans," the classic French green vegetable accompaniment to the *poulet rôti*—and these *haricots verts* are much narrower and less coarse than the familiar American string beans, and they are "new," fresh picked, the first of the June crop; (c) "mashed potatoes," the classic Parisian *purée de pommes de terre,* ineffably lighter, creamier, more buttery than the usual American-style mashed potatoes (since Hemingway added the "mashed potatoes" to the menu after the original manuscript version, he obviously considered this meal carefully); (d) "apple-pie and cheese"—the apple pie could be either a *tourte aux pommes* or a *tarte aux pommes* and there are many traditional French versions of these; *none,* however, involves the combination of cheese with apples in any fashion whatsoever; as correctly averred in the recent *Hemingway Cookbook* (which regards this as a classic French meal): "it is not likely that Jake and Bill had all-American apple pie and cheese, an unheard-of combination in France" (Boreth 74). Clearly, since Hemingway again adjusted his menu in his revisions of the original manuscript, adding "and cheese" after apple pie, his intention was to stress that this was a traditional French meal, with a cheese course served after the salad and before the dessert. It is possible (though unlikely), since Madame Lecomte's restaurant was described by a contemporary source as "shabby," that the now-familiar option of cheese *or* dessert was offered, and given Hemingway's stated menu, Jake had one and Bill had the other; however, they probably had both cheese *and* dessert courses, since this was the restaurant of the *mariniers,* and even hardworking hungry bargemen would endorse the old French proverb: "A dessert without cheese is a beautiful woman with only one eye." Far from being an "all-American" meal, what Bill and Jake eat is a classic traditional and authentic all-French meal, in a very French restaurant, in a very French place, a world away from Montparnasse.

In sum, close reading of this menu reminds us of the importance of detail in Hemingway's work. The same source (Balassi, "Glossary" 76:20–23) that falls into multiple confusion regarding this meal and this restaurant then concludes that this entire scene is somehow an instance of how France is spoiled (as compared to Spain), how France comes off badly in the "France/Spain split in values" (Svoboda, *Crafting of a Style* 82; see also 25:2). The lesson, then, is simple and direct: if we misread Hemingway's details, the local texture of his fiction, we are likely to misread his larger themes and patterns, the universal design of his vision.

77:8 **circled the island:** This is a crucial passage, both because it presents certain difficulties and ambiguities of location (or composition of place), and because in its approach to and perspective on Notre-Dame it represents one of the key examples of symbolic landscape in the novel. Jake says they *circled* the island—how, exactly, did they do this? They leave Madame Lecomte's on the quai d'Anjou, on the north, or Right Bank side, of the island, just east of the pont Marie (1614), the oldest bridge linking l'île to the mainland. It is not clear whether they walk east along the quai d'Anjou or west along the quai de Bourbon. The first sentence that describes the walk implies lapsed time, motion that is not described, as indicated by both "We walked *along*" (emphasis added) and the simple fact that they have suddenly, with no other signal of lapsed time than that word *along,* been relocated to the quai d'Orléans on the far side of the island from the restaurant. The next location clue comes from the sight of old houses being torn down "across the river"—but which way across the river? Depending on exactly where they are, there are *three* different channels of the river they could be looking "across"—toward the Left Bank, the Right Bank, or the Cité. Then they continue to *circle* the island, but the reader may well be confused about which direction they are walking. The next clue is the *bateau-mouche,* the brightly illuminated tour boat that passes them going *up* the river (i.e., east) and under the bridge. Then they look *down* the river toward Notre- Dame before going out on the wooden footbridge, where they stop and look *down* the river at Notre-Dame again. Before they walk on, they look *up* the river again. Hemingway seems to be very precise about his directions here, especially his ups and downs, yet there has been considerable confusion about this, one of the favorite walks in all of Hemingway's fiction. For a detailed analysis of this walk and its implications, the seven-eighths of the iceberg that is beneath the surface, see appendix.

77:9 **bateau mouche:** Still a prominent feature on the Seine, the *bateaux-mouches* have been a fixture of Parisian tourism for well over a century. Large, low-to-the-water riverboats, usually with a combination of open deck and space enclosed by transparent roof and walls for maximum view of the passing sights of Paris, *bateaux-mouches,* in spite of their name, are not "fly-boats," having nothing to do with flies (*mouches*). They are named after Mouche, the district of Lyon where such water buses were first made for the Paris Exhibition of 1867. Their most striking feature is the spectacular illumination of the riverscape provided by an array of floodlights.

77:11 **Notre Dame:** Often said to be the most famous, the most admired, the most visited church in the world (with Saint Peter's in Rome the only contender for these titles), the cathedral of Notre-Dame de Paris is, as the guidebooks describe it, "the parish church of the history of France . . . one of the most perfect works of art of the Middle Ages and of the art of all time," occupying the site at the southeast end of l'île de la Cité that "has been holy ground since the beginnings of history here" (Martineau 97). Standing where a Temple of Jupiter had stood in the first century, and then from the fourth century the first basilica of Notre-Dame, the present cathedral's cornerstone was laid in 1163; the high altar was consecrated in 1189, and construction continued well into the fourteenth century. Although on aesthetic grounds Notre-Dame is often ranked behind the cathedrals of Chartres, Amiens, Rheims, and Bourges, it is generally considered a supremely majestic architectural achievement and flowering of Gothic art as well as the center of French history and religion. During the Revolution the cathedral was badly damaged, much of its sculpture and many of its treasures desecrated and destroyed. Complete demolition was considered. In typical revolutionary fashion, after the interior was pillaged (with crosses, chalices, lead from coffins, etc., melted down for weaponry), it served as a wine depot for the revolutionary army before it was proclaimed a Temple of Reason, with an opera performer enthroned at the high altar as the Goddess of Reason, and ballet dancers for acolytes. Reconsecrated for Christian worship in 1802, it was the setting for the coronation of Napoleon in 1804. During the nineteenth-century Gothic Revival, extensive restoration of the cathedral was carried out under the supervision of Viollet-le-Duc. Victor Hugo's classic work *Notre-Dame de Paris* reestablished the cathedral's prominence in the history and imagination of Europe and the Western world. All this would be common knowledge even among casual tourists, let alone residents of Paris, and it is thus a part of what Jake and Bill are feeling as they stand, for the most part in awed silence, and look downriver at the cathedral.

They are of course looking at the back of Notre-Dame, the famous view of the apse, the flying buttresses, and the flèche (or spire). This is the celebrated perspective, the vantage point of Notre-Dame, featured in thousands of paintings and postcards, a prime goal of tour buses and tour guides, subject of millions of tourist cameras, and a favorite shorthand vignette of Paris nostalgia for moviemakers (e.g., the opening frames of the 1950s Hollywood movie *The Last Time I Saw Paris*). The architectonics of this symbolic landscape—river, island, cathedral—are far more compelling than the street-bound view of the towers and the west front of the cathedral. From the back, for example, the flèche dominates the skyscape, and Jake (and Hemingway) would know that the ball below the cross, high in the sky, is said to contain relics of Christ's Crown of Thorns and the True Cross—brought back from the Crusades by Louis XI, the warrior king known as an exemplary Christian ruler, the saint for whom the island Jake and Bill have just circled is named. (For consideration of the view of the flying buttresses, see the following entry.) And although they cannot *see* the front of the cathedral from where they stand—the tip of the iceberg, the flèche (or "arrow") suggests the omitted things that they know and feel—Jake and Bill know the square in front of Notre-Dame contains the benchmark, the touchstone, the sign in the pavement that declares that Notre-Dame is the "Point zero des routes de France," the marker from which all distances are measured. (Old signs in the countryside of France still indicate, for example, "Paris Notre-Dame 300 Kilometers.") They also know that the square, the place du Parvis-Notre-Dame, is dominated by a colossal monument of Charlemagne and Roland, and that at the west end of the *place* begins the rue Saint-Jacques, the ancient pilgrimage road south that they will walk along a few paragraphs later (see 78:6–7), which they will follow in a few days to Roncevaux, hallowed terrain of Charlemagne and Roland. Notre-Dame, then, is the point of their walk, and the point of departure for their pilgrimage south to Roncesvalles and Pamplona.

77:11 **squatting:** More than a few readers have been puzzled by Hemingway's word choice here. Some have found it an ugly word to describe a cathedral; others find it "a term of intense disrespect" (Balassi, "Glossary" 77:10–11). It is, at first glance, a curious usage in this context. First, we should note that Hemingway seems to have a fondness for applying variants of "squat" to Notre-Dame. Years before *The Sun Also Rises,* for example, he had used the term in an article for the *Toronto Star Weekly,* "Christmas on the Roof of the World," where he wrote about standing on a bridge and looking upriver "to where Notre Dame squats in the dusk" (*By-Line* 112). It is very clear that there is no "disrespect" for the cathedral implied by his word choice here, no ugliness for him in the word "squat." It is a warm, mellow scene, evocative of how "wonderful" it is to stand on a bridge in Paris and take in, through the lovely "softly curtaining snow," the "beautiful" sight of Notre-Dame squatting in the dusk (*By-Line* 112). (In the manuscript of *The Sun Also Rises* he even reused the "dusk" imagery before he finally deleted it; also, in the novel he is looking downstream at the back of Notre-Dame, while in the article he is looking upstream toward the more distant west front and towers.) If we remember that Hemingway teaches his readers to judge words first for their precision, we may have the reason for his attachment to the image of Notre-Dame squatting. The primary signification of "squat," to sit on one's heels, suggests a low or shortened profile, a crouched compression that squares with the etymological root of "squat": to press flat, to press together. If we know, as Hemingway no doubt did, that Notre-Dame, with its uncompleted towers, the spires having never been built, is of considerably less height than many of the great Gothic cathedrals, we may have the key to the rightness of the word. Compare Notre-Dame's profile against the sky, at 223 feet (or 69 meters), with the towers of Chartres at 350 and 375 feet (106 and 115 meters), and Strasbourg at 465 feet (142 meters). While Hemingway's word choice in no way diminishes the grandeur of Notre-Dame, it does suggest his architectural exactitude, and his agreement with Baedeker that Notre-Dame has a certain *lourdeur,* a heaviness, due to the lack of spires on the towers (Baedeker, *Paris* 303).

But there is more than precise description in Hemingway's use of "squatting"— there is a poetic intensity, an evocative mot juste, especially if we keep in mind that we are not looking at the front towers but at the rear perspective, which is dominated by the *arcs-boutants,* the flying buttresses. Among the most admired *arcs-boutants* in the world, they do indeed have, as the guidebooks insist, "une grande hardiesse," a great boldness and daring and elegance (Baedeker, *Paris* 304; Muirhead and Monmarché, *Paris* 108). For decades, when I have lived and sojourned in Paris and had the duty to show friends and visitors the great sights, I have taken them first to the pont de la Tournelle to absorb this downriver view of Notre-Dame. After the appropriate interval of silent meditation, I always ask what the cathedral looks like to them. The answer is almost always rendered in terms of flight—"it looks as if the building is ready for takeoff," "preparing to soar, explode heavenwards," "ready for a space launch." Then I add Hemingway's words—"Notre Dame squatting"—to the view and ask what that evokes. Rarely does the answer reflect any sense that the word "squatting" implies ugliness or disrespect for the cathedral or anything unpleasant. Rather the word seems to suggest for most a sense of something poised to leap, a great crouching living form or force ready to spring forward or up. Unable to take students to whom I have taught this novel to the actual bridge to ponder the actual view, I repeat this experiment in classrooms, sometimes showing them a large photograph of the cathedral taken from the proper perspective, followed by consideration of the text, sometimes reversing the order of photograph-text response, sometimes asking only what the word "squatting" makes them feel. Almost invariably, the responses suggest some variation on the image of a coiled, crouching form imbued with a sense of arrested dynamic motion, a poised frozen kinetic energy, on the verge of some terrific ascension or apotheosis, elevation, or exaltation. It is, then, one thing to observe the relatively low profile of Notre-Dame from the front and call it "squat"; it is a very different thing to perceive the cathedral from the back, "squatting against the night sky." The former is reportorial accuracy; the latter is poetry. And it is appropriate and necessary to note that the cathedral is poised *against the night,* the night that gives Jake certain difficulties (34:24–25), the dark night of the soul—as Hemingway repeatedly describes it (echoing Fitzgerald) in *Under Kilimanjaro*—where "it is always three o'clock in the morning" (219–20, 384). But the cathedral is always there—as are the other churches that Jake evokes, where he prays, confesses, and goes to Mass—*against* the night.

77:12 **wooden foot-bridge:** In 1925, in the approximate location of the present-day pont de la Tournelle, there was a temporary wooden footbridge to the Left Bank. It is often reported in Hemingway criticism that the Tournelle bridge was torn down in 1923, rebuilt, and reopened in 1928. The source of this information would seem to be Noel Riley Fitch's *Walks in Hemingway's Paris,* where it is noted that "La Tournelle was destroyed and rebuilt between 1923 and 1928" (98). However, contemporaneous and authoritative sources such as the 1927 Blue Guide indicate that the bridge was torn down "in 1921 as an obstruction to navigation"; and the 1931 Baedeker indicates that the new reinforced concrete pont de la Tournelle was opened in 1927 (Muirhead and Monmarché, *Paris* 94; Baedeker, *Paris* 307). Such details suggest that Fitch's book, useful tourist guide that it is—and more readily available than 1920s guidebooks—should be used with caution. In the one brief chapter in which this bridge description is given, for example, we read about the renovated "medieval [!] façade" of 29, quai d'Anjou, when in fact there were and are no medieval facades on l'île, the earliest dating from the 1600s; we read that Hemingway "was a regular in 1923" at the offices of the *transatlantic review,* but that was 1924; Fitch misquotes Hemingway's line from "The Snows of Kilimanjaro" about the place de la Contrescarpe quarter: "There was never [sic] another part of Paris that he loved like that"; she gives easy credence to the dubious story about Hemingway's supposed rented writing room on rue Descartes (a story dismissed by Hemingway's most authoritative biographer, Michael Reynolds); she misquotes *The Sun Also Rises:* "It is [was] always pleasant crossing bridges in Paris"; street names are misspelled—rue le Regrattier becomes rue Le Regattier; the foundation date for the University of Paris is misstated or vastly oversimplified; and Jake and Bill's walking route from Contrescarpe is probably mis- construed (89–109).

77:16 **grand:** Bill's brief comment—about Notre-Dame, about the walk they have just made around the island, about all of Paris—suffices to underline the silent awe and admiration that Bill and Jake share. In the manuscript, Hemingway originally had Bill say: "It's pretty fine isn't it?" (*Facsimile* 1:222). In revision, finding the mot juste, he substituted "grand" for "fine," granting a loftiness, dignity, and magnificence to the scene that could not be contained in the merely aesthetic signification of "fine." The revision also deletes the question, since Jake will say nothing, as he always says nothing when he is most moved, whether by landscape or by sacred places (see e.g., 90:13–15, 93:28–29, 117:17, 128:16–25). As Hemingway noted elsewhere, the appropriate response for a Christian in the presence of a great cathedral is silence; it is impossible to write anything, to say anything, since the cathedral itself "says it so completely" ("On Cathedrals" 2).

77:17–21 **We leaned:** In this and the preceding paragraph, Hemingway stresses the duration of the view with these words: "crossed," "stopped," "standing," "leaned," "looked" (three times), "up," "below," "passed us." The view of Notre-Dame, the island, and the river is not a momentary glimpse, but a sustained vision. The passing presence of the lovers, the man and the girl (added in revision), emphasizes Jake and Bill's stillness and adds the shadow of romantic entanglement or profane love and in yet another echoic or paired scene foreshadows the presence of the couple on the raft during Jake's baptismal swimming scenes in the sea at San Sebastián near the novel's end (235:8–11). Still, the cathedral dominates this scene, and the river, too, remarkably *present* in its soundlessness; the bridge of their crossing may be temporary, but the old bridge that obstructed navigation has been removed, and—in a passage that reverberates with the novel's title and biblical epigraph— the river runs to the sea, soundlessly around the cathedral on the island, and the cathedral also rises, against the night sky.

77:22–31 **Cardinal Lemoine:** The twelve-minute walk uphill from the river on the rue du Cardinal-Lemoine to the place de la Contrescarpe is rendered here in two sentences, with no notation of what they pass on their way. Yet since Hemingway's style and the deep structure of his work consistently demands a recognition that geography is the foundation of his "iceberg," and local knowledge is the sonar with which we must sound the depths, it is useful to know exactly what they are walking past. Any good guidebook, such as the kind Hemingway habitually consulted, will inform the reader that Jake and Bill walk past the site of the massacre, during the Revolution, of seventy-seven priests at the Séminaire de Saint-Firmin; to their left as rue du Cardinal-Lemoine crosses rue Monge are the ancient ruins of the Arènes de Lutèce, the second-century Roman arena or amphitheatre, hidden behind street-front walls but easily accessible from rue Monge or the rue de Navarre, the first street to the left from Cardinal-Lemoine. It is, to be sure, no mere coincidence that Jake and Bill, who could have walked several different routes from the river, who know Paris well, who are leaving for Navarre in a few days to attend the bullfights in the arena at Pamplona's Fiesta of San Fermín, choose to walk by the site where the priests of Saint-Firmin (the same saint, native of Pamplona, French priest and bishop) were murdered, near the rue de Navarre and the Roman arena, where, according to legend, bullfights (most certainly bull games) were once staged. The lay of the land, in Hemingway, always signifies. And what this symbolic landscape suggests, contrary to the usual view in Hemingway studies, is the deep and ancient unity of place and religion and culture shared by France and Spain—even down to the same man and saint—and the mysteries of passion underlined with the blood rites of the bullfight *and* the Church.

As Jake and Bill continue their ascent of the sacred mountain of Sainte Geneviève, they come to the place of the counterscarp, the moat that was part of the ancient walled fortifications of Paris. As is often the case, Hemingway's symbolic landscape is layered; to the significations generated by geography and local knowledge, another layer of feeling is added, accessible through the stated details of the text. Light arcs through the square, music sounds from the Nègre Joyeux (the "Joyful Negro," resonating with the image of the exemplary black boxer earlier in the chapter), and at the café called Amateurs the kitchen is *open,* there is a pot of stew, and the girl (one of those "amateurs" who do things not for money but from love) serves an old man, perhaps a *clochard* (or tramp), a plate of stew. The places named in this scene were *actual* places, but it is hard not to read the selected details as part of a carefully rendered *symbolic* landscape.

78:6–7 **Rue Saint Jacques:** After Jake and Bill watch the old man receiving his nourishment from the iron pot, they decide against having a drink and continue their walk, turning right off the square. The street geography here is tricky, and not everyone has agreed regarding the exact route followed. A comparison of this paragraph with the original manuscript version reveals some initial confusion on Hemingway's part, since there he has Jake and Bill walking past the Panthéon and "cutting along" the rue du Pot-de-Fer to the rue Saint-Jacques, a geographical impossibility without considerable out-of-the-way walking and backtracking. Hemingway knew this neighborhood well, having lived at 74, rue du Cardinal-Lemoine, just off the place de la Contrescarpe for the greater part of two years (1922–1923); but, as I can testify, having lived in this neighborhood, it is difficult to remember the directional crazy quilt of short, narrow streets running at all angles, with street names changing every block or two. Yet since there is no textual indication that Jake and Bill are lost or confused about direction, and since Jake at least knows exactly where he is going (to Montparnasse via the rue Saint-Jacques), and he lives in this district, it seems clear that Hemingway, still in the south of France, far away from a neighborhood that has one of the most tangled networks of small streets in Paris, wrote the manuscript passage quickly, knowing that after his return to Paris he could revise and get it right. But he knew, even in his first draft—and this knowledge provides insight into his creative process—that he wanted the rue du Pot-de-Fer and the rue Saint-Jacques in this passage. The rue du Pot-de-Fer had to be there because the "Street of the Iron Pot" provided an echo of hunger being fed from the restaurant's iron pot in the preceding paragraph. And the rue Saint-Jacques was the key to the entire passage, and one of the keys to the entire novel.

The actual walking route, then, given the stated fact that they turn right off the square, seems to be right on rue Blainville; left on rue Tournefort; right on rue du Pot-de-Fer, which leads into rue Rataud after a short block; right onto rue Erasme; and across the rue d'Ulm to a right on rue Louis Thuillier, which runs in to rue des Ursulines, leading to the turn south (left) on the rue Saint-Jacques. Jake and Bill would walk no more than one block (including some very short blocks) on any of these streets, so, though confusing, it is not a long walk (about six blocks). Another route has been suggested in a guidebook to Hemingway's Paris, following rue Mouffetard out of the square to rue du Pot-de-Fer (thereafter the same), but it is hard to see how, following Hemingway's textual signals, the rue Mouffetard could be construed as a right turn off the square (Fitch 107). Moreover, as Jake indicated earlier, the rue Mouffetard has a cobblestone surface, and the streets they walk along here are "smooth" (25:5). In either case, it would seem that the intervening streets do not signify in this symbolic landscape, and what matters is that if one follows "along" the rue du Pot-de-Fer, not literally but symbolically, the route of the nourishing iron pot will lead to the rue Saint-Jacques, two blocks north of le Val-de-Grâce.

Here we should note that earlier in the novel when Jake went through Contrescarpe in the taxi with Brett, they turned southeast on Mouffetard on the ancient Roman road to Italy, where Jake was wounded in the war, the fact that dictates the tone and terms of the taxi ride. Now Jake takes another direction from the ancient fortifications of the counterscarp—south on the rue Saint-Jacques, the ancient pilgrimage road to Spain, the route that prescribes much of the movement, action, and resolution of the rest of the novel.

It is possible—indeed probable—that Hemingway's sentence here about the rue Saint-Jacques is one of the handful of passages in the novel that the reader must decode and thoroughly understand in order to know what the novel finally tells us. Those other passages would surely include the secret-of-the-values scene with the count (59–61), the *afición* sequence with Montoya (131–32), Jake's bullfight homily for Brett (167–68), Jake's prayer scenes (96–97 and 208–9), and what might be called the "Some people have God" passage of Jake and Brett's final conversation

(245–46). Some of these passages have been recognized by commentators as crucial scenes. But this passage, with its signification of the novel's pilgrimage motif, had been overlooked until my work on the subject began in the 1970s. In Hemingway's revisions between the original manuscript and the published text, he added the characterization of the rue Saint-Jacques as "rigid north and south" as well as the allusion to le Val-de-Grâce, and these changes radically transform the passage. I will quote at length from my 1986 essay on the subject, from the sixtieth anniversary "Special *SAR* Issue" of the *Hemingway Review,* because I would not change anything of substance now, and because I want to transmit here the sense of discovery and how the eurekas of literary criticism and the joys of scholarship may be rooted in something other than library research and may spring from close attention to the particularity of the world around us, to the actual and symbolic landscape in and through which we—and the characters of a novel—move:

> During the course of preparing an essay for the 50th anniversary of *The Sun Also Rises* [in 1976], I became convinced that for half a century we had been missing much of that novel. . . . I will record here the anecdotal and topographical origin of that process of conviction. It was 1974; I was living in Paris, teaching a Faulkner seminar as a Visiting Professor at the University of Paris. (Everyone there seemed to think that Hemingway was passé.) For some time I had been deep in Faulkner studies, having long since dismissed (i.e., misread) much of Hemingway in some of the ways that literary criticism had been dismissing and misreading him for decades. I had not read or thought much about Hemingway for a long time; the last time I had read a novel by Hemingway I was living in northern Michigan, on the edge of Hemingway country [in 1961]. . . . In 1974, as a relief from immersion in Faulkner, and because I was then living among the Parisian scenes Hemingway had rendered so vividly, I reread *The Sun Also Rises*. From the window of my apartment on the rue Saint-Jacques, I looked across to the great heavy dome of *le Val-de-Grâce*. Sitting at my regular café on the corner, I brooded the topography of Jake's itinerary; I was particularly puzzled by Hemingway's description of the rue Saint-Jacques—there, in my winding, medieval neighborhood—as "the rigid north and south of the Rue Saint Jacques" (*SAR* 78). Why would the ostensible master of precision so clearly distort the actual conformation of a street that he knew well?
>
> I raised this question one day in conversation at the café, with a Saint-Jacques autochthon, a life-long denizen of that *quartier*. Yes, he knew of Hemingway; no, he had not read his *romans*. I read to him the "rigid north and south" passage, and he pondered the matter in silence over his calvados. He said nothing that day. The next day . . . he asked: "Do you know of Saint-Jacques de Compostelle?" No, I said, what was that? "Do you know, then, Santiago de Compostela?" . . . I said yes, I had heard of it—it was a place in Spain. "More

than a place, my friend. Come, walk with me." We walked a few blocks down the rue Saint-Jacques. He said I was right, the street is not rigid—it is medieval, it bends. The boulevards, the creations of the 19th century, are rigid. He asked me if I knew that Val-de-Grâce was a hospital for wounded soldiers, that it was a monastery founded by Anne of Austria in thanksgiving for the birth of her son after 21 years of marriage. Yes, I knew that. He pointed out the entrance to the famous Convent of the Carmelites and spoke of the associations with St. Theresa of Avila. He identified . . . [a site where] there had been an important hospice for the pilgrims to Santiago de Compostela. (He was not very religious, he said, but he was much in love with history.) He made some point, which I missed, about the [pilgrimage] church of Saint-Jacques-du-Haut-Pas (my mind was wandering to another high pass [Roncevaux] in the novel). In rapid succession he showed me [many things] . . . where St. Ignace de Loyola had been a student [after he was wounded at Pamplona, what Hemingway called the "wound that made him think"—*Death in the Afternoon* 274] . . . the former site of yet another refuge for the pilgrims of Saint-Jacques. I did not know it then—and of course my neighbor-guide did not know this—but I had just been given a tour of touchstones in Hemingway's life and work. As we walked back toward Val-de-Grâce, he said something like this: "So, you see, we are walking the ancient route of millions of pilgrims. Saint-Jacques—Santiago—is a place and the way that takes you there is part of the place. This famous rue Saint-Jacques is a sign we can no longer interpret of the vast, secret ceremony of our civilization, now lost, in this age. It is—how do you say—a *constatation emblematique* of not alone the history, but the art, the beauty, the feeling, the belief—the very spirit of Western Civilization (he spoke this in uppercase). It is, then, rigid north and south only in the strict light of history, in the suffering and joy of the great *pèlerinage*. Although I have not read him, it seems your Mr. Hemingway knew more history and was perhaps more *Catholique* than most Americans. *Après tout,* he was concerned with much more than the surface of things." Yes, I said, it did seem so. That small lesson in topography and history has led to an unfolding of the numinous sense, the anagogical level of Hemingway's work which has been unceasing, which has brought me, through pilgrimages great and small, back to Hemingway, the Hemingway of the true moveable feast (as the church calendar expresses the matter). It is a pilgrim's feast, with *The Sun Also Rises* holding the center, and there is never any end to it. (Stoneback, "From the Rue Saint-Jacques" 2–4)

It is emblematic of the state of Hemingway studies that even the best early critic (and biographer) of Hemingway, Carlos Baker, completely missed the significance of Jake and Bill's walk as well as many other symbolic landscape details in the novel. This is all the more curious since Baker was particularly alert to literary landscape, albeit in the rather old-fashioned conventional sense suggested, for example, by his well-known reading of *A Farewell to Arms* in terms of the symbolism of "The Mountain and the Plain" (*Writer as Artist* 94–116). Remarkably, Baker writes this regarding Jake and Bill's walk from l'île Saint-Louis to the rue Saint-Jacques: "Sometimes . . . the facts seem too many for the effect apparently intended, though even here the reader should be on guard against misconstruing the intention of a given passage." In spite of such admonitions, Baker lets his guard down when he argues that it is "hard to discover, nevertheless, what purpose beyond the establishment of the sense of place is served by Barnes's complete itinerary . . . the walk fills only two pages [actually less than one-and-a-half pages]. Yet it seems much longer and does not further the action appreciably except to provide Jake and Bill with healthy after-dinner exercise" (52). Some readers, it should be noted, wish the walk were longer, or more detailed; and how odd it is that one of the leading Hemingway critics would miss completely the significance of the circling of the island, the viewing of Notre-Dame, and the following of the pilgrimage route, finding all of it nothing more than mere "after-dinner exercise." Baker even laments Hemingway's inclusion (one short sentence) of the meal Jake and Bill eat at Madame Lecomte's, and he concludes that "the inclusion of so many of the facts of municipal or gastronomic geography—so many more than are justified by their dramatic purpose—may seem excessive" (52). But of course he has completely missed the dramatic purpose and the very existence of Hemingway's symbolic geography. Although all serious students of Hemingway are indebted to Baker's important early work on Hemingway, it is clear that he did not apprehend Hemingway's method of rendering *paysage moralisé*, his unique version of modernist landscape principles, the deep structure and form of his oblique, understated, and layered symbolic landscapes constructed under the rubric of the writerly iceberg. James Joyce, another high priest of modernism, recognized his fellow modernist's intricate formal method; "there is much more," Joyce said, "behind Hemingway's form than people know" (Ellmann 708).

In sum, then, Jake and Bill are following the "rigid," undeviating historic pilgrimage route of Saint Jacques de Compostelle, the rue Saint-Jacques, on which millions of pilgrims for more than a thousand years have left Paris, headed south toward Spain and Santiago de Compostela. This brief allusion, this structural clue carefully provided by Hemingway in revision, foreshadows the fact that in a few days (and six pages later) they will leave Paris, following that route through Tours to Bayonne on a train full of pilgrims, and then on to Burguete, Roncevaux, and as far as Pamplona—every place they go a landmark on the pilgrimage route. It is thus most apt that Jake, who, as we learned early in the novel, has "a hell of a biblical name" (22), takes his last significant walk in Paris on the rue Saint-Jacques, the ancient pilgrimage route south, for, as his name also reminds us, he is a *Jacquet* (the French name for a Saint James/Santiago pilgrim) who follows much of the pilgrim's route described in the *Liber Sancti Jacobi*, the famous medieval pilgrim's guide, which may have given Jake his name and primary identity as pilgrim in Hemingway's version of a twentieth-century pilgrimage guide. Jacques, Jake, Jacob—Saint Jacques, Saint James, Sancti Jacobi, Santiago—they are all one and the same name, and Hemingway knew what he was doing when in the manuscript he changed Jake's name from the original "Rafael" (*Facsimile* 1:49). Raphael (meaning "God has healed"), one of the three archangels mentioned in the Bible, would be a curious name for the Jake that we know. Hemingway might have thought he would give too much away with the Raphael allusion to healing in Jake's original name. In any case, since it is his namesake pilgrimage that Jake makes in this novel, and pilgrimage is always about the *process* of healing (rather than the past-tense achieved fact of healing), Jake's naming is as right and revealing as is the naming of Santiago in *The Old Man and the Sea* (a naming that was not an *accident,* as Hemingway reminded some of his friends). The millions of pilgrims who have headed south from Paris on the rue Saint-Jacques will have no trouble interpreting this symbolic landscape.

78:7 **Val de Grâce:** As Jake and Bill walk south on the symbolically "rigid" rue Saint-Jacques, on the ancient Roman road that linked Paris to the rest of the world, on the "winding and picturesque . . . road which in medieval times was the main thoroughfare of the left bank" (Muirhead and Monmarché, *Paris* 159) and was renamed in the thirteenth century to denote its significance as the pilgrimage route, they come to the most striking ensemble of buildings on the street—le Val-de-Grâce—including the famous church, a convent, and a hospital for wounded soldiers, together with museums devoted to the treatment of war wounds. Originally, Val-de-Grâce was the abbey of the Benedictine nuns of Val-Profond, under the patronage of Notre-Dame du Val-de-Grâce; the great domed church was built in 1645–1665. With the Revolution and the suppression of the monasteries, many of the convent buildings became (and remained) a hospital for wounded soldiers. It would be difficult to find a more efficacious emblem for Hemingway's symbolic landscape than le Val-de-Grâce— resonating exactly with Jake's experience, from wounded soldier to pilgrim seeking healing, spiritual grace. This Parisian "Valley of Grace" on the rue Saint-Jacques prefigures Jake's imminent pilgrim passage at Roncevaux or Roncesvalles, the "Valley of Thorns," on the French-Spanish frontier, where Jake (both pilgrim and Fisher King figure) will soon be fishing.

78:17 **Michael:** They turn west off the rue Saint-Jacques on to the boulevard and continue past the usual establishments (noted earlier) to the Café Select, where they meet Mike and Brett. Mike is modeled after Pat Guthrie, a well-known personality of the Montparnasse quarter. One of the best portraits of Pat Guthrie is in the memoirs of James Charters, the famous Montparnasse bartender, who liked Guthrie better than all the other quarterites he knew. Although Charters calls him "Mike," refusing to reveal his real name, he evokes in his chapter "The Sun Also Sinks" a Pat Guthrie who was "lovable" but "quite irresponsible," generous to a fault, and usually broke, who eventually rejected Brett for "an American girl" and after a probable drug binge died of either suicide or an accidental overdose (Charters with Cody 75–80).

78:23 **Bill had gone:** In this second scene since Jake and Brett's last-kiss scene (see 65:3), Brett and Jake ignore each other, making no contact. Bill, still clearly attracted to Brett, ignores Mike and goes right into the bar, where he and Brett continue their flirtation. Jake notes this, as he notices that Brett is stockingless, in the latest sexy Paris fashion of 1925. Throughout the entire scene, Jake and Brett do not speak to each other, except when she sarcastically accuses him of being a poor host, as she turns her eye-wrinkling flirtations from Bill to Mike.

79:1 **a piece:** Since Mike calls Brett "a piece" or "a lovely piece" six times in little over one page, in a scene that is clearly sexually charged, most American readers of the later twentieth century and after are likely to hear what the *American Heritage Dictionary* delicately refers to as "*Vulgar Slang*. A woman regarded as the object of coitus," or what the *OED* calls "U.S. coarse slang—*piece of ass, tail, etc.*" However, since this (according to the *OED*) is an *American* usage that became common around the time of World War II, it is likely that Mike, a Scotsman, is employing the term "piece" in the earlier sense of a "healthy girl"; clearly, Brett (who tells Mike not to be "indecent" only when he suggests they "turn in early") finds nothing "indecent" in his use of the term "piece."

80:8–9 **to the fight:** Of the many revisions—additions and deletions—made to this key chapter, the most substantial revision is the deletion of the six-page manuscript description of the Charles Ledoux–Kid Francis fight, which occurs at this point in the text and concludes the chapter as originally written. It is an extraordinary fight account, one of the best that Hemingway ever wrote, and it could certainly be argued that Hemingway should not have cut the fight sequence.

Ledoux (1892–1967) was much admired by Hemingway, who saw the "Little Apache" fight in 1923, twice in 1924, and on 9 June 1925 witnessed Ledoux's last fight (see 81:1 regarding Hemingway's date change from 9 June to 20 June). Years later, surveying the French boxing scene, Hemingway wrote: "Charles Ledoux was very popular in America and was a great little fighter; one of the best in-fighters that I have ever seen, but his career was interrupted by the war" (*By-Line* 135). Barely over five feet tall, Ledoux fought most of his career as a bantamweight, with some fights in the heavier featherweight division. He held both the World Bantamweight Championship and the European Featherweight Crown; in a career that (even though interrupted by four years of World War I service) included 133 fights, he won 98 (81 by knockouts), lost 23, and fought 6 draws. Considered one of the great French fighters, Ledoux is ranked by *Boxing Illustrated* as the fifth-hardest puncher, pound for pound, in boxing history. Ledoux's opponent on 9 June 1925, Kid Francis, was a young fighter on the rise, a future bantamweight champion who at age eighteen had already compiled an extraordinary record of 38-1-1. Boxing archives give his real name as Francesco Buonagurio and his nationality as Italian, although Hemingway in his 1934 *Esquire* essay, "A Paris Letter," identified Francis, "who fought in the States as an Italian," as a "French featherweight from Marseilles" and ranked him as a fighter in the same class as Ledoux (*By-Line* 135).

In the manuscript version of this chapter's closing scene, Jake and Bill leave Mike and Brett and take a taxi to the Cirque de Paris, where the main bout, the Ledoux-Francis match, is already in progress. They get ringside seats ("Billet de Faveur"—unclaimed complimentary seats for which they pay dearly) and enter the dazzling light of the arena, where everyone is shouting and the action in the ring is intense. Kid Francis, the "tall dark youth," batters the old champion, but Ledoux never quits, "going forward always, ducking, and swaying his head with the punches," until he "pinned the tall dark boy against the ropes and . . . swung with both his hands into the other's body. One two three four, one two three four, one two three four he swung" until the boy slips sideways into the open ring, where Ledoux marches "slowly forward, his eyes on the other's feet, his face covered with blood" (*Facsimile* 1:230–31). The crowd goes crazy, Bill is hoarse, and Jake loses his voice from shouting. "My God," Jake says after one round, "think of missing that." Bill agrees: "We might have missed it all." "My God," Jake says again. "What fools people are." By the final round, Ledoux looks "almost through," but he keeps going after the Kid, "the same look on his face and the same wonderful two handed rallies when he got close . . . ducking and slipping the Kid's returns," swinging with "both his wet soaked gloves." They fight the last round in the center of the ring, neither of them moving back an inch. When the final gong sounds, Jake notes Ledoux's wife rushing to the ring, and Ledoux wiping his face and lips with a towel; then he "leaned down through the ropes and kissed her." "By God she must feel good," Bill says (*Facsimile* 1:231–32). It is an extraordinary portrayal of a great champion's final fight, and the last detail—that kiss through the ropes—underlines the emptiness of the sex-and-booze-driven world of Brett and Mike that Jake and Bill left behind to see the fight, just as that kiss resonates with Jake's final kiss with Brett that ended the preceding chapter.

Jake and Bill leave the Cirque de Paris before the decision is announced—in fact, Francis won on points, although Hemingway never tells his reader this, since Ledoux comes across as the real winner, the true champion. They also leave because there is another fight to follow, and they don't want to "spoil" what they've just witnessed "with a bum one." (Boxing history indicates they were right to leave, since the next fight that night was between two fledgling untested lightweights; Jules Alverel—career record 5-6-1—defeated Harry Corbett—career record 14-20-6.) They leave the arena, talking about how big these five-foot bantamweights look in the ring; they walk along the Champ de Mars—thus back in Hemingway's symbolic landscape—the historic warrior's parade ground in front of the École militaire and "under the shadowy steel of the Eiffel Tour" (then the tallest man-made structure in the world, thus imparting by juxtapositional minimalism a towering stature to Ledoux). As they do so, Bill says: "By God Ledoux is great. Funny how a guy like that can get to you." Jake agrees, saying that he'd seen Ledoux "when he used to be just a hard hitter and then he lost his punch and he was a great boxer and now all he's got is just that he knows everything. Nothing left but his *métier*," to which Bill adds: "And his guts" (*Facsimile* 1:232–34). Clearly, in cutting this scene Hemingway discarded one of his most compelling exemplar figures: Ledoux, the aging ex-champion who has been the "hard hitter," then the "great boxer," and is now the old master of his métier who "knows everything" and still has "his guts." Ledoux, who, although he loses this, his last fight (a fact Hemingway refuses to mention), is clearly in Hemingway's eyes the real winner, might well seem a more engaging and powerful exemplar than Count Mippipopolous and Montoya, than even the "kid" bullfighter Pedro Romero. Why then did Hemingway discard this fight scene?

Hemingway criticism has largely ignored the entire matter. Frederic Svoboda, however, cogently argues that Hemingway wisely cut the scene in keeping with his overall principles of selection and tight organization of the novel. In his revisions, Svoboda observes, "Hemingway carefully developed the novel's bullfight scenes while cutting the similarly exciting and immediate description of the Ledoux-Kid Francis prize fight"; he recognized that although "the prize fight worked thematically in much the same way as the bullfights . . . it contributed little else to the overall structure of the novel" (*Crafting of a Style* 114). In direct opposition to this view, William Balassi has argued that "it is to be regretted that Hemingway chose not to include" the fight scene. Noting the evidence from a manuscript fragment of Hemingway's decision that the fight "was not part of the story," Balassi argues that it *is* indeed a part of the story, especially since Ledoux serves as yet another exemplar, another "role model" for Jake, in terms of how to live well and "keep fighting even after he has 'lost his punch'" ("How It Probably Was" 142–43). Contrary as these critical views may be, I am inclined to agree in part with both of them, especially if the implications of their arguments are extended somewhat.

On one hand, if the fight scene were included, it would provide a powerful capstone—perhaps too powerful—to what amounts to the novel's boxing subtext, which begins on the first page with the account of Robert Cohn's boxing career. In chapter 8 alone, if the exemplary depiction of Ledoux were retained, there would be three separate admirable boxers (Ledoux, Tiger Flowers, and the unnamed boxer from Cologne identified in the manuscript as both "Larry" and William Tate); in a key chapter that sets up the movement to Spain, to the fiesta and the bullfight, this might indeed seem to detract from the paramount importance of the bullfight. Moreover, the example of the aging ex-champion who takes a beating from the "kid" might seem—as image pattern, as *constatation emblematique*—to work at cross-purposes with the novel's last fight, when Cohn the veteran, aging yet still aggressive (and antiexemplary) boxer, who is roughly the same age as Ledoux, ingloriously batters the "kid," Romero, who refuses to quit. It might also be argued that the magnificent Ledoux-Francis fight scene, in its privileged chapter-ending position, would deflect attention from other primary themes treated in this chapter, such as the Brett-Jake relationship and, more important, the symbolic landscape and the first major presentation of the pilgrimage theme.

On the other hand, the loss of Ledoux as exemplar is to be regretted because he would (being roughly Jake's age, or "middle-aged"), with the "kid" Romero and the older wise count, round out a perfect trinity of exemplars of all ages who know how to live life "all the way up," who perform with "grace under pressure." Moreover, Ledoux—or Le Doux, meaning the gentle (mild, mellow, pleasant) one—would reinforce the "noble" and "wonderful" qualities of the unnamed married black boxer from Cologne and Tiger Flowers, the fighter preacher, as well as the domestic tenderness (see Ledoux's kiss) that can coexist with a great fighting spirit. And this would, happily, help to dispel some of the confusion that pervades certain segments of Hemingway's readership about so-called macho activities in a world of wanton violence. Even the loss of the Kid Francis allusions might be regretted, for they might seem to reverberate with Frances's "kidding" of Robert Cohn, with Robert as Frances's "kid" (both adolescent and scapegoat). More important, far from detracting from primary themes, if the fight scene concluded this chapter it would properly deemphasize Brett's world of lust and promiscuity, and it would show Jake beginning his pilgrimage south sustained by an image of a fighting spirit, an indomitable heart.

And there is an even more important reason why we might wish the Ledoux fight had not been cut in revision. It seems to have evaded the notice of all Hemingway biographers and critics that during his composition of *The Sun Also Rises* Hemingway discussed religion and philosophy with the philosopher Ralph Withington Church. Church had recently published *The Essence of Catholicism* (1924) and would later publish six volumes of philosophical studies. In his unpublished memoirs, Church recalled Hemingway speaking about his forthcoming novel as a "pilgrimage to Pamplona." From their discussions it was evident to Church that "Hemingway was deeply interested in the problem of redemption" and held a deep "conviction that Sport . . . afforded a major way to the redemption of man" (Stoneback, "Holy Cross 33–Yale 6" 14–15). While it has sometimes been argued that sport is a kind of substitute for religion in Hemingway, it is more accurate to say that Hemingway's religion subsumes sport, that he consistently deploys the ritual significance of sport—bullfighting (if readers insist, as many do but should not do, on considering it a sport), fishing, boxing—as *convergence* and *confirmation* of the ritual and sacramental vision of his Church. Ledoux's fight is about redemption. Bloodied but unbeaten—even though he loses his last fight to the Kid—Ledoux is victorious. He is victorious in much the same fashion as is another Hemingway character in a short story (or playlet) written during the revision of *The Sun Also Rises*. In *Today Is Friday,* Hemingway characterizes Christ on the Cross, very much as if he were an athlete, with the repeated phrase "He was pretty good in there today." Ledoux was pretty good in there too. Even the most exact and careful writers do not revise ex cathedra; no matter how they have mastered their métier, their revisions are not infallible. That is the final argument *for* retaining the Ledoux fight scene. The final argument *against* including the Ledoux fight scene is rooted in Hemingway's writerly iceberg axiom—the fight *is* still there, beneath the surface; it is alluded to, and thus, as with many other things that are briefly noted in his symbolic landscape, it might be expected that the reader will find out more about it. "Things may not be immediately discernible in what a man writes," Hemingway said in his Nobel Prize address, "but eventually they are quite clear" (Bruccoli 196).

CHAPTER 9

81:1 **20th of June:** As noted in the preceding entry, the actual date of the Ledoux-Kid Francis fight was the night of 9 June. Many Hemingway commentators have addressed the matter of conflicting calendars and inaccurate chronology in the novel, not always with clear principles of aesthetic structure informing their concerns about mere reportorial accuracy. What does it matter that Hemingway moved the date of the fight forward by eleven days? Who would notice, except a few boxing fans with exact calendrical recall? A far more obvious date alteration occurs in chapter 12, where Jake and Bill discuss the death of William Jennings Bryan just after the end of the Scopes trial. The trial, and Bryan's sudden death, amounted to the biggest news story of 1925, and yet Jake and Bill, fishing in late June, discuss Bryan's death, which did not occur until 26 July 1925 (121:22). A contemporary reader, in late 1926, say, might notice that the date was off by a month, although it would hardly affect the thematic thrust of the passage. It would be a most rare reader who would notice eighty years later (in 2006) that deliberately altered date. Even students of history rather than fiction tend to remember the *seasons* of memorable events, not the precise *dates* (unless, like Pearl Harbor Day, the remembrance is tied to the date). And who can give the precise calendrical sequence of any favorite novel? Chronological exactitude is not generally a primary concern of novelists.

Indeed, to judge from the response of students to whom I have taught this novel, who (with rare exceptions) are blissfully unaware of or untroubled by any problem with dates, too much has been made of the calendar conflicts in the novel. Some commentators have even argued that Hemingway is basing the story on his actual journey to Pamplona in 1923 or 1924, contrary to the usual assumption that the novel follows *some* of the events of 1925. Others have argued that Hemingway is composing an intricate composite of several years of experience, or even that he is confused about what happened in what year, and thus the novel's chronology is confused. Such arguments are misleading at best, irrelevant and absurd at worst, since Hemingway is not writing a personal travelogue, an autobiographical narrative, but a novel. Hemingway himself calls attention to time or, more exactly, *timelessness,* when, during the fishing interlude, he has Jake wonder what day it is; his fellow fisherman Harris responds that it's "wonderful how one loses track of the days up here in the mountains" (127:1–3). And timelessness is precisely the point—of fishing trips, fiestas, pilgrimages, bullfights, of all the actions of the novel that take characters out of profane time and into *sacred time,* the rituals and ceremonies of timelessness (see Josephs, "*Toreo*" 91–93). Storytelling is another such ceremony.

In any case, Hemingway did not make *mistakes* about the dates of the Ledoux-Francis fight or the date of Bryan's death. The "incorrect" dates would only be errors in the time-bound realm of journalism. Hemingway had just seen the Ledoux-Francis fight shortly before he went to Pamplona in 1925; and he had just started writing the novel in late July 1925 when Bryan died—and he knew that he wanted to use both events in his fiction. He kept the fight allusion, but in response to the needs of storytelling that are much deeper than mere calendrical exactitude, he moved the fight date forward eleven days because he had to keep the story moving, to get Jake and Bill in motion on the pilgrimage south, and away from Brett. (Imagine another eleven days inserted in the novel at this point.) And all date alterations had to be made in relation to the one fixed unchanging date in the novel—6 July, when the Fiesta of San Fermín begins. He needed the Bryan allusions in Jake and Bill's fishing-trip conversation, so he moved his death back a month. All that the Bryan and Ledoux dates really tell us is that the novel takes place in 1925 and Hemingway altered the actual facts to serve fictional ends. (Readers who are concerned with the essentially tertiary matter of the novel's timetable should consult Kermit Vanderbilt's survey of the matter, "*The Sun Also Rises:* Time Uncertain.")

81:3 **Hendaye:** A town (actually two towns—Hendaye and Hendaye-Plage) in the south of France, Hendaye, where Hemingway often stayed and where he wrote part of *The Sun Also Rises,* is the last town before the French-Spanish border. Since it is just up the road from San Sebastián, the Hendaye origin of Cohn's letter should—and probably did (even though he doesn't say so; there is much Jake doesn't *say*)—arouse certain suspicions in Jake regarding who accompanied Brett to San Sebastián. And Robert's deliberately deceptive letter to a friend tells us more about Cohn's antiexemplary behavior.

81:10 **Bayonne:** See 88:25.

81:11 **Pamplona:** See 93:32.

81:14 **at the bar:** The bar is the Dingo Bar (10, rue Delambre in Montparnasse). Although some Hemingway guidebooks point out that Dingo means "Crazy Man" (e.g., Fitch 140), it should be noted that more primary associations are (1) a wild dog; (2) particularly in the 1920s, a contemptuous term for a person who was a cheat, a scoundrel, a traitor; and (3) to betray or let someone down (in verb form, "to dingo on" someone)—as in this scene, where Brett is about to admit her "dingo" identity to Jake and inform him that she has "dingoed on" Jake, cheated or betrayed him with Robert Cohn. We note, too, that in this scene, unlike Jake's two preceding encounters with Brett, she greets him directly and at least offers physical contact—a handshake (see also 36:19).

82:16 **Chantilly:** A small town forty-one kilometers north of Paris, Chantilly is famous for its château, racecourse, and stables (*grandes écuries*). It is the location of the French Derby, the *prix du Jockey-Club* race in June. Since that would be the time, above all others, to be in Chantilly, Hemingway may imply Bill's presence at the race (even if the novel's date scheme suggests it's a little late for that; but, as we have seen, it is the *event,* not the actual *date,* that matters to Hemingway). In any case, through the reference to Chantilly, Hemingway makes yet another reference to sporting activities; originally, in the manuscript, Hemingway placed Bill out at Versailles, famous mainly for its grandiose palace, a place with no sporting associations. Also the change to Chantilly, which is close to Senlis, whose cathedral spire is visible from the château and racecourse, and adjacent to that village called Saint Firmin (after the famous French bishop San Fermín of Pamplona), provides yet another echo of the symbolic landscape sketched by Hemingway in the novel's first chapter (see 6:31 and 7:2). At the southern edge of town, the Forest of Chantilly, aside from its hiking and horse trails, contains what were once royal hunting grounds and the site of the Château de la Reine-Blanche, the small medieval castle belonging to the mother of Saint Louis—Blanche of Navarre.

82:24 **I'll see:** Brett apparently has family connections with Mike's family, and she will see to it that the money gets sent. (Duff Twysden and Pat Guthrie, the models for Brett and Mike, had intertwined family connections; they were, in fact, cousins.)

82:27 **fish:** Brett, of course, chooses not to fish; she could have no part in the redemptive quest of Jake as Fisher King. At this point, however, she still talks as if she—and Mike and Robert—will be part of Jake's pilgrimage to Roncevaux and Burguete. The reader might have some difficulty trying to imagine what things would have been like if Brett, Mike, and Robert had joined Jake and Bill in Burguete (see also 27:20–21).

83:5 **brothel:** Like the earlier Georgette-Brett linkages (see, e.g., 17:26), this serves as another association of Brett with prostitution.

83:15 **Delambre:** Although this is really a short walk, Hemingway sustains and intensifies its duration through repetition—"We walked up," "we walked along" (twice), in sixteen lines—thus foregrounding Brett's announcement as they walk "*up*" the street about with whom she "went *down*" (emphasis added) to San Sebastián. When Brett says she hasn't seen Jake since she got back—she just saw him twice in the last chapter—she means of course that she hasn't been alone with him in their two preceding post–San Sebastián encounters; but her comment also tells us something about her blindness (in several senses of the term).

83:26 **Congratulations:** In the manuscript, after Brett's who-did-you-think announcement, Jake says: "Really? Oh Duff." The revision turns this emotional response into a sublimely sarcastic retort, and (see the two following entries) Hemingway's changes in this scene underline Jake's increasingly ironic detachment from Brett. This sense of a turning point is reinforced by Jake's careful notation that they have "turned a corner," and by the abrupt cessation of this scene juxtaposed with Jake's observation that he did not see Brett again for three days, probably avoiding her until a brief, necessary trip-planning encounter on the eve of his departure (84:10).

83:33 **good for him:** Jake does not forget this, and Brett's words reverberate later; in Pamplona, Jake tells Bill what she said (102:8), and in Madrid Jake tells Brett—after her affair with Romero—that she was "probably damn good for him" (241:30). He is more ironic, more detached, in that final scene of the novel than is generally recognized, an oversight that might be traced to the failure of readers to see the corner turned in this scene, to remember Jake's ironic detachment here.

84:1 **social service:** In the manuscript, Jake's response to Brett's assertion that their fling "was good" for Robert is lame, free from irony. First, Hemingway wrote: "Just as you think best." He lined that out and wrote: "Do what you like" (*Facsimile* 1:240). Carefully gauging the nuances of Jake's feelings about Brett's conduct as he revised this scene, Hemingway came up with this wonderful, memorably ironic career suggestion for Brett to take up social service, defined by the *OED* as "Service to society or to one's fellow-men, esp. as exhibited in work on behalf of . . . the underprivileged." That Hemingway's use of the term "social service" is memorable is underlined by the fact that the *OED* cites this exact passage as an early usage example, one of many *OED* examples drawn from *The Sun Also Rises*.

84:23 **the Montoya:** See 94:9–10.

84:25 **Burguete:** See 108:23.

84:28 **Gare d'Orsay:** Variously misidentified in Hemingway studies as, for example, "one of five Paris Railway stations . . . now a theatre" or as the "Gare d'Orsay . . . on the quai Anatole France" (Balassi, "Glossary" 84:28; Oliver 115), the gare du Quai d'Orsay, on the quai d'Orsay, was one of eleven Paris railway stations in 1925 and was the terminus for all trains of the Orléans line. In 1986 the magnificent Musée d'Orsay opened in the old train station (on a segment of the quai d'Orsay across from the

Tuileries renamed quai Anatole France), and its most important Hemingway association is that the museum now houses the impressionist paintings and particularly the Cézannes that Hemingway had studied in the 1920s when they were in the Musée du Luxembourg.

84:29 **country was beautiful:** Typically, Jake stresses the beauty of the French landscape, one of a number of such passages that readers enthralled by the false France-Spain dichotomy enshrined in Hemingway criticism should note. Contrary to the somewhat feverish and Francophobic view that recurs in Hemingway studies, there is no specifically French "wasteland" in the novel (see 25:2 and passim).

85:12 **first four services:** Because the train is so crowded with pilgrims, there are five rather than the usual two set lunchtimes in the dining car, and the first four servings have been fully booked well in advance for the pilgrims. Behaving rather like ugly Americans, Jake and Bill try to bribe the dining-car conductor for privileged service, and when quite correctly he declines their request, Bill insults him twice. The conductor naturally pockets the ten francs—exacting the toll for the proffered bribe and the insult, and proving, contrary to the view of some commentators, that not everything is for sale in France. Although he probably understands Bill's insults exactly, since he is the dining-car conductor on a train that routinely carries many English-speaking travelers toward the favorite English destination of Biarritz, he only responds with a curt what-did-you-say: "*Comment?*"

85:23 **Americans:** Bill and Jake are recognized immediately as compatriots by their fellow Americans sharing the compartment. The gentleman from Montana and his wife and son, Hubert, play an interesting role in this scene. On one hand, they seem to be presented as a conventional portrait of a middle-American family—the only such non-expatriate Americans depicted in the novel. Their conversational clichés (e.g., "See America first!"), their joking and winking about fishing trips (that have little to do with fishing), and their mildly anti-pilgrim status all seem to define their role as satirical counterpoint to Jake and Bill, pilgrims (at least Jake is) and passionate fishermen. On the other hand, the satire is not as vicious as it is sometimes said to be. Where Jake and Bill ineffectually try to bribe the dining-car conductor to break in line, to secure privileged early seating, the family from Montana simply occupies some seats in the dining car and manages to get served while Jake and Bill eat sandwiches in the compartment. They do not insult the conductor, as Bill does. Probably Protestant, they nevertheless blend in with the Catholic pilgrims in the dining car. They are anti-Prohibition and thus anti-Puritan. And Jake, at least, is very interested by and concerned about Hubert's passion for swimming, which elicits Jake's most extended conversation in the entire scene, as he warns Hubert about the potentially dangerous waters of Biarritz. Given the bathing and baptismal imagery that pervades the novel, and given the fact that Hubert is the only member of this Montana family who is *named*, Hubert may be intended as a presence who reverberates with the implicit presence of Saint Hubert in the first chapter (see 6:19, 6:31, and 7:2). He's "crazy" about the water; he longs for immersion, like the Lourdes pilgrims, whose goal is Saint Bernadette's sacred spring; he *is* traveling "young," and he's seeing France, not America, first. And he's more polite than Bill.

86:1 **Dayton:** Of all the places that the seven cars of pilgrims could be from, Hemingway chooses Dayton, Ohio, as their hometown, thus setting up an intricate place marker and reverberation on the pilgrim and Puritan themes, since the Scopes trial—subject of an extended conversation in chapter 12 (121–22)—took place in Dayton, Tennessee.

86:2–3 **pilgrimage ... Lourdes:** In spite of the pervasive pilgrimage imagery in the novel, this is Hemingway's first and only use of the word "pilgrimage," thus constituting a major clue to the otherwise understated and submerged—in terms of the iceberg structure—pilgrimage motif. These pilgrims have been to Rome, one of the three great *ancient* pilgrimage sites (with Jerusalem and Santiago de Compostela) of Christendom. However, they are not bound for Santiago, but for Lourdes, the great *modern* Catholic pilgrimage site. The contrast of the Lourdes pilgrimage with the Compostelan pilgrimage is instructive: generally, Lourdes is understood to be a pilgrimage made in a meekly petitionary spirit, especially in quest of *physical* healing, while Compostela is associated with a crusading medieval spirit and a rigorous quest for *spiritual* renewal. Pilgrims reach Lourdes on special pilgrimage trains (and buses and chartered planes); pilgrims approach Compostela, by a much longer and more arduous route, on foot (or horseback or bicycle). For Lourdes pilgrims, there is no specified route; the destination *is* the pilgrimage; for Santiago pilgrims, the *way,* the long traditional overland route (via many secondary pilgrimage sites), is as much the raison d'être of the pilgrimage as is the destination. Jake is much more the medieval than the modern pilgrim—although one might think that given his physical infirmity he would go to Lourdes seeking miraculous cure—but he does not even consider the journey to Lourdes.

Some observers have noted the significance of Hemingway's Lourdes allusions. Michael Reynolds, for example, comments on how Frances Clyne's "early remark about Lourdes sets up the word in our mental matrix preparing us" for this usage. "Do that enough times," Reynolds rightly says, "with enough images and a sense of unity is achieved without following traditional structural devices"(*Novel of the Twenties* 40). Bizarrely, however, in his zeal to illustrate what he is pleased to regard as Jake's "nominal" Catholicism, Reynolds also says: "At both Lourdes and the monastery at Roncesvalles ... Jake turns away" (66). Jake, of course, cannot turn away from prayer at Lourdes, because he never gets anywhere near Lourdes. (As for what really happens at Roncesvalles, see 128:16.) With his characteristic sense of the importance of the historical background to Hemingway's fiction—an important advance over much Hemingway criticism—Reynolds observes: "Lourdes was not a strained reference in 1926. During the summer of 1925, when Hemingway was writing the book, thousands of religious pilgrims crowded special trains to Lourdes, for on 14 June of that summer the Pope declared the peasant girl, Marie Bernadette, a saint" (41). Yet if we are to stress the historical background—and we should—then we should get it right. In fact, Reynolds's version of history notwithstanding, Bernadette, Marie Bernarde Soubirous, was *beatified,* declared blessed and worthy of public religious honor by the pope, on 2 June 1925, and *canonized,* declared a saint, in 1933. She was canonized "not because she saw visions [of the Virgin Mary] . . . but because of her total commitment in simplicity, integrity, and trust." However, the "vast pilgrimage movement to Lourdes[,] . . . the greatest in modern Europe," began not at the time of her beatification or canonization but immediately after her visions of the Blessed Virgin in *1858* (Farmer 43). Reynolds implies that the train Jake and Bill are on is a special pilgrim's train, crowded because of Bernadette's recent sainthood (which did not occur until 1933), and that June of 1925 was a particularly crowded pilgrimage season (because of a canonization that would not occur until eight years later). Actually, June has always been one of the slower pilgrimage months, since the principal pilgrimages to Lourdes are in February, March, August, October, and December. In these months there were, long since established by 1925, *trains spéciaux*—special trains for Lourdes pilgrims—and, in August, the Paris-Lourdes *train blanc* for seriously ill pilgrims (Monmarché 185–87). Clearly, Jake and Bill are not on a special pilgrim train, just a regularly scheduled train that happens to have an unusual number of pilgrims for the low pilgrimage season. Finally, there is the curiously low and wildly inaccurate number of pilgrims given by Reynolds—mere "thousands"—in the summer of 1925 (a pilgrimage season he seems to regard as unusually busy). All the pre-1925 sources agree that from 1870 on, an average of 600,000 pilgrims went to Lourdes each year, and in some pilgrimage seasons more than a million pilgrims per year made the journey. The 1907 Baedeker, for example, notes that in 1903, during the high pilgrimage season from mid-August to mid-September, in one month "there arrived in Lourdes 132 trains of 80,000 pilgrims in all" (*Southern France* 128). Reynolds's strangely low statement of the number of pilgrims notwithstanding, Hemingway knows better; he knows the vast numbers involved in the most important *modern* Catholic pilgrimage, and it is only against that background knowledge that we can truly understand Jake's identity as a Compostelan pilgrim. The long neglected *medieval* pilgrimage in decline since the Reformation, the pilgrimage of Santiago de Compostela, experienced a sudden resurgence and popularity in the late twentieth century, but Hemingway was there—in the 1920s—long before celebrities like Shirley MacLaine were in the 1990s (see also 51:8–9).

86:4 **Pilgrims . . . Puritans:** Bill, ever the humorist, deliberately mixes up Catholic pilgrims with Protestant Puritans and extends the joke later in the conversation when he calls the Lourdes pilgrims a "gang of Pilgrim Fathers" (86:21). Of course, nothing could be further apart than the clichéd grim gray gang of Protestant New England–style Thanksgiving pilgrims (i.e., Puritans) and a train filled with Catholic pilgrims in France. American Puritanism, understood generally as hostility to social and cultural pleasures, was of course a subject of derision among American writers such as H. L. Mencken and Van Wyck Brooks. Even more so, among European writers, America was often dismissed as the Puritan Republic of the West, a dreary life-denying place. The perfect symbol of Puritanism in the 1920s was Prohibition. For many observers, it was unthinkable that an entire nation would actually outlaw one of the oldest human pleasures. Yet Jake and Bill, far from agreeing with attacks on Puritanism by the likes of Mencken, find Mencken and his ilk's anti-Puritanism—their missionary monkey-puritanism, as both Jake and Bill characterize it in a deleted manuscript passage—more offensive than the so-called Puritanism that they attack (see 122:18).

86:30 **wagon:** *Wagon-restaurant* is French for "dining car." Hemingway properly hyphenated it in the manuscript. *Wagon* means "carriage," or "railway car," in French—as in *wagon-lit* ("sleeping car") and *wagon-fumeurs* ("smoking car").

87:13 **fields . . . of poppies:** Again, Hemingway stresses the beauty and fertility of the French landscape. This passage was carefully revised between the manuscript and published versions; in the manuscript Hemingway inserted the sentence about the ripening grain and the fields of poppies, thus creating a tension between fertility and war, since poppies are the flower of remembrance, the memorial emblem of fallen soldiers. The common poppy (not the opium poppy) is a hardy survivor, the seeds of which can be dormant for a long time and then explode in blood-red profusion, as they do on French roadsides, in ploughed fields, and in battlefields. After the Battle of Waterloo, the poppies that covered the battlefield "were said to have sprung from the blood of the troops" who had fallen there (Vickery 288). In World War I at the Battle of Ypres in Flanders, the Germans used poison gas, and thousands died, an event witnessed by an army doctor and poet named John McRae, who penned the famous poem "In Flanders Fields" in 1915. The poem evokes the poppies that suddenly bloomed shortly after the horrible battle, covering the ravaged battlefield with fields full of red poppies. McRae wrote: "We shall not sleep, though poppies grow / In Flanders fields" (Darwin 326). After the war, the poppy became the symbol of remembrance, memorializing the dead and wounded warriors. Jake knows all too well the tension between the fertile green pasture, the river (the Loire), and the ripening grain, and the memory of horror evoked by the poppies—and he still has trouble sleeping.

87:16 **Tours:** A historic city on the Loire River, former capital of the Touraine, and principal city of the department of Indre-et-Loire, Tours is some 220 kilometers southwest of Paris. Tours is celebrated as the city of Saint Martin, bishop of Tours from 372 to 397. His extraordinary popularity in France is reflected in the fact that five hundred villages and four thousand parish churches are dedicated to him. After his death, his cult spread rapidly and widely, and his tomb in Tours became the principal pilgrimage place of the Franks. He died on 11 November, and the spell of fine November weather that sometimes occurs around his feast day is known in Europe as Saint Martin's summer. Between the field of poppies outside Tours and Saint Martin's tomb, 11 November—originally known as Armistice Day to commemorate the end of World War I—is a date that might well cross Jake's mind here in this symbolic landscape. Tours was long a major way station on the pilgrimage route of Saint-Jacques-de-Compostelle (Santiago de Compostela). It is also historically significant for the Battle of Tours, at which the Saracen invasions of Christian territory were repulsed by Charles Martel in 732 (cf. Roncesvalles/Roncevaux; see 108:26).

87:19 **swimming . . . Hubert:** See 85:23.

87:29 **snappers:** Hemingway originally (in the manuscript) had written "Knights of Columbus," which he later changed to "snappers," slang for Catholics (short for "mackerel snappers," or fish eaters). Also, at first, it was Bill who said he was Catholic, but Hemingway shifted to Jake the "I am" assertion of Catholicism, in response to the Montana man's statement about "the power of the Catholic Church."

88:2 **rather difficult:** Jake acknowledges Bill's continuing rudeness (see 85:12 and 85:23), now getting out of hand, and crossing lines that Jake feels should not be crossed, especially in his remark about the Klan (88:6).

88:3 **streams of pilgrims:** Since the Lourdes pilgrimage is centered on the miraculous healing waters of Lourdes, it is apt that Hemingway employs water imagery in describing the *streams* of pilgrims. When Bill buttonholes (or accosts) the priest, he identifies himself (perhaps jokingly) as a Protestant. It might be noted that in the manuscript Hemingway properly used the uppercase spelling of "Father" in addressing the priest, but the capital *F* disappeared in the process of publication (88:4).

88:6 **Klan:** The Ku Klux Klan was originally a post–Civil War secret society in the South organized to reassert white supremacy after the war. Having largely died out before World War I, the so-called Second Klan experienced a great resurgence after World War I, especially in the Midwest, with a reconstituted anti-immigration (or nativist), anti-Catholic, and anti-Semitic focus. Klan membership soared to about four million in 1920; by 1930 that number had declined to about 30,000. Chicago had the largest number of Klan members; although Bill is from Chicago and asserts his Protestantism, he hardly seems ideal Klan material. Yet his Klan threat or insult directed at the priest, in a period of extreme anti-Catholicism, is not funny, for the priest, for Jake the Catholic, or for the reader. Jake notes that Bill is being "rather difficult" (88:2); the priest says nothing but gives Bill a significant look.

88:9 **table d'hôte:** The standard French term (also employed as a naturalized term in English) means literally "the host's table" and signifies a set meal with a fixed menu and price (*prix fixe*).

88:10 **purple:** Jake and Bill joke about why the waiter's jacket is purple under the arms; drinking too much wine or wearing purple undershirts serve as humorous explanations, but the joking might lead the reader to try to figure out exactly what did make the waiter's jacket purple. Perhaps wine has spilled (quite probable in a railroad dining car), and the waiter has cleaned it up with napkins and put the wine-soaked cloths momentarily under his arms; or perhaps he carries an order pad with the usual purplish carbon copy sheets, and while carrying things to and from his tables he has put the pad under his arms repeatedly, thus staining his white jacket. Or maybe there is a buried joke reverberating from this passage: (1) In the next line they enter Bordeaux, world wine capital; (2) Three lines after the purple guessing game ends, they enter the Landes and watch what is likely to be a purple-tinged sunset and look at distant hills, which probably appear, as far-off hills at sunset often do, purple shadowed; (3) A few lines later they are met by Robert Cohn. Thus the waiter's wine stains lead the narrative flow through the purple Landes to the waiting Robert Cohn, and the reader is subliminally reminded that Cohn was earlier summed up in terms of his romantic infatuation with Hudson's *The Purple Land* (see 9:9).

It might also be noted that these four spoken lines about the wine stains carry no dialogue speaker-identification tags, a characteristic Hemingway device that forces the reader to pay closer attention to who says what. Here the device forces the recognition that Bill speaks the first and third lines, Jake the second and fourth lines, and that it is Jake who doesn't want to carry joking too far again, Jake who is considerate of the tired waiter's exhaustion and feelings.

88:15 **Bordeaux:** In 1925, Bordeaux was the fourth-largest city in France and, after Marseille and le Havre, the third most important port, and the center of the French wine trade. An ancient Roman city, it was already famous for its wines in the first century. With the arrival of the Visigoths, wine making and trading declined, but as one authority notes, "Luckily Christianity had arrived first, and . . . it was the Church that preserved a vestige of the old learning and saved the culture of the vine" (Lichine 112). Since their train stops for only half an hour at the Gare Saint-

Jean (or du Midi) on the southern edge of Bordeaux, they do not have time for the long walk into the city center, so they take a short walk in what must have been the quarter surrounding the tenth-century church of Sainte-Croix; and they would be aware of their presence in a place famous for the ancient vineyards surrounding the city, for bullfights, for its importance as a major way station for Compostelan pilgrims, and for its contemporary identity as the seat of the French government when the Germans threatened Paris during World War I and the place—marked by a monument—where the first American troops to participate in the Great War landed in June 1917. Hemingway himself had landed there on a troop ship in the spring of 1918 and before going on to Paris and the battlefields of Italy had "gorged" himself with "red wine and French cooking" (Baker, *Life Story* 40). Later in the novel, in Bayonne, Jake enjoys a bottle of Château Margaux, one of the world's greatest wines, from the vineyards just north of Bordeaux (see 232:31).

88:17 **the Landes:** Some Hemingway commentary to the contrary, the Landes is anything but a wasteland, and the French word *landes* does not exactly mean wastelands, in the general English language sense of a desolate, barren, or ravaged land, or symbolically, a spiritually or culturally barren or hopeless place (see Balassi, "Glossary" 88:17). Given the connotations of "wasteland" in English, especially since T. S. Eliot's immensely influential 1922 poem (*The Waste Land*), *lande,* the dictionary translation of which is sandy moor or heath, would better be avoided as a translation of "wasteland"; if one were indicating a rural wasteland, *terre à l'abandon* would be used, or, for urban wasteland, *terrain vague.* The Landes is the name of a region, a vast, sandy pine-forested plain stretching from outside Bordeaux, where the vineyards give way to sandy pinewoods, to near Bayonne—bounded by the Atlantic Ocean and the valleys of the Garonne and Adour rivers. Pine forests were planted beginning in the 1700s to halt the advance of windblown sand; spectacular sand dunes rise more than sixty meters in places. As Hemingway writes, it is "sandy pine country full of heather," hauntingly beautiful. There are also stretches of oak and cork-oak woods, and interspersed among the forests, extensive sheep pasturage. While there is no substantial farming in the Landes due to the soil quality, the region has commercial importance for its timber and for the production of resin (the pine trees are tapped). The Landes is also celebrated for its hunting, especially duck shooting in its lagoons, and for bullfighting—in the *Courses Landaises,* where, like the *Courses Camarguaises,* the bull lives to fight again; the bull is the hero.

In this landscape paragraph, Jake observes the country closely, as always. Here he moves through an intensity of *looking, seeing, watching* ("watched the country") into a state of *feeling* ("we could feel the country") that connects with the spirit of place. Far from being evocative of a wasteland, this passage is a charged composition of place, of *country* (a word here repeated three times in four sentences), that once again foregrounds the beauty and diversity of the French landscape, as well as the *strangeness* of all country, especially as seen from a passing train window (see also, for example, Hemingway's story "The Porter," *Complete Short Stories* 571–78). As 1920s guidebooks put it, the Landes made a profound and poetic impression on the traveler.

88:25 **Bayonne:** An important port city of southwestern France, Bayonne is located at the confluence of the Adour and Nive rivers, about seven kilometers from the Golfe de Gascogne and the Atlantic Ocean. Picturesque and historic, Bayonne was an important port under the Roman Empire; it flourished in the Middle Ages under English rule from 1154 to 1451 and firmly resisted Spanish incursions in the sixteenth century, when the French made major improvements to the port and strengthened the city's fortifications, an ongoing process that included major seventeenth-century installations by Vauban, the great French military architect. These works continued into the nineteenth century, when the ramparts and citadel assumed their present appearance, unchanged from when Jake and Bill visit the town in 1925. In the 1920s, the population was about 28,000, a mix of French citizens of Béarnaise origin with some French Basques (although most lived south of Bayonne), as well as some Spanish immigrants (Monmarché 58). An important way station on the pilgrimage of Saint-Jacques-de-Compostelle, Bayonne is well known to travelers for its cathedral, its fortifications, its strategic location for excursions into the French Basque country, and its bullfights. It also gives its name to the bayonet, said to have been invented in Bayonne and first used in combat by French Basque troops in sixteenth- and seventeenth-century French-Spanish frontier skirmishes. As symbolic landscape, then, Bayonne evokes war, pilgrimage, bullfights, and frontiers—all primary concerns of Hemingway (and Jake).

88:27 **LaNegresse:** Present in its correct form in Hemingway's manuscript (without the accent mark), this is a typo (introduced in the process of publication) for la Négresse, the station just outside Biarritz.

89:6–7 **near-sighted:** Robert Cohn has trouble *seeing* clearly, a literal fact Jake says he hasn't noticed before and that places Robert in terms of the novel's vision imagery. Of course, Jake has noticed from the outset Robert's metaphorical vision problem.

89:12 **dark bridge:** They get off the train at the Gare du Midi, in the suburban Faubourg Saint-Esprit on the right bank of the Adour, and take the cab across the pont Saint-Esprit, the dark bridge over the Adour, to their hotel in the city center.

89:17 **nice hotel:** This is the same hotel where Jake stays again, after the fiesta, when he identifies it as the "Hotel Panier Fleuri" (232:4). The Hôtel du Panier Fleuri ("1st category," forty rooms) was at 3, rue du Port-Neuf, in the heart of the old town just down the street from the cathedral. Jake stresses that it's nice, the room is good, and the reception is "very cheerful." Given the proximity to the border, and Jake's later meditation on border crossings (see 232–33), the image of the hotel might be taken as Hemingway's deeply embedded formula for French hotels near border crossings: in his 1927 story "Che Ti Dice la Patria," Hemingway ends the tale with the safe arrival in France—after much unpleasantness in Italy; his characters get a hotel room in Menton, just across the border into France, and it is all "very cheerful and clean and sane and lovely" (*Complete Short Stories* 230; see also Stoneback, "Very Cheerful," passim).

CHAPTER 10

90:3 **very clean:** This early-morning scene, like the "pleasant early-morning feeling" in Paris (35:4) and in San Sebastián (234:3), stresses the "bright," "nice" morning feeling of Bayonne, a French city that is either like a Spanish town, only "very clean," or like certain "very clean" Spanish towns (e.g., San Sebastián)—or both. The morning flavor of Bayonne echoes the cheerful, good, nice qualities of the hotel the night before (89:17), as the sunrise echoes the sunset in the Landes the previous evening (88:18). The "dark bridge" of the night before is now the bright bridge of morning, the bridge of the Holy Spirit—the pont Saint-Esprit—crossing the Adour (which may suggest "adore," or worship), the river that rises in the high Pyrenees near Lourdes and flows into the sea just beyond Bayonne. The repetitive emphases on the bridge and the "big river," about to run into the sea, together with the newly washed streets, resonate with the sun-also-rises and rivers-running-to-the-sea mood reflected in the novel's title and the Ecclesiastes epigraph. In the following two paragraphs they buy fishing gear before they go to the cathedral—symbolic landscape indeed.

90:3 **big river:** Actually, Bayonne is on two rivers, the Adour and the smaller Nive, which flows through the city, dividing Petit Bayonne from Grand Bayonne, and runs into the Adour in the heart of town, just west of the pont Saint-Esprit. The Nive also rises in the Pyrenees, one branch just north of the Pass of Roland above Roncevaux, the other branch on the French side of the border near the Irati Forest.

90:13 **cathedral:** Originally Notre-Dame de Bayonne, the cathedral was renamed the Cathédrale Sainte-Marie early in the twentieth century. It was founded in 1140, and after a fire, rebuilding commenced in 1213 and continued into the nineteenth century, when the spires were added to the towers in 1875. Since the cathedral is regarded as one of the finest examples in southern France of the northern Gothic style, Cohn's guidebook remark about it being a good "example of something or other" probably refers to this fact—"du style ogival septentrional," as one 1920s guide has it (Monmarché 60). Jake's response, however, has to do with *feeling,* not guidebook facts; as a Catholic pilgrim and believer, he responds emotionally to the "nice cathedral, nice and dim." He is also surely aware of the cathedral's pilgrimage associations, and of the fact that the equally "dim" cathedral of Sainte-Marie in Pamplona—where he will pray six pages later—conceals behind its "cold, classical façade" from 1783 a fine "austere Gothic" fifteenth-century interior "inspired by the Cathedral of Bayonne" (Muirhead, *Northern Spain* 16; Ayuntamiento de Pamplona 22). We note also that in the manuscript Hemingway wrote: "took a look in the cathedral," and looking *in* is more exact than looking *at,* as the published text has it.

90:16 **Syndicat d'Initiative:** This is the tourist office.

91:5 **café on the square:** This refers to one of the several cafés on the place de la Liberté, the "liveliest open space of Bayonne" with excellent cafés, according to the 1926 Blue Guide (Muirhead and Monmarché, *Southern France* 345). This square is the heart of town, at the confluence of the Adour and the Nive rivers. Their hotel is just up the "busy Rue du Port-Neuf, whose low-pitched arcades shelter the best shops in Bayonne" (345). Again, Jake stresses the "cool, fresh, early-morning smell," and how "pleasant" it is to sit in the café and feel the sea air and the sun and watch the pigeons and the "sun-baked" houses, thus reiterating the earlier sun-sea-river-morning imagery used to evoke the Bayonne landscape (90:3). Like everyone who knows the joy of lingering in a French café, Jake does not want to leave.

91:11 **the bill:** According to the guidebooks, rooms at the Panier Fleuri, one of the best hotels in Bayonne, had increased from two-and-a half francs in 1907 to ten francs in 1926 (plus *taxe de séjour*), but we note that in 1926 the rooms still cost less than one dollar each.

91:15–16 **waiting . . . cockroach:** Three times Jake emphasizes the wait for Cohn until he "finally" comes. While they wait, a cockroach comes in "from the garden," in spite of the fact that it is "really an awfully clean hotel." Maybe there's always a cockroach in the garden. The juxtaposition of Cohn with the cockroach seems more than incidental, and who could blame Jake for wanting to do to Cohn what he does to the cockroach?

91:22 **back of the car down:** They hire a type of half-convertible (*voiture décapotable*) familiar in the 1920s, and, of course, they want the top down, the better to see and feel the country. They pay a great deal, by 1920s standards, for the rented car and driver—four hundred francs (about sixteen dollars, or more than sixteen times the cost of the hotel room in Bayonne). It would have been much cheaper to take the train via San Sebastián, but Jake has planned this trip carefully, and he wants to enter Spain through the mountains, both because that route will provide connection with the *deus loci,* the spirit of place, and because that is what proper pilgrims have done for many centuries. Medieval guidebooks recommended that sick or infirm pilgrims take the coastal route to Pamplona (as Brett and Mike do), but Jake avoids the easy way and plans his pilgrimage along the ancient mountain routes. He is probably surprised to find that the bus service, which followed the same route from Bayonne to Pamplona that they take in the car, did not start until the first of July. But that does *not* imply lack of careful planning on his part—all the best 1920s guidebooks indicated that this bus service began in summer. Since it is almost a week into summer (26 June) when they leave Bayonne, he would have expected the bus service to be started by then. Still, at great cost, he sticks to the route he originally planned.

91:25 **country:** After they pass "lovely gardens," they enter the green, rolling country of "nice farmhouses," land "rich and green," and villages "well-off and clean." This is the fertile, prosperous French Basque country of the Labourd region south of Bayonne (on route D932; see 92:6 for details of the route). A 1920s guidebook described this region as follows: "Labourd is characterized by the extreme gracefulness of its outlines, so pure, so delicately harmonious: structural unities which model its relief, architectural unities so fortunately combined that they seem to wear in themselves the sweetness of life." Among these "lovely scenes," there seems to be "health and happiness spread over" all things in this "calm and peaceful atmosphere: the charm of the Labourdine land" (Lamare 12–13). Again, the beauty of the French landscape described by Hemingway, felt deeply by Jake, makes it impossible for the reader or critic (with even an elementary grasp of geography and basic reading skills) to postulate the existence of a French wasteland in the novel.

91:28–29 **Basque country:** Here Jake does not mean to indicate the *entire* French and Spanish Basque country, but the region of Labourd south from Bayonne to the French-Spanish frontier. In the complete Basque country, covering large areas on both the French and Spanish sides of the Pyrenees, there are many differences—as the details of Jake's journey make clear—of topography, fertility, prosperity, and appearance. Not all the Basque lands look rich and green, nor do all the villages look prosperous and clean (cf. the "gloomy little village" in Spain, 93:16). Travel writing and guidebooks of the 1920s stressed the many differences of the Basque regions. The French Basque province of Soule, for example, is found to have a "less smiling" countryside and a "more austere" life than the rest of the French Basque country (Lamare 13). The prosperous Spanish Basque provinces of Guipúzcoa (San Sebastián is the capital city) and Vizcaya, with their mining and hydroelectric installations, were already in the 1920s less pastoral and agrarian than Labourd, north of the Pyrenees. "As for Navarre," our source continues, in the province of which Pamplona is the capital, only "the valley of the Bidassoa" resembles Labourd in its "small towns of seductive comfort," its "green and fertile fields." Elsewhere in Navarre, setting for most of the novel's Spanish scenes (Pamplona and Burguete-Roncevaux), there is a "harder soil" and "a more severe life is guessed behind the more silent housefronts" (e.g., as in Burguete) than is found on the French northern side of the Pyrenees. As for Basque culture and language, we are told that by the mid-1920s "it is almost entirely banished from Pampeluna [i.e., *Pampelune,* French for Pamplona] and loses ground everyday in the environs," and southern Navarre "is not Basque any more." And the Spanish Basque province Alava is said to be of no interest: "its misery and isolation make it the infirm and desherited relative to which nobody pays any attention" (14). While this volume displays somewhat tenuous translation skills, it offers a far more detailed treatment of the Basque country than do the standard Baedekers and Blue Guides of the 1920s.

91:30 **pelota court:** *Pelota* (Spanish) or *pelote basque* (French) or, more commonly in the Americas, jai alai (a Basque-derived term meaning "joyous festival") is often described as "the national sport of the Basque people." Believed by many Basques to be "the most elegant of all sports," it requires "an astonishing skill, dexterity and strength" (Lamare 50). As this 1920s source puts it, the *pelote* (or ball) is thrown against the wall "either with the hand, either with a kid glove, a withy-glove [basket], a battler [paddle] or a stringed racket" (50). There were many different versions of the game, although some have died out and others are still played only in certain Basque villages. All versions require a court, open or closed, with a high wall, thus the signs on the churches forbidding *pelota,* since the churches would often have the highest walls in a village. Since every Basque village would have at least one court, the prohibition against church-wall *pelota* should not be taken as a negative sign (as some commentators have viewed the matter) reflecting some imaginary repressiveness of the Church, just as the lack of basketball goals affixed to walls of American churches does not indicate religious repression.

92:6 **Spanish frontier:** Dancharia, or Dancharinéa, is the hamlet straddling the French-Spanish border where the French road from Ainhoa (currently designated D20) meets the Spanish road (now N121) to Elizondo, the Puerto de Velate, and Pamplona. The "little stream" is the upper Nivelle. They probably ask about trout in the stream because Jake (or Hemingway) knows that in the mid-1920s it was said that the Nivelle was "not very abundant in fish, except in the upper part of the course, the trout of which is remarkably delicate." The same source stresses: "Fishing-licenses are *compulsory* in Spain," which is apparently not the case in French Basque country (Lamare 72–73; in the next chapter, immediately after Jake and Bill get off the bus in Burguete, the Spanish carabineer demands that they show their fishing permits—109:3–8).

Given the fact that the route Jake, Bill, and Robert follow from Bayonne to Pamplona has been a matter of some confusion in Hemingway studies, it should be clarified here. Jake's recorded details of the journey—the unnamed passes, rivers, and villages, and the directions mentioned—together with a study of detailed 1920s maps and recommended routes, remove all doubt as to the route taken. Is this a curious instance of the operation of his iceberg theory—to *name* nothing, while being exact about the route? Or is it a device to ensure that the good reader will pay close attention to the text, get a good map, and know at all times exactly where the characters are? Place and *placement,* a sense of place and local knowledge, are always important in Hemingway's fiction. In any case, what follows here is an outline of the route followed based on 1920s maps, using current road numbers, and indicating certain important textual clues and historical-geographical facts:

1. They leave Bayonne, headed south on D932 through the Labourdine heart of French Basque country. After about twelve kilometers they come to Ustaritz, one of those villages that "look well-off and clean"; the road here is lined with the beautiful residences of the *Américains,* the term used to describe Basque emigrants who "returned with a fortune from South America" (Muirhead and Monmarché, *Southern France* 393).

2. Two kilometers south of Ustaritz, they bear right on D20, leaving the main road (D932–D918) that goes on to the pilgrimage town of Saint-Jean-Pied-de-Port via the resort town of Cambo-les-Bains. They are now in the terrain of Roland, the French hero memorialized throughout this country; nearby is the Pas de Roland (also called by some guidebooks the Brèche de Roland), the vast cleft or gap in the rocky hills along the Nive said to have been made by Roland's famous sword—Durendal—when the French paladin was returning from Spain. Given the novel's Roland subtext (see 108:26), we might ask why they do not make a detour to visit the Pas de Roland at Ixtassou. For one thing, as all the 1920s guidebooks point out, it had been much disfigured by the railway, and a new road cut through. For another, they are on the most direct route to Pamplona (109 kilometers via D20 and Dancharia), and they want to be in Pamplona in time to get checked into their hotel, confirm the bullfight tickets, and prepare to meet the train from San Sebastián that Brett and Mike are supposed to be on; so they don't have time for detours and touristic visits to famous sites—or lunch. More important, from the perspective of narration, had they detoured to the Pas de Roland, it would have been natural to continue on to Pamplona by the longer route, via Saint-Jean-Pied-de-Port and Roncevaux, and that would have ruined the dramatic approach to Roncevaux in the following chapter. (And Robert would have been with them in Roncevaux and Burguete, a fact that, as lingering image, might spoil the idyllic interlude that begins there for Jake and Bill the next day.)

3. On D20 they pass through the Basque village of Larressore, well known for its production of Basque *makilas,* walking sticks, and continue a few kilometers to where D20 joins D918. In two-and-a-half kilometers they pass through the typical Basque village of Espelette, bear left on D20, and begin immediately the ascent ("and then the road turned off and commenced to climb"—see 92:1–2)

to the Col de Pinodiéta. From this vantage point, as the text indicates, they would see nothing (driving south-southwest) but hills and would sense the sea beyond. After driving a few kilometers on through Ainhoa, D20 brings them to the frontier at Dancharia (see above).

4. They drive ten kilometers south from Dancharia on N121 to the Maya Pass, also called Puerto de Otxondo (602 meters). At the top of the pass, or Col, it's "really Spain" because they can see "brown mountains."

5. Shortly after they come "down out of the mountains," they enter the fertile valley ("grassy plains and clear streams") of the Rio Baztan, and at thirteen-and-a-half kilometers after the Col, they go through Elizondo, the major town of the region and once an independent republic like Andorra. Hemingway omits mention of this lively town, probably because it would detract from the sense of rural isolation developed in this passage.

6. After Elizondo they pass through a "gloomy little village" (this is probably Irurita), and since they start to "climb again" they must be on the cut-off road to Berroeta, after which they continue to climb to the Puerto Velate on N121, at 847 meters the highest pass on their route. After the pass, the road runs (as Hemingway writes) "down to the right," and the view is dominated by what the Blue Guide calls "*un vaste cirque de sierras grisâtre*"—a cirque or amphitheater of grayish mountains—as they enter a more desolate, uncultivated country (Monmarché 77; emphasis added). Jake describes the "brown" and strangely furrowed mountains they see to the south and southwest as they come down from the pass.

7. After they "came out of the mountains," about six kilometers down from the pass, they continue on a straight stretch by the grain fields near Lanz; the stream that the road now follows is the Rio Mediano. Near here there was, in 1925, "an old house, flanked with *turrets*, on the *left* next to a bend" (Lamare 264; emphasis added). This sounds like Jake's "old castle" on the left with the grain growing "right up to the walls." (My travel notes from the late 1970s—"N121 c. 25 K north Pamplona: possible small old castle on left with grain all around between straight stretch after Col, somewhere between Lanz and Etuláin-Burutáin"—may refer to this turreted "old house," which may or may not still stand.) When they cross the plain near Ostiz, where the Mediano flows into the Ulzama (and where 1920s guidebooks say the prevalence of Basque language ends), they would see the big river, the Rio Ulzama, off on the right. Between here and the confluence of the Ulzama with the Rio Arga at Villava, they would have a view of the plateau of Pamplona—"away off"—and the skyline of the churches, from a distance of four to ten kilometers.

Given the textual time indications, together with the morning activities in Bayonne, the waiting for the car (and for Cohn), and their lunch shortly after arrival in Pamplona, it seems to have taken about three hours to drive the 109 kilometers from Bayonne to

Pamplona, over some good roads, some dusty uneven roads, through many villages, and over two substantial mountain passes with many curves and switchbacks.

92:7 **carabineers:** The Spanish border guards carry short-barreled carbines. According to one 1920s source, the Spanish "carabineers are Customs-officers," who also (like the French border officers) wear kepis, the flat-topped and visored cap, and the carbine-armed Spanish officers in Bonaparte hats (bicorn or tricorn upturned brim) are "civilian-guards" (*guardia civil*) or "armed policemen" (Lamare 68).

92:20 **old man:** The old man with the kid goat on his back is like some archetypal figure, some iconographic legend. Perhaps a biblical Old Testament figure, perhaps a pilgrim with his long staff bearing an intended slain offering, he has no passport and does not acknowledge state-determined borders. Jake pays particular attention to him (as his biblical namesake, Jacob, who knew about kid goats, would have; see also Jake's encounter with a goat in Burguete—112:5). Practically speaking, the border guard's confirmation that the old man will "wade the stream" and "go through" confirms the legendary indifference of Basques to the French-Spanish frontier and their reputation for frontier smuggling.

93:28 **asleep:** Much of what we have learned about Robert Cohn is confirmed in this touchstone line: as Jake observes closely the countryside and is moved by its beauty, by images of fertility juxtaposed with history (the old castle and the ripe fields of grain), he seeks silent confirmation, communion, but Robert is asleep. Bill, who knows where they are and what he is seeing, nods in wordless acknowledgment. As Hemingway wrote many years later (in the manuscript of "The Strange Country"), the writer should "make the emotion with the country," and he admonishes himself, regarding the landscape he is creating there, to "make as sound and good as the ride from Bayonne to Pamplona in the Sun" (Stoneback, "Hemingway's Other Florida" 115). Throughout *The Sun Also Rises* Hemingway consistently *makes the emotion with the country,* and if we sleep through the actual and symbolic landscapes, as Robert does here, we miss both the country and the emotion.

93:33 **great brown cathedral:** As was generally the case throughout Europe in 1925, and is still true in some places in Spain and France (where, e.g., centuries-old building codes prohibit buildings higher than the churches or buildings that obscure the view of churches), the skyline of many cities was defined by church towers. The view that Jake describes is particularly dramatic, because Pamplona itself is elevated from the surrounding country. The cathedral, one of the finest examples of French Gothic architecture in Spain, together with the "other churches" (see below), dominates the skyline, a skyline that is "broken" because the numerous church towers are not of uniform elevation or style. Regarding the cathedral, see also 90:13 and 96:30.

94:1 **other churches:** The other churches include San Cernín (also called San Saturnino), San Lorenzo, San Ignacio, San Nicolás, and Santo Domingo, all touchstones in the symbolic landscape of Hemingway's Spain and France. Jake cites the cathedral first since it is built along the outer walls of the city, but the actual skyline is particularly defined by San Cernín. As the contemporary (1998) official guidebook of the Ayuntamiento de Pamplona puts it, under the bold rubric of "Pamplona's Skyline," "The towers of San Cernin [*sic*] are undoubtedly its most recognizable 'skyline.'" "The towers of San Cernin at night," the guidebook adds, "is one of the most beautiful and characteristic views of the city" (26–27). The oldest church in Pamplona, the French Romano-Gothic fortress Church of San Cernín, is described in the Blue Guide as follows: "*San Saturnino*, a 13–14th cent. church on the spot where St. Saturninus or Sernin is said to have baptized 40,000 pagan citizens of Pamplona" (Muirhead, *Northern Spain* 17). According to tradition, Saint Saturninus was the famous third-century French saint who evangelized much of Languedoc before crossing the Pyrenees to preach to the pagans and Romans in Pamplona and elsewhere. With his companion, Saint Honestus (a French farmer from Nîmes), Saturninus converted the wealthy Senator Firmus, father of the boy who would become San Fermín (or Saint Firminus). Honestus, who is sometimes said to be the first bishop of Pamplona, stayed in Pamplona as the teacher of Fermín, who is also sometimes said to be the first bishop of Pamplona. Saturninus (or Cernín or Sernin) went back to France, where, tradition holds, he founded the church of Toulouse and worked many miracles. Saturninus converted thousands in Toulouse, and the Roman priests of this ancient city feared him and incited a mob to tie him to the tail of a wild bull awaiting sacrifice; Saturninus was dragged to his death by the bull through the streets of Toulouse. On the spot of his death was erected a church, Notre-Dame du Taur ("Our Lady of the Bull"), which stands on the rue du Taur, the street in the heart of Toulouse that leads to the place Saint-Sernin and the great Romanesque Church of Saint-Sernin (or Saturninus, or Cernín).

The importance of Saint Sernin the man in the legendary history of *tauromachie* (French for "bullfighting") is evident in the conversation of contemporary aficionados of bullfighting in Toulouse—long an important center of *tauromachie*. Moreover, Saint Sernin, the man and the church, have important connections to Pamplona through their centrality in the development of the pilgrimage of Saint-Jacques-de-Compostelle, or Santiago de Compostela. Saint-Sernin is not only the largest Romanesque church in France but "the most perfect Romanesque building in France," or, again, "one of the finest Romanesque churches in existence" (Muirhead and Monmarché, *Southern France* 360; Baedeker, *Southern France* 79). The church contains the relics of Saint Sernin and, behind the altar, his tomb, resting on bronze bulls. It was begun in 1075 and is said to have served as the model for the Cathedral of Santiago de Compostela, the great pilgrimage center of Spain and "the most important monument of the early-Romanesque style in Spain . . . the whole arrangement is so similar to that of Saint Sernin of Toulouse, that it is impossible to doubt that it is due to French architects" (Baedeker, *Spain* 184–85). The crucial importance of French architects, religious orders, priests, pilgrims, saints, and settlers in the shaping of the Compostelan pilgrimage routes is firmly established and well documented in the history of the pilgrimage. Thus it should come as no surprise that when Pamplona experienced major growth in the eleventh and twelfth centuries, the many French settlers, "devotees of San Saturnino, to whom they consecrated their church and whose name they gave to the new quarter," the Burgo de San Cernín (Ayuntamiento de Pamplona 5), brought their beloved French saint with them and thus cemented the ties (historical and ecclesiastical, pilgrimage connected and bullfighting related) of Toulouse and the French Midi with Pamplona and Navarre. The entrance to Pamplona's Church of San Cernín is flanked by statues of San Cernín and Santiago the Pilgrim (Saint James/ Saint Jacques in his pilgrim avatar, not Santiago Matamoros—the Moor slayer). The church's clock tower serves as official timekeeper of the fiesta—the first rocket announcing the *encierro,* or running of the bulls, is lit when the San Cernín clock strikes 8:00 A.M.—and "El Gallico," the rooster weather vane that tops the clock tower, is one of the "most popular symbols of the city" (Ayuntamiento de Pamplona 26). The church contains a pilgrim hostel, a reliquary of San Saturnino (relics sent from Toulouse), and the chapel and statue of Our Lady of the Way (i.e., the Pilgrimage Way), patron saint of the city.

The official route of the pilgrimage, the Pilgrim's Way to Santiago (generally called, in English, the Way of Saint James) directs pilgrims to enter Pamplona at the French Gate (the Puerta or Portal de Francia), the sole intact sixteenth-century gate to the old walled city, and proceed from the cathedral to the Church of San Cernín, and to pause at El Pozo or El Pocico ("the little well"), where the plaque in the street by San Cernín commemorates the well where San Saturnino baptized the first Christians in Pamplona, where San Fermín was baptized. After praying (or staying at the pilgrim hostel) at San Cernín, the pilgrim might stop at the churches of Santo Domingo (also called the church of Santiago, or Saint James, on the Plaza Santiago, its doors are decorated with iconic Jacobean pilgrim shells) and San Nicolás, the thirteenth-century (much restored in the nineteenth and twentieth centuries) Gothic fortress church that gave its name to another quarter of Pamplona that was heavily settled by the French in the medieval period. Some pilgrim itineraries also recommend a visit to the Basilica de San Ignacio, built on the spot where Ignatius of Loyola was wounded in the sixteenth-century siege of Pamplona—what Hemingway in *Death in the Afternoon* called the "wound that made him think" (i.e., the wound that led to his conversion from a soldier to a saint of the church; 274). Jake, also a wounded soldier and a convert, would know about Saint Ignatius, who moved to Paris, where he lived and studied for years, and who founded his Jesuit order, the Society of Jesus, in Montmartre in 1534. (His birthplace, in Basque country about one hundred kilometers northwest of Pamplona, near San Sebastián, is also an important place of pilgrimage.)

Finally, by tradition, the pilgrim's last stop in Pamplona is at the Church of San Lorenzo and its San Fermín Chapel, where the relics of San Fermín reside and from which the statue of San Fermín is carried in procession at the beginning of the fiesta, on 7 July (San Fermín's Day), which Pamplona authorities still call "the most important day of the fiesta" (Ayuntamiento de Pamplona 46; see 155:3). It was the transfer of the relics of San Fermín from France—where he lived a long time, serving as the first bishop of Amiens (where he is memorialized in the famous cathedral there) and was martyred on 25 September 303—in 1186 (and again in 1386) that led the citizens of the Pamplona quarters of San Nicolás and San Cernín (the so-called French Quarters) to celebrate the festivities of San Fermín every year. Originally, the fiesta began on 10 October, a date set in remembrance of San Fermín's arrival in Amiens. Because of the bad weather that often occurred during the October fiesta—in the fourteenth century, for example, because of the weather, the most important bullfight was held on 25 July, the feast day of Santiago—Pamplona changed the fiesta's date from 10 October to 7 July in 1591. In 2006, Jacobean pilgrims on the road to Santiago are still advised, as they have been for centuries, to make their last stop in Pamplona (before continuing the pilgrimage) at the San Fermín Chapel in the Church of San Lorenzo. Jake's first prayers in Pamplona, in keeping with the pilgrimage traditions, are at the cathedral (see 96–97); before and during the fiesta he prays and goes to Mass several times, possibly at any or all of the "other churches" cited here, and his last prayers before leaving Pamplona are at San Lorenzo, in San Fermín's chapel (see 208:7).

The reader might well ask if Jake, if Hemingway, would know all these legendary and historical details that bind Spain to France, Navarre to Languedoc, Pamplona to Toulouse. The answer is yes, of course, since all the details discussed above are repeated in the best guidebooks and in the folklore and conversation that may be divined and heard on the streets of Pamplona and Toulouse, as elsewhere in Spain and France. The casual tourist, or even some so-called aficionados of the Fiesta of San Fermín, may not know these things; but the alert and attentive traveler (such as Jake, such as Hemingway) would know. The Cernín-Fermín axis of intertwined French and Spanish history and legend is the underpinning, the foundation of Pamplona. In a still larger sense, one of the great shortcomings of Hemingway criticism is the failure of commentators to recognize the depth and the details, the full extent of the way that France and Spain, taken together, inform Jake's life (as well as the overall life and work of Hemingway). Hemingway chat rooms and Listservs that endlessly debate whether France or Spain is more important to Hemingway's life and work, as well as Hemingway criticism and scholarship that posit some imaginary "France/Spain split in values" (Svoboda, *Crafting of a Style* 82), miss the point completely. Real knowledge of geography and history and a sense of symbolic landscape rooted in the local knowledge that Hemingway always stressed provide a salutary corrective for such failures of critical vision. Like Hemingway, Jake *lives* in France and makes *pilgrimages* to Spain; and like Hemingway, Jake loves both countries and understands their profound connections, which are underlined by the ritual-centered terrain of the pilgrimage, the Church, and the bullfight.

94:3 **Pamplona:** The capital of the ancient kingdom and the modern province of Navarre, Pamplona had a population of about 33,000 in the mid-1920s. Hemingway called it a "little town" in his 1923 article "Pamplona in July" for the *Toronto Star* (*By-Line* 86). Pamplona is now a good-sized city of about 191,000 inhabitants and in some ways very different from the place Hemingway first saw in 1923. The Casco Antiguo (the "Old City"), however, remains much the same. Significant changes since 1925 in the old quarters will be pointed out under the appropriate individual entries below (e.g., see 94:9 for the "big square").

In 75 BC, the Roman general Pompey founded on the site of a preexisting Basque settlement the city of Pompaelo (or Pompeiopolis). The first urban center in the Pyrenees, Pompaelo served the Romans as a strategic link between the Iberian Peninsula and the transmontane province of Gaul (or *Gallia Narbonensis,* the forerunner of modern France). The Roman city was not very large, approximately one-third the size of Pamplona's Casco Antiguo, and by the late 200s it had declined and been destroyed by fire. Visigoths occupied the site in 476 and retained it until the Franks took it in 542 and retained possession for most of the period—except for a brief interval of Moorish rule—until Charlemagne's arrival from France in 778 to settle factional disputes related to the Christian reconquest of the Iberian Peninsula and to sack the city (thus the massacre of his rear guard under Roland at the Battle of Roncevaux). It was again in possession of the Franks until 905, when Sancho Garcés I and Sancho II (980) constituted the Kingdom of Pamplona, an important phase in the long struggle for Navarrese autonomy. After a period of Aragonese domination, the Kingdom of Navarre was established. By the later 1000s, Pamplona began to prosper, especially with the arrival of many French settlers, who were granted special privileges in a bid to tempt them to settle. By the end of the eleventh century there were more Franks in Pamplona than there were native-born citizens, and Estella, the next important town forty-five kilometers down the pilgrimage route from Pamplona, had been "founded exclusively for French settlers" (Tate and Tate 56). These French settlers created the new quarter of the city, the Burgo de San Cernín (see above 94:1), and by the mid-1100s the Población de San Nicolás. These two boroughs of Pamplona "preferred the French monarchy" in opposition to the city's third borough, the Navarrería, which demanded an "alliance with the Kingdom of Castile." The "three burgos" of Pamplona "fought until 1423, when King Carlos III, the Noble, unified the three entities" (Ayuntamiento de Pamplona, 5). Or, as another guidebook puts it, "Throughout the Middle Ages, the city was troubled by disputes between the citizens of the old quarter—the Navarrería—who supported an alliance with Castilla, and the freemen who lived . . . in the districts of San Cernín and San Nicolás and favoured the retention of the Navarra crown by a French line" (Miñon-Marquina 361).

Another crucial factor in the growth of Pamplona from the eleventh century onward, directly linked to the arrival of waves of French immigrants after circa 1090 and the creation of the two new boroughs of Pamplona, was the pilgrimage to Santiago de Compostela. From the eleventh to the fifteenth century, the so-called Way of Saint James brought between 500,000 and two million pilgrims a year to Spain—most of them *from* France, and most of them *through* Pamplona. It would be hard to overestimate the effect on the prosperity of Pamplona and Navarre of this first great wave of mass tourism, not to mention the establishment by French settlers of churches and monasteries, hospitals and hospices, all along the pilgrimage route. Thus it is easy to understand why the loyalties of many Navarrese lay with the French. Moreover, why the Kingdom of Navarre was a dependency of the French crown for most of three hundred years until Ferdinand of Aragon (or Fernando the Catholic) took the Spanish part of Navarre and united it with Castile in 1512.

Understanding the history of Pamplona—not through obscure historical sources and learned tomes but from the same guidebooks that Jake (and Hemingway) would assiduously consult—might provide a key to the background, a guide to avoid *mis*-understanding of *The Sun Also Rises.* Local knowledge and attitudes may fill in the rest of the background. For example, on my first trip to Pamplona in 1972, I was told by a Pamplona native, on the train from San Sebastián, that Pamplona "is the most French city in Spain." That was news to me, although I immediately felt the truth of the assertion and, after some time in Pamplona, began to understand what lay behind that view. Later that week, my first conversation about the city's history and sense of place was with a native whose ancestors had come from France and settled in the San Cernín quarter in the twelfth century—and our conversation was conducted in French. Later in the 1970s, my first real understanding of the role of French pilgrims in the history of Pamplona, of the importance of the Jacobean pilgrimage route, or *via jacobea,* part of which, in Navarra, is called the Camino Francés (the "French Way"), and of the immense shaping force of French Cluniac architecture and spirituality, was gained in another conversation (in French) with another Pamplona native who was an authority on the pilgrimage, and whose ancestors had come to Pamplona as pilgrims in the thirteenth century and had settled there. Jake's Spain, the Spain of *The Sun Also Rises,* is Navarra/Navarre, a long way in every sense from Andalucía, from southern Spain. And since Jake—Jacob Barnes, we recall, with his "biblical name" (22:28)—is a Jacobean pilgrim himself, following the *via jacobea,* and he knows exactly where he is, in history and place, so should the novel's readers.

94:7 **the bull-ring:** The Plaza de Toros, which Jake describes as "high" and "concrete-looking," was in fact quite large and new in 1925. It was built and inaugurated in 1922, at which time it accommodated 14,000 people (in a city with a population of about

30,000). Today it holds 19,529 people and is the second-largest bullring in Spain, after the Plaza Monumental de las Ventas in Madrid, built in 1931, with a seating capacity of 22,300.

94:9 **the big square:** Not a square at all but "an imperfect rectangle of almost 14,000 sq m" (Ayuntamiento de Pamplona 8), the Plaza del Castillo (as it is called today), or the Plaza de la Constitución, as it was called in the 1920s, has long been the center of life in Pamplona. Until 1844, for example, when the first bullring was built, bullfights were held in the square. The Gayarre Theater, still standing on the south side of the plaza in 1925, was later demolished, and the appearance of the square was changed with its opening onto the Avenida Carlos III in 1932. Other changes since *The Sun Also Rises* include the replacement of the wooden bandstand in the center of the square with the more substantial *Kiosko* of today.

94:9–10 **Hotel Montoya:** In the manuscript version, Hemingway used the name of the actual hotel throughout—Hotel Quintana—before lining it out and inserting Montoya. The Hotel Quintana was located at the southeast end of the plaza (18, Plaza de la Constitución/Castillo) where the popular Bar Txoko is now located. Three decades after *The Sun Also Rises,* Hemingway wrote about his Pamplona sojourn of 1959: "Our public life was at the Bar Choko under the arcade outside the hotel Juanito Quintana used to own" (*The Dangerous Summer* 139). The Hotel Quintana had forty rooms; in the mid-1920s, rooms could be had in the regular season for five pesetas (or about sixty cents American); the cost of lunch or dinner was six pesetas. In 1925 the Quintana was slightly less expensive than two of Pamplona's other principal hotels, the Maisonnave and La Perla, both of which are still in existence. Hotel La Perla, in a building of historical interest at 1, Plaza del Castillo (at the northeast corner of the plaza), is generally regarded as Pamplona's most traditional hotel; in Hemingway studies and popular lore it is sometimes mistakenly identified as the model for the novel's Hotel Montoya.

94:11 **The driver:** Compare this helpful French driver, who is invited for lunch, with his counterpart, the Spanish driver who drives Jake back to Bayonne in chapter 19 and offers an excessively priced continuation of the ride before Jake dismisses him (232:1–5).

94:15 **Montoya:** Aficionado and hotel keeper, one of the novel's important exemplar figures, Montoya is based on Hemingway's friend Juanito Quintana. Hemingway remained friends with Quintana for decades after the novel's appearance. Quintana is described in *The Dangerous Summer* as "an old friend from Pamplona who was the model for the hotel keeper Montoya in *The Sun Also Rises*" (53).

94:26 **first meal:** In the manuscript, Hemingway wrote, "It was hard to get used to a Spanish lunch" (*Facsimile* 1:264), but later changed that to this observation regarding the "shock" of the "first meal in Spain." The shock, the difficulty, of course, is based primarily on the *amount* of food served. The standard guidebooks of the 1920s usually commented on the size of the servings and often added cautionary statements regarding quality. The Blue Guide, for example, observed: "Except in the chief towns good restaurants are rare, and the tourist generally lunches and dines at his hotel . . . portions are generous. . . . One is often sufficient for two persons. . . . Spanish cookery is rather oily and somewhat highly seasoned and should therefore be treated with respect" (Muirhead, *Northern Spain* cx). More colorful, another 1920s guidebook recommends eating only at the larger hotels and adds this warning: "The Basques cannot possibly claim the art of cookery to be one of their titles of pride, or even of originality; the food is not prepared with much refinement: it is heavy and not easily digested." (Note Jake's observation about how much wine you have to drink "to get it all down.") In the Spanish Basque country, our source continues, "The green oil they use for cooking is an olive oil made with overkept fruits, and which has not been clarified; its nauseous smell and bitter taste spoils the best things"; the food is "excellent" at the "good hotels," but "as for the *posadas* of the Spanish Basque country, we will only advise those with ravenous appetites to go there; otherwise, it will be better for them to put up with boiled eggs and potatoes in their jackets" (Lamare 69). Thus we note that Jake generally follows the guidebook's recommendations, taking his meals at the hotel, and, later, at the *posada* or *hostal* in Burguete, he regards the food with some reservations, and he and Bill take boiled eggs (as the guidebook recommends) for their fishing-excursion picnic (see 110:32 and 121:18). We should add that today, eighty years after *The Sun Also Rises,* bilious or finicky (and mostly British) travel writers to the contrary, one may eat very well indeed in Pamplona and throughout the Basque region, thanks to their privileged location at the intersection of Basque, French, and Spanish culinary traditions and innovations.

95:8 **superior knowledge:** Cohn, as Jake has already noted, has been nervous and awkward since meeting Jake and Bill in Bayonne, because he doesn't know whether they realize Brett went with him to San Sebastián. Since they do know, they are irritated by his attitude of "superior knowledge"; thus Jake enjoys baiting Robert, assuring him regarding Brett's imminent arrival (although he knows better)—and when Cohn (inarticulate in any language) "tried to say" what he wanted for lunch, Jake would not interpret for him. Robert's "superior" attitude, his haughtiness or superciliousness rooted both in his general character and in what he is pleased to regard as his privileged knowledge of Brett, is referred to repeatedly by Bill, who links it with Cohn's Jewishness (e.g., see 96:5 and 162:22).

95:26–27 **Café Iruña:** The best-known and most historic café in Pamplona, the Iruña, at 44, Plaza del Castillo, opened in 1888. (Iruña is the Basque name for Pamplona.) The Spanish counterpart to the legendary cafés Jake frequents in Paris, the Iruña is the gathering point for the Pamplona section of the novel, with more than twenty separate rendered or announced scenes or visits to "the café." Only Robert Cohn prefers another place, the Café Suizo; it is symbolic (and typical of Robert, who is never happy where he is, never really *there*) that Cohn prefers the Swiss (i.e., Suizo) Café (where German is spoken) to the Pamplona (i.e., Iruña) Café (see 100:11).

96:14 **Ayuntamiento:** The city hall, or Casa Consistorial, was built on "a piece of no-man's land" where the three medieval quarters of Pamplona—San Nicolás, San Cernín, and the Navarrería—met (Ayuntamiento de Pamplona 14). The eighteenth-century late baroque and neoclassical facade bears many emblems, in its sculpture and ironwork balconies, of the history of Pamplona and Navarre. In the Hall of Receptions there is a chapel, open only twice a year, which contains relics of San Cernín (San Saturnino) and San Fermín.

96:19 **the story:** This curious sentence, added by Hemingway in revisions made after the original manuscript, may seem at first glance an authorial intrusion that pointlessly calls attention to itself or awkwardly underlines a non sequitur. In fact, it serves as a signpost to remind the reader that there is more to "the story" than what appears on the surface as Jake, Bill, and Robert wait for Brett and Mike to arrive, and it reminds the reader of the symbolic landscape on which "the story" is constructed. While Cohn, the self-absorbed romantic solipsist, goes to the barber-shop, and Bill, the writer, writes letters, Jake enjoys walking alone, "seeing the town again." He goes to the Casa Consistorial, at the literal intersection of the history of Pamplona and Navarre (see 96:14 above), where the archivist's walls are covered with the *history* of *place.* The archivist, the *historian,* has secured Jake's bullfight tickets, his entry to the *ritual* of *place.* As Jake leaves the archivist's office, the porter brushes the dust of the road off Jake's coat (reminding the reader of the pilgrimage from Bayonne), and Jake walks down the street to the cathedral to enact the pilgrim's *sacrament* of *place.* History, tradition, rituals, and sacraments both secular and sacred are all rendered in one symbolic landscape passage that may have "nothing to do with the story" but has everything to do with the novel.

96:30 **the cathedral:** The Cathedral of Santa Maria stands on the site in the oldest quarter of the city where earlier churches had stood, including the Romanesque cathedral consecrated in 1127 that partially collapsed in 1390. Construction of the Gothic cathedral, modeled on the Cathedral of Bayonne, began in the later 1390s and was largely completed by the mid-1400s. Widely admired as one of the finest French Gothic churches in Spain ("l'une des grandes églises élevées en Espagne par l'art gothique français"—Monmarché 78), it has also been reviled—Jake's comment on the facade echoes this opinion—for its unfortunate and "cold, classical façade," the work of the Spanish architect Ventura Rodríguez executed in the eighteenth century, which clashes with the pure Gothic style of the rest of the cathedral. It takes some getting used to, Jake implies, but he has been there before and now he likes it. In any case, he is going to the cathedral to pray, not to study architecture. Inside, before he starts praying, he notes that it is "dim and dark," echoing his description of the Cathedral of Bayonne ("nice and dim"—see 90:15) and underlining his probable knowledge of the connections of the two churches. He notes the "wonderful big windows"—only four original windows from the sixteenth century remain, including the one that depicts San Fermín with saints Peter and Paul. He must also be aware as he prays that he is next to one of the finest Gothic cloisters in Europe, that he is surrounded by the sacred history of Navarre, including the Reliquary of the Sacred Sepulchre of Christ containing a relic of the True Cross (*Lignum Crucis*), sent to Pamplona by Saint Louis, king of France, in 1258. And he must know that he is near the refectory and the kitchen, where medieval pilgrims were fed (as they also were at the cathedral's entrance), and the old pilgrim's hostel, where Jacobean pilgrims were fed and housed or sent on to the pilgrim hostels of San Cernín and San Lorenzo (Tate 81; Arrondo 48). Jake, a proper Jacobean pilgrim, says his first prayers in Pamplona, in keeping with pilgrimage tradition, at the cathedral near the ancient French Gate, where millions of pilgrims had preceded him for ten centuries.

Regarding this entire long prayer-in-the-cathedral paragraph, the following should be noted: (1) Hemingway revised this paragraph extensively, changing the details and the structure of every sentence in the original manuscript, discarding some material, adding new details, working to get it exactly right; (2) This is the most important prayer scene (and contains the longest sentence) in the novel, and arguably the most significant and revealing—albeit widely misunderstood—prayer scene in all of Hemingway's work (see following entries).

97:3 **prayed for:** Quite appropriately, and in theologically sound fashion, Jake prays for everybody he can think of, *including* Robert Cohn, then he prays for himself; when he prays for himself he gets sleepy, so he prays for a good outcome in communally shared activities—the bullfights, the fiesta, the fishing. Clearly, it could be argued that his prayers are "answered" on at least two—the bullfights and the fishing—of the three latter scores, especially in light of the coming action and Jake's later firm assertion that his prayers have indeed been answered (209:1–3). Yet, in spite of the clarity and exactitude of this passage, bizarre misreadings and strangely confused interpretations of this prayer scene abound in Hemingway studies, to such an extent that we may suspect that not only *ignorance* of but *hostility* toward the act of prayer, and toward religion in general, are widespread among the professoriat, the radically secular community of intellectuals who have addressed such matters in Hemingway's work. Typically, one Hemingway biographer, Kenneth Lynn, reads this scene as proof positive of the "failure of Jake's prayers" (313). Lynn seems to think (as do many other commentators) that this so-called failure is related, in part, to the fact that Jake prays for himself. Of course, there is no catechistical proscription against praying for oneself—in fact, Christians are urged to pray for themselves. Lynn and the other commentators who hold contrary views may be swayed by Hemingway's characteristic assertion, made repeatedly in the last two decades of his life, that he no longer prayed for himself, only for others. A representative statement to this effect occurs in *The Dangerous Summer,* where Hemingway writes about his prayers for the bullfighter Antonio Ordóñez: "Antonio knew I prayed for him and never for myself. I was not fighting and I had quit praying for myself during the Spanish Civil War when . . . I felt that to pray for oneself was selfish and egotistical. In case my prayers were invalid . . . and to make sure someone competent was doing it I took out a membership in the Jesuit Seminary Fund Association at New Orleans for Carmen and Antonio." After the ordination of the graduating class, Hemingway noted, they "would pray for them each day" (142). In fact, on 4 June 1959, Hemingway sent a check for $150 to Father C. A. Leininger, SJ, director of the Jesuit Seminary and Mission Bureau, enrolling Ordóñez and his family in the Novena between 23 June and 3 July, when, as Hemingway told Father Leininger, Ordóñez would be "fighting again" after being "wounded seriously" on 3 May. Hemingway added that he "would be grateful that [Ordóñez's] safety and success be remembered not only then but throughout the year" (unpublished letter, private collection). Hemingway's humility, like Jake's, regarding religious practice and spiritual exercises is very much to the point of this scene, as is the practice of praying for bullfighters—as Jake puts it, "separately for the ones I liked."

Consider another strand of critical commentary on this prayer scene. Lynn, again typically, thinks he has demonstrated the failure of Jake's prayers because "Nothing happens" (313). There are two important responses to this kind of assertion: (1) What does the critic expect, demand, to happen? Thunder? Lightning? Miraculous seizure? Glossolalia? Sexual healing—instantaneous resurrection? (2) Do critical presumptions of *omnipotence*—presuming to know what happens or doesn't happen between Jake and God—know any bounds? Apparently not, based on the printed record. John Killinger, for example, asserts that the "very quality of Jake's prayer in the cathedral . . . points up the inefficacy of supernatural communication in our time." Further, he states that Jake "tries to pray, but only the mockery of prayer is left to our day—God is so far removed from the unreasonableness of human events that he is become a mere abstraction" (59, 100). Mockery? Abstraction? To whom, we should ask—to the critic? Certainly not to Jake, to Hemingway, or to any careful reader of the novel. But what else can we expect from a critic who, like Killinger, seems determined—without any textual evidence, without any apparent knowledge of religion or Catholicism or what prayer really is, without even a basic grasp of the spiritual arc of Hemingway's life and work—to prove, as the title (*Hemingway and the Dead Gods*) of his study proclaims, that Hemingway announces the death of God and religion in the modern wasteland. Even a more moderate critic, Wirt Williams, who recognizes what he calls a "submerged God search" in *The Sun Also Rises,* oddly (and inaccurately) writes: "Jake and Brett attempt on different occasions to pray in the cathedral at Pamplona, but are unable to achieve communion, to establish a sense of unity with a deistic power" (57); and again, Williams writes: "He and Brett try unsuccessfully to pray—Jake twice" (52). The inability to read the text accurately here is symptomatic of a larger problem: Jake and Brett do *not* attempt to pray in the cathedral; as far as we know from the text, they are *never* in the *cathedral* together, although they are in church together twice, at least once in the Church of San Lorenzo (see 208:7). There are many churches in Pamplona (see 94:1). While Brett admits the difficulty of prayer for her, she does pray (see 208:13), and there is no evidence whatsoever that Jake tries "unsuccessfully to pray." And what can that curious diction employed to deny Jake's "communion," his "sense of unity with a deistic power," possibly signify but the critic's indifference to the modalities of Christianity and the vocabulary of Catholicism? (Not to mention the fact that literary critics should not be in the business of presuming to pronounce on the validity of another man's communion, especially in the absence of evidence.) Examples of such misreadings of this prayer scene may be found almost everywhere in Hemingway criticism of the past six decades.

Moreover, such flatly inaccurate and hasty dismissals of Jake's praying are often used as a springboard to very large statements about the overall thrust of the novel, forced to serve some procrustean "lost generation" thesis. For example, one of the most influential early Hemingway critics, Philip Young, argued in the 1950s: "One's net impression today is of all the fun there is to be had in getting good and lost. . . . Prayer breaks down and fails, a knowledge of traditional distinctions between good and evil is largely lost . . . and, cut off from the past chiefly by the spiritual disaster of the war, life has become mostly meaningless" (59–60). This passage illustrates perfectly how incomprehension or willful distortion of Jake's prayer scenes can lead to the all-too-familiar leap to meaninglessness. Cars "break down," not prayer. Jake's prayer does not "fail"; the critic does. Traditional distinctions and values are very much alive in Jake's world, as he seeks to *recover* the values that had been lost before the war, the very betrayal of which had caused the war; far from being "cut off from the past," Jake quests radical repossession of what Hemingway elsewhere called the real *old* things, the things that have "come down to us intact from the old days," and Hemingway identifies these things as "the ritual of the church" and the bullfight (*Selected Letters* 237). Since the rituals of the church and the bullfight, which speak volumes about "traditional distinctions between good and evil" and delineate precisely the values that give meaning to life *and* death (passion, honor, courage, decorum, aesthetics, and morality, for a start), are the bedrock foundation of *The Sun Also*

Rises, one's net impression is that this critic, like so many others, has had fun getting lost and has read a novel different from the one Hemingway wrote.

This inventory of critical confusion could be continued at great length, since most commentators who deign to mention the role of prayer or religion in the novel take this approach: prayer fails and religion is defunct, most of the characters are lost and directionless, and Jake—or Hemingway (you can't always be sure who they're talking about given all the biocritical confusion)—is at best a nominal or bogus Catholic, at worst a nihilist or atheist who believes in nothing. The Iron Law of Hemingway criticism almost never fails—decreasing accuracy (and sometimes logarithmical hysteria) in direct relation to increasing religious content. Even the best critics, those who have some understanding of Jake's (and Hemingway's) Catholicism, are affected by this Iron Law. Michael Reynolds, for example, recognizes Jake's "specific Christian virtues" and the fact that "Jake remains Catholic enough" in spite of "the uneven practice of his faith"; yet he, too, misjudges Jake's prayers—"Jake's voice sounds a lot like Huck Finn who never got what he prayed for because he was praying for the wrong things" (*Novel of the Twenties* 26). And Carlos Baker, one of the few critics who is sound and true to the text on the question of Jake's Catholicism, inadvertently reveals the antireligious bias of Hemingway criticism when he writes: "Without apology or explanation, Jake Barnes is a religious man" (*Writer as Artist* 89). Here, at last, is fact. But why should Jake apologize, pray tell? And to whom? The reader? Brett? Robert Cohn? And what should he explain, and who would understand if he did? Montoya, perhaps Romero, maybe the count, but they all know that there are certain matters of passion—such as the bullfight and religion—that one does not expose "to people who would not understand" (131). The curious tonality in Baker's presentation of Jake as "a religious man" may explain why Hemingway noted in a letter that Baker reminded him of someone approaching religion very cautiously with a ten-foot pole (Stoneback, "Nominal Country" 116).

What really happens, then, in this prayer-in-the-cathedral scene? In brief, Jake prays properly and in strict accordance with Catholic teaching. First, he responds emotionally to the ambiance of the cathedral, and then he kneels, assuming one of the "proper postures in prayer," according to *The Catholic Encyclopedia,* since kneeling is a primary outward sign "of the reverence proper for prayer" (Wynne 7). Jake knows that prayer is an "act of the virtue of religion" that may involve praise or thanksgiving, "but petition is the principal act of prayer"; he knows, too, that along with the spiritual objects of prayer, it is fitting "to ask also for temporal things, our daily bread, and all that it implies, health, strength, and other worldly or temporal goods"(Wynne 1–2). It is perfectly proper, that is, to pray for a fine fiesta, good fishing, and money. Under the rubric of "For whom we may pray," Jake is also in strict accordance with the Catholic forms of prayer, since Catholics are instructed to pray "for all, without exception, in high or low station, for the just, for sinners, for infidels . . . for enemies as well as for friends" (Wynne 3). Jake prays for everybody he can think of, even Robert Cohn, even the bullfighters he doesn't like. Since attention is said to be the essence of prayer, perhaps some observers (with little experience of prayer or knowledge of its proper conduct) think Jake's prayers fail because his mind seems to wander during prayer. On this matter, *The Catholic Encyclopedia* instructs that when "attention ceases, prayer ceases" and is "resumed only when the mind is withdrawn from the object of distraction"; however, "one is at liberty to pass from the subject of prayer, provided it be done without irreverence, to any other proper subject" (Wynne 5). If we judge Jake's thinking about the count during his praying to be a distraction from prayer, a loss of the proper *attention*—and this need not necessarily be the case, since the count's presence in Jake's state of mental prayer or meditation may be the very heart of the matter (see following entry)—it is, at worst, a momentary distraction before he returns to the proper form of prayer. Distraction, *The Catholic Encyclopedia* notes, "is wont to happen in time of prayer," but distractions "do not rob prayer of its essential character," nor do they "invalidate prayer," which keeps its "substantial value as prayer" unless the "dissipation of thought is willful" and the distraction stems from irreverence (Delany 1). Clearly, from the perspective of the magisterium, the teaching authority of the Catholic Church—the only perspective that matters here—Jake's prayer does *not fail.*

97:13–15 the count . . . something funny: Jake's mind *seems* to wander during prayer to thoughts about the count. The first question that presents itself here is this: just what is the "something funny" that Brett told Jake about the count? This crucial passage was added in Hemingway's revisions, and it seems very much like a hint of the iceberg depths, a clue to a fact that Hemingway originally left out deliberately under his rubric of the theory of omission, a mystery precisely planted here to force the reader to try to identify the omitted fact. Although the passage is generally passed over in silence by Hemingway commentators (perhaps because it has been regarded as hermetic, insoluble), suggestions have been made in passing, for example, that the "something funny" about the count that Brett told Jake may have something to do with either homosexuality or with the fact that the count was wounded in the same way (or with the same result in terms of sexual activity) as was Jake. The former suggestion strikes most readers as absurd, and there is no evidence for such a conclusion; the latter notion, if the textual evidence is carefully examined, seems at least partially correct. The count, as we know, has been in many wars, and he has been wounded (see 60:7). Although he offers Brett a good deal of money to take a trip with him, there is no evidence that he intends a sexual rendezvous (see 33:6). In fact, the earlier insistent use of the word "funny" as a keyword linked specifically with Jake's sexually incapacitating wound (see 26:30, 27:10, and 31:2) constitutes the firmest kind of stylistic evidence that the "something funny" that Brett has told Jake about the count is that he, too, has been rendered celibate by a war wound. Further, if we bear in mind the count's role as an exemplar of the proper values, an exemplar who may be seen as embodying specifically Christian virtues and spiritual love (see 60:7, 60:31–32, 61:4, 62:22–23, and 64:27), it seems quite probable that the "something funny" about the count that Brett has learned is that he, like Jake, is both a practicing Catholic and a wounded war veteran who has had to come to terms with wound-enforced sexual abstinence.

Thus, it would be doubly appropriate for Jake to think of the count in the midst of his praying. In that case, thinking of the count would not be mind-wandering interrupted prayer, not "distraction" at all, but prayer in strict conformation with church teaching—that is, mental prayer deepened and extended into meditation, as in the recommended spiritual exercises of Saint Ignatius (that wounded warrior who, as Hemingway said, received the groin "wound that made him think" and led to his conversion in Pamplona, a few blocks from where Jake is praying—see 94:1). Thus, meditation on "something funny" (not on "making money") about the count reminds Jake of both his own spiritual needs and how they are connected with his physical disability, a perfectly appropriate subject of prayer. Originally, since Hemingway planned in his manuscript outline to have the count show up in Pamplona, this prayer reference may have been intended to foreshadow some future, more specific revelation about the count and the "something funny." However, since Hemingway changed his mind about having the count present in Pamplona, this reference functions in the published text as a signal harking back to the crucial secret-of-the-values scene in chapter 7. Most of that chapter takes place in Jake's apartment, yet when Jake looks back to the last time he saw the count, he says, "That night in Montmartre," which is across the river, on the right bank, far from Jake's apartment. It is apt that Jake's remembered final vision of the count is fixed in Montmartre (the sacred Mount of the Martyrs, even if the vision does take place in Zelli's, the hellish smoky, crowded, noisy nightclub at the base of the mount), and it recalls how Jake then, as he left the club, *looked back* at the count with the "three girls" (who may be adumbrative of the three Holy Women of Christian tradition); Jake's final intensely remembered vision of the count causes him to regret as he meditates in his first Pamplona prayer that the count is not there (see 64:27). Jake reflects on his principal exemplar—in more ways than have hitherto been recognized—regretting the count's absence, yet knowing that he must, like the count, come to terms with the "something funny" at the center of his experience and live, through "the secret" of getting "to know the values," a life that will enable him to be "always in love" (see 60:31–32 and 61:11).

97:18–20 **rotten Catholic . . . grand religion:** Jake feels a certain shame because he fears his thoughts have wandered inappropriately and he has been distracted from the proper mode of prayer—although this is not necessarily true (see entry above). Whatever degree of unworthiness Jake feels here, he is clearly not *rejecting* the Church, as some commentators have argued. He is *celebrating* the Church. Through prayer, he has come to a conviction of his rottenness, a natural, indeed an essential, condition for anyone who would become a true believer. The Catholic Church is, he says, "a grand religion," and in the presence of that grandeur what can he feel but "rotten"? Suppose he had said: "I was proud I was such a great Catholic"? Would any good Catholic say that? His fundamental stance here is reflected in the words of the familiar prayer, the *Domine, non sum dignus:* "Lord, I am not worthy . . . but only say the word and my soul shall be healed." In all this, Jake is a great deal like Hemingway, who, shortly after *The Sun Also Rises* was published, wrote that he was "a very dumb Catholic" but he had "so much faith" that he "hated to examine into it"; and, for many years, Hemingway would assert that the only way he "could run his life decently was to accept the discipline of the Church," and he could not imagine taking any other religion seriously (Stoneback, "Nominal Country" 127–29).

What Jake means here when he says there is nothing *he* can do about his rottenness may seem somewhat mysterious to some readers, and rightly so, since it is a thoroughly orthodox reflection on the mystery of God's grace, which comes to the sinner, unearned, unmerited, irresistibly, and not on any humanly fixed timetable. Jake, of course, hopes that he will feel more religious the "next time" he prays (and the evidence clearly suggests he does—see, e.g., 150–51 and 208–9). This is the precise function of ritual, of all ceremonial and sacramental forms and modes of being: to carry the person who performs the ritual through the times of aridity and the vagaries of personal circumstance, from one efficacious rite to the next, no matter how much time of dryness (or spiritual aridity) intervenes. Surely it is axiomatic that this is the function of all ritual, the ritualism that pervades Jake's life (and Hemingway's life and work) from beginning to end—whether the rituals of the church, the bullfight, and fishing, or even travel and work, as well as the smaller but no less important ceremonies of dailiness such as wine drinking. One may experience occasional difficulty in prayer before realizing deep connection or communion, or see many bad bullfights before experiencing the ecstasy of the real thing, or fish many streams before finding the living water and the magical trout, or drink many mediocre wines before consuming the transcendent vintage, but it is only the confirmed ritualist who is ready for the promised grace when it arrives. On this subject, one might consult many Christian saints and mystics or, for that matter, Confucius, who understood very well the centrality of ritual in the dimension of the holy, the beauty and dignity of ceremony, and the feeling of magical power that emanates from the authentic ritual gesture. This is what Hemingway meant when he wrote of the "permanent value" of things such as the bullfight and "the ritual of the church," the rare things that had been passed down "from the old days" (*Selected Letters* 237).

In the original manuscript version of this passage, Jake's sense of ritual was more emphatic; he begins to "not feel *very* religious *any more*" (i.e., he feels less religious than he had when he began praying), he says, "So I stood up and half *bent my knee* and *crossed myself*" (*Facsimile* 1:271; emphasis added). That is, he concludes his first ritual—prayer—with two further ritual gestures, the bent knee of worshipful genuflection, and the sign of the cross, a token of faith and an invocation of blessing. Thus he faithfully performs the ceremonies of his "grand religion." In sum, how this key prayer scene could be misconstrued by so many Hemingway commentators as an example of *failed* prayer, or Jake's (or Hemingway's) rejection of religion, will remain a mystery to close readers of the text. For most readers, as for the vast majority of all the students with whom I have discussed this scene, it is straightforwardly the devout prayer, meditation, and ritual of a devout man.

97:23–24 **right hand . . . damp:** In the manuscript version of this sentence, Hemingway had originally written: "as I went out I dipped my fingers in the holy water and crossed myself again and put a peseta in one of the poor boxes to help nail down my prayers" (*Facsimile* 1:271). Thus he emphasized three separate aspects of ritual: the holy water, the sign of the cross, and almsgiving. The holy water font and the alms box are located near the door of the church. As Jake leaves the church, he makes the sign of the cross after dipping his fingers in the holy water and puts a coin in the poor box to seal his intentions. Holy water, blessed by a priest, is an ancient sign of blessing, cleansing, and sanctification. (Note that this fits neatly with the novel's pattern of water imagery.) The sign of the cross is, in Catholic tradition, a life-giving devotional emblem to which effects of grace and power are attributed. Almsgiving for the poor and the needy is a fundamental act of Christian charity, or love, one of the seven traditional Corporal Works of Mercy. In revising the passage Hemingway submerged the physical specificity of the three actions (holy water, sign, and alms), so that readers unfamiliar with the ritual might miss the significance of his damp thumb and fingers. Whether regarded as a characteristic passage of writing by the iceberg theory or an understatement designed to force the reader's participation in the discovery of Jake's devotion, the revised passage is a brilliant instance of the genius of Hemingway's style. While most writers would say something like "he crossed himself and went outside in the sun" (and Hemingway originally said pretty much the same thing), the achieved sensuous precision makes the curious and careful reader *feel* the sign of the cross, physically and imagistically and durationally, as an immediately apprehended emotional and intellectual complex.

We should note that the sign of the cross is actually there in the text—it is not implied or omitted, not the submerged part of the iceberg that is merely hinted at, but very much there, in direct physical rendering. Yet many readers miss it. For many years I have conducted a classroom exercise in which many students have participated. I ask them to describe exactly what happens in this sentence. Around 10 percent (in classes where the students are usually 30 to 40 percent at least nominally Catholic) recognize that Jake makes the sign of the cross at the end of the sentence.

This may or may not suggest the death of religion in the wasteland; more likely it indicates the death of reading in America. By way of contrast, some 70 percent of my students at the University of Paris saw and understood exactly what Jake did, and, in China, at Peking University, at least they all wanted to *know* about that dampness. Some of my students, remarkably enough, have thought that Jake was crying about his wound or about Brett during his prayer and wiped away his tears with his thumb and forefinger. If the reader misses the fact that Jake makes the sign of the cross, and what that means, that reader is likely to miss the import of much else in the novel. The sign of the cross is, according to the teaching of the Catholic Church, "a confession of faith in Christ crucified and an invocation of His Blessing." Jake's precision regarding the sign (as with all signs) extends to the proper form of "two fingers stretched out and the thumb hidden within them, by which the Trinity is symbolized. Take heed," Catholics are instructed, "to make this sign rightly, for otherwise you can bless nothing" (Thurston 3). If the reader of the novel *sees* the sign yet still makes the familiar objection that it is a mere automatic *mechanical gesture,* the proper response is that it is a *ritual gesture* designed to bless and protect Jake and hold him steady until the next ceremony. And with that, it is a charm, a magical sign of that tribal faith that matters so much in Hemingway's world.

This extraordinary prayer sentence ends with Jake's sign of the cross still felt, lingering "in the sun." With 196 words, it is by far the *longest sentence in the book.* Its long flowing rhythms, its stream of devout consciousness (taken together with the preceding long sentence—the actual praying occupies only two long sentences), evoke the novel's central concerns and Jake's emotional and spiritual core. And as the unnamed sign of the cross dries in the "hot and hard" sunlight, Jake "*crossed* over" (emphasis added), thus inhabiting totally the sign and ritual, the sigil of his prayer.

97:28 **bath:** While Jake prays, Robert Cohn bathes. While Jake prays for Robert, Robert prepares to betray Jake yet again with Brett. While Jake engages in the rituals of charity, Robert practices the corporal works of solipsism or self-absorption. The direct shift from Jake's praying to Robert's bathing, shaving, cutting, shampooing, and hair greasing should require no commentary, except to note the skillful juxtaposition of the two actions. Jake makes the sign of the cross and his fingers dry in the sun; Robert makes the signs of the self and his greasy nervous fingers—if he runs them through his hair—will not dry in the night as he sweats Brett's arrival.

98:11 **the worst:** Jake feels lousy over his enjoyment of Robert's nervousness, over his impulse "to devil him" (to annoy or tease him), but Cohn's insufferable behavior brings out what Jake acknowledges to be "the worst" in him. He has, after all, just finished including Robert in his prayers. But, like a good Catholic, Jake feels somewhat guilty over his enjoyment of Robert's nervousness.

98:31 **bet on bull-fights:** To Robert's egregious question about betting on bullfights, Bill answers practically that it's possible, but not necessary. Jake, with his deeper sense of the life-and-death ceremony and passion of the bullfight, is shocked at the question and likens it to "betting on the war." Robert continues to say, to do, and to think the wrong thing at every opportunity.

99:9–10 **send their regards:** In one of three telegram scenes in the novel that are the occasion of ironic or humorous reflection (see also 127–28 and 238–39), Jake devils, or teases, Robert again and enjoys it again when he relays a perfunctory message from Brett and puts the telegram in his pocket without letting Robert see it. It is, after all, his telegram. Jake acknowledges that he is "blind, unforgivingly jealous" but the scene seems to lead to Jake's first real recognition that he hates Robert not as much from jealousy as from his sense of "superiority" because of his relationship with Brett (see 95:8). What triggers Jake's acknowledgment of hatred, however, is a concrete action—"all that barbering," Cohn's primping and preening to get ready for Brett.

99:28 **edge of the cliff:** Throughout the novel, there is a recurrent pattern of edge imagery, sometimes a generalized rising-falling climbing-descending pattern (in the earlier chapters); after this first specifically named use of edge imagery, it recurs several times—when Jake sees Roncevaux from the "edge of the rise" (108:22), when Jake is with Brett at the edge of the "fortifications" in the "shadow of the cathedral" (182:30), when Jake swims in San Sebastián and dives from the "edge of the raft" (238:12), and when he enters Madrid past the "unfinished church on the edge of the cliff" (240:4). The rising-falling and poised-at-the-edge images seem to portend major movements in Jake's heart and soul: the essential rising followed by descending that may lead either to a kind of hell (e.g., the place d'Enfer, with Brett—see 25:2 and 27:27–28), or to the *locus amoenus,* the good place, as in the Burguete scenes (see 108:22). In this scene, being at the "edge," past the "bull-ring," and above the dark river suggests all the tension that will explode, that will be purged during the fiesta.

100:11 **Café Suizo:** Typically, Robert likes the wrong café (see 95:26–27). It is further evidence of Cohn's translocation or displacedness that it is at the Café Suizo—his place—that Robert assaults Jake and Mike (190–91).

100:17 **your ticket:** Robert seems incapable of making plans and sticking to them, of making his word his deed. Given their plan of action, Jake has bought their tickets, but without telling Jake until the last minute, Robert has changed his mind. It is not the trivial cost of the ticket that matters to Jake (as it does to Robert—"I'll get the money back"); it is Robert's vacillation and his absurd confiding that Brett and Mike expected him to meet them in San Sebastián, when, in reality, they would probably do almost anything to avoid meeting him. After this scene, Robert goes—again!—to the barbershop.

101:14 **lying bastard:** Set off by Bill's report of Robert, the "great little confider," talking about his "date with Brett," Jake makes what may be his strongest remarks against Cohn. Bill calms Jake down, and they agree that while Robert is "awful," he is also "nice." Niceness, of course, is not necessarily a great virtue, especially when linked to Robert's other patterns of behavior; but it does make people feel guilty if they are not "nice" in return, and it makes difficult the principled dismissal or exclusion of someone who, although superficially "nice," behaves badly.

101:26 **darbs:** This is Canadian slang, used here ironically, for something or someone outstanding.

102:10 **he slurred:** When Bill slips up, asking why Brett didn't go off with Jake, he slurs over his remark, slurring in the musical sense of seamlessly gliding over a series of notes without a break, covering his accidental evocation of Jake's wound first by suggesting Brett should have gone off with him, and then with humorous self-mocking banter about his face. Similarly, at breakfast in Burguete (chapter 12), Bill covers his crack about impotence with a rapid-fire barrage of puns and humorous one-liners to slur over any direct reference to Jake's wound.

102:27 **he can go to hell:** It seems that various characters are always telling Robert to go to hell, or wishing he would go (e.g., see 39:11, where Jake first tells Cohn to go to hell but then tells him to stick around for lunch). Whether Robert gets back from the barbershop in time to have lunch with them at the Iruña is unclear here, but what matters is that their spirits are lifted as they both look forward to the "swell bus ride" *without* Robert, and to trout fishing *without* Robert.

CHAPTER 11

103:3 **ladder:** This passage marks the beginning of a recurrent pattern of ladder imagery. Perhaps, given Jake's "biblical name" (22:27–28), certain reverberations of the biblical Jacob's Ladder are intended here. In Genesis 28.12, Jacob dreams of "a ladder set up on the earth, and the top of it reached to heaven: and behold the angels of God ascending and descending on it." When he wakes up, he declares: "Surely the Lord is in this place . . . this is none other but the house of God, and this is the gate of heaven" (Genesis 28.16–17). As Jake and the others climb up and down the ladder, ascending and descending four times in this chapter (see also 106 and 109), readers may feel a strong biblical undercurrent in these scenes—and there is certainly a kind of blessedness and communion, though not necessarily angelic, on this bus ride. The bus may not be the house of God (although the Lord is "in this place"), but it is the conveyance that takes Jacob to the Holy Ground of Roncevaux, a version of the "gate of heaven" (see 108:26). Moreover, while the phrase "Jacob's Ladder" has long been so popular it has been used for everything from rope or chain rescue ladders to construction site elevators, from flowers to the runs in women's stockings, its primary signification in Christian exegetical commentary is as a ritual acknowledgment of the place where earth and heaven meet; and in the New Testament the identity of Jacob's Ladder is shifted to Jesus, who becomes the ladder, the way—"Hereafter ye shall see heaven open, and the angels of God ascending and descending upon the Son of man" (John 1.51). Earth and heaven meet in several senses on this rooftop bus ride, and again in the fishing scene in the high country around Roncevaux; and Jake, a Christian who was praying in the cathedral the day before he climbs the ladder, might be aware of the New Testament interpretation of Jacob's Ladder. The pertinent scriptural passages, both the well-known passage from Genesis and the less familiar passage from John, inform two of the best-known hymns—"We Are Climbing Jacob's Ladder" and "Nearer, My God, to Thee." (Hemingway certainly knew hymns well, given his boyhood church-choir experience; see his hymnodic allusions, e.g., in his "Three Shots," "The Last Good Country," and *Under Kilimanjaro*.) And Jake may know "We Are Climbing Jacob's Ladder," with its evocation of the "Soldiers of the cross" who climb "higher, higher" and its injunction to "rise, shine." Jake is a *soldier* who admires what he calls the "grand religion" of the cross, who climbs higher throughout the novel, who knows that the sun *also rises and shines*. And Jake would know—everybody who lived in the English-speaking world in 1925 would know—the story of "Nearer, My God, to Thee" (the hymn of choice for the funerals of several American presidents, and supposedly for the orchestra of the sinking *Titanic*), with its emblems of Jacob's Ladder as the Cross that raises the sinner out of sundown darkness, out of "stony griefs," to the "steps unto Heav'n." The day before he climbs the ladder, Jake has just finished praying, hoping, that he would feel more religious—nearer to God—the next time he prays (97:18–20). And he will (see 209:6).

For additional Jacob's Ladder imagery, see 106:21, 109:2–3, 130:7, and especially the *desencajonada* scene, where Jake and the crowd climb the ladder to get their first look at the bulls who will participate, who will be sacrificed in the mystery and passion of the bullfight. The stone wall of the corral, and the ladder they climb to stand on top, is another symbolic point where heaven and earth meet, where, as Hemingway might put it, the prelude to the ecstasy and communion of the bullring occurs (see 137:27).

103:12 **leather wine-bag:** Varying his terminology, Hemingway refers to the *odre* or *pellejo de vino*—Spanish for a wineskin usually made of dressed goatskin—as wine bag, wineskin, or leather wine-bottle. All readers who have traveled in Spain will recognize the accuracy of Hemingway's rendering of the initiation rite for foreigners, the ceremony of drinking from the wineskin, complete with the spills and misses, and the laughter of the locals and the instruction in the proper manner of drinking from the wineskin.

103:15 **klaxon:** This is the trademarked name of the horn (produced by the Klaxon Company, which also produced other horns and sirens) on many automobiles in the early twentieth century. (The French word *klaxonner* means "to hoot.") Since the horn imitations, the "false klaxons," are heard several times on Hemingway's bus full of Basques headed toward Roncevaux (and one version of legend records that it was the Basques who ambushed Roland at Roncevaux, where the great French hero blew his horn too late), Hemingway probably intends here an ironic foreshadowing of the symbolic landscape that is the setting of the Burguete-Roncesvalles fishing interlude (see 108:26).

104:17 **fine view:** Once again, the wordless communion confirmed in a shared appreciation of the landscape serves as a touchstone for Jake's values. This scene, with the Basque winking and nodding at Bill and Jake as he calls attention to the view, directly echoes the earlier scene where Bill silently nods at Jake to indicate shared appreciation of the landscape while Robert Cohn sleeps (see 93:28). Here, Cohn misses not only the view but the entire ride, since he has backed out of the fishing trip, just waving good-bye to Bill and Jake, so he can attend to his barbering and grooming as he waits for Brett.

104:29 **Arriba:** Hemingway handles the translation of "Arriba!" with his usual economical rendering and contextual clarification of foreign language words: "Lift it up" (see also 105:29).

105:14 **town . . . posada:** Given the landscape details in this paragraph, and the fact that the bus route from Pamplona to Burguete followed the present Route N135, this first town where they make a brief stop at the roadside *posada* (Spanish for inn or tavern) could be either Larrasoaña or Zubiri—most likely the former, fifteen kilometers north-northwest from Pamplona. After this brief stop, they leave behind the "rich grain-fields" around Larrasoaña and enter after a few kilometers the "barren" country around Zubiri, which 1920s guidebooks describe as "in an afflicted country," or in a "pays . . . désolé, africain," (i.e., in French, a desolate and African countryside; Lamare 164; Monmarché 121). For the next, longer stop in Erro, see 106:1.

105:29 **arriero:** Typically, Hemingway translates this word—the muleteer, or mule-train driver—contextually, with great economy.

106:1 **sudden green valley:** After the desolate countryside around Zubiri, the road climbs sharply up to the village of Erro, through which flows the Río Erro. Hemingway emphasizes the suddenness and fertility of this valley, where the grapes, the vineyards, are *touching* the houses. Here he sets the longest interlude of the bus ride, a classic local color scene evoking all the details of place in a country *posada*.

106:13 **aguardiente:** *Aguardiente* is the generic name in Spanish-speaking countries for clear spirits—in grape-growing regions, brandy. Here, given the landscape and the grape references, it probably refers to the local brandy.

106:28 **at once:** Hemingway again emphasizes the suddenness and transience of the "green valley" of Erro before the bus again enters the barren country (108:4–6). In the manuscript he placed even greater emphasis on the brief fertile landscape interval: "Very soon the road mounted out of the high fertile [lined out] green valley" (*Facsimile* 1:293–94).

107:1 **been there:** If the old Basque man speaking here was in America "forty years ago," he went in 1870; after staying, as he says, for fifteen years, he came home to get married in 1885. Several questions are raised by this entire passage and its implicit sketch of patterns of Basque immigration to the United States. First of all, if he came in 1870, he would have been part of a second wave of Basque immigrants in

America. The first wave came at the time of the California Gold Rush (1848), most of them coming to the West Coast from South America, where they had emigrated earlier. These Basques soon began raising cattle and sheep, finally turning almost entirely to sheep since prices were more stable and they could practice transhumance without owning the land on which their sheep grazed. If the old man on the bus came in 1870 it would be likely that he came to work as a sheepherder, since Basques in the American West needed a steady supply of skilled shepherds from the French and Spanish Basque country. His return in 1885 also fits the pattern of emigration return among Basques, since the expansion of cattle ranches in the late 1800s as well as the establishment of national parks in the early 1900s radically reduced sheep transhumance in vast territories, and such employment declined. (By 1921, the immigration quota for all of Spain was reduced to 912 persons a year; by 1924 it was down to 131 immigrants a year. French quotas were higher, however, and French Basque herders continued to emigrate to the American West—primarily California, Idaho, and Nevada—into the 1950s.) All this might suggest that the old man is a shepherd—yet he says he's "been in Chicago, St. Louis, Kansas City, Denver," four cities in four states with almost no Basque population. Did he merely pass through these cities on his way to Nevada and California? Probably so, since he says he "was in" California and he's "been in" the other places. In any case, this interesting minor character plays another variation on the novel's theme of expatriation.

108:1–25 **look at the country:** Of the numerous carefully composed landscapes in the novel (see also, e.g., 77, 91–92, 93–94, 105), this approach-to-Roncevaux landscape may be the one most likely to remind the reader of Hemingway's often expressed admiration for the landscape art of Cézanne. The year before Hemingway composed his landscapes for *The Sun Also Rises,* he had affirmed, in the deleted conclusion of "Big Two-Hearted River" (posthumously published as "On Writing"), that he "wanted to write like Cézanne painted." His protagonist, Nick, wants "to write about country so it would be there like Cézanne had done it in painting." To get the "real thing," you had "to do it from inside yourself," without any "tricks"—"Nobody had ever written about country" the way Cézanne had painted it. Nick feels "almost holy" about his vocation, his commitment to work hard to get the country right ("On Writing" 239). One year later, we see Hemingway writing this Cézannesque landscape. In a fashion similar to the stringent formal principles that govern Cézanne's sense of composition, Hemingway deploys color and light, the volume and shape of rocks and mountains, the rigorous structure of foreground, middle ground, and background, and gives his landscape (as has been said of Cézanne) "a solid framework by carefully placed horizontals and verticals: fence and horizon line, offset by tall trees" (Schmitt 41). Hemingway also seems to be aware here of Cézanne's perceptual theory that held that "landscapes consisted of a fabric of colored patches . . . *taches colorées,* patches of color that the mind immediately translates into a logical framework" (Schmitt 90).

Hemingway arranges colored patches of green, brown, white, red, and gray and refers specifically to the "patches" of sunlight coming through the trees. In the manuscript Hemingway had used "patches" in relation to color a second time in this paragraph— "Far back the fields made *patches*"—before he revised that to the even more Cézannesque rendering: "Far back the fields were *squares* of green and brown" (*Facsimile* 1:296; emphasis added). Indeed, this landscape was one of the most extensively revised passages in the novel, with twenty changes from the manuscript to the finished novel, many having to do with color and shape. (Those twenty revisions do not count the editorially inserted punctuation, including the commas, which may normalize the punctuation but at the same time destroy rhythm and diminish the intensity and flow of the sentences. Hemingway had only one comma—after "flattened out"—in the manuscript version of this entire paragraph.)

Moreover, the concerns of Cézanne's (and Hemingway's) landscapes are "not merely visual, but visionary," the quest to render, in color and form (and words), "the emotions aroused in him by the landscape" (Schmitt 41). For Cézanne, that vision has to do with the "kind of divine illumination with which his landscapes are suffused," as the poet Joachim Gasquet stressed in the 1890s, and this is especially true of his mountain landscapes, his more than seventy-five paintings of mont Sainte-Victoire, which for many observers reflect a sense of "the divine and the numinous," evoking a "sacred aura" (Schmitt 87). Hemingway's landscapes somehow achieve a similar visionary aura, and indeed he seems most indebted to Cézanne's paintings of mont Sainte-Victoire. In Hemingway's Roncevaux landscape, the distant monastery, its shape and color, on the shoulder of the far-off mountain, functions as do Cézanne's faintly discernible buildings in the shadow of his sacred mountain, to anchor the landscape, to underline the emotions felt at the crossroads of the sacred and the secular, the eternal and the transient, the divine and the human.

Finally, we should note that Hemingway's landscape is not static, not a fixed composition, since Jake, his observer, is moving through the picture in a bus. This will remind some readers of the deleted conclusion of "Big Two-Hearted River," where Nick knows "just how Cézanne would paint this stretch of river" and, "seeing how Cézanne would do the stretch of river," steps into the stream—"moving in the picture" ("On Writing" 240).

108:26 **Roncevaux:** As Jake and Bill approach the sacred mountain of Hemingway's Cézannesque landscape (see above), the mode of apprehension of country shifts to *paysage moralisé,* to symbolic landscape informed by literary and historical allusion. As narrator giving geographical identification, Jake properly identifies the place by its Spanish name, Roncesvalles, since it is located in Spain, some twenty-one kilometers from the French border. As pilgrims, as students of literature and history, Jake and Hemingway identify it in conversation by its far more familiar and celebrated French name—Roncevaux.

Famous for many centuries in European history, literature, and art, Roncevaux is the place where Charlemagne's rear guard, under the command of the great warrior Roland, was, on 15 August 778, ambushed and massacred by treacherous Saracens in league with local Basques, or merely by Basques rolling boulders down from the heights of the Pass of Roncevaux, or by heroic Spaniards resisting Frankish invasion—depending on which version of the legendary battle the reader consults. The most famous telling of the story is, of course, in the national epic of France, *La Chanson de Roland* (*The Song of Roland*). Roland is there depicted as the ideal Christian knight, exemplar of all the chivalric virtues. Although the vast commentary on the *Chanson* often differs in its analysis of Roland's character, most scholars stress his exemplary loyalty, courage, and true (or justifiable) pride, and many see him as a personification of *Humilitas* and *Virginitas,* humility and chastity. In order to grasp the nuances of Hemingway's Roncevaux-Roland allusion, a good place for the student of the *Chanson* to begin is with Gerald Brault's landmark edition of *The Song of Roland,* published in 1978 in commemoration of the twelfth centenary of the Battle of Roncevaux; Hemingway would likely have known the classic J. Bédier edition of 1921 (or an even earlier edition). In Brault's commentary, Roland's chastity and virginity are stressed: "Throughout the Middle Ages Roland, in legend and song, never weds nor does he dally with women" (1:100). Brault also emphasizes "the deep spiritual significance" of the *Chanson,* its vision of life as "Joy mixed with Suffering," its "Christomimeticism"—how "Roland's *passio* is the central fact" and his "suffering and death is an imitation of Christ" (1:40–42). Brault stresses, more generally, how the poem views life "as a series of difficult choices, the correct response requiring one to follow the hard road," how its central "agonistic metaphor" envisions life as "a never-ending Roncevaux that must be faced with courage and with faith" (1:43–44; Brault also deals with many centuries' worth of misreadings, which have been legion). The emphases in Brault's analysis on Roland's loyalty, chastity, and courage, on commingled joy and suffering, on Roncevaux as an emblem of the hard road of life that must be traveled with courage and faith, resonate significantly with Jake's character and experience.

In any case, the core image of the *Chanson* depicts Roland fighting courageously to the death against overwhelming odds at Roncevaux. As many schoolchildren once knew—for generations, indeed centuries—Roland has a famous sword, Durendal, and a legendary horn, Oliphant, which can be heard for a great distance, many leagues. And, as nearly everyone once knew, Roland blows his famous horn too late, and by the time Charlemagne, hearing the horn at last, returns to Roncevaux, Roland and all his warriors are dead on the battlefield. In a series of essays and conference papers, beginning more than three decades ago, I have argued that the importance of the Roncevaux allusions (and setting), the submerged presence of Roland in the novel as an implied exemplar at the heart of the landscape *exemplum,* the *paysage moralisé* of Roncevaux, must no longer be overlooked as an important key to the novel, even if it might seem to be one of the more deeply submerged parts of Hemingway's iceberg. To students who asked why Hemingway doesn't *name* Roland, I used to reply that he doesn't need to because it is impossible to say Roncevaux without thinking of Roland. But they had never heard of Roncevaux or Roland, and they were not convinced. Nor were they convinced that Hemingway would know about Roncevaux and Roland. And since evidence was not available in the 1970s that has since surfaced (e.g., in Hemingway's letters and manuscripts—see below), my argument had to be couched in the terms that I used, for example, in a 1976 essay:

> To imagine that Hemingway would not have known of the deeds of Roland at Roncevaux, indeed to think that he had not read the *Chanson* during his time in Paris or before, is to posit the illiteracy of an extremely literate young novelist. Even if he had not carefully read the *Chanson,* he could have read about it in his friend Ezra Pound's *The Spirit of Romance* or in Henry Adams' *Mont-Saint-Michel & Chartres* to name only two of the familiar and fashionable manifestations of "medievalism" and discussions of the *Chanson* that were current in the early twenties. Pound noted its poetry and dignity, and its "championship of Christianity against Paganism [which] makes it almost as much of Christendom as of France." Adams discussed at length its "directness, simplicity, absence of self-consciousness," and noted Roland's folly as well as his "courage, loyalty and prowess." Roland, then, is type and paradigm for Jacob Barnes who wrestles courageously with the angel of his fate in the country around Roncevaux. (Stoneback, "Hemingway and Faulkner" 137; see also Stoneback, "Hemingway on the Road" and "From the Rue Saint-Jacques")

In retrospect, I recognize that my earliest arguments about the importance of Roland and Roncevaux in the novel may have presented the matter, implicitly at least, as something to be regarded under the rubric of Hemingway's style of omission, his iceberg theory of writing. Now I would argue that what Hemingway criticism often takes to be submerged motifs, present only under the rubric of his iceberg style, are in fact perfectly straightforward allusions that have become indecipherable due to the tides of history. This recognition, and the simplest explanation of it, may be traced to a conversation I had with my grandmother in the early 1980s. I knew she had been an avid reader of Hemingway's books as they were published from the 1920s to the 1950s.

As we leafed through *The Sun Also Rises,* I uttered the word "Roncevaux," with no further commentary, and she merely said, with the haunting force of long inburnt memory: "*Ah que ce cor a longue haleine.*" (That's the way she wrote it down for me; Brault's edition renders line 1789 of the *Chanson* as "*Cel corn ad lunge aleine!*" and translates it as "That horn has been blowing a long time!" [1:110–11]; early versions cite the Old French closer to my grandmother's version—and Hemingway's, see below—translated as "Ah that horn has a long breath.") That is, Jake's notation of the approach to Roncevaux made her think of Charlemagne's famous words in the *Chanson* as he hears the dying fall and call of Roland's horn. When I asked her where she had learned the famous line, she said, "as a girl," in the equivalent of eighth or ninth grade before World War I. As we went on to discuss the *presence* of Roland in Hemingway's novel—she seemed to think it was obvious—it became clear to me that the understanding I had labored to attain through scholarly effort was something she had possessed as a matter of course since girlhood. And she was not a scholar, not a writer. Since she was only a few years older than Hemingway, I realized that he must have possessed the same early knowledge of Roland and assumed that his readers in 1926 would also. Thus, what may sometimes seem to be the submerged part of the iceberg is really the tidemark of the decline of cultural literacy.

Evidence that surfaced later confirmed that epiphany. For example, in a 1924 letter, Hemingway urged his friend William B. Smith to make a trip with him—"drive down all through France and over the Pass of Roland"; in other letters, he alludes in military terms to Roland's battle—"I could come through the pass of Roncevaux." And, in the middle of a 1956 letter to Harvey Breit, Hemingway writes (with no commentary or contextualization): "Ah que cet cor a longue haleine," a version of the famous line very close to the one that lived in my grandmother's memory (*Selected Letters* 136, 687, 870; in a curious footnote to this last letter, Carlos Baker writes: "How this handsome line came into EH's possession is not clear"—but it *is* clear, and the cultural literacy of the early 1900s explains it). Hemingway used this line again in the manuscript of *The Garden of Eden;* David Bourne looks at the mountains beyond Hendaye, in the south of France and thinks, "beyond them would be Navarra and Navarra was Navarre. Ah que ce cor ha longue haleine"—but the heavily edited published version deletes the Old French quotation, removing completely that famous image of Roland's horn (*Garden of Eden* 44). Here, readers are deprived of the recurrent and haunting presence of Roland in Hemingway's creative imagination, probably because the editor did not know what the quotation means, where it's from, and what it signifies—a kind of double whammy of cultural illiteracy. (It may strike some readers as analogous to editorial deletion of T. S. Eliot's core vision in *The Waste Land*—"Datta. Dayadhvam. Damyata."—because editors or readers don't understand the foreign language, or, say, deleting "spangled" from "The Star-Spangled Banner" because "spangled" is no longer an everyday word.) And then there is Hemingway's summary of *The Sun Also Rises,* in an inscription of his novel to a friend, as a "small study in promiscuity set against travel scenes in Navarre and a fishing expedition in the Pass of Roland" (See Stoneback, "From the Rue Saint-Jacques" 6). It may be that years after *The Sun Also Rises* was published Hemingway began to recognize that some readers were not getting the point of the Roncevaux interlude, of his Roland-haunted symbolic landscape.

In 1935, in an article for *Esquire* entitled "Notes on Life and Letters (Or a Manuscript Found in a Bottle)," Hemingway responded to what he took as disparaging remarks in William Saroyan's first book, repeating Saroyan's name over and over in a humorous attack, saying: "Mr. Saroyan . . . I don't charge you a nickel for this and every time they see the name Saroyan it makes an impression on them. . . . How that name will echo. Listen!" And at the heart of Hemingway's attack is this: "Soon the world will echo to it like Roland's horn at Roncevaux. (You can use that some time in a piece. It's in Spain but that's the French spelling. I give it to you, Mr. Saroyan. For nothing, kid. It's a literary reference)" (159). The implication of the "kid" Saroyan's (and his generation's) cultural illiteracy is very much to the point here. Hemingway's generation would need no explanation of Roland or Roncevaux. William Faulkner, Hemingway's contemporary, in the concluding lines of his novel *Flags in the Dust* (written in the year after *The Sun Also Rises* appeared), memorably attributed a quality of "glamorous fatality" to the name of his Sartoris protagonists, a quality like the "dying fall of horns along the road to Roncevaux" (433; see Stoneback, "Hemingway and Faulkner" 154–60). Faulkner, never known for understatement, omission, or any form of iceberg principle in writing, offers no explanation of his Roncevaux allusion—because he assumes his readers will understand the reference, just as in 1957, speaking at the University of Virginia, Faulkner explained simply that Snopesism (modern amoral rapacity) will not prevail because "when the battle comes it always produces a Roland" (*Faulkner in the University* 34). That is a reference that I must—in 2006, as in 1970—explain to students. For the generation of Faulkner and Hemingway—as for many generations before, including my grandmother's—no explanation was necessary. We should have recognized long ago, and some early readers obviously did, that Jake is, as Hemingway later put it, on a "fishing expedition in the Pass of Roland."

The title of the first chapter of a contemporary guidebook declares in bold print the important thing about Roncevaux directly: "CAPITALE SPIRITUELLE DE L'EUROPE" (Del Burgo 7). As most contemporary guidebooks covering this region do, this volume stresses that Roncevaux is a "spiritual capital of Europe," an important place of pilgrimage not just for pilgrims on the route of Saint-Jacques/Santiago but for the pilgrimage to the place of Roland's death, as well as the regional pilgrimage to Nuestra Señora de Roncesvalles—the so-called Queen of the Pyrenees. In the twelfth century, the famous medieval pilgrim's guide, the *Liber Sancti Jacobi* (a possible source for Jake's name—see 78:6–7), linked Charlemagne with Saint Jacques/Santiago/Saint James and "outlined the fabled deeds that spanned the pilgrim road, reaching an apocalyptic climax on the pass at Roncesvalles where Roland . . . died"; and relics of the great battle "were distributed amongst sites that later became centers of pilgrimage." The mythic version of Charlemagne and Roland as Saint-Jacques/Santiago pilgrims "was thus cultivated to persuade the 'warrior' aristocracy not to disregard this way of salvation" (Tate and Tate 22). Some of the secular tourist guidebooks of Hemingway's time were less enthusiastic; in its brief description, the 1926 Blue Guides, for example, called Roncevaux "a miserable hamlet surrounding a half-ruined Augustinian Abbey" and pointed out that it was here "in 778 that the rearguard of Charlemagne's retreating army, led by Roland and the 'twelve peers' of France, was cut off and overwhelmed by stones hurled from the rocks above" (Muirhead and Monmarché, *Southern France* 394–95). Not a very enticing entry likely to encourage a casual tourist to visit, the description is notable mainly for its French/ Spanish designation of Roncevaux/Roncesvalles and for its inclusion in a guide to southern France. An early Baedeker's *Southern France* mentions the "magnificent" approach on "The Road to Roncevaux" and the "valley famous for the defeat of Charlemagne's rearguard in 778, and the death of Roland, better known in poetry than in history" (68–69). Other Baedeker's guides make brief mention of the pilgrimage to Roncevaux.

Guidebooks with a more narrowly regional coverage give more detail. For example, the 1928 *Illustrated Guide-Books: The French and Spanish Basque Country* describes the Battle of Roncevaux, and then the actual place as it was in the 1920s, including details of various buildings such as the Gothic Royal Collegiate Church of Roncevaux (the Iglesia de la Real Colegiata), with its collection of relics that are the goal of pilgrimages, a church "considered in Spain as one of the most famous sanctuaries of Christendom; it ranks next to Jerusalem, Roma and Saint-Jacques-de-Compostelle, under the protection of the Holy See and under the direct patronage of the King of Spain." Also mentioned is the "*Chapelle du St. Esprit,* where formerly were buried the pilgrims from Saint-Jacques-de-Compostelle who happened to die at Roncevaux," and where masses are held for Roland and "the doughty knights of Charlemagne who are supposed to be buried there." After some details about religious processions at Roncevaux, the guidebook writer concludes: "There is only a Spanish inn at Roncevaux: to get more comfort, it is better to go to Burguete" (Lamare 163). In a more recent guidebook to the Saint-Jacques/Santiago pilgrimage route, we read: "At the foot of the mountain, Roncesvalles appears like some medieval apparition amongst beech trees and oaks." Aside from Roland and Charlemagne, the place owes its fame to the Royal Hospital and Pilgrim's Inn, and the writer quotes a verse from a twelfth-century "Ode to the Hospital of Roncevaux": "It opens its gates to the sick and the sound / both to the catholics and the pagans / jews heretics, beggars and the vain, / and embraces them all as if they were its brothers"—"Marvellous charity," the guide writer exclaims, "without limits of land nor ideological or religious frontiers: if it were not like this, it would not be charity . . . !" The same writer praises the collegiate church, "presided over by the Virgin of Roncesvalles under a canopy of embossed silver," and the library and museum, which contain such relics as Roland's maces; and he also notes the tiny "pilgrims' church," the Chapel of Santiago, and the Chapel of Sancti Spiritus (*le Saint-Esprit,* Holy Spirit), also known as Charlemagne's Silo, the mortuary building where the remains of Roland and his knights, and later pilgrims, are said to be buried (Arrondo 40–41). It is clear from all the guidebooks that the main reasons to go to Roncevaux/Roncesvalles are perhaps for its literary and historical associations and, more important, for pilgrimage—as a pilgrim of Saint-Jacques/Santiago, a pilgrim of Roland, the exemplary Christian knight, a pilgrim of Nuestra Señora de Roncesvalles/Notre-Dame de Roncevaux. It is equally clear that one does not go to Roncevaux for the fishing. There were many good trout streams within reasonable distance of Pamplona, and if fishing the Irati River were one's primary goal, there were places to stay much closer to the Irati than Roncevaux-Burguete (see 117:30). Jake, then, comes to Roncevaux as a pilgrim, not merely as an angler—in Roncevaux he is more Fisher King than Fisherman.

It is worth noting here that Hemingway wrote the first draft of this chapter, as we can tell from his dated and place-designated manuscript notebooks, in Hendaye, France. The scholar who has studied most closely the day-by-day writing of the manuscript of *The Sun Also Rises,* William Balassi, concludes that what he designates Sessions 22–33 of the composition process, covering pages 59 to 111 of the published text, were written in Hendaye on 10–17 August 1925, and this, the first of the Roncevaux-Burguete chapters, "was probably the last of the material written during Hemingway's Spanish vacation since he returned to Paris on 18 August" ("Writing of the Manuscript" 75; see also Balassi, "How It Probably Was" 157–64). Although it is not helpful (or accurate) to see Hemingway's eight-day period of intense writing in Hendaye, in the south of France, characterized as part of "Hemingway's Spanish vacation," the more important point has to do with *what* he wrote and *where* he wrote it. Hendaye is just north of the French-Spanish border, across the Bidassoa River from the old Spanish town of Fuenterrabia. There is a minor tradition to the effect that Roland fought and died at Fuenterrabia rather than Roncevaux; it is not a widely current belief and it may have its source in the work of a few British writers. For example, in a well-known passage from *Paradise Lost,* John Milton evokes how Charlemagne's "peerage fell / By Fontarabbia," and Sir Walter Scott, in *Marmion,* invokes Roland with these much quoted words: "O, for a blast of that dread horn, / On Fontarabian echoes borne!" (Darwin 345, 418). As noted above, David Bourne, Hemingway's writer-protagonist in *The Garden of Eden,* walks around Hendaye and thinks of a line from *The Song of Roland:* "Ah que ce cor ha longue haleine." And then, thinking of Roland's long-breathed reverberating horn (and perhaps remembering Scott's line with the inauthentic place designation), he wishes he were at the place where it really happened: Roncevaux.

At the very least, it is interesting that Hemingway wrote this Roncevaux scene in Hendaye, in the place that a variant legend held to be the location of Roland's death. It is also possible that he stayed on in Hendaye to be in the proximity of Roncevaux (about one hundred kilometers away) as he wrote his first Roncevaux chapter. In Balassi's manuscript study, he notes that Hemingway wrote pages 84–89 (the pilgrim scene on the train) on 14 August, when he "decided to make Bill a Catholic, then changed his mind and instead made Jake a Catholic" ("Writing of the Manuscript" 75). Perhaps Hemingway was indeed hearing the echo of Roland's horn, at least in his creative imagination, during his time at Hendaye. And given how close he was to Roncevaux, he may have gone there from Hendaye to check some details before he left for Paris. On 15 August, the date of Roland's death in 778, there are—every year—ceremonies and special pilgrimage masses held at Roncevaux in honor of Roland. Was Hemingway there during the composition of *The Sun Also Rises*? Quite possibly so, and if he was, he might have witnessed a smaller-scale version of what I saw on 15 August 1978, the twelve-hundredth anniversary of Roland's death: a vast crowd—the newspapers estimated thirty to forty thousand—of mostly younger Europeans (French, German, Italian, Scandinavian, and, of course, Basque and Spanish) in a festive mood, with many songs sung and chanted bits of old poems, and some even blew long and haunting notes on antique hunting horns. There were religious and secular ceremonies, much music and dancing, and even a reading of *The Song of Roland* conducted by members of the pilgrimage associations of Santiago/Saint-Jacques. And, as the newspapers observed, it was "sobre todo, una fiesta"—above all, a fiesta indeed, with its rich blend of the sacred and the profane. I talked to many who were there that day, and although few seemed to be the penitential pilgrims one often sees at Roncevaux religious processions, and for some it was the Basque Fiesta at Orreaga (the modern Basque name for Roncevaux), they all knew exactly where they were and why they were there: they were Roland pilgrims, some said, and others said they were Nuestra Señora de Roncesvalles pilgrims, and all knew they were at a numinous place on the pilgrimage of Saint-Jacques/Santiago and they were there, one way or the other, because of Roland. It was a typical fiesta, and although there were no bullfights, it was like Pamplona's, a fiesta with its rich blend of the sacred and the secular: pageantry and ritual dealing with life and death—Hemingway's primary motif in *The Sun Also Rises*. As even a recent *New York Times* article recognized—in a travel essay on Seville's Holy Week (*Semana Santa*) ceremonies, from solemn religious processions to the celebration of "resurrection on Easter morning and the year's first major bullfight later that afternoon," followed by the drinking and dancing of the Feria—there is something "deep and reassuring" for even the nonreligious participant in the ritual transformation of mundane place "into a sacred place." The *Times* even gets the bold-print headline right: "A Moving Ritual . . . blends the sacred and the profane" (Clarey 1, 9). We must bring some such understanding to our reading, not only of the Fiesta of San Fermín but to all the sacred places of *The Sun Also Rises*. As Hemingway knows, and Jake knows, Roncevaux is a sacred place, and Jake the Fisher King inhabits deep time in its numinous landscape (see 170:15–16).

Cultural literacy, recognition of what Roncevaux means (and why Hemingway would set important chapters of his novel in that Roland country), is not lost completely, not in Europe, where even food and beer carry the Roland brand name, which employs Rolandesque iconography (swords, horns, allusions to *The Song of Roland*). In an undergraduate class on *The Sun Also Rises* a few years ago, a student brought in a jar of mustard; the label on the crock read: "Roland: Moutarde a L'Ancienne. Product of France." And on both sides of the label was printed an extensive passage (parts of forty-five lines!) from *The Song of Roland*, including a passage about Roland blowing his horn. Since Americans are inveterate readers of food labels, maybe "nutrition facts" will take on a new meaning, maybe there is hope that we can reinvest, *ingest,* our lost cultural literacy. Those who know the Parable of the Mustard Seed (Matthew 17.20) may continue to have faith that mountains can be moved.

108:30 **It's high:** If readers consult a detailed map (always a good idea for close readers who wish to decode exactly a Hemingway text), they will see that at the precise place where Jake says the altitude "must be twelve hundred metres" (i.e, somewhere between the "edge of the rise" and where the bus levels "down" into the stream valley on the straight stretch of the road to Burguete), it is about 900 meters. When they level down and cross the bridge they are at 860 meters. Burguete is at 960 meters, and just beyond, Roncevaux (the church and the "monastery," or complex of religious buildings) is at 981 meters. Two kilometers up the road the famous mountain pass of Roncevaux (also called the Port or Col Ibañeta) is at 1,057 meters, and the mountaintops on either side of the pass range from 1,266 to 1,280 meters. Why does this matter? Because Jake's reliability as narrator and travel guide, his exactitude regarding all matters of place from churches to wines to bullfights to altitude, is an essential part of his character. Some readers might hastily conclude that Jake is way off here regarding the altitude, since at the spot when he says it "must be twelve hundred metres" it can only be about 900 meters. But who would give the altitude reading of a bus in motion? Clearly, Jake is looking off at the "high" place, near the mountaintop, where, as widely believed, Roland fought and died—and that place is at about 1,200 meters. Jake's vision is centered on the *elevated* place, and his altitude assessment is neither incorrect nor exaggerated. Note, too, that Jake *sees* Roncevaux about six kilometers in the distance, and Bill does not. This signifies, among other things, that Jake knows where he is going. (For a more detailed discussion of this question, see Stoneback, "From the Rue Saint-Jacques " 6–8.)

108:33 **crossroads:** This is the point where route C127 intersects with N135, the road they are on. The small bridge they cross is over the Rio Urrobi, the headwaters of which are near Roncevaux; from this point, the Urrobi flows south twenty kilometers to empty into the Irati near Itoiz. Given the iteration of "crossroads and crossed,"

Jake's landscape details may be read symbolically. In the manuscript Hemingway had written "cross roads," his usual idiosyncratic spelling that serves to emphasize the "cross" (see, e.g., his short story "Black Ass at the Cross Roads," *Complete Short Stories*).

109:1 **Burguete:** Guidebooks of the 1920s generally devote one sentence to Burguete, describing it as a "market-town" of some size, and noting that it has one "very fair" or "up-to-date" hotel—the Hostal Burguete, where Jake and Bill stay (see below). More detailed regional and pilgrimage guidebooks tell us some interesting information: "Historiquement, Burguete fut le premier village édifié dans cette plaine et fut appelé Villa de Roncesvalles (*Villa Runcievallis*). . . . Au XIIe siècle, l'on réserve le nom de *Villa o Burgo de Roncesvalles*. . . . Le diminutif de Burguete apparaît pour la première fois dans un document de 1476. Burguete est donc antérieur à Roncevaux, et porta son nom avant lui (Burgo de Roncesvalles)" (Del Burgo 16–17). Thus, in brief, Burguete is in reality (and had long been in name) the *village* of Roncevaux, as opposed to the religious buildings and pilgrimage complex just up the road. In the fifteenth century the "Burg of Roncevaux" acquired its diminutive form, Burguete, and dropped its Roncevaux place designation. This clarifies the confusion, for example, that I felt when I came up from Pamplona and first stayed in Burguete in 1973; I asked the innkeeper how far it was to Roncevaux, and she told me: "You *are in* Roncevaux." Or, as a pilgrimage guide puts it, "a step or two further" down the road from the "ecclesiastical buildings at Roncesvalles" the pilgrim comes to Burguete, where the "present-day hotels rest on the foundations of old hospitals" (i.e., establishments that existed to serve the pilgrims of Roncevaux and Saint-Jacques; Tate and Tate 72).

109:3 **school-yard:** Over the years several of my Hemingway students have said that they hear an echo, in this line where the bus passes the church and the school yard, of Emily Dickinson's famous poem "Because I could not stop for death." They may be right—Dickinson's "Carriage" that passes the school yard, her fields of grain and "Setting Sun," her evocation of timeless time or short "Centuries," and her concern with Death, Immortality, and Eternity resonate with the details of Jake's carriage or bus ride as he passes fields, crossroads, and the school yard and, as the sun goes down, steps into the numinous landscape of Roncevaux, a timeless place where the *deus loci*, the spirit of place, echoes Death, Immortality, and Eternity.

109:4 **carabineer:** In the manuscript, Hemingway wrote "carabiniere." See 92:7.

109:13 **the inn:** At least since the 1970s this inn has been called the Hostal Burguete; in the 1920s it was called the Hotel Burguete and was one of six hotels listed in regional guidebooks. Standard guidebooks such as Baedeker and the Blue Guides listed only this hotel, no prices given, and noted that French was spoken by the inn-keepers. I stayed in this inn in the 1970s, and again in the 1980s, and it was not much changed from the 1920s, when Jake (and Hemingway) stayed here. Since the 1920s an upper story has been added to the building; but the interior descriptions, the details, and the ambiance, including even the family (the *same* family in the 1970s) that ran the hotel, were recognizable as described by Hemingway (see following entries). We should note, too, that the hotel, at least its foundation and original stories, is most likely a building that originally existed to serve pilgrims (see 109:1). Thus Jake and Bill are staying in a pilgrimage hostel.

Since one of the possible uses of this study, given the close attention to details of travel and place, is as a guidebook for the traveler wishing to follow today in Hemingway's steps, it might be noted that the landscapes and places depicted by Hemingway, perhaps more so than any other writer, seem to compel readers to visit the actual places. And many have written of such travels, creating a kind of sub-genre of Hemingwayana. For an engaging and informative account of the current Hostal Burguete and its history, based on observations made in the 1980s and 1990s, see the book by the Hemingway enthusiast and traveler Robert Burgess, who de-votes eight chapters to the details of the Burguete section of the novel (291–365).

109:19–20 **Nuestra Señora de Roncesvalles:** In the manuscript, Hemingway wrote "big framed steel engraving of the silver"—then crossed out "silver"—"Nuestra Se-ñora de Roncevalles. It was a beautiful silver virgin and"—then he lined these last seven words out and continued with the description of the wind as it appears in the published text. This deletion conforms with Hemingway's consistent practice as he moves from manuscript to published text of *understating* his religious details; he leaves the crucial signpost there but eliminates Jake's emotional and aesthetic response to the "beautiful silver virgin." In addition, had he left Jake's response to the engraving in the text, it might have suggested the response to the actual Virgin, the famous statue of Nuestra Señora de Roncesvalles (Notre Dame de Roncevaux) under the high altar canopy of the church of Santa Maria, the Gothic collegiate church just up the road at Roncevaux. Known as the Queen of the Pyrenees, this extraordinarily beautiful Virgin has long been the object of pilgrimages undertaken by residents throughout the Pyrenees from both sides of the French-Spanish bor-der. Carved from cedar, the statue is plated in silver, except for the face and hands, and ornamented with gold and precious stones. The most venerated object in the church, it was created in France circa 1300. (The church itself is considered an out-standing example of Parisian Gothic.) Local knowledge and tradition maintain that it is a faithful image of the ninth-century apparition of the Virgin Mary at Roncev-aux. It is said that the Virgin appeared to local shepherds some years after Roland's death, and the two events are linked in the popular imagination that has inspired so many pilgrimages to Roncevaux (see 108:26 and Del Burgo 75, 95–100). Hemingway undoubtedly knew this information and had seen the actual statue in the church (as Jake might have, too, on a previous visit). But in the rendered action of the novel Jake has not yet been to the church that he visits two chapters later (see 128:16). And, to Hemingway's creative radar, the deleted response to the "beautiful silver virgin" must have seemed an extreme reaction to a hotel room decoration. In 1973 when I stayed in what the Hostal Burguete called "Hemingway's Room," all the furniture and the room location (second floor, facing Roncevaux) that Jake notes here were the same, and Our Lady of Roncevaux was hanging on the wall. I would not have called her a "beautiful silver virgin"—at least not until the next day when I first saw the real old thing, the statue in the church. (For discussion of the Hemingway Room as it appears more recently, see Burgess 306–9.)

109:27 **upright piano:** The upright piano that Bill plays to keep warm was still in the Hostal Burguete the last time I was there (in 2006), and the innkeepers still proudly pointed to it as the piano Hemingway played. (Hemingway did not play the piano.) When I first played this piano in 1973, I was shown a fake inscription inside the top lid reputed to have been made by Hemingway—with his name spelled wrong and an impossible date lightly carved into the wood. On a later visit, around 1980, I noticed they had glued on the inside of the lid a photograph of Hemingway obviously taken from a newspaper or magazine. On another visit to the inn, in 1992, the piano was even more out of tune, and when the innkeeper offered to move things piled on top of the piano to show me the evidence that Hemingway had played the piano, I politely told him not to bother, as I had seen it years ago. Perhaps the more interesting and unanswerable question here is what was Bill playing? (See Burgess's chapter "The Piano" for details on the piano in more recent times, 315–25.)

110:4 **too much:** Jake is right—they *are* being overcharged for a basic room (with bathroom down the hall) in a simple small-town inn. At the Montoya/Quintana in Pamplona they had paid five pesetas for a room, and lunch or dinner was six pesetas (see 94:9–10). At the Panier Fleuri, one of the best hotels in Bayonne, they had paid ten francs, or less than $1.00 in 1926 (see 91:11). At the mid-1920s exchange rate, the steep twelve pesetas that they must pay in Burguete was about $1.70. The "fat woman" tells him it's her "big season" (a line added after the original manuscript); Jake notes that they are the only people staying there. Jake decides to make it up in wine. For those intent on finding a nonexistent "France/Spain split in values" in the novel (see 25:2 and passim), the price-gouging, suspicious, rum-skimping, bottle-counting demeanor of this innkeeper should be contrasted with the "nice" hotel, "good" room, and "very cheerful" hotelkeepers at the French Hôtel Panier Fleuri. Hemingway's additions (the "big season" excuse for price jacking in an empty hotel, the lack of rum in the punch, the counting of the empty wine bottles) after the manuscript version emphasized the overcharging and skimpiness of the Burguete hotel.

110:32 **hot vegetable soup:** This excellent traditional soup of the Pyrenees includes chopped onion, sliced leeks, minced garlic, sliced cabbage, green beans, green peas, and white beans cooked with a large piece of cured ham. It is still served at the Hostal Burguete today, and they sometimes call it "Hemingway Soup." (A recipe for the soup is printed in Boreth's *The Hemingway Cookbook* 84.) As for the rest of the menu, the fried trout would be the version of *Trucha a la Navarra* that they serve (and I have eaten several times) at the Hostal Burguete (where they still tell you, as they told me in 1973 as in 2006, it was Hemingway's favorite dish). There may be as many variations on the classic country-cooking *Trucha a la Navarra* as there are country inns that serve trout—in the 1920s, from the local river; today, most likely from hatcheries—as their specialty throughout the Spanish and French Pyrenees, but it always involves trout fried in olive oil and layered or stuffed with cured Serrano ham—and it is almost always very good. It's difficult to say exactly what that "some sort of stew" was, but the wild mountain strawberries had to be delicious, as they always are when one is walking in the mountains around Roncevaux. Smoking and reading in bed, Jake feels good, a well-fed pilgrim in the good place, free, and far removed from the anxieties created by Brett's presence.

CHAPTER 12

112:1 **morning:** This is one of several bright, clear, dewy-fresh cloudless morning scenes that echo the novel's title.

112:3 **old diligence:** Literally, an old horse carriage, or stagecoach, metaphorically, this is a reminder of the attentive care and assiduity necessary in dealing with problems, making progress on a hard road the old traditional way. In the manuscript Hemingway called it a "relic" from the old days, but here in this country of many sacred "relics" that were the goal of pilgrimages, that must have seemed too obvious an allusion (or maybe he rejected the ironic mixture of sacred and profane relics), so Hemingway changed it to something "left from the days" before buses. Perhaps this diligence also echoes the last horse carriage we've seen in the novel, the "horse-cab" in Paris, after Bill jokes about giving Jake the "stuffed" horse-cab for Christmas (see 73:1 and next entry), and they take their last "ride" together before the final taxi ride in Madrid in the novel's closing scene.

112:5 **goat:** This goat, together with the near-biblical goat on the old man's back at the border crossing (see 92:5), may add up to one of Hemingway's characteristic paired symbolic scenes. There are many significations associated with goats, from the he-goat Devil to the lasciviousness of the domestic goat to the sharp-sighted watchful mountain goat that represents Christ seeking his beloved, the Church, or the all-seeing God (Metford 110). And this goat, on the roof of the old diligence, may remind us, too, of the horse carriage in Paris that Bill is going to stuff for Jake (see 112:3). If recurrent echoic scenes add up to something (although literature is not math), then maybe the old man with the goat on his back is a type and paradigm of Jake, with a goat on the roof of the "stuffed" carriage associated with Brett, the emblem of lasciviousness that Jake must get off his back, must sacrifice (as Jake will seem to "sacrifice" Brett in Pamplona, watching her go off with Romero, although he cannot be held solely responsible for that). Yet sometimes, especially in the early morning, a goat may be just a goat, especially the kind of nosy and humorous goats that watch what you are doing.

112:16 **trouty:** This small stream is the Ansobi, a tributary of the Urrobi; it flows behind the Hostal Burguete and still, in the 1970s, did not "look trouty," and local inquiry indicated that there were no trout in it. (Fishermen, however, know what that might mean. And on one visit in the 1970s or 1980s I saw trout in it.) In the manuscript, after "trouty," Hemingway had written: "It did not have any look of reserve at all. It was just a flat, fairly fast moving brook winding behind the houses and under fences and willow trees" (*Facsimile* 1:306). This may be, for some readers, one of those inexplicable and regrettable deletions, sacrificing as it does the exact and poetic image of a stream that lacks the "look of reserve." But then, given Hemingway's stylistic preoccupations, it may be the very principle of "reserve" that sometimes requires the sacrifice of poetry.

113:6 **asked her . . . that:** Originally, Hemingway had written "I told her to get coffee for us and that we wanted a lunch"; but when he changed "told" to "asked," he did not appropriately revise the rest of the sentence (*Facsimile* 1:306).

113:31 **irony and pity:** This motif (and joke) sets the tone in the opening pages of this chapter. In a little over one page, Hemingway repeats the phrase, or some variation thereof, eleven times. As the context makes clear, "irony and pity" is the literary catchphrase of the hour—"They're mad about it in New York"—the latest American buzzwords used by such essayists and literary journalists as H. L. Mencken and Gilbert Seldes, following after Anatole France, the French writer who had earlier popularized the "irony and pity" formula (see 50:32). In April 1925, three months before he began writing *The Sun Also Rises,* Hemingway wrote a letter filled with literary gossip to John Dos Passos in the States, asking: "What's all this about Pity and Irony. Never heard of them" (*Selected Letters* 158; see also following entry).

114:1 **Bill singing:** The proper title of the song tune Bill sings is "For Me and My Gal." Immensely popular throughout the 1920s (and long afterward), it was first published during the war (1917) and was a big hit in 1917–1918. Like many popular wartime songs, it would appeal to a soldier's longing for home and normalcy, for domesticity; the song, as everyone once knew, evokes a wedding day, with the church bells ringing, and the future dream of a "little home for two, for three or four or more in Love-land, for me and my gal." The actual words of the song, from Jake's perspective (and from the view of many wounded soldiers), provide the perfect subtext for a series of variations, replete with irony and pity, on the things Jake will never have: a wedding, a wife, a home with kids—and the bells will never ring in "Love-land" for Jake and Brett. Why does Bill sing his song first thing in the morning? Maybe it's the unspecified tune that he was playing the night before, a tune lively enough to warm him up. Maybe the sheet music was on the hotel piano. The illustration on the cover of the 1917 sheet music of "For Me and My Gal" features a naked Cupid with a quiver of *arrows* on his back, peering through a curtain at a man kissing a woman in a wedding veil, with the parson who presides at their wedding watching them kiss. The parson (appropriately for 1917) looks a good deal like Woodrow Wilson. Maybe he also looks like the count, who, after telling his story about *arrow* wounds, instructed Brett about "love" and played Cupid, asking Brett and Jake: "Why don't you get married, you two?" (61). And that scene and chapter end with Jake ringing the bell to his apartment building, going home alone after having kissed Brett goodnight (65:8). It should also be noted—although Hemingway commentary has sometimes wrongly held that Bill's ironic ditty cannot be sung to the tune of "For Me and My Gal" and this may tell us something about Bill's (or Hemingway's) flawed musical ear—that Bill's words are perfectly (and wondrously ironically) singable to that tune. James Hinkle, for example, in "What's Funny in *The Sun Also Rises*," asserts that "There is no way Bill's words can be made to fit that tune" and, misconstruing this, discovers further misconstrued "humor" based on his dismissal of Bill's musicality (118–19). Literary critics are generally not noted for their singing skills, but the reader can rest assured, based on the forty-year singing-songwriting career of this literary critic, that Hemingway selected exactly the right tune for Bill's song. And the rhyming word for "pity," although unprintable in the 1920s, should be obvious. In addition, the close reader might wonder if the ellipsis after Bill's "When they're feeling . . ." indicates an authorial ellipsis or Bill's omission of the word—after all, who would walk into a hotel restaurant belting out the word "shitty"? Probably not even Bill, not in the 1920s, not even in a small hotel in a foreign country where the word might not be understood. In the manuscript, Hemingway wrote, "feeling _____," perhaps indicating that *Bill* left a blank space in his song (308). Writing to his editor, Maxwell Perkins, during the final preparations for publication, Hemingway noted: "If the Irony and pity ditty bothers there are a couple of things you could do—reduce the size of the dashes and omit periods after them. Or just run it all in together. No dashes and no periods. Do whatever you like with it. I don't care what happens to that as long as the words are not changed and nothing inserted" (*Selected Letters* 215).

114:11 **Fratellinis:** A famous family of French circus performers, stars of the Cirque Medrano in Paris, Albert, François, and Paul Fratellini are often credited with refining and defining the role of clowns in the circus. Albert Fratellini in particular was regarded as an extraordinary comic actor; Picasso was said to be a regular visitor to his dressing room at the Cirque Medrano. In the early 1920s, Darius Milhaud, the avant-garde French composer, and his "Group of Six" young French composers, together with their poet companions, often went to the Cirque Medrano to admire the poetry and creativity of the Fratellini performances. Bill suggests that they are no longer the latest art craze, having been supplanted by "irony and pity." Circus clowns also know a good deal about "irony and pity." Hemingway alludes to the Fratellinis in *The Torrents of Spring* (56), and in the opening chapter of *Death in the*

Afternoon, explaining how the death of horses by disembowelment in the bullring can be regarded as comic, he writes: "It is as comic when what is trailing is real as when the Fratellinis give a burlesque of it in which the viscera are represented by rolls of bandages, sausages and other things" (7). Apparently Hemingway had seen the Fratellinis perform a circus bullfight burlesque.

114:12 **buttered toast:** Readers, perhaps especially American readers, are often puzzled by these two curious sentences about the toast, which may seem to make no distinction in spite of the difference implied by Hemingway's second sentence beginning: "Or, rather." In fact, the distinction is there: although "buttered toast" would suggest to most American readers the familiar soft bread, just toasted, still warm, with melting butter, what the girl actually brings is the cold, pretoasted, and very crisp continental version of toast—the familiar French *pain grillé* or some Spanish version thereof. Thus the point of these two seemingly odd and attention-getting sentences that may strike readers as awkward is to emphasize Jake's precision of observation of details, his exactitude of description—certainly one of his major character traits.

114:21 **Primo de Rivera:** The Spanish general established, with the approval of King Alfonso XIII, a dictatorship in 1923, ruling Spain until 1930, when he was forced into exile.

114:23 **the Riff:** The mountainous coastal region of north Morocco (also spelled Rif), where the Riffian Berbers revolted against Spain in 1921, declaring independence and creating the Republic of the Rif. At the time Jake says this (the summer of 1925), the Spanish are indeed in a "jam" in the "Riff," having been driven back to their coastal enclaves by the Riffian troops. (In late 1925, however, a joint force of Spanish—led by Primo de Rivera—and French troops counterattacked, and the Republic of the Rif was dissolved in 1926.) Jake puns on the three previous mentions of the raspberry jam the girl has brought them, and Bill dismisses Jake's pun as "very poor." However, Bill doesn't get the depth of Jake's joke, which probably includes Jake's sense of "riffing"—in both comedy and music a phrase, newly current in the 1920s, for extending a passage—in a "jam session," another term for improvisation that appeared in the 1920s. Thus, Jake, way out in front of Bill in the punning game, riffs on the jam and gives him a metaphorical "raspberry" but plays along with his "irony and pity" game by saying "something pitiful" (Robert Cohn) before trying to retreat from all the joking because it's "too early in the morning."

115:16 **expatriate . . . soil:** By this point in Bill's hilarious riff on the latest literary trends in New York, he has shifted from "irony and pity" to the absurdity of American journalistic complaints about expatriate writers, who, having given up their

American roots, will never write anything worthwhile. Bill stresses the word "expatriate," repeating it four times, as if it's a *dirty* word. Still, some readers (as the experienced teacher of this novel will know) persist in confusing the word "expatriate," which simply means one who lives abroad, with "ex-patriot," as a designation for someone who has lost his or her patriotic love of country; and these same readers will sometimes take seriously Bill's humorous charges that Jake has abandoned his American roots for phony European standards. Bill, of course, is mocking not Jake but the American writers who make these kind of sweeping statements about expatriate writers, and Bill's list of these "complaints" (sex obsession, excessive drinking, café malingering, etc.) sounds exactly like what some reviewers who read the novel as an *endorsement* of some imagined "lost generation" way of life would later say about *The Sun Also Rises*. Hemingway, knowing what some of his readers would say, fends off future criticism by mocking it in advance. It is interesting, too, that Bill would repeat the American cliché about losing touch with the soil just as they are about to embark on a long walk and fishing excursion that is, in fact, the essence of being in "touch with the soil," and that Bill would utter the New York banality about being ruined by "fake European standards," in a book that is about recovering the real old standards, values, rituals, and traditions of France and Spain that were no longer understood in America. While many American writers, including Mencken, one of the novel's favorite targets, echoed the theme of the debilitating effects of expatriation, Hemingway may well have had in mind here the writing, in general, of Van Wyck Brooks, and specifically Brooks's 1925 volume *The Pilgrimage of Henry James*, which argued that James was ruined by expatriation, never becoming the great writer he might have been had he remained in the United States. It seems that Hemingway read the Brooks book not long before he began work on *The Sun Also Rises*, since Scott Fitzgerald wrote to Brooks in June 1925: "I read the James book, so did Zelda + Ernest Hemingway" (*Correspondence of F. Scott Fitzgerald* 170). Thus Brooks's thesis about the enervating European pilgrimage of James probably helped to inspire not only Bill's riff on expatriation, and his allusion to Henry James, but also Hemingway's anti-Brooksian authentic pilgrimage motif and structure in the novel he was about to write (see following entry).

115:27 **Like Henry's bicycle:** Although there was no mention of this in the manuscript, Hemingway added in the typescript: "Like Henry James' bicycle." Responding to editorial insistence that the allusion be deleted, Hemingway wrote to Maxwell Perkins: "As for the Henry James thing—I haven't the second part of the Ms. here—it is over at Scott's—so I can't recall the wording. But I believe it is a reference to some accident that is generally known to have happened to Henry James in his youth." He assured Perkins it was not a "sneering" reference to James (another Scribners author), just the use of "an historical example"—and the bicycle was just a non sequitur (*Selected Letters* 208–9). But Hemingway yielded to Perkins's objection and removed James's last name, thus rendering an already cryptic allusion even more so. There had long been a vague rumor to the effect that James suffered, in his youth, an obscure injury to his groin, which left him impotent. Fitzgerald, in his 1925 letter written in response to the Van Wyck Brooks book on James that Hemingway had also read (see above entry), asked Brooks: "Why didn't you touch more on James [sic] impotence (physical)?" (*Correspondence of F. Scott Fitzgerald* 170). Although much has been written on James's "wound," it remains obscure and in the realm of speculation—something that has indeed been worked "up into a mystery," as Bill advises Jake to do regarding his "accident" and the rumor that he is impotent. Of course, some Hemingway critics to the contrary (see Oliver 166), Jake is not *impotent*, but dephallused (see 30:26). In any case, James (via Van Wyck Brooks) may have provided a kind of model for Hemingway's conception of Jake, both his sexual dilemma and his European expatriation and pilgrimage.

115:29 **being impotent:** Jake is not hurt by Bill's "crack" about impotence because he is not impotent. Definitions of impotence do not usually cover the lack of a penis. Here, after Jake wants to get Bill started again, twenty-four lines of the original manuscript are deleted, including the passage that immediately followed "start him again": "It is funny that a thing that ninety nine times out of a hundred you yourself never even think about other people should mind so. It is imagination I suppose. Bill has plenty of that" (*Facsimile* 1:312–13). Does this deleted passage suggest that Bill can only guess, imagine, the exact nature of Jake's wound? The rest of the deleted passage lamented the fact that, for some people, "Sex explains everything"—and nobody's allowed to believe they're having fun without it because "Everybody's frustrated" (313). In place of these deleted lines, Hemingway inserted the next eleven lines on the bicycle-tricycle-joystick.

116:1 **joystick:** Jake knows about airplanes and joysticks; both Jake and Bill obviously know that early tricycles did not have handlebars, but a steering post somewhat similar to a joystick, and they both engage in elaborate wordplay here: Jake cannot pedal-*peddle* his missing joystick, Bill wants to *lay* off that subject, and Jake is just standing *up* for the tricycle. Not all commentators have agreed regarding the influence of James Joyce on Hemingway, but Robert Gajdusek, for example, has argued that Joyce is a major influence, and he sees this chapter as "the most textually dense and Joycean chapter of the novel" ("Hemingway and Joyce" 27). He notes that the "point about the joystick of an airplane is that it is at once a sensual tool and a device facilitating elevation or descent," and, since it appears in a passage that focuses on both "Henry James's supposed impotence . . . and Jake's dephallused state, it has a strong sexual connotation. Additionally, in many planes the joystick is at once a stick *and* a wheel (masculine and feminine). Historically, the joystick was originally the Joyce stick, taking its name from its inventor, a man named Joyce—a fact that Hemingway undoubtedly knew. Therefore, Hemingway's joystick is his Joyce stick—or Joyce trick?—a way of reconciling masculine and feminine possibilities in one image even as it allows one to mediate between or reconcile air and earth, abstract masculine and physical feminine realms" (27). For Gajdusek, then, the joystick-Joyce stick-Joyce trick is central to this entire sequence, focused as it is on gender/sex ambiguities, on lesbians and homosexuals, and on the Civil War as a "psychic split" (see following entry) that announces Hemingway's concern with the "integrative synthesis of masculine and feminine" (27).

116:11 **in New York:** Bill—and Hemingway—are probably not as concerned here with the "integrative synthesis of masculine and feminine" (see preceding entry for Gajdusek's Jungian interpretation) as they are with how things are in the literary scene in New York, where Bill could not tell Jake how much he likes him without being taken for "a faggot." (This, too, serves as commentary on the Jamesian international theme, the contrast of American and European culture.) Obviously, Bill does not think that Lincoln and Grant and Davis were homosexuals—but he is mocking those in New York who would make such arguments. In New York, as a long passage deleted from the manuscript has it, "Sex explains it all" and this idée fixe is enough to "make you sick"; "And every literary bastard in New York never goes to bed at night not knowing but that he'll wake up in the morning and find himself a fairy" (*Facsimile* 1:314). The deleted passage has Bill and Jake repeatedly affirming that they are free from such sex-centered obsessions and are genuinely happy. Jake says: "Ninety percent of the time I'm happy. Honest to God." They agree on the "swell time," the "damned good time," that they can have away from sex-obsessed New York, where everybody is stuffed into one sex/gender closet or another. Given all the literary allusions in this chapter, it is engaging to note one surprising allusion that is lost by this manuscript deletion. Jake says: "We're a couple of bright young Polly [crossed out] glad girls." Clearly, Hemingway had started to write "Pollyannas" then understated his allusion only slightly by referring to the almost-as-legendary "glad girls." Eleanor H. Porter's *Pollyanna,* a 1913 novel that became an almost instantaneous children's literature classic, was an immense best seller and had gone through more than fifty printings by the mid-1920s. The very words "Pollyanna" and "glad girl" became commonplace within a few years, first as terms to describe someone who is always happy, cheerful, optimistic, someone who by playing the "glad game" could be happy in spite of the most disastrous circumstances—or injuries, we might note, since it is often forgotten that Pollyanna is badly injured in a car accident, can't walk, can't feel anything in her legs, and embarks on a slow recovery. Pollyanna insists that we must feel our happiness, our "glad game" of joy and pleasure in life in spite of our losses and brokenness. Of course, subjected to the acids of modernity, to the corrosiveness of such literary posturing and fashions as the "irony and pity" syndrome, Pollyanna eventually became a derogatory term and entered most dictionaries as a synonym for a naively or blindly optimistic person. In fact, the real Pollyanna, like Jake, is tough—in Hemingway's memorable phrase from *A Farewell to Arms,* "strong at the broken places" (249)—utterly alive, and happy "ninety percent of the time," as Jake says. In the manuscript, after Jake says they're "bright young glad girls," Bill says: "The hell we are. I wasn't kidding were you?" "No," Jake says, "but it just made me a little embarrassed to tell the truth" (*Facsimile* 1:315). And the truth is Jake *is* happy, especially when Brett's not around; most readers, especially first-time readers of the novel free from the infection of any "lost generation," degenerate-expatriate, irony-and-pity thesis-ridden de/reconstruction of the novel, *feel* Jake's happiness. Pollyanna, then, the true Pollyanna, takes her place as yet another wounded quester and Fisher King avatar, another Jamesian pilgrim, another of the many literary allusions that provide the iceberg foundation for this chapter—a chapter that nearly everyone agrees is one of the *happiest* chapters in the novel.

116:16 **The Colonel's Lady:** This is Bill's New York–style parody of the closing lines of Rudyard Kipling's famous poem "The Ladies": "For the Colonel's Lady an' Judy O'Grady / Are sisters under their skins!" (Darwin 298). Although Kipling's poem is about taking "fun" where one finds it and how one "must pay for [one's] fun," and what one can "learn about women," and although *Lady* Brett Ashley had her title from a husband who commanded a ship (as per the deleted first chapter of the novel), he is not a colonel, she is not the colonel's lady, Judy O'Grady is nowhere to be found in the novel, and Brett is not a lesbian. That is, this literary echo provides no deep-layered interpretive resonance; the point of the allusion is Bill's mockery of what the New York literary scene would make of Kipling, of everything.

116:32 **path crossed a stream:** Given the precision of the novel's text regarding this hike, it is easily possible to follow Jake's route today, to find it little changed from the 1920s. For example, we know here that Jake and Bill have walked *up* the main road toward Roncevaux (about a half-kilometer), crossed a meadow onto a sandy path, and are here crossing the first stream, the Barranco de Arranosina, which flows down from Roncesvalles parallel to the road. The information on the entire route of the hike presented here is based on three sources: the text of *The Sun Also Rises,* a topographical map of the Roncesvalles quadrant, and my firsthand knowledge of the area dating back more than three decades. This last source of local knowledge is grounded in local inquiry and double-checking, extensive walking in the country here discussed, tours of back-country trails with the local forest ranger, and so on. It should be noted, however, that the conclusions reached here and in the following passages concerning the hike—that is, the essential geographical conclusions—can be confirmed by any good map and text reader without ever leaving home. It is particularly gratifying for the sharp-eyed Hemingway aficionado who follows this route today that many of the details Jake notes (tadpoles in a sand-bottom stream pool, cow bells in the woods, ancient beech trees, wild strawberries, fields of yellow gorse, etc.) are still the defining details of the landscape today. For a more detailed discussion of the hike, see Stoneback, "You Sure This Thing Has Trout in It?"

117:5 **faster-flowing stream:** The Barranco de Soralucea joins the Arranosina (see above) to form the Rio Urrobi. After crossing the stream, the path joins the "road." Hemingway's text and all detailed maps, including those from the 1920s, agree that this is a dirt "road," a *camino,* that they follow, not a *senda* or *itinerario de ascension,* that is, not a hiking trail but a route suitable for farm animals and—today, for the most part—some farm machinery and jeeps.

117:9 **beech wood:** As they enter the woods, Jake notes carefully the very old and big trees, with their visible roots and twisted branches—a feature of the magical woods all around Roncevaux/Roncesvalles. Jake, of course, suppresses all emotion and adjectival rendering of what the woods make him feel, but for an idea of what Hemingway felt in this Rolandesque landscape, see what he wrote nearly thirty years later in *The Dangerous Summer* when he revisited the woods of this country: "I had expected it would all be cut and destroyed but it was still the last great forest of the Middle Ages with its great beeches" (138). While it is not *exactly* the same woods that Hemingway describes decades later, it is the typical "beech wood" of the region. What signifies is Hemingway's association of such woods with the real old thing, the "last great forest of the Middle Ages." Here, Jake says nothing, rendering the details that make the emotion, what he and Bill clearly feel (and Bill says): "This is country." This echoes the charged landscape moment in Paris when Jake and Bill stand on the bridge and look at another great sign of the Middle Ages, the cathedral of Notre-Dame; Bill says "It's pretty grand," and Jake says nothing, although he has indicated through his details of place and his silence that he feels as much, or more, than Bill does (see 77:16).

117:22 **height of land:** Here, they are at the Collado (hill, or small eminence) de Nabala; they have ascended 123 meters from Burguete and covered a little over four kilometers. Hemingway describes with verifiable precision the route that goes along the "shoulder of the ridge of hills"—the woods, the clearings, the cattle, even the wild strawberries on the sunny side of the ridge are still there. In the manuscript, Jake and Bill pick some wild strawberries, thus echoing the wild strawberries they were served at the inn. Why would Hemingway delete the few words that indicated that they actually picked some wild strawberries? This may be a small but telling instance of the way Hemingway's style forces the reader to participate in the action, the sequence of fact and motion being described, to force the reader, as it were, to pick the strawberries.

117:30 **course of the Irati:** When Jake says they see the Irati bluffs "way off," he means *way* off—at least thirteen to sixteen kilometers as the crow flies. This is a very distant prospect, not of the Irati River but of the topographical features that indicate the Irati Valley. When Jake explains to Bill how far it is, Bill says, "That's a hell of a hike," and Jake replies: "It's too far to go and fish and come back the same day comfortably." This—especially that "nice word," *comfortably*—is the first clear textual indication that they do not fish the Irati. For never has there been a more comfortable fishing, reading, eating, talking, sleeping afternoon than Bill and Jake are about to have. Contrary to one of the most fondly held beliefs of many Hemingway readers and most Hemingway commentators, they do *not* fish the Irati on this hiking excursion. And this fact has certain important implications that have generally been overlooked. If indeed, as most readers of the novel seem to believe, this entire two-chapter Burguete-Roncevaux interlude is about fishing the Irati, then why do they stay so far from the river? In the 1920s there were inns right on the Irati where they could have stayed, in several different locations on the river only a few kilometers farther away from Pamplona than Burguete. For example, at Orbaiceta, a town right on the Irati, there was in the 1920s what the guidebooks described as a good country inn (see, e.g., Monmarché 117). In Orbaiceta—at the end of the road (in 1925), seventeen kilometers west of Burguete—and other villages on the Irati, Jake and Bill could walk out the door of their inn and be on the banks of the Irati in five minutes, as opposed to the six-hour (minimum round-trip) walk to the Irati from Burguete. Thus, what a vast majority of readers and commentators have taken to be the Irati fishing expedition in *The Sun Also Rises,* and by extension, the Irati-centered mountain interlude before the fiesta, is not about the Irati at all. It is about what Hemingway called a "fishing expedition in the Pass of Roland" (see 108:26). They stay where they stay, Burguete-Roncevaux, because it is the heart of Roland country. And they fish where they fish, the Rio de la Fábrica (see following entry), because it is the closest good fishing to the Pass of Roland.

118:8 **Fabrica:** Tired when they come down the steep road into the Fábrica valley, Bill and Jake fish there, in what locals in this country generally refer to as the Fábrica. To be more exact, Jake fishes the Itolaz branch of the Fábrica, and Bill, since he fishes downstream, since he fishes longer than Jake, and since he catches bigger trout, works his way downstream past the confluence of the Txangoa branch of the Fábrica with the Itolaz, to the bigger water, to the deeper holes. All the details of the fishing passage (the white house on the hill, the dam, the falls, the spring, etc.) confirm the location, still exactly verifiable today, on the Fábrica. Yet there is one astounding omission: Hemingway completely omits a village. Known variously as Fábrica or Fábrica de Orbaiceta, it is the most striking feature of the valley of the Fábrica, where Jake and Bill walk and fish. There are abundant ironies and complexities in all this: *Fábrica* means factory, and when they fish the river of the Factory, they are at the hamlet called Factory, a distinct village with a number of houses (in Fábrica proper and the adjacent Barrio Larraun), an old hostel, an old church, government buildings where the forest ranger lives, and the like. But most striking of all are the extensive ruins of a large eighteenth- and nineteenth-century factory on the Fábrica, sprawling more than one hundred meters along the small river—the factory that gives the village, the valley, and the river their names. An important site for the manufacture of firearms and munitions to supply the Carlist guerrillas, it dates back before the early years of the Carlist wars. Most 1920s guidebooks with detailed coverage of the Pyrenees indicate the ruins of the factory—in Spanish guidebooks, the *antigua fábrica de armas de fuego hoy día en ruinas,* and in French guidebooks, the *Fonderie de canons* or *les anciennes fonderies royales.* And these same guidebooks clearly indicate the old route, the *chemin muletier,* or mule path, that Jake and Bill follow from Burguete-Roncevaux to the ancient royal arms foundry at Fábrica. When I first explored this country, rather hurriedly, in 1973 I did not own any period guidebooks (essential for anyone wishing to retrace the steps of Hemingway and his characters), nor was I looking for a ruined factory, because like everybody else I assumed Jake and Bill were fishing the Irati. Everybody knew, or thought they knew, there wasn't any factory in the mountain idyll of *The Sun Also Rises* and on Jake and Bill's hike—no factory, no village, no ruins. In subsequent visits I learned, with the help of local inquiry and much hiking, exactly where Jake and Bill fished by the factory and how they came there. In 1992, I led more than one hundred Hemingway Conference attendees on this guided hike, thus putting to rest, for some Hemingway scholars at least, the old confused notions about where the fishing takes place.

But the critical questions remain. What is Hemingway up to? Why this major calculated omission of a village and a large, ruined factory? One obvious answer is that he does so for aesthetic reasons, to avoid the intrusion into his mountain idyll of civilization, a village—a *factory* village at that—and to erase any trace of the machine in Eden. This seems a reasonable view, yet it feels wrong or limited, given the way Hemingway constructs the entire landscape and *names* the river and the valley; after all, the scene would work well without the jarring, counter-idyllic mention of the river and the valley of the Factory. Thus, it seems like more of a trademark Hemingway theory-of-omission fabrication (or defabrication), a deletion intended to make the reader feel more than is understood and to urge the reader to participate actively in decoding the action. Thus, nothing could be more apt, more resonant with the novel's deepest patterns of signification, than the fact that Jake as Fisher King, Jake as wounded war veteran, should fish, read, sleep, talk, eat, and ponder his Catholicism and his love for Brett in and by the banks of the river flowing through the village of the ruined war munitions factory. It is neither accidental nor incidental. It is somewhere near the base of Hemingway's iceberg. Such things, as Hemingway said in his Nobel Prize address, may not be "immediately discernible" in what he writes, but eventually they will be seen and understood. (For further commentary on these matters, see Stoneback, "You Sure This Thing Has Trout in It?")

118:18 **fish bait:** Jake fishes with worms, Bill with artificial flies. An unfortunately recurrent view in some discussions of the novel's fishing scenes is the absurd notion that Jake's character is somehow diminished because he fishes with worms. For one commentator, Jake's bait fishing shows him to be a "hollow man," a lazy, debilitated character who lacks passion, a pseudosportsman who believes in nothing and is adrift in his empty, meaningless world. All these conclusions are based on the fact that he fishes with worms; moreover, the same critic apparently has something against sleeping and reading, since he thinks that Jake is lazy and slothful for doing that after he fishes (Ward 21–25). Such vermiphobic nonsense need not be dignified with a response, except to note that it has nothing to do with what's actually in the novel and is imposed on the text from the egregious stance of the fly-fishing purist, a view more appropriate to certain fishing magazine columns than to literary criticism dealing with great novels. Such critics need to put away the fly book and read Hemingway's actual book, and if they can conquer their disdain for the lowly worm and all natural bait—a disdain not shared by Hemingway or Jake or Nick Adams, to mention only three fine sportsmen—they may yet come to see that Jake is the committed, engaged, ethical, moral, spiritual, sporting, and passionate center of the novel. And even exemplars are allowed to sleep. (For more detailed discussion of this matter, see Stoneback, "You Sure This Thing Has Trout in It?" 122–26.)

119:1 **spring:** This spring, or *fuente,* is on the path that descends along the Itolaz, just above the village of Fábrica. It is indeed very cold, a good place to overchill cheap wine. Hemingway readers who aspire to retrace his steps are cautioned against certain local guides who take tourists to the wrong spring, beside the paved road by the Irati (a good distance from the actual spring), and tell them it is the spring of *The Sun Also Rises.* Even generally careful Hemingway travel books have perpetuated this confusion; one such book mixes accurate information with contradictory location and a photograph of the wrong spring (Burgess 348–50).

119:8 **driving logs:** The remains of such a dam on the Itolaz branch of the Fábrica were visible in the 1970s.

120:9 **A. E. W. Mason:** Alfred Edward Woodley Mason (1865–1948) was a best-selling British writer whose immensely popular novel *The Four Feathers* (1902), set during the 1890s war in the Sudan, was the most filmed novel of the twentieth century, with seven versions, including two silent films made before the appearance of *The Sun Also Rises.* The "wonderful" short story Jake is reading here is "The Crystal

Trench" (first published in the 1917 collection *The Four Corners of the World*). In the manuscript this literary allusion is developed more extensively.

121:1 **lazy bum:** In one of Hemingway's typical echo lines, Bill repeats exactly the line—"You lazy bum!"—that Jake, up early digging for worms, had said to Bill that morning when he found Bill still in bed (113:10).

121:4 **wading:** Bill's trout are bigger because he has been downstream wading the deeper water beyond the confluence of the Itolaz and Txangoa branches of the Fábrica.

121:18 **hard-boiled eggs:** As they unwrap the *little* (another indication of the skimpiness of the inn in Burguete?) pack lunches, they find the hard-boiled eggs that some 1920s guidebooks recommended as a safe food to eat at such inns (see 94:26). This passage also resonates with the "hard-boiled" motif developed earlier in the novel (see 73:29 and 34:24).

121:24 **Bryan's dead:** One of the key allusions in this highly allusive chapter, this reference to William Jennings Bryan ("the Great Commoner"), and the development of the Bryan motif throughout this extended comic passage (121–24), is a widely misunderstood crux in the novel. The confusion surrounding the Bryan sequence ranges from superficial matters of chronology (the date of Bryan's death and the novel's time scheme) to more complicated questions concerning Bryan's identity (secular and religious), his image in both popular culture and intellectual circles from the 1920s on, and how these matters may be obfuscated by an important deletion from the more developed manuscript treatment of this material.

Bryan (1860–1925) was a major force in American politics from the 1890s through the first two decades of the twentieth century. A little-known Nebraska congressman in the early 1890s, he achieved national prominence and celebrity at the 1896 Democratic National Convention with his "Cross of Gold" speech, one of the most famous orations in American history. It earned him the Democratic nomination for president in 1896, when he lost to William McKinley after being denounced by Republicans as a dangerous radical. He ran for president two more times, losing to McKinley again in 1900, and to William H. Taft in 1908. He supported Woodrow Wilson in 1912 and served as Wilson's secretary of state until 1915, when, because of his antiwar principles, he resigned as American war fever rose after the German sinking of the *Lusitania*. For two decades he was the champion of activist politics and policies to better the lot of working people, and as his most recent biographer stresses, he transformed the Democratic Party "into the citadel of liberalism we identify with Franklin D. Roosevelt and his ideological descendants"; moreover, he had a central role "in writing every party platform through 1912" (Lingeman 10).

How, then, did the image of Bryan evolve from a leading liberal progressive to the caricature of a reactionary religious fundamentalist that has been the prevailing view of Bryan since the 1920s?

The answer is simple: the so-called Scopes Monkey Trial of 1925, and the media circus that surrounded what is often described as one of the biggest news stories of the twentieth century. In late May 1925, John T. Scopes, a young high-school teacher in Dayton, Tennessee, was indicted for teaching his science classes the theory of evolution—"certain theory," the indictment read, "and theories that deny the story of Divine creation of man as taught in the Bible and did teach thereof that man descended from a lower order of animals" (*New York Times* 26 May 1925:1)—in violation of Tennessee law.

The trial began on 10 July, featuring Bryan for the prosecution and Clarence Darrow for the defense, and it dominated world headlines throughout the month of July. On 21 July, Scopes was found guilty and fined one hundred dollars. On 26 July, still in Dayton, William Jennings Bryan died suddenly.

Given the calendar established by the novel, it is 28 June when Jake says Bryan is dead. They left Paris on 25 June, stayed in Bayonne that night, crossed the Pyrenees to Pamplona on 26 June, and checked into the Hostal Burguete on 27 June. Of course, Jake could not have read of Bryan's death in the newspaper the day before he here announces Bryan's death, since the Scopes trial had not even begun yet, and it would be another month before Bryan's sudden death after the conclusion of the trial. Critical explanations of Hemingway's chronology juggling have ranged from the sublime to the ridiculous. It is ridiculous to suggest that Hemingway was merely being sloppy or miscalculated by a month the date of the biggest news story of the year and the season in which he wrote the first draft of his novel. Consider that on his birthday, 21 July, the very day the Scopes trial ended, Hemingway had started writing the novel. (He began writing on 19, 20, or 21 July; see Balassi, "The Writing" 73, and *Facsimile* 1:xv.) He wrote this Bryan sequence one month later on 21 August (Balassi, "The Writing" 76). Given the fact that birthdays often serve as efficacious mnemonics, and the seasonal proximity and intensity of Hemingway's writing of the manuscript, it seems absurd to suggest that Hemingway forgot or confused the date of Bryan's death.

Many explanations of the novel's time discrepancies and anachronisms have been rooted in biographical readings of the novel, for example, the fact that Hemingway blended his memories of both his 1924 and his 1925 excursions to the Pyrenees and Pamplona: "The biographical reader," Michael Reynolds observes, "would say that Hemingway conflated two summers at Pamplona into one novel" (*Novel of the Twenties* 89). But this is merely to state the obvious: that novelists almost always conflate and manipulate time as they invent from their experience. Reynolds proposes a more elaborate, perhaps sublime, explanation for Hemingway's chronological discrepancies; he argues that Hemingway is playing deliberate "time games" with the reader in a book "where time is out of joint," "having a bit of fun with Einstein's experiment," and creating a fictional world anchored in "a quantum universe of probabilities" where "nothing is absolute, nothing certain but the speed of light" (89–91). It is an interesting, if far-fetched, argument. Hemingway is certainly aware of his narrative time games (see, e.g., 127:2–3), but there is an older, simpler response to the matter: the rules of storytelling have never required factual accuracy, mere chronological precision. The novelist, the storyteller, has always been free to shift events in time as the demands of storytelling dictate. Moreover, most readers remember events and news stories such as the death of Bryan not by exact dates (except in the rarest cases, e.g., 7 December 1941) but by approximate calendrical sequences—memory is *seasonal*. Thus, even in the very next year after Bryan's death, most readers would remember that he died the previous summer, but few would recall the exact date. Obviously, Hemingway shifted the date of Bryan's death not to play an Einsteinian time game with the reader, as Reynolds would have it, but simply because he felt a narrative urgency to work in the Bryan material, to introduce into his fishing interlude both rich comic material and an important religious motif (see following entries; see also Stoneback, "For Bryan's Sake," passim).

122:10–11 **holy mysteries of the hencoop:** Having adopted the rhetorical stance of a fundamentalist preacher, Bill hilariously illustrates his "sermon" by rearranging the order of his lunch—"First the chicken; then the egg." Waving and sucking his drumstick (the chicken), he accentuates what would now be called a creationist point of view, humorously counseling against "evolutionist" fondling (with "simian," monkey- or ape-like, fingers) and questioning of the "holy mysteries" of God's creation, thus providing a succinct objective correlative for the entire action of the Scopes Monkey Trial.

122:17 **God's first temples:** This is a direct quotation of a passage from a famous poem of the 1820s, "A Forest Hymn," by William Cullen Bryant (1794–1878), whose nature poems were widely taught and memorized by schoolchildren for over a century— and at least until the 1950s, when I had to memorize several Bryant poems in the sixth grade. The first line of "A Forest Hymn" is echoed here: "The groves were God's first temples." The poem goes on to praise God's "creation, finished, yet renewed / Forever," a view that would not trouble most fundamentalist creationists. Hemingway expects, no doubt, that the reader will note the associational process in Bill's rhetoric, the name linkage—Bryan-Bryant—and perhaps reflect that Bryant wrote precisely the kind of nature poetry that Bryan would have memorized as a schoolboy and Hemingway did. In 1915, at Oak Park High School, Hemingway memorized Bryant's "Thanatopsis" and "To a Water Fowl" (Reynolds, *Hemingway's Reading* 104).

122:18 **that's Mencken:** This curious apparent non sequitur (who is the "Lady" who is being admonished not to swallow Mencken? And why?) was added in revision. In the manuscript, this paragraph concluded: "let us kneel and say 'A nice week's work, Lord'" (333). The radical shift of focus from Bill's manuscript echo of the creation story of the book of Genesis to his admonition not to swallow Mencken ends the gentle mockery of creationism and shifts the target of the satire to evolutionism, to the anti-fundamentalist point of view represented by Mencken. Earlier in the novel, Hemingway established Mencken as a satiric target, as the source, for example, of Robert Cohn's bemused view of Paris, or the ostensibly fashionable opinions of "many young men" who cannot think for themselves (see 42:5). Commentary on Bill's Bryanesque Monkey Trial homily has generally emphasized Hemingway's ostensible mockery of fundamentalism and ignored the role that Mencken plays in this passage. Even one of the more astute commentators on this scene, Scott Donaldson, who sees that Bill "makes fun" here of both "Bible Belt morality" *and* Mencken, nevertheless stresses what he regards as the ridiculous "know-nothingism of what are currently called 'creationists'" and fails to come to terms with Mencken's presence in this passage or with Hemingway's complex response to the Scopes trial ("Humor" 36–38).

The Scopes trial was generally viewed in the 1920s (and often since) as a contest between fundamentalism and modernism, as a duel to the death between scientific or scientistic materialism and Christianity, as the ultimate instance of (in Willard Gatewood Jr.'s words) "modernists and fundamentalists at Armageddon" (331). "If the Scopes Trial was," Gatewood continues, "'the biggest and best newspaper story since the war' in the United States, it was only slightly less so in Europe. Failure to comprehend its meaning led many in Europe to join some Americans in viewing the disturbance as nothing more than a comedy—a source of considerable hilarity and amusement" (410). This view may account for the tone of Bill's humorous Bryanesque sermon. Yet Hemingway knew it was hardly a simple either-or, modernist-or-fundamentalist question. Resistance to the naturalist/materialist sensibility epitomized by Bryan's opponent, Clarence Darrow, and by Mencken and his boob-baiting so-called modernism was not limited to Southern fundamentalists. Such resistance in the 1920s and after included among its ranks, for example, received Roman Catholic opinion and the neo-orthodox Protestant ethics and theology of Reinhold Niebuhr, as well as a long list of the most important literary figures of the period, including the Vanderbilt Agrarians, T. S. Eliot, William Faulkner, Ezra Pound, and William Butler Yeats. To this list of those who saw the matter in a more nuanced light, who would weigh in against the side of the question represented by Mencken's secularist anti-Bryan ranting and advocacy of Darrow, I would add Ernest Hemingway. Indeed, if we look carefully at the actual Scopes trial transcripts, we see Darrow emerge, in all his arrogance and condescension, in what amounts finally to his banal stance of prelapsarian American innocence, as yet another champion of the myth of progress, a tunnel-visioned, legalistic, and quasi-philosophical version of naive American boosterism and materialism. It is a matter of record that journalistic coverage of the Scopes trial (including Mencken's essays on the subject), in its pseudocosmopolitan zeal to champion Darrow and debunk Bryan (and the redneck caricatures who were imagined to be his supporters), falsified and distorted what actually transpired. The process of debunking Bryan culminated in the immensely popular, misleading, and slick play (1955) and movie (1960 and 1999) *Inherit the Wind.* Ultimately, the curious transformation of the image of Bryan in the popular imagination from a leading liberal progressive to the caricature of a reactionary religious fundamentalist may be traced to Mencken's writing on the Monkey Trial, as he christened the Scopes proceedings. And Hemingway, following the controversy as he wrote *The Sun Also Rises,* would likely be more sympathetic to the Catholic view expressed, for example, by a professor of animal biology (who was also a Catholic priest), George O'Toole, who wrote in his 1925 study *The Case against Evolution:* "Evolution . . . has brought us materialistic monism, in whose barren soil nor faith, nor idealism, nor morality, nor poetry, nor art, nor any of the finer things of life can thrive. To its dystelic and atomistic view Nature has ceased to be the vicar of God, and material things are no longer sacramental symbols of eternal verities" (353). As Bill and Jake pursue and consume their "sacramental symbols" (e.g., fish, wine) and meditate on "eternal verities" (e.g., love, religion—see 123:29 and 124:9), what they are not going to "eat"—or *swallow*—is clear enough: Mencken and all that he represents.

And it was even clearer in the original manuscript. There, after Jake says, "Utilize a little of this" in the following line, Bill says: "God . . . You know Menken [sic] and these birds get worked up about all that monkey business. . . . They're old. They don't realize that all that stuff Puritanism and all hasn't anything to do with us any more." Jake replies: "Let the people believe what they want." "Sure," Bill says, "If they want to believe in heaven and hell and seven day Creation—fine. That's all to the good." The dialogue continues:

"But don't try and ram monkeys down their throats."

"No. Don't be Monkey Puritans."

"They're all missionaries."

"Sure. Monkey missionaries."

"No really. They're all Puritans. They're absolutely intolerant. . . . "

"Sure. Missionaries are all right. They admit what they're trying to do. It's in their faith—"

"But these people that preach tolerance and letting people alone and then want to carry tolerance with a flaming sword" (*Facsimile* 2:333–35).

This crucial and definitive dialogue provides a view of the Scopes Monkey Trial and the media circus surrounding it that may surprise many Hemingway readers, especially those predisposed to Mencken's view of Bryan as an old fool and Darrow as a champion of right thinking. Contrary to the usual assumptions regarding the novel's Bryan sequence, this deleted passage shows Hemingway, and Bill and Jake, making certain judgments regarding Mencken and his ilk that were familiar enough in 1925 but have been all but banished from public discourse and popular culture as defined by what some would call liberal orthodoxy (although there is nothing *liberal* about it). First, we note that Bill defines Mencken's views as passé, the *old* worn-out platitudes of a naturalist/materialist view of experience that has nothing to do with the modern world that Bill and Jake inhabit. Put another way, far from representing avant-garde "modernism," Mencken and his kind represent a rearguard premodern view, both in the writers they champion (e.g., Theodore Dreiser and Sinclair Lewis, with their naturalist and social Darwinist thesis–ridden fiction) and in their views regarding the Monkey Trial. The spiritual openness expressed in Hemingway's manuscript—"let the people believe what they want," it's "all to the good"—is tellingly characteristic of the religious readiness of the *literary modernism* of the 1920s, as is the resistance to the ostensibly liberal but truly Puritanical and absolutely intolerant preachers of tolerance who want to ram the politically correct views of pseudoscientific "evolutionism" (scientistic as opposed to scientific study of the theory of evolution) down the throats of the people. Hemingway's formula—Mencken the Monkey Missionary—succinctly expresses a cultural syndrome that is as apt today as it was in the 1920s. The reader may well lament the disappearance of this manuscript passage from the published novel. Indeed, this textual crux, occurring at the exact center of the novel, constitutes one of the most substantial deletions from and longest additions (122:17–124:29) to the manuscript. Hemingway's addition of the humorous page-and-a-half of dialogue that follows the "that's Mencken" line, although retaining a certain Catholic and religion-centered motif, submerges the serious Mencken-monkey-missionary point in favor of apparently nonsensical comic banter that requires careful decoding to recognize the thrust of the satire (see, e.g., 122:24).

In sum, given the decline of cultural literacy (and thus the ability to interpret topical allusions to events of the 1920s), Hemingway's Mencken motif may be too deeply submerged, and the reader may not have the necessary evidence—without the deleted manuscript passage—to take an accurate sounding on the entire Bryan/Scopes Monkey Trial sequence. Evidence to this effect may be found in one of the more extraordinary moments of an academic career—in 1982 I presented a conference paper concerning Hemingway and the Scopes trial that was delivered in the very Dayton, Tennessee, courthouse, and from the very podium, where Bryan and Darrow contended in 1925. My case was, in brief, that readers have not recognized the extent to which Hemingway's Bryan sequence in *The Sun Also Rises* is pro-Bryan, anti-Mencken. (The paper, entitled "'For Bryan's Sake': The 'Tribute' to the Great Commoner in Hemingway's *The Sun Also Rises*," was later published under the same title.) The formal respondent to my paper delivered in Bryan's old courtroom was Cleanth Brooks, one of the most distinguished literary critics of the twentieth century, a critical presence more daunting than Darrow. Well versed in the 1920s history of the Scopes trial and how the mockery of Bryan and the South engaged in by Mencken and other journalists during the trial was one of the driving forces that caused the Vanderbilt Agrarians—Donald Davidson, Andrew Lytle, John Crowe Ransom, Allen Tate, Robert Penn Warren, and others—to coalesce and compose their famous manifesto, *I'll Take My Stand,* a defense of the South, of religion and region, and of literature and the arts, Brooks praised my anti-Mencken argument but seemed less than thoroughly convinced that Hemingway had presented enough evidence in the novel to support it. At the time, I had not yet studied the manuscript of the novel and was thus unaware of the deleted Mencken-monkey-missionary passage cited above. It was all I would have needed to convince Cleanth Brooks of my argument, for Hemingway's view of Mencken expressed there is *exactly* the view of Brooks and his Agrarian colleagues at Vanderbilt, with some of whom I had studied at Vanderbilt in the 1960s.

Finally, then, it seems necessary in 2006 to insist that we read the Bryan sequence correctly. Nothing in the novel is more timely or up to date—scarcely a day goes by when the national media do not have a feature story on "creationism," "evolutionism," and "intelligent design," on some school or courtroom case that resonates with the Scopes Monkey Trial. More often than not, as is to be expected, the news coverage alludes to Bryan as a reactionary old fool, to Darrow and Mencken as great crusaders for the truth, for common sense. Rarely does any reportage, on any side of the question, possess the acuity of Hemingway's image of Mencken the Monkey Missionary. Why, then, does Hemingway, in revision, add that curious sentence: "Don't eat that, Lady—that's Mencken"? Clue: Bill is not talking to *Lady* Brett Ashley, who is nowhere to be found in this scene. He *is* addressing Our Lady, Notre Dame, the Blessed Virgin Mary—standing in here for the Church and all believers—saying don't *swallow* the preaching of Mencken, the flaming, intolerant, puritanical, overzealous, anti-Christian missionary who wants to ram all that monkey naturalism/determinism down your throat. (See numerous Catholic allusions, including to Our Lady, in the following entries.)

122:24 **Holy Cross:** The College of the Holy Cross in Worcester, Massachusetts—the oldest Catholic college in New England (1843)—is the first of four Catholic colleges and universities mentioned in this humorous half-page "education sequence," with its various incongruous and funny lists of who attended what college. Of course, Bryan, a more-or-less fundamentalist Protestant, and Bill, apparently a mainline Protestant, and Mencken, an anti-church agnostic, did not attend a Catholic college together. Hemingway seems to be choosing the names of his Catholic institutions with his usual precision. This would not be the only time he would make symbolic use of Holy Cross. In the summer of 1926, he published *Today Is Friday,* his playlet centered on the effect that the Crucifixion of Christ has on three Roman soldiers. In the copy of the limited edition booklet of *Today Is Friday* that he gave to his friends Gerald and Sara Murphy, he wrote a long inscription about a trip he made with Archibald MacLeish to Zaragoza, site of the venerated shrine of Nuestra Señora del Pilar, with its strong associations with the pilgrimage of Santiago de Compostela. Hemingway noted that MacLeish, his Protestant friend, with his "fine legal mind," attempted to "take away" from Hemingway, among other things, the popes and the Holy Grail, giving "in exchange a great Yale football team." And Hemingway notes with pleasure that the next Sunday he read that Holy Cross ("or some place like that") beat Yale 33–6: "So I wrote Archie a pneu and said I was sending back his great Yale team . . . and would he return me by return post all the Popes [and] . . . the Holy Grail." In other words, Hemingway's Protestant friend MacLeish tries to talk him out of his Catholicism, but Hemingway resists his legalistic arguments and delights in the fact that Holy Cross trounces (note that score—33) MacLeish's mainstream Protestant Ivy League team. It signifies immensely that Hemingway wrote this long inscription in a copy of his drama about the Passion of Christ, and he stresses that Holy Cross and the Holy Grail triumph over Yale and football (see Stoneback, "From the Rue Saint-Jacques" 5–6).

122:25 **Frankie Fritsch:** Frank Francis Frisch (not Fritsch; 1898–1973), famous as "The Fordham Flash," was one of the great infielders in baseball history. He played short-stop and second and third base for the New York Giants (1919–1926) and the St. Louis Cardinals (1927–1937) and was inducted into the Hall of Fame in 1947. In 1925, during the season in progress as Jake and Bill talk about him, Frisch batted .331 for the Giants. Fordham University (so named in 1907), another famous Jesuit institution, was established (1841) in Rose Hill, in the Bronx, as St. John's College. Proud of its religious heritage and its academic excellence, it also boasts a strong baseball tradition, beginning in 1859 when it established the first intercollegiate baseball program. Frisch's nickname, "The Fordham Flash," no doubt has more to do with his legendary fiery athletic competitiveness and base-stealing prowess than with any implication of the flash of religious illumination. Nevertheless, given Hemingway's strategy of allusion, the submerged iceberg complexities of his prose, it may not be too far-fetched to discern yet another echo of T. S. Eliot's *The Waste Land* in this religion-suffused passage. In Eliot's opening movement, he quotes the Wagnerian lyric *Frisch weht der Wind* ("fresh wafts the wind"), evoking Tristan's unhappy love for Isolde (line 31). In a passage that builds toward an expression of Jake's unhappy love for Brett, the fresh wind of Frisch the Fordham Flash resonates in Hemingway's subtext. And while Frisch was not the most famous fisherman in the roster of baseball's greatest, his name and institutional identification provide an echo of Jake's quest and identity as a distinctly Eliotic Fisher King. These allusions, after all, are the heart of the novel's fishing chapter. If much of this will be recognized only after multiple readings, it is the very stuff of the modernist style that Hemingway learned from his most important writing mentor, Ezra Pound, who was well aware of the risk of sacrificing comprehension to nuance, a risk that the strategy of allusion always entails.

122:27 **Loyola:** There are numerous Jesuit colleges and universities named Loyola in the United States and abroad, but Hemingway probably has in mind Loyola University in Chicago. Founded in 1869 as St. Ignatius College, this third Jesuit institution that Hemingway inscribes in this humorous education sequence serves as a reminder that as they fish and attend the fiesta in Pamplona, they are very much in Saint Ignatius of Loyola country. Ignatius (1491–1556) was born in the Basque country of northern Spain, was wounded in the siege of Pamplona (like Jake, he received a groin wound, what Hemingway called "his wound that made him [Ignatius] think"—see 94:1), and after his conversion and various pilgrimages moved to Paris, where he founded the Society of Jesus, or the Jesuit Order, in Montmartre (see 22:30). Jake's whimsical observation that he went to Loyola with Bishop Manning may be a reference to the bishop who was one of the leaders of the mid-nineteenth-century Oxford Movement—Henry Edward Manning (1808–1892). This Bishop Manning finally left the Church of England for the Roman Catholic Church over a doctrinal dispute on the question of baptismal regeneration. Insofar as Jake's spiritual progress may be seen to parallel Hemingway's (and Manning's), the drift of such an allusion would be clear. Or the reference may be to another Bishop Manning, the well-known William Thomas Manning who became the Episcopal bishop of New York in 1921. This Manning, of course, was not a fundamentalist (although he was attacked as such by Mencken for his opposition to divorce); occupying the usual middle ground of Episcopalianism, this Bishop Manning accepted the *science* of evolution, if not the *scientism* of social Darwinism and other "evolutionisms." Whichever Manning he refers to, in a novel that is much concerned with *unmanning* and makes numerous jokes about it (including the bulls-steers dialogue in the following chapter), Hemingway has chosen his bishop's name appropriately, especially given his humorous "enrollment" with Jake at Loyola, an institution founded by the Order created by the wounded soldier who had been "unmanned" at the Battle of Pamplona before his rebirth as a great religious leader and, ultimately, a saint. Hemingway was well acquainted with the Jesuits; he had subscriptions to Jesuit magazines and sent donations to Jesuit charities (see Stoneback, "Nominal Country" 127–31). As he reported in *The Dangerous Summer*, he prayed regularly for Antonio and Carmen Ordóñez, the bullfighter and his wife, but took out some additional prayer insurance: "In case my prayers were invalid . . . and to make sure someone competent was doing it I took out a membership in the Jesuit Seminary Fund Association . . . for Carmen and Antonio. There was a class graduating who, when they were ordained, would pray for them each day" (142).

122:30 **cock-eyed:** Again, Hemingway's stylistic presence on the cutting edge of word usage is underlined by the fact that the *OED* cites this usage of "cock-eyed" as the earliest example of the word to mean, in its American sense, "drunk" (see also 9:32, 14:5, 34:24, 59:29, 64:4, and 84:1). With his usual precision, Hemingway—given Bill's response "On wine?"—incorporates the double meaning of the word (i.e., drunk, as well as its earlier meaning of absurd or ridiculous).

123:9 **Anti-Saloon League:** Still in existence, the Anti-Saloon League, founded in Ohio in 1893, was an important force in early twentieth-century politics due especially to its moralistic crusade against the sale of alcoholic beverages. Aligned with other so-called temperance (more accurately, prohibitionist) organizations, the Anti-Saloon League was instrumental in pushing the so-called dry law, and their missionary anti-alcohol zeal resulted in the passing of the Volstead Act in 1919. With the end of the Prohibition era in 1933, the influence of the Anti-Saloon League waned, although they were still active in churches, soliciting "temperance" pledges as late as the 1950s. Bill's mockery of the Anti-Saloon League extends the motif of the puritanical intolerance of the "monkey missionaries" that was developed in the deleted manuscript passage discussed above (122:18).

123:10 **Notre Dame . . . Wheeler:** America's best-known Catholic university, Notre Dame (in Notre Dame, Indiana) was founded in 1842 as the University of Notre-Dame-du-Lac (French for "Our Lady of the Lake") by members of the French Congregation of Holy Cross. Thus the fourth and final reference to Catholic institutions in this two-page education sequence harks back, with its evocation of Notre Dame/Our Lady, to the beginning of the anti-Mencken satire, with its admonition to Our Lady not to swallow Mencken's diatribes (122:18). Jake, of course, is being deliberately absurd when he says he went to Notre Dame with Wayne B. Wheeler (1869–1927), the ultimate Protestant, puritanical, prohibitionist, anti-alcohol missionary. Known as the "Dry Boss," Wheeler was the driving force of the Anti-Saloon League, and through his development and application of single-issue pressure politics and lobbying (known as "Wheelerism"), he became an immensely powerful national political figure. Wheeler began his crusade against alcohol when he was a student at Oberlin College, the Protestant (historically Presbyterian) college that since its founding has been associated with social activism. Since members of Hemingway's family had gone to Oberlin, and it was where they wanted him to go, he was certainly aware of its reputation for missionary activism in social causes, and he must have known that Wheeler was one of its most famous graduates. Given Wheeler's proud boasts of his tactics of deception employed to bring about Prohibition, his alliances, for example, with business leaders who believed their employees would work harder if they were alcohol-free—John D. Rockefeller (see 124:26) was a major supporter of Wheeler's Anti-Saloon League—Bill's transformation of Wheeler from an Oberlin graduate to "class president" of Austin Business College is not only humorous but socially and politically acute. If there was an Austin Business College in 1925, there seems to be no record of its existence in a time when so-called business colleges were generally ephemeral and insubstantial local institutions. (The current Austin Business College, founded in 1971 in Austin, Texas, has no connection to what may be Bill's invention.)

123:29 **ever in love:** After fishing, after a lunch well fueled with wine and good humor, both Bill and Jake are sleepy. But before they go to sleep, Bill raises two of the most serious questions that a good friend can ask—about love and religion. Jake acknowledges that he has loved Brett—"Off and on for a hell of a long time"—but now it's *really* over and he doesn't "give a damn any more." Since the accumulated evidence of the text supports this sense of finality (see, e.g., 65:3), the reader is meant to take Jake's assertion here not as evasion or rationalization but as resolution and reconciliation regarding his wound, his life, and his impossible love of Brett. This passage was not in the original manuscript. Instead there was a long passage (fortunately deleted) in which Jake retells the A. E. W. Mason story he had been reading before lunch (120:9). A sentimental story of love, fidelity, and betrayal, it has little connection with Jake's experience. In fact, Jake tells it mainly so that he can tell a better "mountain" story of his own; the entire deleted passage (six-and-a-half pages, *Facsimile* 2:335–41) has much more to do with Jake (or Hemingway) and the craft of writing. Had it remained, this passage would have destroyed the timing and pace, convoluted the theme and imagery, and blurred the thrust of one of the novel's most important and masterful chapters. Hemingway's deletion of this material about the art of storytelling, then, is one of the surest signs of his mastery of narration.

124:9–10 **Catholic . . . Technically:** Jake's response to Bill's question may be one of the most misunderstood passages in the novel. The simplest reading of Jake's one-word response to Bill's wondering if Jake is *really* a Catholic is that Jake *really* doesn't want to talk about it, just as he'd rather not talk about Brett and love. Even if he were not sleepy, relaxed, lying on the ground looking up into the trees, and feeling at peace with the world, Jake's natural reticence would not dispose him to talk about love and religion. Such an understanding of this narrative moment may suffice. However, since the passage is sometimes read as an indication that Jake is not really a Catholic, that he doesn't believe in or truly practice his faith, his religion, Jake's response must be considered carefully. The word "technically" may have many meanings, but all of them have to do with *technique,* with the careful practice of an art or craft, the execution or performance of something in relation to formal or practical details; and the older sense of "technical," with regard to a thing skillfully done, or a person "skilled in or practically conversant with some particular art or subject" (*OED*), should not be overlooked either, especially in a novel so concerned with, say, the technique of bullfighters, the style or technique of all things, including the chilling and opening of bottles of champagne. To take Jake's response—technically—as an indication that he is some kind of a skeptic about his Catholicism is to miss the point entirely. The Catholic Church places great emphasis on not just the right matter and the right intention but also the "right form" when it comes to "the technicalities of Sacramental theology" (Cross 1198). In going to confession and Mass, Jake practices the technique, the form of two of the major sacraments of his church—penance and the Eucharist. As the "laying on of hands" scene with Montoya (131–32) and the swimming scenes in San Sebastián (235–38) demonstrate, he is also alert to the sacramental overtones of secular activities that serve as analogues to the sacraments of confirmation and baptism. Moreover, in the disciplined form of his prayers and his making of the sign of the cross (97), his attention to "eating, giving, and blessing," he practices the technique of "Sacramentals," that is, "certain religious practices and objects akin to the Sacraments," but of less importance in the matter of grace (Cross 1199). Indeed, Jake knows (as Hemingway said of himself) that "the only way he could run his life decently was to accept the discipline of the Church" (Stoneback, "Nominal Country" 127). Discipline and technique, in terms of the sacraments, the sacramentals, and much else in life, are synonymous.

Thus, Jake's answer that he is *technically* a Catholic makes perfect sense and confirms his devout Catholicism (amply demonstrated elsewhere in the text), especially coming as it does at the end of a long passage that pivots on Protestant-Catholic contrasts. Protestantism, in many of its manifestations, is most notable for the manner in which it discards technique, form, and discipline, for its celebration of the individualized gesture over the technique, the form, rooted in tradition. Thus this passage illustrates—as directly as Jake ever says anything—and underlines through the linguistic structure and repetition, that he *really* is over Brett, and he *really* is a Catholic, practicing all the forms, the technique, of what he calls his "grand religion," hoping, as every pilgrim must, that he will become something more than the "rotten Catholic" he has said he is (97:18–20; see also 208:7 and passim).

124:26 **Jo Davidson:** Davidson (1883–1952) was a highly successful American sculptor best known for his busts of leading public figures such as Woodrow Wilson, Franklin Delano Roosevelt, and Albert Einstein. In associating Jo Davidson with President Coolidge and the leading businessmen/industrialists of the day, Henry Ford and John D. Rockefeller, Bill mocks the "dream" of art that becomes business, the mere pursuit of success. Hemingway met Jo Davidson in 1922, at a conference in Genoa where Davidson had come "to make some portrait heads of the leading foreign statesmen" (Baker, *Life Story* 89). He must have known him in Paris, too, for Davidson executed a well-known bronze of Hemingway's friend Gertrude Stein, in a Buddha pose, in 1923. In 1925 Hemingway wrote to Stein from Austria to say that he had grown "a fine Jo Davidson beard"; to Sylvia Beach, he wrote that his beard "looks like a cross between Jo Davidson and Christ," and he jokes that they want him to play Moses in the Oberammergau play (*Selected Letters* 146–47). The motif of art and its corruption by business is compressed, together with *dreaming* and religion, into one allusion to a sculptor best known for his commercial success.

125:17 **Saint Jean Pied de Port:** An important staging area on the pilgrimage of Saint-Jacques-de-Compostelle (Santiago de Compostela), Saint-Jean-Pied-de-Port, named for its position at the foot of the "port" or Pass of Roncevaux/Roncesvalles, prospered due to the pilgrimage trade. Before the Revolution, it was the capital of French Navarre. Although Harris, one of the novel's minor exemplary characters (see 130:4), professes disinterest in the pilgrimage (128:16), he has done the proper pilgrim trek, walking the thirty-one kilometers from France, over the Pass of Roland, and down into Burguete.

125:19 **twice to the Irati:** That is, they made two excursions to the Irati that are *not* rendered in the action, as this chapter's fishing scene on the Fábrica has been described. It is incorrect to conclude, as Charles Oliver has, that there is error or confusion here: "Unless Hemingway meant to indicate that they spent the night, he probably had the Fabrica [sic] River in mind as the location for all their fishing" (170). This is simply wrong, as they could easily have arranged for a ride from Burguete to the Irati for the day's fishing, and a ride back that would get them home earlier than their long walk from the Fábrica does (see 117:30).

125:19 **no word:** Closing the chapter with this reminder of the absence of Robert, Brett, and Mike underlines one reason why it has been such a pleasant interlude.

CHAPTER 13

126:10 **Dear Jake:** This chapter begins with a pointed contrast of the letter writing of Michael and Robert (see 127:31). All the days and dates given here further complicate the already untenable calendar, although readers are rarely interested in mere reportorial calendrical accuracy in fiction. Hemingway, of course, is aware of the calendar problem, even underlining it when he refers to "how one loses track of the days" (127:3; see also 81:1 and 121:24). For a useful explanation of why the novel's calendar is askew, see Svoboda (*Crafting of a Style* 24–25).

127:9 *into:* The italicized emphasis of "into" here is best understood as one of the errors introduced into the text during the process of publication. Note the textual repetition here of three forms—"*into*," "in to," and "into"—in a twelve-line sequence. In the manuscript, Hemingway wrote "in to" for all three instances. The italicized "into" should definitely not be read in a contemporary sense—getting *into* Pamplona, as one might say now: "I'm getting *into* bullfighting"—a usage that did not enter the language until the 1960s. As James Hinkle points out, in arguing his case for a new edition of the novel with printer errors and proofreader insertions removed, this occurrence of *into* "has not been right since Hemingway's original manuscript where he wrote 'in to' (two words) which is what the context calls for. Somehow this got changed in the typescript to one word. The first edition reproduced the typescript's incorrect 'into.' In the second edition 'into' inexplicably appeared in italics—which makes no sense at all—and in italics it remains. One can imagine the written note to the second edition typesetter, underlined for emphasis, which brought about the confusion" ("Dear Mr. Scribner" 46; for another instance of the need for a corrected text, see 12:19–20).

127:31 **Vengo Jueves Cohn:** The reader is here invited to compare Cohn's message with Mike's on the preceding page; as always, when Cohn's conduct or style is measured against almost any standard, he comes off badly. Letter writing has its rules of etiquette, and the sending of messages is best done according to a code of conduct; both Jake and Bill mock the style and the codeless conduct of Robert's message— "What does the word Cohn mean"; "lousy telegram"; "He could send ten words for the same price. 'I come Thursday'"; "gives you all the dope that's of interest to Cohn"—and the telegram as an emblem of solipsism.

128:16 **through the monastery:** Jake, Bill, and Harris walk the two-and-a-half kilometers from Burguete up to Roncesvalles specifically to tour the famous cluster of religious buildings there, the destination of millions of pilgrims for nearly a thousand years (see 108:26, 108:30, 109:1, and 109:19–20). Inaccurate and absurd misreadings of this passage abound in Hemingway criticism; many commentators read the passage carelessly, attributing the reactions of Harris and Bill to Jake; even one of Hemingway's better readers, Michael Reynolds, writes that at Roncesvalles "Jake prefers to visit the bar rather than the monastery church" (*Novel of the Twenties* 66; see also 86:2–3). There is not one shred of textual evidence to support this assertion. Here is what actually transpires: Harris, though apparently not a devout pilgrim, has recently walked the thirty-one kilometers from Saint-Jean-Pied-de-Port (125:17), the ancient pilgrimage town on the French side of the Pass of Roland; Harris says he has intended every day to get to see the religious and pilgrim's landmark site of Roncevaux/Roncesvalles, and he says twice it is a "remarkable place." We cannot know from the text the exact reason that Harris finds Roncevaux so "remarkable," although we gather from his remark about "those sort of places" that his emotion is rooted more in his lively sense of history and a historical awareness of Roland and the pilgrimage than in the pilgrim's spiritual sense of numinous place. And it is *after* they tour the monastery that he notices the pub across the way. Bill, an American Protestant, a literate and well-educated writer, doesn't disagree with Harris's emphasis on how "remarkable" Roncevaux is, presumably because he too appreciates its extraordinary place in European history. Bill does say that it's not "the same as fishing"—after he has walked there to go through the monastery. And what does Jake say? Jake says nothing—as he usually does when he differs with what is being said or finds the matter more complicated than the conversation allows (not to see this is to miss one of the controlling principles of Hemingway dialogue). It is not necessary to read Jake's mind here—we know what a Catholic pilgrim would feel at one of the most venerated pilgrimage sites in the world. His silence is the most appropriate response. And why would he bother to argue with Bill's comment that seeing Roncevaux "isn't the same as fishing," when Jake, the wounded Fisher King of the novel, the pilgrim quester, knows that, in the anagogical sense, *fishing is exactly the same as visiting the pilgrim's shrine.* Jake says nothing, but we know what he *sees* at the monastery—various objects reputed to be Roland's, horns and swords, a reliquary containing thorns from Christ's Crown of Thorns, the venerated icon of the Virgin Mary—Nuestra Señora de Roncesvalles (whose image adorns the wall of Jake's room in Burguete)—and many objects evoking the pilgrimage of Santiago. When they have finished their tour and they spot the "pub" (apparently the small pensione, Casa Sabina, still in the same place today)—and what would be more appropriate after touring such a "remarkable place" than to share some sacramental wine—Jake says they are "standing in front of the old chapel of the monastery." Jake would know that this "old chapel" was built over the rock that Roland split with Durendal, his magical sword, and that Roland and the Paladins were buried there, according to tradition. Actually, there are two "old chapels" at Roncevaux, and we might assume here that Jake is standing in front of the oldest chapel, Sancti Spiritus, also known as Charlemagne's Silo. But they may be standing in front of the thirteenth-century Chapel of Santiago, known as the "pilgrim's church," which is the best preserved monument at Roncevaux and looks more like a chapel than Charlemagne's Silo, a rather odd structure that resembles a farm building and once served as the mortuary for pilgrims who died at Roncevaux. In any case, the two "chapels" are right next to each other; whichever one Jake refers to, the allusion underlines both the Roland and the Santiago-pilgrim motifs. The motifs are contiguous, as are the chapels.

129:8 **fun since the war:** Harris's statement seems to indicate several things: (1) He, too, is a war veteran, possibly, like Jake, a wounded veteran; (2) Because of the war, he hasn't had much "fun"; (3) Or, *since* the war he hasn't lived as intensely as he did *during* the war, a familiar theme among war veterans. In any case, as one of the novel's minor exemplars, his war experience is an important credential. Again, Hemingway reminds the reader that this is a war novel, however understated the war as pervasive background for all that is felt and said and done may be (see 17:4).

130:4 **dozen flies:** Note how Harris conducts his ritual act of friendship and farewell: he accompanies Jake and Bill to the bus and gives them both an envelope containing a dozen of his own hand-tied flies, a highly symbolic act confirming their brotherhood in the community of fishermen. Like all Hemingway exemplars, Harris is generous—he wants to give away what he has made. Also note that he climbs the bus ladder with them just to say farewell; this variation on the novel's Jacob's Ladder motif suggests that Harris is one of those ascending-descending "angels" (see 103:3, 106:21, 109:2–3, and 137:27).

131:9 **Villar bulls ... Miuras:** Montoya refers here to two well-known breeds of fighting bulls in the early twentieth century. Villar bulls, bred at the *ganadería* (a ranch where fighting bulls are raised) of the Villar family, became known around 1910 as ideal fighting bulls. In his nonfiction masterpiece on bullfighting, *Death in the Afternoon,* a work that every reader of *The Sun Also Rises* should consult, Hemingway writes: "I remember a corrida of Villar bulls in Pamplona in 1923. They were ideal bulls, as brave as any I have ever seen, fast, vicious, but always attacking; never going on the defensive. They were big but not so large as to be ponderous, and they were well horned. Villar bred splendid bulls but the bullfighters did not care for them.

They had just a little too much of every good quality" (161). Then, the Villar breeding stock was sold to another rancher, who sought to make his bulls "acceptable to the bullfighters," and by 1927, Hemingway writes, the Villar bulls "were smaller, had less horn"; by 1928 they were "still smaller, the horns further decreased and they were not so brave" (161–62). Regarding Miura bulls, Hemingway writes that the same process of breeding the bulls to be "less dangerous and more acceptable to the bullfighters" has resulted in bulls that have the "appearance of the old deadly Miuras without their ferocious and crescent intelligence which made them the curse of all bullfighters" (129–30). Later in the chapter, after Montoya has seen the bulls, he shakes his head, telling Jake the Villar bulls are "all right," "not too good" (144:32–33).

131:11 **desencajonada:** Hemingway skillfully deploys first the Spanish term for the unloading of the bulls (*desencajonada*) then two pages later provides his English translation—"unloadings" (133:8)—followed by an expository passage that explains the action of the *desencajonada* (133:9–24). In general, in the fiesta section of the novel, Hemingway's prose becomes less allusive and layered, more expository and explanatory, as he takes great pains to define clearly what is about to happen and to render action directly.

131:12 **hand on my shoulder:** One of the crucial scenes in the novel, this two-page passage (131–32) confirming the bond between Jake and Montoya, rooted in love of bullfighting, is very carefully constructed. Characteristic of Hemingway's style, repetition dominates his most highly charged scenes (see e.g., 20:16, 31:2, 46:25, 58:22, and 75:1). Three times in this scene, Hemingway notes Montoya's "embarrassed" demeanor, his self-consciousness over actually *talking* about the secret of *afición* that he shares with Jake; this threefold repetition of embarrassment is repeated in another key scene with Montoya (see 171:17). And five times in this page-and-a-half scene, Hemingway repeats the description of the *touching*, the laying on of hands. Five times early in the same sequence, he stresses Montoya's *smile*, the smile that acknowledges the *secret*—a word repeated three times in two sentences (131:15–17). The interwoven threefold pattern (smile, secret, touching) of repetition subtly shifts its emphasis from the smile, the outward sign of the secret, to a definition of the secret (love of bullfighting), to a confirmation of the passion and the spiritual significance of the shared secret through touching. (In this highly stylized scene, Hemingway exaggerates the recognition ritual of aficionados in order to foreground the importance of the shared passion. See also the following entries.)

131:28 **Afición means passion:** It should be noted that in *Death in the Afternoon*, six years after *The Sun Also Rises*, Hemingway changed and deepened his definition of "afición" to read: "love of bullfights. It also means the entire bull ring public, but is usually used in this generic sense to denote the most intelligent part of the public"

(412). Also, in the explanatory glossary of *Death in the Afternoon* Hemingway modified the novel's definition of an aficionado—"one who is passionate about the bullfights"—to this: "one who understands bullfights in general and in detail and still cares for them" (412). Nevertheless, even if the later definitions are more precise (as appropriate for a nonfiction *treatise* on the bullfight), the passage most Hemingway aficionados remember and aptly quote as a key passage in the *novel* has to do with *afición* as passion. The numerous variations that Hemingway plays on the theme of passion constitute the novel's leitmotif, the dominant theme, from the early posing of the question of how to live "life all the way up" (10:19) to the secret-of-the-values scene with the count (60:31–32) to this crucial scene, and on through to the novel's conclusion (see also 8:12, 32:22, 97:3). With passion, much is understood, shared, forgiven. Without authentic passion, there is nothing, only fakery and confusion (see the following entry).

132:17 **simulate it or confuse it:** Along with the fundamental distinction here between passion and mere excitement, the confused imitation of passion, and the fakery of the phony, this passage clearly states, in line with other American-European contrasts in the novel, that most Americans lack true passion. Jake Barnes is the exception; Robert Cohn is the rule. For other variations on this theme, consider Prohibition (the "dry law") versus communion, aridity versus ceremonial wine drinking, and see 116:11, 122:18, 123:9, and 123:10.

132:20 **oral spiritual examination:** Here the rites and sacraments of the aficionado are marked with a specific linguistic and sacramental convergence with the rites of the Catholic Church, not just in the language Hemingway employs—"oral spiritual examination"—but also in the sacrament of confirmation, the laying on of hands, "the rite whereby the grace of the Holy Spirit is conveyed in a new or fuller way to those who have already received it in some degree or fashion at Baptism" (Cross 327). Thus this carefully constructed passion scene, with its fivefold repetition of the "actual touching" and "putting the hand on" the fellow initiate, reminds the reader of what Hemingway had in mind when he discussed in a 1926 letter to Maxwell Perkins his projected book about bullfighting—"a matter of life and death"—and how it is "the one thing that has, with the exception of the ritual of the church, come down to us intact from the old days" (*Selected Letters* 237; see also 97:3 and 97:18–20).

133:27–28 **SOL, SOL Y SOMBRA, and SOMBRA:** The cheapest bullfight seats are *sol* (sun), the most expensive *sombra* (shade). As Hemingway put it in the explanatory glossary to *Death in the Afternoon,* "*Sol y sombra:* sun and shade; seats in the bull ring which are in the sun as the fight commences but will be in the shade as it progresses. Midway in price between the seats in the shade and those in the sun, they afford a considerable saving to any one who must watch expenditure closely" (482–83).

134:6–7 **intensity of feeling:** In this passage and the scene that follows, Mike's genial self-deprecating character, his civility and sense of humor, and his "intensity of feeling" that he manages to get even into a handshake are all stressed in contrast to Robert Cohn's awkward solipsism, his graceless self-importance that makes him shake hands, absurdly, "because we were back" (he's the one who has been away); but, given Cohn's self-absorption, there is no other world than the one he is the center of. Jake asks him, with an appropriate edge in his voice, where he's been, that is, why he didn't show up in Burguete. Robert doesn't even have the courtesy to ask if they had good fishing. (Mike does, twice.) Instead, Robert absurdly insists that *he* had to go to San Sebastián to get Brett and Mike (see following entry). The reappearance of Robert reintroduces tension into the flow of the action, a tension that has been missing during the Burguete-Roncevaux interlude, where, for thirty peaceful pages, Robert has been absent. (And, of course, for fifty pages Brett has been absent.) This scene, then, up to the unloading of the bulls, shows Mike's character at his best (and Robert's character at his typical worst) before Mike turns on Robert in the scene following the *desencajonada*. (On the "lovable" and "generous" but irresponsible traits of Mike's character, see 78:17.)

134:11 **What rot:** Three times in ten lines Brett exclaims, "What rot" to express her contemptuous dismissal of Robert's ridiculous assertion that he "brought" Mike and Brett to Pamplona, and that he had to go to San Sebastián to "bring" them (see 142:9).

134:27 **those dear days:** Mike's ironic characterization of the war here echoes inversely Wilson-Harris's observation a few pages earlier that he has not "had much fun since the war" (129:8). The reader does not learn much about Mike's war experience, except that he was in the war—perhaps as a cavalry officer (his "horse bolted")—and that he had earned medals that he "never sent in for" (135:14). Whatever his war experience had been, his humorous self-deprecating character forbids boasting and requires ironic understatement, and he tells only the "war stories" that, as he says three times in this scene, "reflect discredit" on him. (Brett tells these stories, too; but she, no doubt, heard them from Mike. The emphasis on the stories that "reflect discredit" implies that there are other stories, too, war stories that neither of them will tell.)

135:23 **bloody gazette:** Mike's indifference to the *London Gazette,* the British government publication in which official announcements of such matters as promotions and medal recipients were made, suggests his attitude to the war.

135:27 **Henry Wilson:** Sir Henry Wilson (1865–1922) was the British director of military operations before the war, and a general with various titles and commands during the war, including British representative to the Allied Supreme War Council, where he worked closely with Marshall Foch, the allied supreme commander. After the war, he was Britain's head military advisor at the Paris Peace Conference. In 1922, he retired from the military as field marshal and entered Parliament. A prominent opponent of Irish independence, he was murdered by IRA gunmen on the morning of 22 June 1922. He had just unveiled a new war memorial at London's Liverpool Railway Station; returning home, he emerged from a taxi and was shot nine times. (The assassins were caught and executed in August 1922.) When the allusion to Henry Wilson is understood, Mike's story of the medals he'd earned but didn't bother to claim, and the dinner that he attended that the prince (later King Edward VII) and the king (George V) did not attend, and at which "no one wore any medals" due to the assassination that morning of Wilson, while told humorously, reflects seriously on questions of war and peace, on war memorials. The presence of Henry Wilson in the narrative might also be responsible for Hemingway's naming of Wilson-Harris, fishing companion of Jake and Bill. (Hemingway also alludes to Henry Wilson in his short story "A Way You'll Never Be," where the shell-shocked Nick quotes that "great soldier and gentleman, Sir Henry Wilson,"—see *Complete Short Stories* 313.)

136:15 **military cove:** "Cove," like "chap," is common British slang for "fellow." Cove and chap are "nearly equivalent in meaning, save that *cove* belongs to a lower and more slangy stratum of speech" (*OED*). Mike uses the lower form in disdain for the excessively military chap who cared so much for his medals; that is, Mike disdains all war honors, including his own, which he does not bother to claim, and borrowed medals that he gives away to girls in a nightclub.

136:24 **bankrupt:** Mike's humorous reply to Bill's question about how he went bankrupt—"Gradually and then suddenly"—and his statement of the cause ("False friends") lead Brett to ask for another story that "reflects discredit" on Mike: the fact that he was blind drunk in bankruptcy court. Many readings of Mike's character suggest too easily that his fiscal bankruptcy functions as a sign of his moral bankruptcy. It may well be that his generosity to false friends led to his financial bankruptcy. And his ostensible blindness, or drunkenness, is not always what it appears to be (see 143:2) and is sometimes a cover for his profoundly moral impulse to rebuke bad conduct—as in the scene with Robert that follows the unloading of the bulls.

137:27 **ladder:** Three times in two sentences Jake stresses the ladder, and the entire unloading scene is framed by the climbing up and climbing down, thus resonating with the pattern of ladder imagery established earlier in the novel (see 103:3). Resonances of biblical Jacob's Ladder imagery are here suggested by the ascent to see the bulls, who will be sacrificed in the mystery and passion of the bullfight, the "ecstasy," as Hemingway puts it in *Death in the Afternoon*, that has everything to do with death and immortality, that is, "while momentary, as profound as any religious ecstasy" (206). The stone wall of the corral, and the ladder they climb to stand on top, is a symbolic point where (as in biblical images of Jacob's Ladder) heaven and earth meet, where, as Hemingway might put it, the prelude to the ecstasy and communion of the bullring occurs. The *desencajonada* is the first phase of the ritual and sacrifice that culminates in the bullring; if it is not exactly analogous to a Station of the Cross as followed by a Christian meditating on the Passion of Christ, it is, as Hemingway presents it, the first meditative station of the bullfight. It is also, in a less elevated sense, "one of the most interesting of all phases of bullfighting to see the steers work . . . in all the many operations connected with the raising, transporting and unloading of fighting bulls" (*Death in the Afternoon* 107–8).

137:30 **up the ladder:** Clearly, since they are walking across the grass and don't start up the ladder until the next page (138:5), this line should read, "As we came up to the ladder," which is how Hemingway wrote it in the manuscript (*Facsimile* 2:374). The omitted "to"—clearly an error that occurred during the process of publication—confuses the sense of the passage.

138:16 **see the bulls:** It seems that Brett thinks the crowd has gathered because something exciting (e.g., the goring of a steer) might happen; but, of course, the crowd has gathered to *judge* the bulls. Jake stresses this even more clearly in the manuscript, where he says: "They only want to see the bulls" (375). Brett anticipates excitement; Robert is impatient for things to start. Jake is the only one of his group who understands the event, but, as she later does at the bullfight, Brett listens to Jake's instructions regarding what to watch.

140:11 **the steer came up:** Since much nonsense has been written about the role of the steer in this scene, it is worth noting the craft of the steer in picking up and calming the bulls. In his explanatory glossary to *Death in the Afternoon,* Hemingway made this entry: "*Cabestros:* the trained steers used in handling fighting bulls. The older and more experienced these are the greater their value and usefulness" (423). This appreciation of the trained steer should be remembered in the following scene, where everybody—except Jake—talks loosely and ignorantly about steers.

141:13 **being a steer:** Robert, with no apparent appreciation for the skill of the steer and no ironic awareness that the bull's presence in the corral carries the sign of his certain and imminent death while the steer will live to practice its craft, makes the silly statement: "It's no life being a steer." Mike, in rare form now, picks up on Robert's statement—"I would have thought you'd loved being a steer, Robert"—and mocks him five times with that image in less than a page of ensuing dialogue.

Since this scene has been so overinterpreted and so deeply misread, since most high-school seniors and college freshmen (and some college professors) quote the pervasive misleading and superficial study guides as well as the rampant, confused Internet interpretations of *The Sun Also Rises* that present Jake as a steer, and since term papers that discuss Jake as a steer are bought and sold on the Internet, in contexts that sometimes indicate only the fuzziest grasp of what a steer is and no grasp of how exactly Jake is wounded, it is necessary to read this scene very carefully. Indeed, even serious Hemingway commentators such as Michael Reynolds have steered students down this primrose path of incomprehension; in a passage that discusses how "the bullfight ritual is used metaphorically in the novel" Reynolds states three times in rapid succession that "we know that the real steer is Jake Barnes" (i.e., not Robert), "Jake Barnes is the castrated steer whose main job at Pamplona is to keep the men" (i.e., the man-bulls Mike, Bill, and Robert, in Reynolds's reading) "from fighting with each other," and Robert finally "turns on Jake, the steer . . . just as the bull gored his pacifier" (*Novel of the Twenties* 35–36). Yet mere rhetorical assertion and iterative insistence, and all the dime-store deconstruction and K-Mart criticism of Jake as steer, must not be accepted as substitute for close reading of the actual text.

First, we might recall the exact nature of Jake's wound. Then we should remember Hemingway's insistence, in his interview with George Plimpton, that Jake's testicles were intact and he had all the "normal feelings" of a man, and that whoever said Jake is "emasculated precisely as is a steer" must have been "a little bit screwy" (see 30:26). Then we should read the scene closely and see that there is absolutely not one word or implication or gesture that in any way associates Jake with a steer. Robert is the only one associated with steer-like behavior, for the way he hangs around Brett, and that association comes only from Mike's humorous mixed-up metaphor, which is certainly not meant to, or sufficient reason to, set off the frenzy of symbol mongering, the riot of extended metaphor fabrication and near-allegorical exegesis that embraces the idée fixe of Jake as steer that haunts Hemingway criticism at all levels. Examine Mike's metaphor of Robert as steer following Brett around, and the conclusion, if this were the allegory that some critics make it out to be, must be that Brett is the bull, and also that Mike doesn't understand steers, whom the bull follows, and not vice versa. Even Mike's passing fancy of Robert as steer will not hold up, since Robert so clearly lacks the skill, training, and disciplined conduct of the *cabestros* that Hemingway and Jake admire. Robert is not a steer, Jake is not a *cabestro,* and none of them is a bull, not even Brett. It is high time to bury all the imaginary steer metaphors that exist, not in the novel, only in the criticism, and recognize Mike's "steer" jibe at Robert for what it is—a half-drunken joke, not an interpretive key.

142:12 **Why aren't you drunk?** Mike adds to the list of particulars of Robert's bad behavior—his following Brett around San Sebastián, his boring presence there where even though Mike asked his friends to invite Robert to parties, no one would—the fact that Robert doesn't really drink. Then, underlining Robert's cheapness, the last thing Mike says before Cohn leaves is "Robert Cohn's going to buy a drink."

143:10 **did behave very badly:** Although Jake has said they were all embarrassed by Mike's mockery of Robert, and Brett has chided Mike for his conduct, when Robert's gone, Brett says to Jake, "I'm not saying [Mike's] not right, you know"; they are "all friends together," and they agree that Robert has behaved very badly. Mike was not as drunk as he acted and, on balance (though this is one of those points of the code of conduct that readers will have to decide for themselves), Mike is right to say that either Robert "must behave or get out." But as Jake says, how can he tell Robert that?

144:9 **Circe:** Robert's association of Brett with the enchantress who detained Odysseus and turned his men into swine should be taken not as a springboard for critical interpretations of Brett as Circe but for the "ridiculous" assertion of one of those "literary chaps" that it is. If men are swine around Brett, it is due to their own natural swinehood. In fact, the laughable nature of Robert's ever so literary name for Brett reminds the reader of Robert's literary identity at the beginning of the novel—a third-rate imagination wrapped up in romantic escapism. Thus Jake and Brett agree, implicitly, that Mike could be a good writer, better than Robert Cohn.

145:23 **nobody has any business:** Bill, not particularly fond of Robert himself ("he makes me sick, and he can go to hell"—see 102:26–27), thinks Mike has gone too far in attacking Robert. Jake apparently disagrees, since he does not respond and changes the subject to the bulls.

146:11 **from the war:** It's a pleasant enough dinner, with Brett looking lovely, Robert happy looking at her, and Bill and Mike being "very funny." The muted war motif of this entire chapter—from Harris's statement about fun at the beginning, to Mike's story of the war medals, to the allusion to the assassination of Sir Henry Wilson after his dedication of a war memorial—is brought full circle when Jake compares this dinner to wartime dinners: the "ignored tension," the "feeling of things coming" that nobody can prevent. When the fiesta explodes two chapters later, the things foreshadowed in this chapter begin to happen very quickly.

CHAPTER 14

147:3 quite drunk: This is one of the few times in the novel that Jake is drunk, which may account for the feeling of the loosening of "the pressure" in his head (aggravated by the reappearance of Brett after her long absence from the novel), the "oversensitized state" of his mind (149:15). There are numerous important things to notice about this brief chapter, the shortest in the novel: It is the only chapter in the book that contains no spoken words, not one line of dialogue rendered; It is easily the novel's most meditative movement or passage, extensively and intensively; It contains Jake's most concentrated philosophizing and provides important insights into his "fine philosophies" (149:24); It tells the reader a great deal about Jake's aesthetic sensibility (as he reacts to his reading of Turgenev) and his linguistic sensitivities (as he thinks about languages, "inflected phrases," and how his friends talk). The formal beauty and necessity of this *silent* introspective chapter, after two very talky chapters (the humorous dialogue of chapter 12 and the tense dialogue of chapter 13) and before the fiesta explodes in the first sentence of the next chapter, tell us a good deal about Hemingway's technique of pacing, his art of narrative disposition, his genius for the organization and timing of storytelling. We note too the careful internal structure of the chapter, with just under three pages devoted to a scene where Jake is "quite drunk," balanced by a nearly equal amount of text that stresses how "quiet" everything is, how for two days before the fiesta explodes, it is "a quiet life and no one was drunk" (150:31).

147:5 Turgenieff: Ivan Turgenev (in the now-standard spelling) was a nineteenth-century (1818–1883) Russian writer who was one of Hemingway's favorites. He borrowed two titles—*The Torrents of Spring* and "Fathers and Sons"—from English translations of Turgenev titles. In *A Moveable Feast* Hemingway writes about checking out books from the rental library of Sylvia Beach's Paris bookstore, Shakespeare and Company: "I started with Turgenev and took the two volumes of *A Sportsman's Sketches*"; later, as he waits for Scott Fitzgerald to arrive in Lyon, Hemingway reads from the first volume of *A Sportsman's Sketches* in bed and feels "happy being with Turgenev in Russia until I was asleep" (36, 159). Turgenev's style was celebrated for its understatement, for exact observation and description, for avoidance of rhetoric—qualities that no doubt appealed to Hemingway (and Jake). Reading Turgenev is also an apt setup for Jake's meditation on women and Brett, since Turgenev was a never-married expatriate who lived a long time in Paris, where he sustained a long-term passion for a married woman. Even more apt is the subject matter of the Turgenev that Jake reads—sportsman's sketches, including, as Jake says in the manuscript, one about a hunter, and another about "two men fishing" (*Facsimile* 2:396). Yet, since it is the country becoming "very clear" that matters most, that loosens the pressure in Jake's head and makes him feel he "would always have" that country, Hemingway discards the inessential information about the actual sketches Jake reads. Jake's meditation on Turgenev's rendering of country is reminiscent of Nick's meditation on writing country in "On Writing," the deleted conclusion of "Big Two-Hearted River": "You had to do it from inside yourself. Nobody had ever written about country like [Cézanne had painted it]. He felt almost holy about it" (*Nick Adams Stories* 239). Trying to keep from thinking, Jake rereads Turgenev's country until it becomes "very clear" and he has it for always, and then, holding that in his head, Jake is able to stop thinking and go to sleep. This is the meditative landscape formula that informs the writing of country, of landscape, and of cityscape throughout *The Sun Also Rises*.

147:16 **heard them laugh:** One of the only sounds heard in this otherwise silent chapter is Brett and Mike laughing, possibly at something Robert has said or done.

148:5 **bright idea:** Jake's joke about the electric light, not in the manuscript, is a later addition.

148:6 **to hell with:** Hemingway made extensive revisions to the manuscript version of Jake's meditation on Brett and women, cutting a great deal of detail about his feelings about Brett, and, finally, inserting these lines that assert "to hell with" Brett and women. Deleted details include Jake's assertions that he's "pretty well through with" Brett, that since she went off to San Sebastián with Cohn "she had lost something" and was now "vulgar," and that she has "killed" off Jake's feelings for her. Jake calls this a "good thing" because he doesn't want to love any woman, wanting no "grand passion" he can't do anything about. He reviews the entire history of his relationship with Brett and concludes that it's "not so hard to build up a world that women did not have any importance in. It is a damned good world." But, even though he is "all straightened out inside," Brett remains his "best woman friend" (*Facsimile* 2:397–401; see 232:16–19 and 235:25). Perhaps the proximity of Jake's long internal monologue to the Turgenev allusions led Hemingway to follow the lesson of the master and work toward understatement and economy by cutting much of Jake's meditation on women. Although the alert reader will already have reached the conclusion that Jake is through with Brett by the end of book I (see, e.g., 65:3), those readers who believe that Jake remains in a state of perpetual anguish over Brett throughout the book would have profited from the inclusion of the deleted passages.

148:24 **fine philosophies:** Jake's current philosophy, that you pay in some way for everything that's any good, that the world is a "good place" to invest in, will probably not come to seem as silly as his earlier "philosophies" that he has discarded. In the manuscript, he says at this point: "At thirty you should know something. The proof was that I was fairly happy now at thirty and I had been miserable at twenty four" (*Facsimile* 2:404). In later revisions the crucial following lines about learning as you go along, learning "how to live in it," and thus maybe learning "what it was all about" were added. This well-known and little understood passage has often been taken to be a key statement of some kind of pragmatic, relativistic, make-it-up-as-you-go-along code. It is nothing of the kind. From everything we know about Jake, we learn that his "how" of living is the rituals, the ceremonies that, if followed far and faithfully enough, may lead to the "all." All the rituals and sacraments in which Jake participates, mastering the *how* of living, whether ceremonies of food, wine, travel, fishing, the bullfight, or the Church, hold him steady, providing his stay against the irritable demand for certainty, the insistent fundamentalist or Puritan or gnostic urge to immanentize the eschaton, to know all the answers *right now.* This passage, then, is an exact rendering of the pilgrim's code: "Perhaps as you went along you did learn something." And as Jake goes along, as we see two pages later, we see that his pilgrimage to Pamplona embodies his current "philosophy" and belief as he participates in the sacraments of his Church (150:32).

149:3 **immorality:** Like a good Christian, Jake here practices examination of conscience. He assesses in particular Mike's bad behavior toward Cohn, not to judge Mike's conduct but to come to terms with the fact that he *liked* watching Mike "hurt Cohn." In the manuscript he acknowledges that he "hated Cohn now," and "Cohn was acting badly now," but he is doing so through "ignorance of the rules and a sort of stupidity" (*Facsimile* 2:402). Jake's primary concern is the self-disgust he feels over taking pleasure in Cohn's discomfort, which must be, he concludes, "immorality." No doubt that occasion of self-disgust is one of the things he repents when he goes to confession in the next two days (150:32).

149:20 **next two days:** After Jake goes to sleep, Hemingway indicates not only passage of time with the textual space but a profound change in narrative *attention,* a shift from the introspection of Jake's meditation to close observation of external details that is characteristic of the deep structure of Hemingway's art of storytelling. We note that during these *quiet* two days, which occupy the last two pages of the chapter, Jake pays close attention to many details: gateposts, holes dug by workmen, fitted numbered timbers, stiff-legged horses, sun-baked fields, old women sweeping, Gypsy camps, stuffed peasant-saddlebags, a man with a hose watering the gravel walks, girls and officers walking in the evening paseo, high white clouds, the fresh, cool air after the rain, and the view. As poets often maintain, one of the fundamental impulses of all poetry, all writing, is to praise the observed details of things that happen, that *are;* and such description demands observation so intense that—as Czeslaw Milosz observes—"what we paid no attention to, because it struck us as so ordinary, is revealed as miraculous" (383). Such "revelation of reality," such "exceptional sensitivity to the rich materiality of things" that, when "truly seen, seen intensely," remains with us forever (like Turgenev's country), leads not to the mere placid embrace of the physical world but, for a Catholic writer like Milosz (and Hemingway), to a profoundly spiritual place where "dread and reverence can exist within us simultaneously" (383–87). As is often the case in Hemingway's prose, here and in many other passages, his attention to detail in the rendered landscape approaches a condition of revelation, a sense of the miraculous, which functions as an objective correlative for the protagonist's inner state of being. Jake, quietly observing details, reading the newspapers, going to church, walking to the Gypsy camp (where Brett has her fortune told), is poised—in simultaneous dread and reverence—on the brink of the fiesta.

150:9 **gypsies:** See 23:7.

150:9–10 **aguardiente:** See 106:13.

150:31 **quiet life:** See 147:3.

150:32 **church a couple of times:** In two days, Jake goes to church twice—quite probably, after he goes to confession (with Brett tagging along), he then goes to Mass (alone).

151:2 **language:** In the manuscript Jake says he told Brett his confession would not be interesting and "besides it would have to be in Spanish" (*Facsimile* 2:410). The final revision—"in a language she did not know"—extends the reference to include both Spanish and the language of the Church, two languages Brett does not know.

151:10 **felt quite friendly:** In spite of the fact that Cohn's behavior has not changed—he's still overly concerned with "trying to get a shave," and he follows Jake and Brett to church, lurking outside—Jake feels very friendly to him. In other words, Jake's examination of conscience earlier in the chapter—his concern over his own "immorality," his feelings toward Cohn (see 149:3)—has led to his confession of sins—the sacrament has served its purpose, and Jake again feels "friendly" toward Robert.

CHAPTER 15

152:1 **6th of July:** Originally held in October, the Fiesta of San Fermín was moved to the first week of July in 1591 because of the frequent bad weather during the older autumn celebrations. The fiesta has its origins in the liturgical calendar's October celebration of the saint's day, beginning in 1186, when relics of San Fermín, or Saint Firmin, were brought from Amiens, France. Largely a religious festival at first, the fiesta gradually expanded to include bullfights, especially after a new relic of San Fermín was brought from France in 1386. At that time, a bullfight was held in the city square on 10 October; however, the year's major bullfight was still held on 25 July, the feast day of Santiago (Saint James). After 1591, when the saint's day celebrations were moved to 7 July, the "casual concidence of religious solemnity, the hustle of the fair [livestock] and the bulls on the same dates gave the Sanfermines the appearance we now perceive" (Ayuntamiento de Pamplona 40). For San Fermín the saint, see also 6:31, 77:22–31, and 82:16.

152:1 **the fiesta exploded:** As Hemingway stresses in this first paragraph about the fiesta, with his description of the peasants coming into town from the hills and the plains of Navarre, the fiesta was still in 1925 a largely local and regional Navarrese event. Compared with today's influx of many thousands of tourists from all over Europe, America, and Asia, the fiesta then attracted very few tourists. A survey of early twentieth-century guidebooks reveals very little touristic information that would draw tourists to Pamplona for the fiesta: The 1913 Baedeker's guide to Spain does not mention the fiesta in its Pamplona entry; The 1921 Blue Guide to the Pyrenees has one sentence recommending the fiesta, which takes place, the guidebook tells us, from 7 to 12 July and has very good bullfights; The 1928 *Illustrated Guide-Books: The French and Spanish Basque Country* recommends the fiesta (noting that it takes place 7–12 July), evoking the "great excitement of the mob" at the corrida and *encierro,* and noting that it draws "crowds of foreigners" (Lamare 267). Since the latter guidebook dates from two years after *The Sun Also Rises,* the influence of the novel may already be detected. Compare these early guidebooks with the current edition of a standard tourist guide, the Michelin *Green Guide: Spain,* and the fiesta's changed identity is underlined; in a separate highlighted entry entitled "The

'Sanfermines,'" the guide notes, in part, "The *feria* of San Fermín is celebrated with joyous ardour from 6 to 14 July each year. Visitors pour in, doubling the town's population, to see the great evening bullfights and enjoy the carefree atmosphere (described by Hemingway in *Fiesta, The Sun Also Rises*)" (Miñon-Marquina 361). Thus, even the guidebooks take note of the changes wrought in the fiesta by Hemingway's novel. The official contemporary guidebook of the Ayuntamiento de Pamplona, under the headline "The Fiesta Meets the World," puts it this way:

> Until the early 1920s, the Sanfermines was a fiesta known only to the local people. . . . Music on the streets, acrobats and tightrope walkers were the counterpart to the religious offices. The streets were busy with stockbreeders from the surrounding villages making deals. At night, bonfires were lit. The bull contests took place on the day after the day of the Saint, and would last all afternoon. The second decade of the present century [i.e., the twentieth] saw the arrival of tourists from surrounding provinces and the first foreigners, captivated by the legend of the encierro. Ernest Hemingway played a key role with his novel "Fiesta" ("The Sun Also Rises") in this dissemination process. (41)

Writing about the fiesta more than thirty years after *The Sun Also Rises*, Hemingway says in *The Dangerous Summer* a number of interesting things that illuminate these matters and, more generally, the novel's rendition of the fiesta: "It's a man's fiesta and women at it make trouble, never intentionally of course, but they nearly always make or have trouble. I wrote a book on this once. . . . I've written Pamplona once and for keeps. It is all there as it always was except forty thousand tourists have been added. There were not twenty tourists when I first went there nearly four decades ago. Now on some days they say there are close to a hundred thousand in the town" (135–36). And they are there largely because of this novel.

152:17 **mass in the cathedral:** Jake goes to the 11 AM Mass, apparently accompanied by none of his friends; but he is at the crowded Mass, with "many people," with the locals, making the proper preparations for the fiesta, which leads him to remind the reader: "San Fermín is also a religious festival." It is his third time in church in three days.

153:14 **the rocket:** After Mass, Jake joins Bill and Robert at the Café Iruña (see 95:26–27). In keeping with the explosion and rocket imagery, and other military metaphors, Jake notes that the café is "like a battleship stripped for action"; the good tables and chairs have disappeared, and the furniture of the fiesta is in place. Then the noontime rocket announces the beginning of the fiesta. Some commentators on the novel have referred to this as the *Chupinazo*, the first loud rocket fired from the balcony of the city hall, followed by dozens more. This is an anachronism, and it is not what Hemingway here describes. The current form of the *Chupinazo* is a recent tradition, begun in 1941; before that, there was the more or less spontaneous noontime firing of rockets in the Plaza del Castillo (see 94:9).

153:16 **Theatre Gayarre:** See 94:9.

153:26 **riau-riau:** The "music" that accompanies the *Riau-Riau* (generally capitalized) is the Astráin Waltz. The *Riau-Riau* refers specifically to the shout made repeatedly by the dancers after the stanzas of the waltz, which is played over and over, are completed. In a larger sense, *Riau-Riau* is the popular name for a fiesta tradition that was begun in 1914. An event known as "The Vespers" had long been the first official religious and civil ceremony of the fiesta; the mayor and officers of the city council would take the "Vespers Walk" from the city hall to the Church of San Lorenzo, where Vespers (the traditional ceremony of the sixth canonical hour of the church, held variably over the centuries at different hours, usually a late afternoon or evening prayer service) was celebrated in the San Fermín Chapel. In 1914 the *Riau-Riau* protest tradition began, in which crowds of dancers would impede the progress of the city officials dressed in their official finery, shouting insults and ridicule at them and impeding their progress as their procession moved through the streets toward the Vespers ceremony in the Church of San Lorenzo. At first, according to most historical accounts, the *Riau-Riau* dancers delayed the procession for about an hour, as was generally the case in the 1920s; gradually, over the years, the "demonstration" grew larger and more raucous—so that in some years the mere half-mile procession took over three hours to accomplish—until the mayor canceled the *Riau-Riau* in 1991. Although various attempts to revive the tradition (in alternate forms) have been made since then, it is still in an official state of suspension and is not acknowledged in the official program of the fiesta.

154:11 **club of some sort:** A distinct and joyous feature of the Sanfermines is the *peñas*, each club having its own identifying characteristics—as Hemingway notes, matching clothing, large banners—but also an emblem or coat of arms, an official song (played repeatedly by the *peña*'s own *charanga*, or band), and its own bar or venue for festivities during the fiesta. The first official *peña* at Pamplona was El Trueno in 1852. Of the currently existing *peñas*, the oldest is La Única, established in 1903. Their "uniform" consists of a blue-and-white-checked shirt, green scarf, green sash, and green-laced espadrilles (Ayuntamiento de Pamplona 55). The name of the blue-smocked and red-scarved *peña* described here by Hemingway has proved impossible to verify. But, of course, the red scarf and sash have become emblematic of the fiesta.

154:18 **foreigners:** This exchange, in its final form, may be taken as yet another indication of Cohn's lack of a sense of *place*, of knowing where he is, or as an index to his self-centeredness—does he think that the local dancers and musicians of the *peña* are "foreigners"? To a solipsist, they would be. However, we note that in the manuscript, the dialogue attribution of this and the following line is reversed: Bill asks where the foreigners are, and Robert says: "We're the foreigners." Had Hemingway retained that, Bill's question about the foreigners would be a joke, and Cohn's reply would be an indication that he didn't get the joke. Moreover, in the manuscript, Hemingway identifies the true local perspective when Jake adds that the foreigners are "everybody that's come in from outside of Pamplona" (*Facsimile* 2:416–17).

154:30 **consequences:** In this paragraph, Hemingway succinctly defines his understanding of the concept of fiesta. At the beginning and end of the passage, he underlines that it lasts "for seven days," as it did in the 1920s, though it "lasts" longer now. Hemingway's repetition of "seven days" resonates with the most frequently employed Christian symbolic number: "As a combination of four (the earth) and three (the heavens or the Trinity), it symbolizes the universe" (Metford 225). And, of course, there are the seven days of Creation, the seven seas, the seven sacraments, the seven cardinal virtues, the seven deadly sins, and many other sevenfold groupings. This passage also points to how the fiesta makes everything "quite unreal," and the effect that unreality has on a sense of "consequences," and that unreality, that sense of having entered another world, has much to do with the sense of time, the seven days of the fiesta when time is unreal, blurred, nights and days turned inside out, as if the fiesta participants have entered another dimension. This is precisely the world of sacred time, sacred place, the world of pilgrimage, the world that a fiesta centered in religion and the bullfight exists to create; or, as Allen Josephs puts it: "The very reason for the fiesta is, of course, to stop profane time, clock time, historical time. . . . A fiesta is time out of time, sacred time, original time, primal time, *illud tempus* to use Mircea Eliade's term" ("*Toreo*" 93). In the manuscript this paragraph is more than twice as long as its final form: Jake ponders the "strange things" that happen to "English and Americans [who] have never had any seven day fiestas," the way that fiestas are "dangerous" and "reckless," and he cannot decide "whether the danger grew up out of the recklessness or the recklessness out of the danger." He wonders if the fiesta caused "what happened" or if it was just "the natural progress of events starting in Paris"; he seems certain that the "fiesta made every one a little crazy," particularly through its "effect of speeding up the natural tendencies through this insistence on the unimportance of consequences" (*Facsimile* 2:420–21). For seven days, time both slows down and speeds up, and the fiesta's *insistence* on timelessness consigns mere "consequences" to some profane time-bound realm. This may well be Hemingway's best explanation for why everybody does what they do during the fiesta—why they behave badly, why Jake does what he does—but he leaves most of the exposition on the cutting-room floor and trusts finally to his pared-down understated summary of time, unreality, and consequences.

155:3 **big religious procession:** Jake gets this wrong, as he does certain other details of the fiesta. The "Vespers Walk," or procession (see 153:26), is the *first* procession of the fiesta, but it is not "*the big* religious procession" (emphasis added). That has always occurred, of course, on the saint's day, on the morning of 7 July—the morning after the procession described here. Usually described in the literature of the fiesta as simply "the Procession," it begins at 10:30 AM, when the statue of the saint ("a 15th-century statue . . . worshipped by the people of Pamplona"), with a reliquary containing relics of San Fermín, is paraded in grand procession through the streets of the old city. As the official city guidebook puts it, "July 7th, San Fermín's day, is the *most important* day of the fiesta. . . . Thousands of people, dressed immaculately in white, accompany the image of the Saint. . . . [The people of] the city surround him showing their admiration, devotion and acknowledgment. It is *the moment* of the *tradition*" (Ayuntamiento de Pamplona 46; emphasis added). But the actual "big religious procession" is not described by Jake, because he and all his friends are in bed, sleeping until noon the next day (see 161:19). The critical question that this information raises is this: does Hemingway know this, and in having Jake misstate the matter and sleep through the "big procession" the next morning, does he intend some character-revealing point about Jake, some aspect of the unreality of fiesta time that has already affected Jake? Biographical evidence on how well Hemingway knew the precise details of the fiesta in the 1920s is impossible to come by, largely because the biographers themselves have only vague notions about the fiesta. As a fiesta participant who has only attended four fiestas—one more than Hemingway had attended when he wrote the novel—I can attest to the unreality of time that makes it difficult to keep straight and recall accurately events, days, and times and causes confusion regarding exact schedules of processions and other events. And at my first two fiestas I can recall asking many American and British aficionados, some of whom had attended as many as thirty fiestas, exactly where and when the big religious procession was. None of them could tell me, in other than the vaguest terms, and none of these tourists seemed to place any value on what the locals regarded as "the most important day of the fiesta," the very "moment of the tradition." Yet since there are photographs (from the 1950s) that show Hemingway at the authentic "big religious procession" (on 7 July), that show him crossing himself and kneeling with the Pamplona locals as the statue of the saint passed, we know what he felt about the procession.

As for the smaller Vespers procession on 6 July that Jake here describes, he gets right the presence of the civil and religious dignitaries, the *Riau-Riau* dancers, and the "great giants." It is curious that he calls the giant figures "cigar-store Indians"; they are not wooden carvings, but papier-mâché figures; they are not "thirty feet high"—the tallest of the figures is twelve feet eight inches (Hemingway was closer in the manuscript, where he said they were "twenty feet high"). When the bearers raise them up, they can be close to fourteen feet high—perhaps the point is they seem much larger to the fiesta observer. (The same figures of the "giants" have been used since 1850.) Jake says there is "a King and Queen"; in actuality, there are four kings and four queens—one each representing Africa, America, Asia, and Europe. Also in the procession are the *Cabezudos* (the big heads), the *Kilikis* (six-foot figures representing local officials), and the *Zaldikos* (horse-shaped figures)—the same figures having been used throughout the twentieth century, except for two *Zaldikos* added in 1941. However, since Jake is observing from back in the crowd, he probably cannot see these much shorter figures.

155:18–19 **Brett was stopped:** Contrary to what Hemingway commentators have often said or implied, Jake is not turned away at the door of the church. Rather, as he attempts to participate fully in the ceremony (and enter a church for the fourth time in three days), Brett is turned away for sartorial reasons that operate thematically and symbolically, continuing the religious contrast between Brett and Jake, and leading directly into the chanting street-dance around Brett as "image." Unable to get into the Church of San Lorenzo and pray before the image of San Fermín in his chapel, Brett becomes the image that is danced and chanted around before she is elevated to her seat on the "high wine cask" in the dark wine-shop—her church, her high altar.

156:3 **leather wine-bottle:** See 103:12.

156:7 **wreath of garlics:** The local men who dance around Brett wear wreaths of garlic, they hang a wreath around her neck, and when Robert passes out in the wine shop they put a big wreath of garlic around him. Since Hemingway makes repeated mention of the garlic—five times in five pages—he probably wants the reader to be aware of the reputed magical and healing properties, the many superstitions and rituals associated with garlic, worldwide, for many centuries. These properties include, of course, repulsion of vampires and witches, and more generally, evil and the devil, and there is the European notion that a racer who has eaten garlic cannot be passed by his competitors, and the Spanish notion, some say, that a bullfighter might eat garlic to keep the bull from charging too close. Garlic was also widely used in World War I as a battlefield antiseptic. Although some of these garlic properties may resonate with this scene, none of it adds up to a particularly coherent pattern, unless we conclude that Brett and the men dancing around her, and Robert, are protected from evil by the garlic. There is also the fact that wreaths of garlic are a highly visible feature of the Sanfermines and many other French and Spanish fetes and fiestas. Perhaps, given the invitation to unreality and suspended consequences that fiestas evoke, all fiesta participants need all the protection from evil they can get. Or maybe it's just a matter of health.

158:2 **Nada:** Discussing this passage under the rubric of Hemingway's humor, James Hinkle writes: "Religion is put in its place by one brief comment" ("What's Funny" 111). Yet, in his zeal to uncover "jokes" in the novel, and his general impulse to downplay religious motifs, the joke may be on the critic. In fact, since this is the small unimportant procession—not the "big religious procession" of the next morning (see 155:3)—some locals might well dismiss it as nothing. In any case, what the unnamed wine-shop commentator says hardly amounts to putting religion "in its place" and represents nothing but his own view. Jake ignores the comment.

158:13 **Anis del Mono:** This is a well-known Spanish anisette with a famous label bearing a depiction of a monkey or *mono*. The story goes that the distiller was given a present of a monkey from America; the monkey lived in the distillery, and by the end of the nineteenth century, the distillery and its product were widely known as the "distillery and anisette of the monkey." The Anis del Mono monkey was the subject of widely circulated vintage posters produced between the 1890s and the 1920s. Since Robert has passed out from drinking Anis del Mono, perhaps he is identified with the "monkey" from America.

159:19 **It's tomorrow:** Mike's reply to Robert's question about time is one of the many small ways that Hemingway suggests the translocation of dimensions during the fiesta, the access to another kind of time (see 154:30).

160:6 **race through the streets:** Although Hemingway doesn't use the word until a later description of the event, this is the novel's first *encierro,* the running of the bulls. As the official Pamplona guide states, "Leaving religious offices aside, the running of the bulls is the central event of the Sanfermines. It is also the event which has made the fiesta famous" (Ayuntamiento de Pamplona 50). Certainly some aficionados would quarrel with this characterization of the *encierro* as the "central event," with the seeming elevation in importance above the bullfights themselves. Yet, in terms of popular culture and media coverage of the fiesta, the statement is accurate. In *Death in the Afternoon,* Hemingway defined the *encierro* as follows: "the driving of fighting bulls on foot, surrounded by steers, from one corral to the corral of the ring. In Pamplona the running of the bulls through the streets with the crowd running ahead of them from the corral at the edge of town into and through the bull ring into the corral of the ring. The bulls to be fought in the afternoon are run through the streets at seven o'clock in the morning of the day they are to be fought" (437). Until 1924 the *encierro* was held at 6 AM, from 1925 through 1973 at 7 AM, and since then at 8 AM. The running of the bulls is a feature of many bullfighting towns in Spain and the south of France, but Pamplona's is the most famous and most deadly *encierro*. Since 1924, thirteen runners have died in the *encierro* and thousands have been wounded. In contrast, not one bullfighter has died in the ring in Pamplona.

Jake's expository details here concerning the running are precise and accurate regarding the rockets announcing the progress of the *encierro*, the appropriate posture of the fallen man, and the like. Eight belled steers run with the bulls, and three more are released two minutes later to pick up any bulls separated from the herd. The route from corral to corral is 848.6 meters, the average duration of the run is three minutes and fifty-five seconds, the average speed of the bulls is twenty-four kilometers per hour, and there are usually from 2,000 to 3,500 runners. Each segment of the route has its own name and features; Jake is here watching the *encierro* pass below him on the Estafeta stretch, one of the narrowest and most crowded places, where, as Jake notes, the runners are "packed close together."

161:19 **before noon:** Because they all sleep until noon (or later), Jake's group completely misses the truly "big religious procession" (see 155:3), the traditional heart of the fiesta for the Navarrese. From 10 AM on, while they slept, the grand procession wound through the streets with the statue of Saint Fermín at the center of the event; at 11:40 AM, the saint was returned to his chapel in the Church of San Lorenzo, followed by a High Mass, which is in progress as they sit at the café.

161:25 **This hum:** As the hour of the bullfight approaches, even the café seems to be part of "this hum," a kind of massed mystical mantra, a droning Om-like incantatory hum, and they are "in it," "part of it."

162:1 **mind the horses:** Both Robert and Brett are advised to stop watching the horses when they're hit—as Jake says in the manuscript, "Just don't watch when it's repulsive" (*Facsimile* 2:436). Before 1928, the horses were unprotected by padding and their death was a frequent occurrence. A typical guidebook of the period, written of course from an Anglo-American and generally anti-corrida perspective, observes: "The great blot on the bull-fight has always been the torture of the horses. Until 1928 these, usually worn-out crocks of little value and no spirit, were exposed unprotected to be gored by the infuriated bull, and if they escaped with life, their ghastly wounds were often roughly sewn up or stuffed with tow and they were goaded to face the terrifying ordeal once more" (Muirhead, *Northern Spain* cxiv). In *Death in the Afternoon* Hemingway addresses in considerable detail the "complicated" matter of "why the death of the horse in the bull ring is not moving" and "tends to be comic while that of the bull is tragic" (6). Writing after the introduction of protective padding, Hemingway notes that the number of horses killed will be greatly decreased, but padding will in "no way decrease the pain suffered by the horses." Repeatedly stressing the "minor comic-tragedy of the horse," Hemingway sees the introduction of padding as "the first step toward the suppression of the bullfight. The bullfight is a Spanish institution; it has not existed because of the foreigners and tourists, but always in spite of them and any step to modify it to secure their approval, which it will never have, is a step toward its complete suppression" (8).

162:4 **bored:** Bill, and later Mike, gives Robert a hard time regarding his utterly inappropriate remark that he might be *bored* at the bullfight. Indeed, why is he even there at the fiesta if he feels this way? The answer is obvious: so he can follow Brett around. It seems that Robert (and Hemingway) has been reading the Baedeker guide to Spain, where we find this regarding the bullfight: "Many visitors will agree with Mr. Finck, who writes: 'Six bulls were to be killed; I left after the third had been butchered, and his carcass dragged out by the mules—equally disgusted and *bored* . . . [with] the most unsportsmanlike and cowardly spectacle I have ever seen" (xxxv). This passage, with its textual emphasis on "*bored,*" is from the 1913 edition, the very edition that Hemingway owned (Brasch and Sigman 18). Robert gets all his ideas from books, especially guidebooks that trivialize place and tradition—even his boredom is inauthentic and secondhand (see also 90:13).

162:30–31 **meet Pedro Romero:** In Hemingway's earliest draft of the novel, which begins with the material of this chapter and the meeting with the bullfighter, he is called Cayetano Ordóñez or Niño de la Palma, the real name and professional name of an actual bullfighter whom Hemingway had seen in his first season as a matador—1925. When Hemingway made the next phase of his revisions, he changed his exemplary matador's name to Antonio Guerra, or Guerrita, a close name echo of the actual and great nineteenth-century matador Rafael Guerra, who was also known as "Guerrita." In his final revisions, Hemingway changed his name to Pedro Romero, thus evoking the eighteenth-century torero often referred to as the greatest matador in bullfighting history. Why the name changes, and what do they signify? First, consider the actual Cayetano Ordóñez (Niño de la Palma), the young bullfighter who, in his first season in the ring, had so impressed Hemingway. Here is what Hemingway wrote about him six years later: "If you see Nino de la Palma the chances are you will see cowardice in its least attractive form; its fat rumped, prematurely bald from using hair fixatives, prematurely senile form" (*Death in the Afternoon* 88). In one season, he "raised the most false hopes and proved the greatest disappointment"; in 1925 he "looked like the messiah who had come to save bullfighting," but in 1926, after his "first real goring [that] had taken all his valor," he had the "most shameful season any matador had ever had" (*Death in the Afternoon* 89–90). Yet there is no question that the Niño de la Palma of 1925 serves, in part, as a model for Pedro Romero; referring to *The Sun Also Rises,* Hemingway writes in *Death in the Afternoon:* "I tried to describe how he looked and a couple of his fights in a book one time" (89). Writing about Antonio Ordóñez in *The Dangerous Summer,* Hemingway notes: "I had known his father Cayetano years before and had written a portrait of him and an account of his fighting in *The Sun Also Rises.* Everything that is in the bull ring in that book is as it was and how he fought. All the incidents outside the ring are made up and imagined" (50). Allen Josephs, who has admirably traced the Nino-Guerrita-Pedro Romero name evolution and its role in the transformation of the novel from factual to mythical terrain, suggests that Hemingway's statement needs "to be taken with a grain of salt" ("*Toreo*" 94).

Surely a skilled writer of fiction might want a little insurance against the factual disappointments of subsequent history (see Hemingway on Cayetano's disastrous 1926 season, above). And just as surely, it was in part the burden of significance, the weight of the fundamentally religious claim of messianic redemption that the author wants his exemplary matador to carry that led Hemingway to remove him even further from contemporary and factual history by making his final name-change to Pedro Romero. With that change the novel claims its mythic terrain. Pedro Romero, the great historical but chronologically far-removed torero, the matador who killed 5,600 bulls *recibiendo*— receiving the bull, the "most difficult, dangerous and emotional way to kill bulls; rarely seen in modern times" (*Death in the Afternoon* 474; see also 220:11)—is exactly the right name to carry the burden of grace under pressure and the mythic signification that Hemingway invests in his exemplary bullfighter. And the name change—from Niño (the "Kid") to Guerra/Guerrita ("war/little warrior") to Romero ("pilgrim")—signifies in other ways, too, a progress that also adumbrates Jake's pilgrimage.

163:5 **monastic partition:** A highly charged scene, rendered in painterly fashion as if in some old master portrait—the "little light" coming in the dark room with the "monastic partition" where the boy bullfighter in his white linen seems "very far away and dignified," "straight and handsome and altogether by himself"—this striking initial portrait of Pedro Romero radically foregrounds his presence and builds anticipation, as Montoya says, of how he will be "in the ring." In fact, this scene is the *core image* of the novel (in the sense most famously employed by William Faulkner when he said that *The Sound and the Fury* grew from the core image of a little girl with muddy drawers up in a tree)—the first scene that Hemingway wrote in his earliest draft of the novel was, in fact, a version of this page, which remains, in spite of all his revisions, remarkably close to the original: "monastic partitions," dark room, the boy in the "white shirt and gold pants . . . seeming far away and dignified" (*Facsimile* 1:5). Hemingway retains the key painterly details of the dark room, adds the light coming from the window, and intensifies the portrait of Pedro Romero: the shirt becomes white *linen,* the bullfighter is now *very* far away, and instead of the more generalized original image of the boy "standing, straight and handsome, looking the essense [sic] of torero" (6), Hemingway renders him "standing, straight and handsome and altogether by himself." It is useful to remember that this is the novel's core image, and that the first sentence of the first draft of the novel was this: "I saw him for the first time in his room at the Hotel Quintana in Pamplona" (5).

164:8 **a real one:** Using one of the novel's repeated iconic gestures, Montoya only needs to nod to Jake to communicate their shared passion, their recognition that Romero is the first "real one for a long time."

164:18 **kike:** Jake uses the new keyword associated with Robert (see 162:4)—bored—and Bill utters his most vulgar and offensive anti-Semitic epithet. Two pages before, it was Cohn's use of the word "bored" that got to Bill and led him to link the stance of boredom with Robert's Jewishness, with his observation that "He's got this Jewish superiority so strong" that he thinks he'll get no other emotion from the bullfight than boredom (162:22–24). Of course, the attitude of boredom regarding bullfights is not limited to any one group and was indeed standard in guidebooks of the era (see 162:4). The anti-Semitism of Bill, Mike, and others is a reflection of the widespread cultural anti-Semitism of the period, not an indicator of the author's anti-Semitism (see 3:1–6 and 10:32). In the novel's intricate pattern of alternating and shifting responses to Robert's behavior, especially by Bill, Brett, Jake, and Mike, Bill's attitude here contrasts with his defense of Robert when Mike was attacking Cohn two chapters earlier (141–45), the scene that made Jake feel disgusted and led to his meditation on "immorality" (149:3).

164:33 **sort of jota:** As he is concerning everything around him, Jake is a careful and informed observer of Basque and Navarrese dances. He doesn't just respond to Bill with the observation that they're dancing a "sort of jota"—he notes in the preceding paragraph the "intricate play of the feet" that they could not see (because of the crowd they can only see the jumps), and in the next descriptive paragraph, when they can see the dancers, he devotes eight sentences to the intricate steps of the dance. The Basques, of course, are well known for their striking folk dances. Guidebooks of the period sometimes devoted special sections to the subject. For example, one guide notes that in Navarre "they have nationalized a foreign dance called the *jota.* This was naturally handed down from Aragon, where the jota is the popular dance, to the neighbouring valleys where it has become the Navarrian jota." Lamenting the disappearance of many traditional dances, our 1928 source notes that some dances remain very popular, "especially the Basque jump or *mutchico* which . . . is composed of some twenty figures, each one with a step and a music of its own: Mutchicoac, Laphurtarrac, Chibandarrac, etc." (Lamare 47). Generally overlooked by commentators on the novel, dance and music play a major role in *The Sun Also Rises,* from the *bal musette* scene in Paris (see 19:16) to the fiesta. And just as the rituals of religion and the bullfight are at the center of the fiesta, the music and dancing in the street provide the driving rhythm of the fiesta that conducts participants into sacred place, sacred time (see 154:30).

165:33 **bored:** The relentless insistence on Robert's boredom continues and is repeated five times in the next twelve lines. He finally admits he did not like the bullfight but says it was "a wonderful show." Although it demonstrates a certain lack of perspicacity to characterize the bullfight as a *show,* everything seems to be a show for Robert, his show.

167:11 **the second day:** In this two-paragraph explication of the second day of bull-fighting, Hemingway's prose takes on an expository exactitude as he explains for the reader the details of the bullfight; the effect is redoubled by the fact that this passage shows Jake in his role as teacher, his pedagogic function, which, though more understated elsewhere, pervades the novel. Jake explains to Brett, through precise attention to the bulls, horses, picadors, and Romero's capework, what it is "all about," the "definite end" worked toward, so that she might see more than a show with "unexplained horrors." He stresses repeatedly the importance of working close to the bull, avoiding the tricks and the fakery, and he thinks that Brett sees "how something that was beautiful done close to the bull"—with courage, in the authentically imminent presence of death—"was ridiculous if it were done a little way off." Hemingway's exposition here requires no interlinear commentary, except perhaps to wonder if Brett really does see what Jake hopes she sees. After the first corrida, we learn that Brett really sees Romero's green trousers; after this second corrida, Mike says he's afraid Brett is falling in love with Romero and Jake says he "wouldn't be surprised" (168:25).

We should also note that insofar as the bullfight functions as an analogue for behavior, a metaphor for conduct outside the bullring, this first extensive passage of bullfight commentary underlines how "all that was faked turned bad," how a technique (translate to personal style) that simulated danger (or passion) gives "a fake emotional feeling." Indeed, this passage, which stresses how Romero "had the *old* thing, the holding of his purity of line through the *maximum* of exposure" (emphasis added), is certainly an emblem for moral behavior and should be considered, with the secret-of-the-values scene with the count (see 60:31–32 and 61:4), as one of Hemingway's crucial definitions of how to live fully. Jake, like the count and Romero, has the *old thing,* the solid traditional values (e.g., courage, honor) of his religion and his *afición* to sustain him. And was there ever anyone who exposed himself more—he doesn't *have* to invite Brett to Spain, nor does he *have* to create and orchestrate the entire trip, the group pilgrimage, as he does (he could go alone)—while striving to hold the "purity of line" of his conduct?

168:15 **next day:** In four short end-of-chapter sentences, Hemingway succinctly compresses time yet relates it to fiesta time, which keeps on "all day and all night." The *first* "next day" does not matter because Romero does not fight. The *second* "next day" there is no bullfight.

CHAPTER 16

170:5 **bad weather:** In the rain and the fog, everything is dull and gloomy, even the shapes of things are changed, and the bad weather of the first paragraph of this chapter functions as Hemingway's symbolic weather forecast, foreshadowing the fog that settles over the action by the end of the chapter.

170:15–16 **Val Carlos dancers:** Again Jake pays close attention to the dancing and music in the street and this time he specifies exactly the costume and the name of the dancing group: the Val Carlos dancers. Valcarlos (in the standard spelling for the past two hundred years) is eighteen kilometers north of Roncevaux/Roncesvalles, just south of the French-Spanish frontier. Hemingway separates the place name to emphasize that the dancers are from the Valley (Val) of Charlemagne (Carlos), where the "epic remembrance of Charlemagne inundates" the modern pilgrim, where the "air and the mountains of this valley of Charles . . . exude highly dramatic reminders" of the emperor Charlemagne (Arrondo 38), where in fact the local people claim to hear in certain winds even today the sound of Roland's legendary horn resounding from the distant battlefield at Roncevaux. Just as Roland blew his horn too late, it is already too late for Jake, or anybody, to call for help, to prevent what is about to happen. In his typical fashion, Hemingway intensified, gave clues to, his Rolandesque symbolic landscape (see 108:26) by adding the presence of the Val Carlos dancers to this scene after the original draft.

171:17 **embarrassed:** Again, as in the scene where Jake and Montoya confirm their shared *afición,* the threefold repetition of embarrassment on Montoya's part signifies that he is self-conscious and ill at ease because he is on a mission of *afición,* one aficionado asking another how to prevent a bad situation for the young bullfighter, who might be spoiled by association with rich tourists (see 131:12 and 131:28). In the earliest draft, where this passage is part of the novel's opening scene, Jake (then "Hem") and Montoya (then Quintana) talk a good deal more; they are both so "impassioned" that they would have "gone big in a Y.W.C.A. lecture"; they "both love bull fighting and when once in twenty years a kid comes along with everything in the world and people would wreck him to make a nymphomaniacs holiday"—this is something to get "pretty well worked up" about (*Facsimile* 1:23).

171:18 **the American ambassador:** This American ambassador (to Spain) was Alexander Pollock Moore (1867–1930), earlier the editor and publisher of the *Pittsburgh Leader* and the fourth husband of the famous singer and stage actress Lillian Russell (who died in 1922). Moore served from March 1923 to December 1925. The fact that, as Jake says, everybody knows "them" may suggest the corrupting power, for a vulnerable Romero, of a group of American media-entertainment plutocrats and their hangers-on. In the novel's earliest draft, the American ambassador (his name is not given here, either) sequence is more extensive; he arrives on the square in "a big Rolls Royce," gets no reception, and stands there "looking big and solid and rather cunningly stupid," accompanied by two women, "one tall one in blue, perfectly dressed shanty Irish looking, sort of a White House hostess and the other a cute little short one, the kind . . . capable of taking any man away" (*Facsimile* 1:10–11).

171:30 **Grand Hotel:** The most expensive accommodations in Pamplona in the mid-1920s were at the Gran Hotel, so naturally the American ambassador and his friends would stay there. The "Grand Hotel business," as Montoya calls it on the next page, can ruin a young bullfighter very quickly—"in one year they're through" (172:12–13).

172:4 **message:** Montoya is very pleased with Jake's suggestion that the invitation not be delivered to Romero; this contrasts with the displeasure Montoya will feel with Jake's complicity in delivering Brett's "message" to Romero later in this chapter.

172:17 **collects bull-fighters:** Again, in Jake's awareness of how certain women collect and ruin young bullfighters, there is direct foreshadowing of the sequence of events that is irrevocably in. motion by the end of the chapter.

173:33 **Ronda:** A small city in the south of Spain, Ronda was celebrated in the guidebooks of the 1920s as one of the most picturesque places in Spain; it is famous for its bullring, said to be the oldest in Spain, and for its claim to be, as Hemingway put it in *Death in the Afternoon*, "one of the cradles of modern bullfighting, and the birthplace of the historical Pedro Romero"—"one of the first and greatest of professional fighters" (43)—and his famous bullfighting grandfather (Francisco Romero) and father (Juan Romero).

174:17–18 **work . . . apart from himself:** Hemingway stresses Romero's sense of his craft, his art, its separateness from personality. Like a true artist, Romero's art has nothing to do with the merely personal; it exists in the dimension of technique, tradition, and passion—not ego.

175:3 **arrobas:** In Spain, a unit of weight equal to just over 25 pounds, or 11.5 kilograms. Thus, the bulls described here—weighing 26 arrobas or less (about 650 pounds or 299 kilograms)—are small. As Hemingway notes in *Death in the Afternoon,* bulls are weighed "after they are dressed, drawn, skinned, heads and hoofs and all parts of the meat that has been damaged cut away. This latter state is called *en canal* and for many years the weight of bulls has been judged when they are in this state. . . . The dressed-out or *en canal* weight of a bull is estimated as 52½ per cent of his live weight" (444). Hemingway also asserts that a 26-arroba weight "is as small as bulls should be fought if the animal is to be imposing enough to give real emotion to the corrida" and that the "ideal bull" should be from 26 to 30 arrobas, with "an absolute minimum of 25 arrobas"(445). In 1925 the taurine *Reglamento* (the codified rules of Spanish bullfighting) required that the minimum weight of the bull in a first-class bullring had to be 570 kilograms (Mandel 9). That is to say, the bulls here discussed—if indeed they *are* 26 arrobas, and both Romero and the bullfight critic doubt it—barely meet this *minimum* weight (using Hemingway's 52 1/2 per cent *en canal* figure above, a bull of 26 arrobas would have a live weight of exactly the 1925 minimum of 570 kilograms). Largely because of Belmonte's stylistic innovations that required "a smaller, faster, more responsive bull," underage and underweight bulls were sometimes fought; in the 1930 revision of the taurine *Reglamento* minimum weights were drastically reduced (from 570 to 470 kilograms in first-class bullrings), and reduced yet again in 1959 (Mandel 10; see also 215:28).

175:21 **muy borracho:** Hemingway's art of contextual translation makes it clear that Mike is *very* drunk. A "bad drunk," as we have been told earlier, Mike has passed that "certain point" where he becomes "unpleasant" (see 148:30–33). Shouting, "Bulls have no balls" three times in a public place, in the presence of a bullfighter and a bullfight critic and other aficionados, highlights Mike's bad conduct in contrast with Romero's "very nice manners"—and may lead the reader to wonder what response Romero's code of manners would dictate if he understood what Mike was saying. Of course, given Mike's foreknowledge of what Brett is about to do with Romero, an inevitability that he knows from experience he cannot prevent, Mike may have good reason to get drunk.

177:4 **did not even nod:** Montoya's interrupted smile and sudden distant demeanor contrast sharply with his conversation with Jake shortly before, when he and Jake agreed about the need to protect Romero from "this Grand Hotel business," from drunken foreigners and women who collect bullfighters (see 171:18, 171:30, 172:4, and 172:17). Seeing Romero drinking and laughing, sitting between the bare-shouldered

Brett and Jake, Montoya leaves the room without even a nod. Does he hold Jake responsible? Or is he just shocked to see Jake's participation in the scene, given their recent impassioned talk and Jake's suggested action to protect Romero from the Grand Hotel crowd?

178:8–15 **lady of title . . . lady love:** Jake reiterates aspects of Cohn's character and conduct that were established earlier in the novel, not just his romantic escapism, his silly pseudochivalric "childish drunken heroics," but the quality of *abstraction* involved in his "affair with a lady of title" (see 50:15, 50:24, 50:32, and 51:14–15). As usual when he's ready to fight over somebody he knows nothing about (i.e., Brett), Robert stands up, ready to hit Mike, "to do battle for his lady love," thus echoing earlier and later scenes that underline Robert's only rendered *action* in the novel—violence (see 38:9, 39:14–15, and 190:32–33). When he's not ready to hit someone—Jake or Mike or Romero—his extraordinary passivity, his following Brett around, his refusal to go away, and his apparent pleasure in being insulted are his defining characteristics.

179:5–6 **complicated fireworks:** With the military band playing, and the fire balloons falling among the people in the bad weather, it is impossible not to read this scene as an objective correlative for the "complicated fireworks" that are about to fall into the lives of Jake (the wounded warrior whose plane crashed) and his friends. "Globos illuminados [sic]," Mike says in another threefold repetition, but there is nothing *iluminado*—filled with light, infused with grace or knowledge—in the crashing globe, the sphere, the world of the rest of the fiesta, except what happens in the bullring.

179:31 **some English:** In the manuscript version, there were more tourists; the big cars "kept coming," the chauffeur-driven cars "bringing the haute monde from Biarritz and San Sebastian"—"a terrible looking lot" in their "golf clothes—loud tweeds and looking pink and white as though they all had facial massages" (*Facsimile* 1:19). And there were busloads of tourists not of the haute monde. In the finished novel, Hemingway somewhat downplayed the numbers: "Some English and Americans"— their "golf clothes" now "sport clothes"—and some of the women staring at the "quaint" locals through their lorgnons, their short-handled eyeglasses so indicative of their condescension, since the word "lorgnon" is derived from the act of *leering*. Decades later, recalling the Pamplona of the mid-1920s, Hemingway wrote: "Pamplona [in 1959] was rough as always, overcrowded with tourists and characters, but with a hard core of all that is finest in Navarre. For a week we averaged something over three hours sleep a night to the pounding of the war drums of Navarre, the piping of the old tunes and the dancers swirling and leaping. I've written Pamplona once and for keeps. It is all there as it always was except forty thousand tourists have been added. There were not twenty tourists when I first went there nearly four decades ago. Now on some days they say there are close to a hundred thousand in the town" (*The Dangerous Summer* 135–36). Here Hemingway downplays the numbers even further, yet surely, by all contemporary accounts, and in Hemingway's own manuscript accounting, there were far more than twenty tourists when Hemingway was in Pamplona in 1923–1925. It is natural, of course, for the travel writer or the person who considers himself a knowledgeable traveler to exaggerate the uniqueness of his own discoveries of place. And the vast crowds in Pamplona today, so many of them with copies of *The Sun Also Rises* in their backpacks or in their memories of high school and college, are due, in large part, to the influence of the novel.

181:21 **Everybody behaves badly:** Again, the novel's focus is on behavior—or manners and morals, one of Hemingway's prime subjects—as it is consistently from the first chapter. Everyone agrees that Cohn has "behaved very badly," and finally he's been driven away, only to lurk nearby under the arcade. Brett wonders if she's been "rude enough" to Robert; she's "sick of him" and certain that "nobody else would behave as badly," that Jake "wouldn't behave badly." Even Mike gets off the hook somewhat; Brett says, ironically, he's "been lovely," but Jake twice insists: "It's been damned hard on Mike." And Jake knows that "Everybody behaves badly," given the "proper chance"; indeed, that "chance" is already in play, and Jake knows it, and he does behave badly, in spite of Brett's certainty that he is incapable of bad behavior. Does this mean that Jake the Pilgrim, Jake the Catholic, Jake the Exemplar, Jake the Teacher, is somehow a failure in these roles, a morally and spiritually bankrupt betrayer of the very values and beliefs he holds most dear? Hardly. For the knowledge that there are no plaster saints in the real world, the deep sense of human limitation that guarantees everyone will behave badly in certain circumstances, is central to the vision that makes an authentic pilgrim/Catholic/exemplar/teacher. (On conduct and consequences, and how the danger and recklessness of fiesta time affects everybody's behavior, see 154:30.)

182:31 **shadow of the cathedral:** Of the three times that Jake is alone with Brett in Pamplona, two scenes are in church, and the third is this scene, where they sit, not touching, not talking, in this symbolic landscape at the edge of the abyss with the "shadow of the cathedral" behind them. They walk to the fortifications at "the *edge* of town" (emphasis added), sit on the wall above the "dark pits," and look across the dark plain and up to the mountaintop lights of another fort. Below them, the river, high and "black and smooth," flows to the sea. Brett is at the edge, ready to fall, and Jake is on the edge of complicity; behind them are the "trees and the shadow of the cathedral," emblem of Jake's ultimate code. This symbolic landscape is part of the recurrent pattern of edge imagery throughout the novel (see 65:3 and 99:28).

183:16 **goner:** Four times Brett says she's a goner, doomed; five times she repeats she "can't help it," "can't stop" it. It should be noted carefully that Jake objects to every assertion she makes that she's a goner and can't help it, essentially telling her to have some volition, exercise some will, resist: "don't do it," "you ought to stop it," "you oughtn't to do it," "you don't have to do that." He knows that Brett once had a strong will; in a last-minute cut from the novel's galleys, Jake refers to Brett taking care of Mike when they first met, through "the exercise of her then very strong will" (Svoboda, *Crafting of a Style* 101). When Brett tells him not to be difficult, he just says, ironically, "Sure." In the manuscript, he adds: "I just wanted to register an objection" (*Facsimile* 2:466). Indeed, he does object, firmly, but what can he do to stop it? Maybe when Brett tells him not to be "difficult," she is afraid that he's going to "start proselyting," try to convert her, make her see that religion offers some hope of changing her ways, a way of disciplining will and choice (see 209:7). Readers inclined to take at face value Robert's later absurd assertion that Jake is a "pimp" should read and reread this scene (see 190:32–33).

184:12 **bitch:** In yet another instance of Hemingway's trademark treble repetition, Brett declares three times that she's "such a bitch." Jake's laconic response— "Well"—functions as agreement on the subject of her bitchery at the same time that it says yet again, well, then, don't do it. This passage reverberates in her best-known line at the end of the book about "deciding not to be a bitch"—of course the appropriate response to her later assertion is if she could *choose* then, why does she say she has no choice in this scene? (See 245:16–17.) We note, too, that Jake will *not* ask Romero to come to their table: "*He came* over to our table" (emphasis added)—there is nothing Jake can do to stop the mutual drivenness of Romero and Brett, their willed assignation.

185:21 **his hand:** The phrase "he showed his hand" has at least a double meaning. And it was when Brett "gave him her hand" that he felt her readiness to play out the hand. There are multiple additional overtones to the focus on Romero's hand. First, Brett, who had earlier had her fortune told at the Gypsy camp (151), now tells Romero's fortune. She takes his hand, spreading the fingers; he spreads his hand, the hand that is foregrounded by a sixfold repetition in little more than half a page. She says she sees in his hand thousands of bulls and a long life. When Romero says he's "never going to die," Jake, always attentive to small ceremonies of the supernatural, taps three times on wood to counter Romero's overbold assertion and to purchase silently some good luck for Romero. If we remember that Romero's namesake, the historical Pedro Romero, did indeed live a very long life—recorded variously as between eighty-five and ninety years—and did indeed kill an extraordinary number of bulls (nearly 6,000) we see Hemingway's mythicizing transformation of his fictional bullfighter in operation. And the buried allusion to the historical Pedro Romero, in this scene that centers on the reincarnated Romero's hand, will remind some readers of Goya's celebrated portrait of the actual Pedro Romero, with its remarkable attention to Romero's right hand, an unusually large, forceful, yet delicate hand that Jake is probably describing here: "very fine and the wrist was small." The Goya portrait reflects, as Allen Josephs aptly puts it, "the assured grace, the understated elegance, the paradoxical delicacy of the prominently displayed right hand that dispatched 5,600 bulls in his long and unmarred career" ("*Toreo*" 96).

187:8 **hard-eyed people:** Jake says he must "find our friends and bring them here." Romero gives him a "final look" to verify the understanding. The "hard-eyed" aficionados watch him leave, and to say the moment is "not pleasant" is profound understatement. Readers who agree, essentially, with Robert Cohn, who think that Jake has just set up Brett with Romero and is thus guilty of a deep betrayal of the code of the aficionado should consider whether the whole affair had an air of inevitability, that, with or without Jake, the rendezvous of Brett and Romero was willed by both of them and would have happened. After all his objections, what else can Jake do? When he comes back twenty minutes later, Brett and Romero are gone. The three empty glasses are on the table, not to suggest that the cognac made them all do it but as the iconic sign of complicity, which is not the same thing as intentionality and causality. Jake, a good Catholic pilgrim, knows the difference; knows that either nobody is responsible for anything or we're all responsible for everything; knows that the necessary Christian choice of our complicity, our braided-togetherness, is the foundation of grace and redemption; knows that, as Robert Penn Warren puts it:

The recognition of complicity is the beginning of innocence.
The recognition of necessity is the beginning of freedom. (*Brother to Dragons* 214)

CHAPTER 17

188:3 **thrown out:** Events move quickly from bad to worse, right from the first lines of this, the most violent chapter in the novel: ejection from a bar by the police, after four near fights there, flows seamlessly into Robert's punching out Jake and Mike, the unreal night that is followed by the deadly morning *encierro* in which a man is killed and twenty people taken to the infirmary for injuries, and finally the news of Cohn's massacre of Romero.

190:7 **Fundador:** At the Café Suizo, Robert's preferred place (see 100:11 and 95:26–27), they sit down to have a Fundador, a brandy. *Fundador* means "founder," and it is the brand name of the oldest (1874) and one of the best-known and most widely marketed so-called Brandies de Jerez. When Robert comes in and stands there demanding to know where Brett is, the reader is fully primed to expect Robert's next action. From the first sentence of the book, we have been learning what kind of a boxer he is, watching him stand up, ready to hit somebody. When Jake, early in the book, tells him to "go to hell," Robert stands up, ready—absurdly—to hit Jake unless he takes it back (see 39:14–15). Here Mike tells Robert to "go to hell" four times in eight lines—with some typically funny dialogue effects: "Oh, go to hell!" followed by "Is that where she is?" Thus we know Robert's aggression is imminent: first his preselected target, Jake, and then Mike. Before the chapter is over, he will have assaulted all three of the men in the novel who know Brett far better than he does.

190:32–33 **you damned pimp:** In the manuscript, after Robert's verbal assault on Jake, Hemingway started to follow the charge of "pimp" with a comeback possibly to be spoken by Jake: "You damn panderer"—but he crossed it out, apparently immediately, before he closed the quote and gave dialogue attribution (*Facsimile* 2:478). If Hemingway intended that Jake would call Robert a "panderer" in response to the charge of "pimp," he may have had in mind a possible distinction in the two terms, "pimp" meaning simply a procurer, "panderer" suggesting a male prostitute or just someone who caters to the sexual desires of others and exploits their weaknesses. In the long and clouded usage history of both words, the distinction is possible. Thus, replying to Robert's ridiculous accusation of "pimp," Jake might have been about to say that Robert was just a male whore exploiting Brett's weakness. But the fuzziness of the distinction wouldn't work, and besides, having been called a pimp, given the circumstances, there is nothing for Jake to do—certainly talk and wordplay would be inappropriate—but swing at Robert.

Far more important here is a close consideration of Robert's accusation, which many Hemingway commentators carelessly read as fact, as all-encompassing symbolic truth. It is simply not true that Jake is, in any sense, a pimp. All the scenes leading up to Brett and Romero's assignation show Jake counseling Brett against it; he receives nothing from Brett or Romero for his very peripheral role as an observer of an affair that was going to happen, one way or the other (see 183:16, 184:12, and 187:8). He has also proselytized Brett, as she plainly states later, trying to get her to convert to his faith as a way of reforming her behavior (see 209:7). Yet even Michael Reynolds, in his introductory-level study of the novel, repeatedly states that Jake acts "as Brett's procurer," claiming that readers must be "sorely disappointed with Jake's debasing role as procurer," because "a sexually maimed war veteran who pimps for a sexually rapacious woman has little chance of appearing admirable for the general reader" (*Novel of the Twenties* 31, 50). In other words, Reynolds, like so many other commentators, takes Robert's "pimp" accusation as a statement of fact, in defiance of all the details in all the scenes leading up to Robert's verbal and physical assault on Jake. And, in such a reading, Jake is *debased* by his pimphood, deprived of whatever exemplar/aficionado status he has established—indeed, for some readers, his narrative authority is called into question. To accept as truth Robert's charge suggests that we should accept Cohn, not Jake, as an arbiter of morality, a judge of conduct; and if we do that, then I suppose we'd have to accept Cohn not only as the moral arbiter but also as the key stylistic and aesthetic authority, the touchstone of values and taste in the book. Thus we must be content to read only the trashy books he reads (and writes), to get all our ideas about life from such books rather than from good books and experience; we must resolve to be bored at bullfights; to sleep through and miss magnificent landscapes; to be concerned like good solipsists only with our physical appearance as we follow like sick puppies the person around whom we have erected a silly romantic fantasy, a person who has no real interest in us; to be gluttons for punishment as we act pathetic and ridiculous in every identifiable category of experience. And then, frustrated by our own stupidity and ignorance of any code of conduct, we must retaliate with violence toward everybody who has tried to be decent to us in spite of our bad behavior and beat them to a pulp. No, Robert Cohn is *not* an exemplar. And Jake is *not* a pimp. Pimps don't pray with, don't proselytize, their close associates or their clients (see 209:7). And Brett is *not* a prostitute.

191:29 **Cohn in jail:** After Robert knocks Jake out, knocks Mike down, and leaves to find Romero and try to destroy him, Edna somewhat humorously says she wishes

Bill had been there so she could have seen him get knocked down too. Even in his groggy condition Jake doesn't wish that on Cohn.

192:9 **borrowed a hundred:** When Jake hears that Mike has borrowed money from Montoya, he knows that the unreality of the fiesta has gone too far, and it all seems "like some bad play." The only thing left to redeem the fiesta is Romero's final performance in the bullring.

192:24 **everything looked new:** In his post-knockout state of concussion, Jake remembers the only other time he felt that way: after being kicked in the head in a high school football game. All the old warm familiar details of place were "new and changed," "different," and "strange"—as Pamplona now is to him. Even his feet seem far away, and the only familiar thing is his phantom suitcase.

194:2 **Please forgive me:** Three times Robert begs Jake for forgiveness. Jake just wants "a hot bath in deep water." Yet, groggy as he is, he listens to Cohn's crying, how "funny" his voice is, and twice notes the detail of Robert's white Princeton-style polo shirt. Finally, on Robert's third plea for forgiveness, Jake says it's "all right." And it probably is with Jake, since as a Christian he knows the necessity of forgiveness and reconciliation. When Robert, in a sign of some never-outgrown attribute of a schoolboy code of sportsmanship (as suggested by that white Princeton polo shirt), insists on shaking hands with Jake, we might expect Jake to hit Cohn (as Romero later does when Robert tries to shake his hand after knocking him down)—but no, Jake will even shake hands, though his handshake does not likely signify reconciliation, maybe just the contents of that phantom suitcase—the way things were before everything was "changed" (see 192:24). All Jake wants is a bath, deep water, but he'll have to wait until he gets to San Sebastián for that (see 235:5–7).

197:14 **anything happen at the encierro:** After the long action description of the *encierro*, so precisely described in translucently descriptive prose that no clarification is necessary, Hemingway, in a brilliant narrative transition, introduces the nonaficionado waiter who speaks for all the voices not heard in the temporary otherworld of the fiesta, those who question what may seem mere recklessness and danger, the risking of life, "all for fun." The waiter's voice does not undercut all the other voices that embrace the world of the aficionado, but it is the voice of the mundane world that must be heard, that must raise the necessary questions that may lead to comprehension of the fiesta imperative of dramatizing life and death, passion and ecstasy, and tragedy. The runner who possesses the fortitude, the physical and spiritual courage to engage in a ritual confrontation with primal forces, with death, does not do it "all for fun."

198:15 **Vicente Girones:** There was no one killed in the *encierro* at Pamplona in 1925. In 1924 the first documented death (of a total of thirteen from 1924 to 2000) in the running of the bulls occurred. His name was not Vicente Girones, and he was not from Tafalla; he was Esteban Domeño, a bricklayer from Sangüesa. Hemingway's fictional victim is from the small town of Tafalla, thirty-five kilometers south of Pamplona, a former residence of the kings of Navarre; it is a town of many aficionados, with a small bullring and a local fiesta. The vivid portrait of the funeral rites for Girones, the emphasis on his wife and two children, with the ellipses-driven insistence at the second of the three family repetitions, adds up to a profoundly moving portrait of the death of a runner. Objections that have been raised to the effect that Jake couldn't possibly know all the details presented in this paragraph completely miss the point. He could have read in the newspaper the details of his age and place, that he was a farmer from Tafalla who left behind a wife and two children (the kind of newspaper report that Hemingway probably read about Esteban Domeño in 1924), and then—knowing well the ceremonies of San Fermín, the rituals of the *peñas,* the details and motion of the train ride "down grade around the *edge* of the plateau" (emphasis added) and through the fields of grain to Tafalla—added the bright particularities of place that make the story. (Since I know these exact details from only four visits to Pamplona and two train rides from Pamplona to Tafalla, Jake could easily have known them.) Moreover, what writer worth reading (e.g., Hemingway), what storyteller worth listening to (e.g., Jake), would not be capable, when moved by a vignette, a brief image of life on the edge that had to be told, of inventing from experience and knowledge whatever details were necessary to make the compelling story of Girones's life and death and burial complete. From the muddy ground at "the *edge* of the town" (196:3, emphasis added) by the bullring where Girones is gored to the *edge* of the plateau where his funeral train bears his body down through the fields of grain to be buried in the abiding earth, the prose tells the story, in miniature, of the novel that Hemingway said was not some "bitter satire but a damn tragedy with the earth abiding forever as the hero" (see epigraph directly preceding 3:1; on the patterns of edge imagery throughout the novel, see 65:3, 99:28, and 182:31). The story of Girones must be well told, not to support the nonaficionado waiter's complaint but to prepare the way for Romero's complete and perfect sacrifice in the bullring later the same day. The bull that killed Girones, Bocanegra (the "black mouth" of death), will be sacrificed not just for Brett and for Romero himself but for Vicente Girones, and for all humankind.

199:6–7 **ear . . . cigarette-stubs:** Brett disrespects the ceremony of the bull's ear and the honor accorded to Romero by "popular acclamation" and, in turn, conferred on Brett by Pedro. That she discards the symbol of *afición* along with her cigarette butts may lead the reader to further question whether she has any real interest in the ritual and ceremony of the bullfight, as opposed to what's in "those green trousers" of Romero's that "she never took her eyes off" (165:17–18). And this instance of a typical Hemingway device, the paired echoic scene, should certainly lead the reader back to the key scene in chapter 7, just before the count's lesson on the secret of the values, where Brett is shown flicking her cigarette ashes on Jake's rug (see 57:13).

201:16 massacred the poor, bloody bull-fighter: In his final act of violence before finally going away, Cohn massacres Romero—he "nearly killed" him—knocks him down "about fifteen times," but Romero keeps getting up. Years of quizzes and exams administered to first-time readers of the novel have confirmed for me that this recounted fight scene is what crystallizes and epitomizes reader reactions to Cohn and Romero. Even casual, superficial readers remember Cohn's brutality and Romero's courage getting up repeatedly to be knocked down again. Not one of the thousands of readers who have discussed this scene in my classes for nearly four decades has ever maintained that there is anything admirable about Robert's conduct here; most see him as not only brutal but also ridiculous or pathetic in his insistence—yet again (see 194:2)—that a man he has just "massacred" should shake hands. Readers clearly see that Robert, the ostensible winner of the fight, is the loser, "ruined" by Romero (203:1). When Cohn, absurdly, wants to pick Romero up and carry him to the bed, Romero says he will kill him, and he will "kill him anyway" if he doesn't get out of town. And when Robert leans down to try again to shake hands with the floored bullfighter, Romero hits him again. That final blow culminates a scene that illustrates what Hemingway meant when he wrote, years later in *The Old Man and the Sea,* these words that summarize the conduct, the honor, the courage, and the endurance of Hemingway's most famous exemplar—Santiago: "A man can be destroyed but not defeated" (103).

If this last fight scene introduces a tension into the narrative—will Romero the exemplar be able to fight in the final bullfight?—that tension is resolved when Romero does appear, and his transcendent performance in the bullring is made all the more extraordinary by the fact that he has been "massacred" by Cohn's undisciplined brutality the night before.

203:30 he'd kill her: All these details about Lord Ashley—who came back from the war, slept with his loaded gun, made Brett sleep on the floor, and told her he would kill her—remind us that Brett, wounded by irrational violence, was a war victim too.

204:25 Was anybody killed in the ring: The word "kill" reverberates through the closing pages of this chapter. The closing reminder of the death of Vicente Girones in the *encierro* is juxtaposed with the implicit fear that Romero, after being "killed" by Cohn, might be killed in the ring.

CHAPTER 18

205:5 **Sight-seeing cars:** Here, obviously, "car" means bus (*autocar* means "bus" in Spanish). Tourists continue to stream into Pamplona for the last day of the fiesta (see 179:31).

205:15 **music in the street:** The ever-present dancers, now "quite drunk," the pounding drums and the shrilling pipes, and the "hard-voiced singing" drive the fiesta toward its final ecstasy.

207:14 **Brett was radiant:** Aside from Jake's joke—carried by the juxtaposition of Brett's radiance with the bright sun—we learn that even though Romero's people are "very angry" with Brett, she is very happy: she *has* Romero, she has been nursing ("looking after") him, and Cohn has left town.

208:7 **San Fermin's:** This is the Church of San Lorenzo, with its San Fermín Chapel, where Brett was turned away on the first day of the fiesta. Apparently she is properly attired this time. In the manuscript, immediately after Jake notes that many "people were praying" as his vision adjusts to the light, Hemingway wrote: "I dipped my fingers in the fount and touched Duff's [Brett's]. She did as I did and we went in and knelt and prayed" (*Facsimile* 2:517). Clearly, this indicates that Jake performs the sacramental actions of his faith, wetting his fingers and making the sign of the cross as he enters the church to pray. The striking part of the image is that it shows Jake again as teacher, as technique exemplar, instructing Duff (Brett) in the proper forms, wetting her fingers for her, after which she makes the sign of the cross as he does. When they leave the church, Jake notes: "Duff followed me through the usual small ceremonies" (*Facsimile* 2:517). Had these details remained in the text, they might have clarified Brett's remark about Jake's "proselyting" (209:7). Also, it should be recalled that, by tradition, pilgrims following the Way of Saint James, the Santiago pilgrimage, are advised that their last act of devotion before leaving Pamplona should be made at the San Fermín Chapel in the Church of San Lorenzo (see 94:1). It is the last day of the fiesta; Jake leaves Pamplona the next day—as always,

Jake the Pilgrim performs the ceremonies, large and small, of his church and the pilgrimage tradition (see 124:9–10).

208:23 **any good:** Throughout this post-prayer conversation, Hemingway makes brief but finely nuanced revisions to what Jake says, both within the manuscript itself and in later revisions. Here, after Brett says church never does her any good, Jake originally replied: "It helps me sometimes. But not when I'm with you." Then he crossed that out completely, replacing it with: "It works sometimes"—then that is lined out (*Facsimile* 2:518). After the final revisions, Jake makes no reply; his silence as they "walk along" allows readers to conclude what they will about Jake's thoughts concerning church doing "any good."

209:2 **Have you:** Brett's statement about never getting anything she prays for, and her question to Jake about the effect of his prayer, is carried over unchanged from the manuscript. Once again, it is Jake's response that is precisely calibrated through several revisions. First his response to her question is: "Sometimes." Then Hemingway lines that out and inserts: "I think so." The final version is much more affirmative: "Oh, yes." In the manuscript, after Brett says, "Oh, rot," Jake says, downplaying his devoutness, "I just do it so as not to overlook any bets" (*Facsimile* 2:518). This is heavily crossed out. All the revisions in this sequence tend to underline and intensify Jake's religiousness.

209:6 **I'm pretty religious:** In the manuscript, after Brett says Jake doesn't look very religious, he replies: "I am though. Quite" (*Facsimile* 2:519).

209:7 **proselyting:** Brett uses the variant form of "proselytizing," the act of trying to convert someone to a religion or a doctrine. In the manuscript details deleted from the final text, we see some of the concrete actions Jake takes in his apparently ongoing process of proselytizing Brett—showing her how to follow him through the "small ceremonies" of his church (see 208:7). We note Brett's emphasis on *today*—her plea to Jake not to start trying to convert her *today*, as if she's saying, don't start that again, at least not *today*. She clearly implies that he has preached, evangelized, proselytized—tried to convert her before. She knows Jake is "pretty religious," but she doesn't want to hear his sermons *today*.

209:27 **He bowed:** On his last appearance in the novel, Montoya bows but does not smile. If Jake had been alone, without Brett, would Montoya have spoken to Jake? They have not spoken since the "Grand Hotel business" passage (see 171:17 and 171:30), when they confirmed their deep communion and shared *afición* that was established in the key passion-definition scene (see 131:12 and 131:28). When Jake checks out of the hotel the next day, he may or may not see Montoya in the lobby or the restaurant. All we are told is this: "Montoya did not come near us. One of the maids brought the bill" (228:16–17). (This is a strong statement. Montoya is, as Hemingway described him in a letter to his editor, Maxwell Perkins, a "highly moral hotel keeper," *Selected Letters* 240.) Does Montoya regard Jake as primarily or peripherally responsible for the corruption of Pedro Romero? It seems impossible to determine the degree of guilt assigned, based on the evidence of the text. Near the end of *Death in the Afternoon,* in his closing apostrophe to Spain, Hemingway saluted Juanito Quintana, the model for Montoya (see 94:15), in these words: "Quintana, the best aficionado and most loyal friend in Spain, and with a fine hotel with all the rooms full" (274). In whatever fashion Montoya assesses the behavior of Jake, then, he is being judged by the very highest standards of the "best aficionado" in Spain.

211:9 **fiesta boiled over:** Repeating the image twice in four lines, Jake notes that the fiesta has "come to the boiling-point" in the streets and is now boiling over *toward* the last bullfight in the ring. For Jake and his friends, the fiesta had "boiled over" the previous night.

211:9 **toward the bull-ring:** The next eleven pages (211–21) take place in the bull-ring, the novel's longest sustained scene in one precisely delineated location. In one sense, Allen Josephs is correct in calling the exemplary Romero's "perfect sacrifice" in this scene, the death of his last bull, "the precise center and climactic moment" of the novel (*Toreo* 97). While this scene is a moral and spiritual crux, it is not the "precise center" of *The Sun Also Rises*—that comes in the second-longest scene in one location, the fishing interlude by the Fábrica, with its humorous and serious motifs of quest, religion, and love enacted at the exact mathematical center of the novel (118–25). And, in a traditional literary sense, the final bullring scene is certainly not a *climax,* but more of a *denouement* that involves a reversal, a *peripety,* a triumph for Romero in the ring after he has been "massacred," beaten to a pulp the night before, and a move toward *resolution* (sealed in San Sebastián in the next chapter) for Jake, the novel's chief protagonist. In another sense, the novel, like many modernist works, confounds traditional plot expectations and designs. Most of the novel's understated catastrophes and wounds (including the great ur-wound of the war) take place off stage. While the novel does exhibit certain aspects of tragicomedy, its most insistent motif and deep structural design is anchored by the notion of pilgrimage, Jake's progress toward renewal, a fundamentally religious motion that is confirmed and underlined by the action of grace and passion in the bullring, by the sacrifice and shedding of blood that make possible the ecstasy and redemption, the sense of immortality *with* the abiding earth.

In *Death in the Afternoon,* six years after *The Sun Also Rises,* Hemingway suggested that after his early initiation into the mysteries of the bullfight, he wrote about it although it was "much too complicated," and maybe he should "have waited ten" years before trying to write about it (3). This has sometimes been taken to indicate that he was dissatisfied with his treatment of the bullfight not only in the vignettes of *In Our Time* but also in *The Sun Also Rises*. I do not think this is what Hemingway actually means in his rather clouded statement about complexity and his "then equipment" as a writer; in fact, the following eleven pages of the novel contain, in my view, his finest writing ever, of the bullfight as *rendered* action (even if it is more the *telling* of conventional narration as opposed to the *showing* in the avant-garde modernist bullfight vignettes of *In Our Time*.) It seems safe to say that the vast majority of Americans, and millions of readers all over the world, had their first and efficacious initiation into the bullfight, the corrida, the world of *toreo*, particularly through this culminating bullring scene of *The Sun Also Rises*. They have not gone to Pamplona by the millions all these years because of *Death in the Afternoon* or *The Dangerous Summer*. In the novel, Hemingway creates the concrete action that makes the reader feel much more than is stated; it is the property of all great fiction to make the reader feel emotion that is not easily translated to words and formulas. *Death in the Afternoon* is an essential *supplement*, in this sense, to the novel, for it is there that Hemingway articulates the nature of Romero's triumph in this bullring scene:

> the faena that takes a man out of himself and makes him feel immortal while it is proceeding, that gives him an ecstasy, that is, while momentary, as profound as any religious ecstasy; moving all the people in the ring together and increasing in emotional intensity as it proceeds, carrying the bullfighter with it, he playing on the crowd through the bull and being moved as it responds in a growing ecstasy of ordered, formal, passionate, increasing disregard for death that leaves you, when it is over, and the death administered to the animal that has made it possible, as empty, as changed and as sad as any major emotion will leave you. (206–7)

Every serious reader of *The Sun Also Rises* should consider *Death in the Afternoon* essential reading, a required secondary text, just as every aficionado of the bullfight should note carefully Hemingway's use of religious language when he describes matters of *afición*, should see the convergences of the Church and the arena, should hear what Hemingway means when he says that the ecstasy that happens in the bullring is a "momentary" instance of "religious ecstasy." Hemingway knows that the central mysteries of the Church are concerned with the "growing ecstasy of ordered, formal, passionate, increasing disregard for death" that will change you in ways that are not "momentary." Jake knows it, too, and the bullfight serves him as convergence with and confirmation of his overarching Christian quest, his Catholic vision, and his Catholic pilgrimage.

211:11 **callejon:** Throughout this bullring scene, when Hemingway introduces a term the reader may not know, such as *callejón,* he immediately defines it ("the passageway," etc.) almost as if he were writing his explanatory glossary for *Death in the Afternoon.* That is, in matters pertaining to the bullfight, Hemingway's style is less driven by understatement and allusion than it is in the novel's non-bullfight sequences. The prose of the bullfight passages, for the most part, has an expository exactitude that requires no footnotes, no interlinear commentary (see 167:11). Even when the information presented may be inaccurate or misleading (e.g., see 215:28 and 216:23–24), its *presentation* serves the primary purpose of the scene: the exaltation of Romero's work in the bullring.

212:9 **three matadors:** Juan Belmonte (1892–1962) and Marcial Lalanda (1903–1990) were highly regarded matadors who, critical assessments of their work aside, were leading bullfighters of their eras. The point here is that Hemingway uses two *actual* and highly esteemed matadors as foils to underline the "greatness" of his *invented* matador, Pedro Romero. The reader is given the information necessary to establish the context in which to judge Romero. Readers who wish to know more about Belmonte and Marcial should consult *Death in the Afternoon,* which contains numerous references and photographs of both men. (See also the following entry.)

215:26 **flashes of the old greatness:** Hemingway's portrait of Belmonte is essentially a set-up job, an attack on one of the great bullfighters of the twentieth century in order to elevate, for the purposes of fiction, the performance of Pedro Romero. Often considered the creator of modern *toreo* and the major revolutionary influence in the creation of the *art* of bullfighting, Belmonte achieved early fame, from 1914 on, "due to his reckless, aggressive style. He took unbelievable risks and was injured in almost every fight. Purists decried his lack of polish and complained that his injuries were unnecessary and the sort of thing that gave bullfighting a bad name. But his apologists lauded his strong personality, and the crowds rushed to see the passionate daredevil" (Mandel 74–75). By 1919 he had achieved artistic polish and, always maintaining "his revolutionary closeness to the bull," he fought a remarkable 109 corridas, a record that stood until 1965 (Mandel 75, 492). Yet "the public that had once rushed to see him risk his neck objected to his newly acquired control and authority, which they read as coldness, self-interest, and, most damning, lack of *afición*" (Mandel 75). Clearly, although Hemingway had not seen the early work of Belmonte, who retired (the first time) in 1923, he here echoes this stream of opinion concerning Belmonte's performance in the ring. Belmonte came out of retirement in 1925, and Hemingway saw him in Pamplona on 11 July with Marcial Lalanda and Cayetano Ordóñez; Belmonte's performance that day was disappointing (Mandel 76). Although Hemingway does not follow exactly the details of that corrida as contemporary accounts record it, and he obviously manipulates certain details to serve his narrative purpose of exalting Romero, this bullfight scene is based on that corrida.

In his notation of Belmonte's former "greatness," his ability to give the "sensation of coming tragedy" by working always in "the terrain of the bull," Jake (and Hemingway) sets Belmonte up as an actual standard against which to measure the performance of the fictional Romero, whose "greatness" is defined in opposition to the "flashes of the old greatness" of the once-great matador who has come out of retirement. But in stating that Belmonte's actual work in the ring is all "discounted" in advance because *he* has chosen "two small, manageable bulls without much horns," Jake (and Hemingway) engages in a falsification, at best an obfuscation, that even the demands of storytelling may not justify (see the following entry).

In sum, as Miriam Mandel has it, in "*The Sun Also Rises* Hemingway attacks Belmonte . . . and denigrates his performance in order to exalt Romero" (77). In *Death in the Afternoon* Hemingway presents a more balanced portrait of Belmonte. He praises his "great revolutionary style" (212) and his perfection in his work with the cape and muleta (175), yet blames him for the "modern technique of bullfighting" that requires "an almost made-to-order bull" (161). And Hemingway also "wrote that Belmonte is 'The only living bull fighter that I unreservedly admire'" (Mandel 78). Belmonte retired for the second time in 1927 after a bad goring. He came out of retirement again when he was 42 years old and fought (mostly in Portugal) from 1934 to 1937. He died in 1962, taking his own life in the year after Hemingway's death.

215:28 **picked the bulls:** This passage, together with the following sentence, implies (or allows the casual reader to believe) that Belmonte has picked the "two small, manageable bulls without much horns" that he will fight. Indeed, Belmonte might have picked the bulls for the entire corrida but not the two bulls he would fight; that would be determined at the *sorteo,* which is the regulated process of (as Hemingway defined it in *Death in the Afternoon*) "making up the lots and drawing of the bulls before the fight to determine which bulls shall be killed by which matadors" (483). It could be argued that Hemingway's prose here is ambiguous, that he means to suggest that the *sorteo* does not matter because Belmonte picked the bulls, and *all* the bulls were small and manageable "without much horns." This supposition might seem to be supported by the earlier conversation Jake has with Pedro Romero and the bullfight critic about the weight and horns of the bulls (see 175:3). Yet a few pages after the derogatory passage about Belmonte picking the bulls we learn that Romero's second bull was "a good bull, a big bull, and with horns" (219:25). Clearly, since that bull might have been Belmonte's (as determined by the drawing of lots at the *sorteo*), the reader must conclude either that Jake (and Hemingway) does not understand the *sorteo*—which seems unlikely—or that to serve the narrative drive to downgrade Belmonte the process of picking the bulls is falsified or deliberately obfuscated.

216:4 **the greatness:** The rendering of Romero's action in the ring, how he does everything "smoothly, calmly, and beautifully," how all his passes are "linked up, all completed, all slow, templed and smooth," is more than sufficient to demonstrate how this is "perfect bull-fighting" (even with his first bull), how it is "like a course in bull-fighting" with "no tricks." For a more complete understanding of Romero's "greatness" the reader should see Hemingway's discussion, throughout *Death in the Afternoon,* of the "valor, art, understanding and, above all, beauty and great emotion" (206), the "pundonor," which means "honor, probity, courage, self-respect and pride" (91), the qualities that Romero here exemplifies. As for the "religious ecstasy" that can occur when "greatness" informs the bullfighter's work, consider another key passage from *Death in the Afternoon:* "It is impossible to believe the emotional and spiritual intensity and pure, classic beauty that can be produced by a man, an animal and a piece of scarlet serge draped over a stick. If you do not choose to believe it possible and want to regard it all as nonsense you may be able to prove you are right by going to a bullfight in which nothing magical occurs; and there are many of them. ... But if you should ever see the real thing you would know it" (207). Romero's final bull represents the "real thing," the magic and the "spiritual intensity."

216:13 **His first "quite":** As he does consistently throughout his essentially expository descriptions of the bullfight scenes, Hemingway immediately defines the term "quite" after introducing it in this passage. In his *Death in the Afternoon* glossary, he defines it more precisely: "*Quite:* from *quitar*—to take away—is the taking away of the bull from any one who has been placed in immediate danger by him. It especially refers to the taking away of the bull from the horse and man after he has charged the picadors, by the matadors armed with capes and taking their turns in rotation; each one taking the bull after a charge. The matador who is to kill the bull makes the first *quite* and the others follow in order" (471).

216:23–24 **color caught the bull's eye:** Given the long-term confusion over the color blindness of bulls (over whether they "see red"), and given a certain confusion in Hemingway's rendering of this scene as he moves from Romero's first "quite" (see preceding entry) with the first bull that Belmonte is to kill to a description of Romero's first bull that does "not see well," it is necessary to read carefully this three-page passage (216–18). Hemingway repeats five times in less than two pages some version of his formulation regarding the ability of bulls to see color; in this first instance, he writes that "the color caught the bull's eye." Describing the next bull, Jake (and Hemingway) further confuses the matter by characterizing the "bull that can't see the color" (217:25)—and again "the bull who could not see the colors of the capes, or the scarlet flannel of the muleta" (217:28–29)—as a bull with "impaired" vision. That is, Jake attributes the inability of this second bull to see color to a vision defect, not to the normal condition of color blindness in bulls. On the question of color blindness in bulls and the role of cape and muleta color, one authoritative source notes: "Over the centuries, muletas . . . have changed in color, from the earliest, which were white, to later ones in red, yellow, and blue. Changing the color of the muleta . . . often does have good results . . . because the bull, although color-blind, does distinguish between light and dark. The argument, however, is that the bull is attracted to the muleta's movement, not its color. Be that as it may, by the time Hemingway came to the bullfight, muletas were red, and red they remain to this day" (Mandel 42–43). Bulls, then, although extremely sensitive to movement and light/dark color contrasts, are accurately said to be color-blind. Since the preponderance of scientific evidence (as well as the testimony of bull breeders) confirms that bulls are color-blind, or have a form of protanopia (inability to see red, for example) due to the deficiency of cones, or photoreceptors in the retina of the eye, it seems clear that Jake (and Hemingway) has his facts wrong in this scene. And, as I can attest from the reactions of student readers to this scene, the transition from the first bull (who is said to see the color) to the second bull (whose inability to see color is said to be a vision defect), further clouds the issue.

219:22 **not touched his spirit:** The reader is here reminded, just before Romero's final triumph with the bull, that his grace under pressure is all the more compelling because of his smashed face and battered body—but his spirit was untouched by Cohn. Like the novel's other wounded exemplars—the count, Jake—Romero is strong at the broken places, and his spirit epitomizes the secret of the values.

220:11 **his feet firm:** Romero kills the bull *recibiendo,* receiving the bull's charge while his feet are firmly planted, the dangerous and difficult technique of killing so rare in the twentieth century. One of the more interesting changes between the manuscript version and the final text occurs in this passage. In the manuscript Romero kills *volapié,* not *recibiendo;* Hemingway describes how Romero executes "perfectly the three tempos of the volapié the best thing I know to watch in bull-fighting." First he wrote, "the most beautiful thing," but crossed that out (*Facsimile* 2:547). *Volapié* means "flying while running." Years later, Hemingway's long glossary entry in *Death in the Afternoon* gives a definition in which he says nothing about it being the "most beautiful" or the "best thing" to watch in bullfighting; he does note that it is the usual "method of killing bulls in modern times" (493). Did Hemingway change his mind about the beauty of *volapié?* Or did he decide to stress the difficulty and danger of the old tradition, the "real old stuff"? (See 19:16.) More likely the latter, since the entire thrust of the book is concerned with recovering the *old values* that had been lost. He also probably wished to stress the difficulty and danger, the authentic confrontation with death, more than beauty of execution. But, above all, he wanted to complete the mythicizing evolution of his bullfighter exemplar by reminding those who would recognize the allusion of his namesake, the historical Pedro Romero, who killed all his bulls *recibiendo* (see also 162:30–31).

221:17 **hard-boiled eggs:** Again, as in Paris and in the Burguete/Roncevaux fishing scene, Jake and Bill eat hard-boiled eggs (see 73:29 and 121:18–20). Given the fact that Belmonte, after his dismal performance, is eating soft-boiled eggs, this probably resonates with the novel's overarching "hard-boiled" motif (see 34:24). And Jake and Bill are rather hard-boiled, undaunted, regarding all that has transpired during the fiesta.

222:7 **absinthe:** This two-page absinthe drinking scene at the end of the fiesta echoes the Pernod drinking scene with Jake and Georgette the prostitute at the beginning of chapter 3. After the first "pleasantly bitter" absinthe, things seem "better." After the second absinthe, things seem like "a wonderful nightmare," and Jake feels "low as hell." After the third absinthe, which he drinks too fast, Jake is "very drunk." The sequence of three absinthes here is reminiscent of Oscar Wilde's famous pronouncement on the three-stage progress of absinthe: After the first one, things seem as you wish they were (for Jake, that's pleasantly bitter but better); After the second, you see things as they are not (for Jake and Bill, a wonderful nightmare); And after the third, you see things as they really are—horrible (see 15:9). When Jake finishes his third absinthe, he learns that Brett has left town with Pedro Romero on the 7 PM train.

222:30 **feel like hell:** In another instance of Hemingway's use of threefold repetition, Jake says three times in ten lines that he feels like hell. It seems much more than mere coincidence that "I feel like hell" are the exact words of the "3rd Roman Soldier" in Hemingway's drama centered on the Passion of Christ, *Today Is Friday*. Hemingway wrote that playlet in May 1926 as he was working on the revisions of *The Sun Also Rises*. Having witnessed the Passion, the extraordinary grace under pressure of Christ on the Cross—underlined by the second Roman soldier's insistent repetition: "He was pretty good in there today"—the third Roman soldier has been profoundly moved, "feels like hell," and may well be on the brink of conversion (*Complete Short Stories* 271–73). In the manuscript version of the novel, Jake says: "I feel like hell" twice, and he feels "rotten" once. At some later point the final revision brings Jake's "feel like hell" repetition into exact accord with the Roman soldier's iteration. Given the simultaneity of the composition of *Today Is Friday* and the revision of *The Sun Also Rises*, it seems more than likely that there is a deliberate intertextuality. After the passion of Romero—who was "pretty good in there today"—Jake has a "hollow gone feeling" (*Facsimile* 2:551). And, absinthe aside, feeling like hell may be the necessary prelude to feeling renewed, redeemed, as Jake so clearly does in the baptismal swimming scenes in San Sebastián in the following chapter.

223:31 **seven o'clock train:** In 1925, of course, the bullfights did not start at 18:30 and end at about 20:30, as they do today. Oral local inquiries in Pamplona suggest that the bullfights started at either 16:00 or 16:30 in the 1920s, although I have been unable to find documentary evidence to confirm a starting time. Even if the bullfights started as early as 16:00—or more likely at 16:30, a common starting time for corridas in the 1920s—and ended about two hours later, this would only leave an hour for Pedro Romero to be carried on the shoulders of the crowd, for Pedro and Brett to return to the hotel, clean up, change, pack, and get to the train station to catch the "seven o'clock train." Of course, Romero is *running* toward the exit, and when the crowd hoists him they are *running* out the gate; the hotel is only a few blocks away, and Brett and Pedro might have done most of their packing and arranged for a waiting cab before the bullfight, so it is possible they could catch the train at 19:00. In any case, the timing stresses their precipitate departure, their haste in leaving town. Belmonte, it is to be noted, also catches a seven o'clock train, bound for Barcelona. As Brett goes upstairs to her room, Belmonte (who did not have a heroic exit from the bullring) comes into the hotel dining room, already in his "street clothes." He does not eat much, but the men with him eat "a big meal" (221:16–23). There is no indication that they are rushing to catch their "seven o'clock train." Perhaps all this amounts to another instance of Hemingway playing fast and loose with time; or perhaps it is a narrative slip. Yet, regardless of the exit time from the bullring, which would almost certainly be not much earlier than six and as late as six thirty, Hemingway's train timetable inevitably stresses the hasty departure of Brett and Romero, and of Belmonte.

224:10 **did not mean anything:** What does Jake mean? That the fiesta, which in a sense has meant everything to him, no longer means anything? Or that the fiesta does not *signify*, rather it just *is*—a fiesta should not *mean* but *be*? Or that now that the heart of the fiesta is over, after the big religious processions, after the last of the bullfights, after Brett and Romero are gone, the fiesta has finished its job— Jake's purgation, his catharsis, is complete? Although the world is a little blurry at the edges, it is not "wheeling any more"; it is "very clear and bright." And, after a few days in San Sebastián—"a good place to get all straightened inside again"(see 235:25)—after some swimming and serenity to round off his summer pilgrimage, he can go back home to Paris.

CHAPTER 19

227:1 **fiesta was finished:** The first lines of book III and the novel's final chapter reiterate that it is "all over," and again, after a sketch of Pamplona returning to normal, the cleansing of everything—notice the water imagery—Jake seals it: "The fiesta was over."

228:16 **Montoya:** See 209:27.

228:23 **out of Spain:** The return to the lush green countryside of France echoes the rich, green, and clean landscape evoked as they left France on their way into Spain (see 91:29–30).

229:2–3 **a very Ritz place:** This seemingly curious form, in a context where today one would generally say "a very ritzy place," appeared in the manuscript as "a very Ritz like place" (*Facsimile* 2:561). The *OED* cites Hemingway's "a very Ritz place" as one of the earliest such usages to indicate luxury. The uppercase form "Ritzy" (and "Ritz-y") began to be used in the 1920s, and the lowercase form, "ritzy," having more or less shed its direct association with the great luxury hotels of César Ritz, appeared by the late 1930s. In any case, Bia*rritz* is a very ritzy place. It may seem curious, given the animosity expressed by various characters toward the Biarritz tourists during the fiesta, that they go to Biarritz for a drink (see 188–89; see also 171:17, 171:30, and 179:31). Of course, it's Mike, the big spender, who makes the suggestion, and Biarritz is more his sort of place than Bayonne, and Biarritz is just down the road from Bayonne.

229:21 **I'm stony:** Having lost at dice, unable to pay for the round of drinks, Mike has to admit he's "stony"—stony broke or stone broke. He has no "credit along the coast," but he does know a pub in Saint-Jean-de-Luz (a short distance down the coast) where he can run a tab, or live "on tick," until his allowance comes. Note Bill's change in attitude and Jake's concern when he learns that Brett has no money with her.

230:31 **villages farther down:** Again the beauty of the landscape is stressed—the green headlands, the forest, the ocean—as they take a pleasure ride along the Corniche Basque before turning back to drop Mike in Saint-Jean and get Bill to his train in Bayonne.

232:2 **Don't kid me:** This scene serves effectively as the introduction to a series of France-Spain contrasts in the pages that follow (see the following six entries; also 235:30–32 and passim). The Spanish taxi driver has raised the agreed-upon "fixed" price by 25 percent, from 150 pesetas to 200 pesetas. Jake doesn't like it, and he rejects the driver's bargaining and outrageous offer to take him to San Sebastián (not far, and not far out of the way) for 50 pesetas. Given the price-gouging greediness of even the driver's second offer of 35 pesetas (a room and dinner at most of the better hotels in San Sebastián cost less than that), Jake dismisses him, inscribing with his rod case his mark on the dusty car, the "last thing that connected" him with Spain. This scene echoes the reverse journey, from Bayonne into Spain, when the French driver is characterized as helpful, apparently quite pleasant (since he "stayed for lunch" with Jake and the others), and, most significant, he makes no problem over his charge and does not attempt to raise the agreed-upon fare (91–94). Since all too many commentators on the novel have professed to discover a "France/Spain split in values," in which France is the wasteland and Spain is the good place, and the French people are corrupt and materialistic while the Spanish people are natural and innocent and uncorrupted by money, all who insist on such false and nonexistent dichotomies need to consider carefully not only the rich, green, clean landscapes of France but the drivers who conduct Jake and his friends across the border. There is no French wasteland, and it is clear, in these paired scenes, which driver anyone would prefer, which one is more unpredictable and materialistic (see also 25:2, 76:12, 84:29, 88:17, 91:25, 94:1, and 110:4).

232:4 **Hotel Panier Fleuri:** Here at the Panier Fleuri, where the hotel reception is "very cheerful," Jake gets the same room he had the night before he left France (see 89:17). For commentators who must seek a France-Spain contrast in values (see preceding entry), there are recurrent and contradistinguishing details involving hotels on opposite sides of the border. Jake's only French hotel (he stays there twice, before and after two border crossings) was nice and clean, and the French proprietors were "very cheerful." In contrast, just across the border at Burguete, the inn is "cold" and overpriced, and the innkeeper is "fat" and rather devious, and stingy with her rum (see 110:4). And at the Hotel Montana in Madrid, the maid is "sullen" and dull faced, and the proprietress, a "very fat woman" with "stiffly oiled" hair, is defensive and insistent and "short and commanding" (see 240:14). Who is materialistic, who is pleasant, and who is sullen in these cross-border hotel scenes that resonate with precisely the opposite significance attributed to them in the spurious scheme of the so-called France-Spain split in values? To be sure, there are pleasant and civilized hotels on both sides of Jake's actual borders—for example, the Crillon in Paris and the Palace in Madrid; my point here is not the converse of the usual absurd argument regarding France.

232:16–19 **safe, suburban feeling . . . San Sebastián:** It feels "strange" to be in France again, with its "safe, suburban feeling" (i.e., in Bayonne). Jake wishes he'd gone home to Paris with Bill, but that "would have meant more fiesta-ing." Paris is not safe, not suburban. San Sebastián, where it "would be quiet," might seem safe and suburban, too. Readers looking for France-Spain contrasts must tread cautiously in interpreting this complicated passage. First, they must desist from assuming that "suburban" was the pejorative term in 1926 that it has since come to be (largely since the 1960s) for some who employ the term. (Did Hemingway, a child of that safe suburb, Oak Park, really disdain his pleasant suburban place, removed from the violence of nearby Chicago?) And then, it must be understood that San Sebastián, the least Spanish of Spain's resorts, was a very pleasant, safe, cosmopolitan small city with a truly international clientele and history. Parks and monuments bear inscriptions in French and English. Even the names of the hotels, as printed in the fashionable guidebooks in English, told the story: the Hotel Continental, the Hotel de Londres et d'Angleterre (Hotel of London and England), the Hotel du Palais (Palace), the Reina Victoria (Queen Victoria), the Hotel de Francia (France Hotel), Hotel de Paris, the Family Hotel, and so on; many of the restaurants and cafés were international in menu and style. And when the city expanded with the demolition of its walls in 1863, everyone knew that Napoleon III and his empress, Eugénie, who often came down to San Sebastián from Biarritz, were the first celebrities to pass through the first break in the walls. The point is that San Sebastián cannot be conscripted to serve in any false pattern of France-Spain contrasts, for it is exactly the same as the part of France that has that "safe, suburban feeling," just as Pamplona and Paris are seen as identical for their "fiesta-ing." As Jake reiterates, it would be "quiet" in San Sebastián; it's a good place to swim; and, as he says in a manuscript line unfortunately deleted from this paragraph, it was a good place to "soak in the sun and get straightened around inside again" (*Facsimile* 2:569; see 148:6 and 235:25).

232:31 **seemed very carefully apportioned:** French and Spanish meals have also been forced to serve in the design of the supposed cross-border split in values, and the meal that has received the most attention, by way of misreading, as some putative token of French meagerness or avariciousness is this meal in Bayonne. Since so many unfortunate generalizations have been made on this score, we might first consider briefly all the meals in the novel to see what pattern, if any, really is present. In France, nine meals are mentioned, and five are characterized. Dining in the bois de Boulogne with Brett and the count, Jake notes that "it was a good dinner" and food has "an excellent place in the count's values"; at Madame Lecomte's on the île Saint-Louis they have a "good meal," and Jake gives the complete menu, the only time in the novel he does so. Other meals in France are characterized as "good" and "pleasant," and at this Bayonne restaurant, where "one eats very well," Jake has "a big meal for France" (61, 76, 232). This last is the *only* reference to *quantity* in the notation of French meals; all other characterizations have to do with *quality*.

In contrast, seventeen Spanish meals are mentioned, and only five are characterized. The meal notations are brief, and they are mostly concerned with *quantity*: "the first meal in Spain was always a shock" (94); at Burguete, they have "a *big* bowl . . . of soup . . . *some sort* of a stew and a *big* bowl" of strawberries (110–11; emphasis added). In Pamplona, they have "a *big* meal . . . the first meal of the prices being *doubled* for the fiesta" (159; emphasis added); finally, in Madrid, Brett and Jake leave the Palace Hotel bar, since lunch would be "rotten" there, and go to Botín's. Jake announces that "it is one of the best restaurants in the world," but his only comment on the lunch is "I ate a *very big* meal" (245–46; emphasis added; see 245:32). The pattern, then, such as it is, stresses *quantity* in Spain, *quality* in France. Maybe Hemingway's meal notations are more axiological, even theological, than we have recognized. Gastronomy is a matter of quality, not quantity; gastronomy is founded on taste, which is one of the regnant values of *The Sun Also Rises*. And the deadly sin is gluttony, not gourmandise.

As for this meal, at the modest unnamed café/restaurant in Bayonne where "one eats very well," this scene may be one of the most frequently misinterpreted passages in the novel. Typically, Frederic Svoboda (*Crafting of a Style* 81) reads this as a scene that foregrounds the "easy" money-centered values of France (in opposition to Spanish values and "the real values that Jake espouses"). Admittedly, it is hard to tell what this reading might indicate other than the dangers of rigid application of a thesis—Svoboda's "France/Spain split in values" (or the France-Bad Spain-Good Law)—but the argument continues; for Svoboda, this scene underscores "the French waiter's love of money" (in opposition to some ostensible "real" values that Spanish waiters embody?) and some presumed negativity thought to reside in Jake's inscription of this meal as "carefully apportioned." What actually transpires in this scene? Jake eats a "big meal" that *seems*, "after Spain," to be "carefully apportioned." In one sense this represents no more, no less than the culmination of the France-Spain qualitative-quantitative meal pattern just noted. In another sense, it relates significantly to one of the novel's primary motifs—the arc of experience from the *mesuré* to the *démesuré*, from decorum to excess. To imply, as Svoboda and others have, that *mesuré*, that careful apportionment, that moderation or decorum are somehow negative qualities associated with France is to miss the point utterly. (Hemingway was not joking when he said that *The Sun Also Rises* was a "tract against promiscuity," and the category of the promiscuous includes indiscriminate eating and drinking.) Indeed, *mesuré* is the luminous, profoundly positive essence of France, as it is of Jake's character in its most exemplary sense. It is *mesuré*, careful apportionment, properly understood (and in fertile creative tension with passion) that is the foundation of *places* that are, like Hemingway's French border town, Menton, "very cheerful and clean and sane and lovely" (in contrast to the Italy left behind in "Che Ti Dice la Patria," *Complete Short Stories* 230). It is *mesuré* that defines Jake's life year-round in France, with a week of necessary excess, purgation, a brief interval of fiesta in Spain. Just as surely as Ash Wednesday follows Fat Tuesday (and one without the other is mere chaos or mere asceticism), Jake longs for "quiet" and simplicity and *mesure* after the fiesta.

So we are with Jake, in Bayonne, enjoying his "carefully apportioned" meal and a bottle of Château Margaux: "It was pleasant to be drinking slowly and to be tasting the wine." Château Margaux, of course, has for centuries been one of the greatest wines of France (and thus of the world); legendary for its elegance and finesse and perfect balance, this Margaux is as emblematic of France as any key French fact or symbol in the novel, and it is very much to the point that Jake, in his happiness at reentering France, selects, drinks slowly, and tastes deeply his Margaux. And one more matter might be noted: Château Margaux is the precise product of tradition, passion, art, and discipline cultivated in the *terroir* of the vine, just as Pedro Romero's performance in the bullring is the precise product of tradition, passion, art, and discipline cultivated in the terrain of the bull. There is no "France/Spain split in values," not for Jake, not for Hemingway, not in this novel, and not in the actual or symbolic landscape of the abiding French and Spanish earth.

233:4 **Izzarra:** The waiter recommends "a Basque liqueur called Izzarra [sic]." Izarra is generally regarded, in France, as an unfortunate counterfeit of the classic French liqueur Chartreuse, or, in the gentle phrase of an authority on spirits, "a Basque attempt to reproduce Chartreuse" (Lichine 271). For Jake, it is repellent, looks like "hair-oil," and smells like Italian *strega,* and he refuses the offered glass. He orders, most appropriately for his French homecoming, a *vieux marc* (or *eau-de-vie de marc*), a representative drink of "la France profonde," the deep heart of France. He has a second marc after his coffee. At this point, as some critics would have it, our supposedly avaricious French waiter gets friendly, a ploy "to increase the size of his tip" (Svoboda, *Crafting of a Style* 81). Nothing of the kind happens, although some readers, with wearisome insistence on the imaginary France-Spain paradigm, argue the contrary (see preceding entry). What actually happens is this: the waiter seems "offended about the flowers of the Pyrenees," Jake's mockingly reiterated epithet for the repellent Izarra, so Jake overtips him. *Then,* not before, the waiter is "happy." We might note also that this waiter is probably not French, given the fact that he recommends the Izarra (it is hard to imagine a French waiter doing so) and, moreover, the fact that he is offended by Jake's rejection of the "flowers of the Pyrenees"; given, that is, the action of the scene as well as the setting, the waiter must be Basque.

233:14 **simplest country to live in:** After Jake overtips the waiter, we get the generally misconstrued sequence of observations about France, "the simplest country to live in" because things are on "such a clear financial basis." In France, nobody complicates things by being your friend for some "obscure reason"; spend a little money, Jake believes, and the waiter will like him and appreciate his "valuable qualities" (more humorous wordplay), and it will be "a sincere liking . . . [with] a sound basis." Jake also overtips at his Bayonne hotel because he wants "a few good French friends" there to make him welcome if he ever comes back: "their friendship would be loyal." Of course, Jake also overtips in Spain; but there, for "obscure" reasons and because "you could not tell about anything" in Spain, he does not always get what he pays for. There is nothing in this scene to suggest that France is any more materialistic or money centered than Spain, that the French are any more avaricious than the Spanish. What the scene does tell us is that there are certain values that prevail in France—soundness, sincerity, loyalty, "simple" (as opposed to "obscure") friendship—dictated by a code that is, in part, the same as Jake's stated code: "Just exchange of values. . . . Enjoying living was learning to get your money's worth and knowing when you had it" (148:14–21). The point is that it is generally preferable, except maybe for two weeks or so a year (Jake's vacation time in Spain when he doesn't mind too much *overpaying* for things like taxis and hotels), to get what you pay for; this is surely better than paying for what you don't get, or getting less—or more—than you bargained for, surely better than not being able to "tell about anything." To be sure, Jake's vision has greater amplitude than the exchange-of-values passage suggests; his code or creed includes and is centered on matters of passion— the Church, the corrida, fishing, sport (boxing, bicycle racing), art (architecture, literature, writing), and pilgrimage—that transcend getting "your money's worth." But the "world is a good place to buy in" (148:22), and Jake knows that buying in and getting what you pay for are the foundation of everything else. Jake is, in most matters, a rather accomplished axiologist—a student of the nature of values.

233:29–30 **I hated to leave France:** Because life is "so simple in France," and simplicity is what Jake wants after the complications of the fiesta, he feels "like a fool" to be going back into Spain. Although San Sebastián (see 232:16–19) is "simple" and "safe," too, Madrid will not be.

234:18 **police bulletin:** In the 1920s, and well into the later twentieth century, many European countries required tourists to fill out a "police bulletin" card, a form of registration with the local authorities, when they checked into a hotel.

234:24–25 **had lunch . . . read a while:** In the manuscript version of this scene, Jake commented on both the lunch and his reading. Predictably, he comments only on the "great amount" of food and contrasts the quantity with "that measured French feeling" (see 232:31). More interesting is the fact that he tells us what he read during lunch, "through the meal"—"Borrow's Bible in Spain" (*Facsimile* 2:575). The complete title of the 1843 best seller by the English writer George Borrow (1803–1881) is *The Bible in Spain, or the Journeys, Adventures, and Imprisonments of an Englishman in an attempt to circulate the Scriptures in the Peninsula.* Immensely popular for many decades, *The Bible in Spain* is a curious mixture of travel writing, cultural commentary, fiction, and missionary accounts of the Gospel enterprise on which Borrow was sent by the Bible Society (of England), which entailed overseeing the printing and distribution of Spanish editions of the Bible throughout Spain. Borrow's account covers a lot of ground, with scenes in Santiago de Compostela, Madrid, and all over Spain, and vignettes of bullfighters, priests, Gypsies, Basque peasants, and all kinds of characters. As is always the case in Hemingway's fiction, what his characters are reading tells us something important about them, and it is most revealing that the first book Jake reads, two days after the fiesta is over, is *The Bible in Spain.* And, in another passage deleted from the manuscript, he alludes to Jake reading Borrow again a few pages later (see 235:25). The passage, now lost except to those who know the "iceberg" of textual history, seems an unfortunate deletion—but then maybe Hemingway decided it gave too much away and revealed too much about Jake and religion.

234:28 **the Concha:** La Concha ("The Shell") is the semicircular bay, long celebrated by guidebooks as one of the most beautiful and noble bays and beaches and swimming places of Europe, on which San Sebastián is centered. The bay is considered to be shell shaped, thus the name. The shell is also the universally recognized symbol of the pilgrim on the Way of Saint James/Saint Jacques, the Santiago pilgrim. The traditional phrase in many European countries, "to wear the shell," signified one's identity as a Santiago pilgrim. As we have seen, one of the keys to the novel is Jake's identity as a Santiago pilgrim, and the deep structure of the novel—geographically and thematically—is determined by the pilgrimage route of Santiago (see especially 78:6–7; see also 16:31, 22:28, 86:2–3, and 94:3). Thus, it seems inevitable that Jake, even though he feels like a fool to be going back into Spain, must enact his Santiago pilgrim status by coming to San Sebastián for his post-fiesta cleansing and swimming. There are, after all, fine beaches in Biarritz and Saint-Jean-de-Luz, where Jake had been the day before. But no, his swimming must be done in La Concha, in the Bay of the Pilgrim's Shell.

235:5–7 **I dove, swam . . . lay on the hot planks:** It has seldom been noticed how important swimming and sunbathing are in Hemingway's work, in general, and in this scene. Heliophilia—love of the sun and sunbathing—became fashionable in the 1920s, and in a novel called *The Sun Also Rises,* heliophilic details certainly deserve close attention. Many observers have noted in passing the baptismal overtones of the swimming scenes. Although the San Sebastián swimming scenes have rarely been contextualized in terms of the novel's overall religious pattern, Robert Lewis noted more than four decades ago that Jake "makes almost a ritual, like baptism, out of bathing," and his swimming, "after the disappointing, fight-marred end of the partly pagan fiesta," represents Jake's return "to the fertile sea for purification" (32). And in my own writing on this novel I have briefly noted what I called, some two decades ago, the "quasi-sacramental reenactment" of baptismal rites and Jake's swimming, which I referred to as "ritual cleansing after the fiesta" ("From the Rue Saint-Jacques" 19). By this I meant to suggest that Jake's swimming is a secular variation on the theme of baptism, at best a symbolic renewal of his baptismal vow, since as a practicing Catholic Jake would have been baptized long before this scene in San Sebastián. It should also be said that Jake's swimming serves as a culmination of the novel's pattern of bathing imagery and as a fulfillment of his need for a deep bath that last night of the fiesta (see 192:4). Recently, I have examined closely the pattern of natatorial and heliophilic details—the swimming and the sunning action—with more attention to the bodily acts of swimming and sunning, and the language used in these paired beach scenes at La Concha (see "Dignity of Movement" 64–67). In brief, we note in this first swimming scene how Jake dives, swims underwater, comes up "with all the chill gone," and pulls himself up onto the raft in the hot sun. He watches the couple on the raft, the girl browning her back with the strap of her bathing suit undone; he listens to this couple talk and laugh as he soaks up the sun. Then he dives deep and swims through the "dark shadow" that the raft makes underwater. The couple on the raft may serve as a reminder of Brett and Cohn and their tryst in San Sebastián, but Jake is able to dive to the *bottom* with his "eyes open," swim through that "dark shadow," pull himself *up* on the raft again, this time paying no attention to the couple, before diving again. The translation of the symbolic subtext is obvious: Jake has been to the bottom over the Brett-Cohn affair, but now, eyes open wide, having no illusions, he has come out the other side of that "dark shadow"—and the chill is gone; the sun is bright. For further reverberations of these motifs, see the paired swimming scene two pages later (237:33).

235:20 **Café Marinas:** Actually the Café Marina, one of several elegant cafés with their own orchestras, it was located at 23, Alameda, near the casino. In the manuscript, Hemingway first wrote "Cafe Marinas," and the second time he wrote it correctly: "Café Marina" (*Facsimile* 2:570, 578).

235:25 **listened to the music:** As the details here suggest, Jake is in a relaxed, contemplative mood after his swim, listening to the music at the Café Marina. This sentence takes the place of one of the more telling deletions from the manuscript, which shows Jake thinking, the second time, that San Sebastián is "a good place to get all straightened inside again" (see 232:16–19; see also 148:6). Then he thinks about the books he has with him—"a Turgenieff" (see 147:5) and "two Mrs. Belloc Lowndes." Marie Belloc Lowndes (1868–1947) was a best-selling mystery writer who regularly appeared on lists of the best Catholic authors; her 1913 novel, *The Lodger,* was a huge popular success and was made into a film by Alfred Hitchcock in 1927; the big 1926 movie based on her work was *Shameful Behavior?* She was also an early crusader for women's rights and a leader of the Women Writers Suffrage League. Her brother, Hilaire Belloc (1870–1953), was the prolific Catholic author known as the "Defender of the Faith" who figured in a scene cut from the beginning of *The Sun Also Rises* and later used in *A Moveable Feast* (85–88; see also appendix). And the last book named is *The Bible in Spain,* the second mention of the classic work by George Borrow (see 234:24–25). Then Jake thinks: "I could get Tauchnitz if I wanted them." Tauchnitz was a German publishing firm celebrated since the mid-1800s for its Library of British and American Authors, a collection of thousands of titles familiar to travelers and widely available in hotel libraries at proper hotels throughout Europe in the early twentieth century. His meditation on the "fun" he will have reading, eating, and swimming leads him to this conclusion: "Then I could go back to Paris and get to work again. Paris would be nice and it would be fun to eat out at the Parc Montsouris and at the Quatre Sergents de la Rochelle again. It was always fun to get back to Paris" (*Facsimile* 2:579). Since this passage conveys some telling information, aside from the always-welcome lists of what Hemingway's characters are reading, one wonders why Hemingway deleted it. Does it make Jake seem too happy? Does the repetition of the treble-deleted image of getting "straightened inside again" reveal too much and work against Hemingway's iceberg aesthetic, which refuses to overwhelm the reader with thematic insistence on what should be obvious to the attentive reader? Does his obvious love of Paris, of his home and his work, *tell* too directly what Hemingway *shows* so clearly in the first nine chapters (though some readers somehow manage to miss it)?

235:28 **Tour du Pays Basque:** One of the major events in multiple-stage bicycle road-racing since 1924 (and still today), the Tour de Pays Basque (in Spanish, *Vuelta al País vasco*) in 1925 took place on 6–9 August. Since it is mid-July when Jake is in San Sebastián, we see Hemingway yet again manipulating chronology to suit his narrative purposes (see 121:24). Surely Jake knows (and Hemingway knows) that he is more than three weeks off in his dating of a major sporting event—but that doesn't matter in storytelling, in the creation of fiction. In fact, Hemingway himself was in San Sebastián during the Tour de Pays Basque in 1925; on 8 and 9 August when the racers had completed the arduous 270-kilometer stage (winning time: ten hours and forty-two minutes) from Pamplona to San Sebastián, they were preparing for the early-morning departure on the ninth for the final 173-kilometer San Sebastián stage. As we know from Hemingway's manuscript notations (see *Facsimile* 1:133), he was in San Sebastián working hard on *The Sun Also Rises,* writing most of chapter 7, including the key secret-of-the-values scene with the count, Jake, and Brett (see also Balassi, "The Writing" 74). In fact, it seems very likely that Hemingway witnessed the dinner he describes here, the Belgian and French bicycle racers and their conversation, and certain details that are very exact. Of course, Hemingway might have read some of the details in the newspaper and invented the rest. But since Hemingway was a great fan of bicycle racing, he may well have availed himself of the opportunity to observe the team at dinner and have some good conversation with the team manager. In any case, Jake gets it right here—that is, that the leading riders are all Belgian and French, and that they would have contempt for the Spaniards, who—in 1925, as opposed to the 1990s when Miguel Induráin, a native of the Pamplona region, won the Tour de France five years in a row—"did not know how to pedal." In all the stages of the 1925 Tour de Pays Basque, the top ten riders were all Belgian and French. In fact, we can even identify who was at the dinner Jake observes. Jake describes the man who has, on the eve of the last lap, "a matter of two minutes lead" and has had a painful attack of boils (not recorded in the archives), a foreshadowing of the next day's event in spite of his joking about it. This was the Belgian rider Joseph Pé, who had a two-minute lead when they left San Sebastián the next morning, but by the time they reached Bilbao he had to settle for second place, well behind another Belgian rider, August Verdyck. In third place was Marcel Bidot of France. These riders, along with seven others who were in the top ten (eight Belgian, two French), are no doubt among those who are present for this dinner at the "long table," so carefully observed by Jake.

235:30–32 **bicycle-riders . . . paid close attention to their meal:** This meal, this entire scene with the bicycle riders and their companions, has sometimes been interpreted in skewed fashion in attempts to force it into the procrustean schema of the imaginary France-Spain values contrast thought by some readers to inform the novel (e.g., see 232:31, 233:14, and passim). For Frederic Svoboda, this entire scene represents the "intrusion" of inauthentic French values into the idyllic San Sebastián setting (*Crafting of a Style* 83). The team manager, Svoboda insists, is "chauvinistic," he "pontificates" on France, and the upshot of the scene is "Jake's rejection of bicycle racing" (83–84). There is more than one thing wrong with such a reading. First of all, the team manager may well be a Belgian, as most of the riders present clearly are (see preceding entry). And then, if the Belgian or French team manager is so offensively "chauvinistic" and pontifical, why does Jake choose to have coffee with him out on the terrace? Why does Jake linger and then choose to have a cognac with him? (Is that an inauthentic French "intrusion"?) Because Jake loves bicycle racing. Because Jake agrees with most of what the team manager says—the Tour de France has long been regarded as "the greatest [and most demanding] sporting event in the world." Given recent sport history, and the extraordinary Tour de France triumphs of Lance Armstrong, more Americans now know this, what Hemingway (and Jake) knew in 1925: "There were no other sports which called for as much from a man day after day," as Hemingway wrote in a deleted manuscript passage (*Facsimile* 2:582–83). Those readers who think that Hemingway constructs this scene to make an invidious cross-border comparison here between the "sports" of France and Spain, between bicycle racing and bullfighting, need to recognize two things: Hemingway, a passionate cycling fan, would not mock bicycle racing (which this scene does not do)—and bullfighting is not a sport.

Jake certainly agrees with the team manager on another score, on getting "back to Paris," and the emotion expressed in the phrase "There is only one Paname." (*Paname*, French argot for Paris, has been defined, and its derivation identified, in various ways: what one who loves Paris calls it; the universal city of the soul or spirit, the center of the world, or *axis mundi;* and so forth.) Readers of *The Sun Also Rises* have all the evidence needed to know that Jake loves Paris, his home, and the evidence is everywhere that Hemingway loved his Paris, "always beautiful . . . the city I love best in all the world" (*By-Line* 337). There is no mockery, no irony, at the expense of France in this entire scene. The French girls are "good-looking"; all the French and the Belgians are paying "close attention to their meal" and "having a good time." And the fact that Jake sleeps late the next morning and misses the race departure (even earlier in the morning than the running of the bulls that he sleeps through in Pamplona) does not indicate what Svoboda calls "Jake's rejection of bicycle racing" any more than sleeping through the *encierro* implies a rejection of *toreo.* The team manager is right: "Few people know France." But Jake does.

236:24 **Bottechia:** Ottavio Bottechia, the Italian rider, was the only non-French, non-Belgian rider in the top ten after the first stage from Bilbao to Pamplona. But, in spite of his sixth-place position, just two minutes behind the leader, he dropped out of the race before the Pamplona–San Sebastián stage.

237:33 **you could never sink:** This paired scene, a typical Hemingway device, echoes the swimming scene the day before (see 235:5–7). At first glance, the two scenes seem very much the same; they are exactly the same length, they seem to evoke the same pleasant feelings of swimming and sunbathing, and they seem to work together to emphasize the sense of post-fiesta cleansing that Jake longed for. Yet Hemingway's craftsmanship should never be underestimated, and his repetition is always incremental, his echoic scenes always nuanced. In the first scene, there was a couple on the raft and a dark shadow in the water. In this scene, Jake has the raft to himself, and there is no shadow in the water. In the first scene, Jake does not look at the sky; here, floating, he notes: "I saw only the sky," and looks up at the "high headland." In the second scene, even the water seems different: "quiet," "buoyant," "lightening"—qualities not noted in the first scene—it feels as "though you could never sink." There is a radical difference in the two scenes; it would be hard to argue that the first scene (with the girl's undone bathing suit and browned back, and the "dark shadow" of sex focusing the scene) is "baptismal," and it is easy to see that this buoyant, unsinkable scene, suffused with imagery of baptismal regeneration and grace, has specifically sacramental overtones of baptism. Consulting a good definition of the sacrament of baptism might help clarify the matter (see, e.g., Cross 124–26), but it is here rendered *naturally*, in the lexicon of the sun and the water. Even Jake's diving is different in the two scenes. He is now poised on the "*edge* of the raft" (emphasis added), and he dives "cleanly and deeply" into the water, where there are no dark shadows. That is, in the theological paradigm, as in the Christian existentialist (Kierkegaardian) paradigm, he is poised over the abyss, unafraid, making the leap of faith. This penultimate *edge* image further develops one of the novel's dominant motifs, the recurrent edge imagery that pervades the book (see, e.g., 65:3, 99:28, 182:31, 198:15, and 240:4).

Both swimming scenes are stylistically remarkable for the extraordinary sibilance of the prose, the alliterative concentration of *s* words that shapes the sentences: "smooth sand," "surface," "shadow," "strap of her bathing-suit," "swam slowly," "swells," "sink," "swam slowly and steadily into shore," and, of course, "sky," "surf," "salt," "sea," "sun." Indeed, a prosodist might scan these prose-poem passages as alliterative verse, bearing in mind that all this sibilant sinuous *s*-centered swimming and sunning take place in San Sebastián. We note, too, that in the second swimming scene, where sex has been removed from the picture, Jake does not name the Concha, avoids that hard *k* sound that is present in the first scene; and Concha, evocative of the Santiago pilgrim shell, is also—even in English—"another term for the vulva" (*OED*). Abruptly, the swimming is ended, as Brett's two telegrams arrive from Madrid. The close reader will also note that the serene *s*-drenched prose comes to a sudden end with Brett's telegrams, composed of harsh *k* and *t* sounds, not one single *s* in her message.

239:13 **all shot to hell:** This may be another of Jake's wry jokes, his witty wordplays: "San Sebastian all shot to hell." Saint Sebastian, after whom San Sebastián is named, was a Roman soldier and a secret Christian who was "shot to hell," ordered shot to death by arrows (a favorite subject of Renaissance artists). But Saint Sebastian, patron saint of soldiers, survived. Jake, who knows his saints, was also wounded in a "rotten way" in Italy, "on a joke front" (31:1–2).

239:19–20 **LOVE JAKE:** Jake receives the two telegrams (and the concierge waits for "another tip" after the second one is delivered) from Brett in rapid succession and immediately books his berth on the Sud Express for Madrid, the famous Grandes

Lignes (and the fastest) train from Paris to Madrid (via San Sebastián). Then he sends his message to Brett—he'll be there in the morning—and signs it "LOVE JAKE." Readers have sometimes interpreted this as a suggestion that he is not yet over Brett, that he is somehow still under her spell. This seems a confused reading of the situation. We know that Jake was concerned when he learned from Mike the day after the fiesta ended that Brett has no money with her (see 229:21). We also know that Jake places great importance on "the values"—and one of the values is certainly loyalty, generously assisting old friends who are "in trouble." And when one knows and lives "the values," as the count teaches, one is "always in love" (see 60:31–32 and 61:4). Thus, in a spirit of loyalty and charity, Jake cuts short his serene retreat in San Sebastián and rushes off to help Brett in her "trouble," whatever it may be—and, of course, signs his message with love. At this point in the manuscript, there follows a long passage in which Jake thinks about what he is doing and why, including an awkward digression on the aristocracy and manners and how Americans can have no conception of such a code of behavior. He tells himself there is "no use belly aching about it"; he'll just go and "get this Madrid thing over with"—it's the right thing to do (*Facsimile* 2:591). Wisely, Hemingway deleted this four-page-long passage, which, though it contains such interesting lines as "you learned a lot about a woman by not sleeping with her," is tonally confused, diffuse, written in clotted prose, and, in part, runs contrary to the established thrust of Jake's situation (*Facsimile* 2:593). For a good discussion of the manuscript deletions and revisions from here to the end of the novel, see Frederic Svoboda (*Crafting of a Style* 84–95).

239:27 **Avila and Escorial:** Just before Jake reaches the "end of the line," two sentences suffice to inscribe the entire actual and symbolic landscape of his train journey. He mentions Avila, best known for its associations with Saint Theresa of Avila, one of Hemingway's favorite saints, whose famous works (e.g., *The Interior Castle,* her classic meditation on prayer and contemplation) he knew (see Stoneback, "Nominal Country" 121, and *Selected Letters* 811). Her statue, used in processions, is kept in the convent in Avila, where she was prioress. Escorial, the village and the famous monastery, Jake evokes in a phrase (typical of the guidebooks), "gray and long and cold"—and it is exactly that, built of whitish-gray granite, immense (675 feet long), and architecturally cold and austere, as most authorities agree.

240:4 **unfinished church on the edge of the cliff:** With a good period map of Madrid, Jake's route from the Estación del Norte can easily be traced. He climbs "up through the gardens" (the Jardines de Palacio), by "the empty palace" (Palacio Real) and the "unfinished church on the edge of the cliff"—the Catedral de Nuestra Señora de la Almudena, on which construction began in 1895; when Jake passed it in 1925, only the lower part was open for worship. Then, in the "high, hot modern town," the taxi coasts down to the Puerta del Sol, the Gateway of the Sun. The same

Baedeker's guide to Spain that Hemingway owned describes the Puerta del Sol as "the largest and most animated plaza in Madrid" and notes that it "derives its name from an old gateway, which . . . commanded a view of the *rising* sun" (*Spain and Portugal* 61; emphasis added). In the few short pages allotted to Madrid, Hemingway does not have room to evoke in great detail, and name, its landmarks. More important than the exact identification of Hemingway's unnamed landmarks, in this case, is the economy with which he sketches a symbolic landscape. Climbing up through the garden (suggesting the recovery of innocence, redemption?), he passes the "empty palace" (symbol of postwar chaos, bankrupt monarchies, and the rise of dictatorship?) and the "unfinished church." First, we should note that the unfinished church functions as a metaphor that is both theologically exact—since the Church is regarded in most accounts as "unfinished" until the Parousia, the Second Coming, when Christ is united with the body of his followers, his Church—and suggestive of Jake's relationship to his Church as unfinished, though his pilgrimage continues, as such pilgrimages must. Then we must see the location of this actual church building—on the edge of the cliff—and recall the pervasive pattern of edge imagery, with variations throughout the novel that point to and increasingly clarify Jake's situation and the novel's deepest concerns (see, e.g., 237:33). Readers who may not yet be fully convinced that Hemingway so carefully constructs his edge motif will want to consider carefully that this key phrase—"the empty palace and the unfinished church on the edge of the cliff"—was added in Hemingway's final revision, *after* the manuscript, *after* the typescript, in the last phase before the published text (see Hinkle, "Dear Mr. Scribner" 59). The Church (i.e., not just the building, but the communion of believers), then, may be poised on the edge, unfinished; and it may be challenged by its proximity to and juxtaposition with the "high, hot modern town," but it is still, and always, under construction—as is Jake's pilgrimage, his vision, his life. With such knowledge, it is a smooth ride to the Puerta del Sol, the Gateway of the Rising Sun, which signifies more than just heliophilia and the abiding earth, since the sun, in Christian iconography, is an emblem of the Son, the symbol of Christ (Metford 234). This *paysage moralisé,* sketched in two sentences, paints the symbolic landscape of the entire novel in miniature. And it serves as the penultimate sign—the last is Jake's assertion five pages later that "Some people have God. . . . Quite a lot" (245:20)—that *The Sun Also Rises* is a profoundly religious, exact, and exactingly Christian novel. And the symbolic landscape continues through the last motion of the novel, as Jake turns onto the "Gran Via" (see 247:11).

240:7 **San Jeronimo:** This is the street of Saint Jerome (c. 342–420), monk, writer, and Doctor of the Church, known for his great passion and sarcastic wit. In his famous dream that intensified his devoutness, he was self-accused of preferring literature to religion. In his writing, he was known for bringing "topographical material to bear on the interpretation of the sacred text" (Cross 719). In art, he is often depicted in a cave with a lion at his feet, holding the stone that is the "sign of his voluntary penance"—a good thing, one Renaissance pope said, for without such penance this passionate writer and sarcastic wit so beset with temptations of the flesh "could scarcely be considered a saint" (Farmer 224–25). Perhaps the shops on Saint Jerome's namesake street here, with awnings down and windows shuttered, suggest his famous cave. Cartography may tend toward exactitude in Hemingway, but symbolic landscape always matters more than mere accurate description (see 77:22–31, 78:6–7). Jake—with his passion and sarcastic wit, his love of literature mixed up with his love of religion, his penchant for blending topography with sacred text, his temptations of the flesh, his penance after the fiesta—seems rather like a Saint Jerome figure, for, as Hemingway often reminded us, there are great depths in his writerly iceberg; what we get from his work is the "measure" of what we bring "to the reading," and, as he said in his Nobel Prize address, "things may not be immediately discernible" in his writing, but when we understand his "degree of alchemy," things will be "quite clear" (Bruccoli 120, 196).

240:10 **HOTEL MONTANA:** *Montaña,* of course, signifies mountain, but nothing about this cheap hotel (no Hotel Montana is listed in the many 1920s guidebooks I have consulted, not even those that list the cheapest pensiones) is elevated. In the manuscript, Hemingway called it "a cheap hotel" (*Facsimile* 2:595). The elevator doesn't work; the maid is "sullen"; the proprietress is "very fat" and oily haired; and the humor of the scene, based on cross-language tourist phrasebook exchange, is hackneyed and not terribly funny (although Jake's translations—"rigidly selectioned," "upbringal of my bags"—serve their comic purpose and remind us how precisely Jake hears and responds to everything that is said, a useful reminder just before his last dialogue with Brett). Readers concerned with the spurious notion of a pattern of Spain-France contrasts (with France always on the downside of the comparison) should consider the scene carefully. But that is not Hemingway's purpose, since he does not construct such a pattern (which matters only to the critics who, in defiance of textual evidence, have invented it). The importance of the scene lies in the way it stresses Brett's "trouble"—she's stuck in a cheap hotel with no money—and in the comic relief before the tension-filled conversation with Brett.

241:20 **she kissed me:** This is the first kiss since early in the novel, in Paris, before Brett went off to San Sebastián with Cohn (see 65:3). Then, Jake noted, "we kissed"; here Jake emphasizes, twice in the same sentence, "*she* kissed *me*" (emphasis added). Hemingway had originally written, "I kissed her" in the manuscript, but several of the changes made to this scene deemphasize the physical contact and increase Jake's sense of distance (*Facsimile* 2:598–99). Of course, as a loyal friend summoned to help a friend "in trouble," he holds her, comforting her.

241:30 **damn good for him:** It is difficult to assess precisely Jake's tone in this hotel-room scene, generally, and in this particular exchange. It amounts to echoic dialogue that resonates with what Brett said when she returned from her fling in San Sebastián with Cohn: "I rather thought it would be good for him" (see 83:33). And Jake's sarcastic response then—"You might take up social service" (84:1)—informs his response here. In fact, in this two-page hotel-room scene there are twelve instances where Jake makes a one- or two-word response, and five silent nonresponses, to things Brett says. Tone is everything, and Jake's responses throughout the scene range from the matter-of-fact to the curt to the ironic. What Jake *says* does not necessarily correspond with what he *does* in this scene—he holds her close and feels her trembling smallness, her crying, as any loyal friend would do.

242:16–17 **didn't have a sou:** Reference to a former French coin of small denomination, this common phrase (even in English) is the equivalent, as the context makes clear, of saying, "I didn't have a penny." Readers inclined to judge Brett harshly, and there are many of them, should note that though she has no money, she refuses Romero's attempt to give her "a lot of money," saying she has plenty and would not "take his money." This point of Brett's honor serves as yet another reminder that she is not in any sense a prostitute, as some commentators have argued (see 17:26, 33:6, 190:32–33).

242:24 **Gib:** This is common British conversational usage for Gibraltar, the small British enclave and crown colony near the southernmost tip of Spain. Since 1704 a crucial military installation controlling the Strait of Gibraltar, the key to the Mediterranean, Gibraltar has long been a contentious issue between the British and Spanish governments.

243:2 **wiped out that damned Cohn:** Although it seems strange and contrary to the felt time of the narrative, Brett was with Cohn much longer than she was with Romero.

243:9–10 **one of these bitches:** This passage harks back to Jake's conversation with Montoya, when they agree about "this Grand Hotel business," about the women who collect and ruin young bullfighters (172:12–13), as well as to Jake's conversation with Brett shortly thereafter, when she keeps saying she's a "goner" and can't help herself even though, as she says three times, she feels "such a bitch" (184:12). Thus the overall context requires the reader to ask, in response to Brett's repeated assertion here that she won't "be one of these bitches that ruins children," but hasn't she already been "one of those bitches," hasn't she already collected and ruined Romero? We know what Montoya's answer would be, but we cannot be absolutely certain of Jake's response.

243:30 **the bill had been paid:** Several questions are raised by the fact that Romero has paid Brett's hotel bill. Is this cheap hotel the place where they stayed together? If so, why such a cheap place when he had a "lot of money"? When she sent him away, where did he go? Is he still in Madrid?

243:32 **Palace Hotel:** They go to the Palace, long one of the luxury hotels of Spain; book their berths on the Sud Express (the night train, which means they will be back in Paris the next day); and go into the hotel bar for martinis. Affected by the "wonderful gentility" of a fine hotel bar, where bartenders are counted among the only "polite" people left, Jake and Brett politely conduct a tense conversation, punctuated by martinis (inscribed in the text six times as three rounds are consumed), which stand in as an emblem of good manners. Brett tries hard not to talk about Romero, and Jake tries hard not to talk about God, after Brett's dismissal of God (see 245:19–22). At each key juncture, the martinis come to the rescue at a tense moment. Brett tells Jake to think about the fact that she was in school in Paris when Romero was born. Jake replies sarcastically: "Anything you want me to think about it?" Martinis are ordered. Jake reminds her that she wasn't going to talk about it, that she'll "lose it" if she talks "about it."

245:2–3 **bung-o:** "Bung-o," or "bung-ho," according to the *OED*, is an "exclamation used at parting or as a drinking toast" that appeared in the mid-1920s. (Again the *OED* and Hemingway serve each other well and his role on the cutting edge of usage is confirmed, since the second-earliest example given by the *OED* is from *The Sun Also Rises*.) Perhaps Jake's more emphatic and quite rare exclamatory reply—how many times in the entire novel does tight-lipped, understated Jake say anything with an exclamation point?—"Bung-o!" suggests that his usage is both a drinking toast and an "exclamation used" at *parting,* at the farewell scene where he essentially says: Goodbye, Brett. (She is going back to Mike; Jake is going home, back to work.)

245:16–17 **deciding not to be a bitch:** Along with the God statements in the following lines (see next entry) and the last sentence of the novel (see 247:17), this is surely one of the novel's most memorable and frequently cited lines. Nearly four decades of student reactions lead me to believe that it stirs up more disagreement among readers than any other single line. In brief, most readers either buy into the line, reading it straight as a sign of a certain quality of moral fineness and genuine renunciation, or they see it as glib rationalization of a situation that was impossible for Brett—letting her hair grow long, becoming "more womanly," and ending her promiscuity, which she would surely have to do if she married or even lived with a bullfighter. Renunciation or rationalization? For many years, I have surveyed readers on this question—sometimes on tests, sometimes in class discussion—and the overwhelming majority, about 70 percent, have been very hard on Brett, insisting she's more or less still a "bitch" and her so-called renunciation is really just rationalization of her own needs and desires. And the vast majority of these unforgiving readers tend to be women, while men usually fall into the other camp, willing to see Brett's renunciation as genuine, as sacrifice and self-denial, as doing the right thing for moral reasons. At this point, I ask, why does it have to be either/or, renunciation *or* rationalization—why can't it partake of both modes of conduct, mixed, inextricably bound up with each other? When I point out that Brett, although she freely admits to her bitchery earlier, may have genuinely *decided* not to be a bitch, and the very fact of *deciding* something, exercising her will and power of choice, represents a moral advance over her earlier stance of helplessness, volitionlessness, and inability to help herself or stop things from happening (see 183:16), and when I note that she *does* refuse Romero's money, that she *does* send him away—if we grant her credibility—some readers in the unforgiving camp come over from the either-or category to the either-and-both category. But not many. I have the greatest respect for the reactions of first-time readers, the gut feelings of casual readers who read for *story* only, who read to sort out their feelings for characters, good and bad, and to cheer when these characters get what they deserve (in Brett's case, they seem to think, that would be Mike and more of the same old promiscuity). Yet, on balance, this conclusion of many first-time readers (and more than a few seasoned commentators) seems rather severe, too hard on Brett. I am willing to grant Brett the authenticity of what she says here, a certain genuine decency and self-abnegation. It may be "pretty to think so," but there is more evidence for this conclusion than there is for Brett's might-have-been proposal in the final lines, which Jake finds "pretty" to think.

245:19–20 **instead of God. . . . Some people have God:** This is surely one of the best-known bits of dialogue in American literature. Unfortunately, all too many readers hear and remember only Brett's statement: "It's sort of what we have instead of God." We must settle here for a brief look at one misreading of this passage that is emblematic of the misdirected thrust of much Hemingway criticism, as reflected by the appallingly misleading editorial commentary in one of the most influential anthologies of American literature for the last fifty years: *The American Tradition in Literature.* The editors develop in their introduction to Hemingway their primary theme—that Hemingway's work is always about the courage with which we face death. Then, almost as an aside, and certainly a non sequitur, but presented as a universally recognized truth that summarizes Hemingway's life and work, we are told this: "Lady Brett knew the code: 'It's sort of what we have *instead* of God'" (Perkins and Perkins 1195). The irresponsibility of this remark—as slippery as greased okra—is terrifying, if we still believe that literary criticism is more about illumination than obfuscation, if we think of the millions of students and teachers who have formed their views of Hemingway from this volume—and it is *millions,* since the remark has remained in the anthology, unchanged, for fifty years now. It is irresponsible in various ways, from the insidious unacknowledged addition of emphasis to that "*instead,*" to contextual distortion, to the misrepresentation of the character of Brett and, by implication, Jake. At best, we might say of Brett's renunciation of Romero—which is the "it" that Hemingway's text refers to, a fact also distorted in the context—that it's sort of what *she* has instead of God. Jake's response, which many critics conveniently overlook, is that some people indeed have God: "Quite a lot."

Clearly, as the novel takes pains to demonstrate (in the surface text, as in the subtext and the symbolic landscape), Jake is one of these people. When Jake says this, Brett replies: "He never worked very well with me." In the manuscript, Jake tells Brett: "There's lots of time yet" (*Facsimile* 2:612). Hemingway changed Jake's rather preacherly statement to an offer of another martini, no doubt because he doesn't want to open the possibility of Brett accusing Jake—again (see 209:7)—of proselytizing, trying to convert her to his faith.

The other piece of slippery reading in the anthology's one-liner typifies another familiar wrenching of the novel—Brett knows the code? Brett, who from beginning to end is shown to be careless and disorderly and promiscuous, in every sense of the term? Brett, who is judged across a spectrum ranging from the smallest detail—flicking cigarette ashes on Jake's rug—to larger symbolic forms of dishonor—discarding the bull's ear given to her, a symbol of Romero's art in the bullring, leaving it in a hotel-room drawer with cigarette stubs? This Brett—who gulps and cannot taste the fine champagne that the count urges her to drink slowly, who cannot comprehend what he has to say about values and being "always in love"—she knows the code? If so, it is an odd code, and it's not Jake's, not Montoya's, not the count's, not Hemingway's. In this acute novel of manners, Brett's behavior is mostly mannerism, when it is not blind promiscuity—at least until the end. One of the main thrusts of the novel is to differentiate between Jake's character and behavior and Brett's, to draw distinctions—as this scene so clearly does—to scrutinize and discard Brett's glib "one of us" rubric. All this is not to say that she is not engaging, compelling, and one of the most vivid characters in our literature; or that I would not buy her a martini in Madrid: that is precisely the problem that drives the action of the novel. (But I would not take her fishing.) Jake, however, does take her to church (almost like fishing) twice, and here, in his largely disremembered response to her dismissal of God, he chooses not to proselytize again, but he does witness for his faith.

245:32 **Botin's:** As Jake tells the reader, Botín's "is one of the best restaurants in the world"; it is also one of the oldest restaurants in the world, having been in operation since 1725. Although there are widely scattered restaurants that claim earlier dates than 1725—in England and China, for example—Botín's, as one authority notes, "is in the *Guinness Book of World Records* as the oldest restaurant continuously under the ownership and management of the same family" (Mandel 83). Another source states that "Casa Botín" is "the oldest continuous restaurant in the world" and notes its "culinary tradition of country fare that remains unmatched" (Boreth 97). The actual "World Record" certificate reads: "Guinness Book of Records. Earliest Restaurant. Casa Botín. Opened 1725." Although some contemporary guidebooks mistakenly suggest that the restaurant owes its fame to Hemingway, who also alluded to Casa Botín in *Death in the Afternoon*—"I would rather dine on suckling pig at Botin's than sit and think of casualties my friends have suffered" (104)—Botín's was celebrated long before Jake had to ask the Palace Hotel barman for directions to the restaurant. Nineteenth- and early-twentieth-century guidebooks (Baedekers, for example) recognized it as one of the best typically Spanish restaurants. The specialties of the house have long been, as they are still listed on the menu today, roast suckling pig (*cochinillo asado*) and roast baby lamb (*cordero asado*). Anyone who has been to Casa Botín will come away with a strong sense of history or tradition and authenticity, from the superb specialties cooked in the eighteenth-century cast-iron and tiled wood-fired stove and oven to the aroma of *place* that lingers in memory, the aura that declares: this is the real old thing. (Thirty-three years, alas, after this writer last dined at Botín's that is what I remember best—and the taste of that roast suckling pig.)

Hemingway's selection of Botín's for the final meal of a novel in which the *food-scape* is an essential part of his symbolic landscape is a perfect choice. Casa Botín resonates with and underlines Hemingway's concerns with taste and tradition, sense of place and history, and what he called the "real old stuff" that has been handed down "intact from the old days" (see 19:16 and 97:3). And even if Jake is redundant in praising the "young suckling pig" (all suckling pig is young), even if he has to ask directions to the *earliest* and one of the best restaurants in the world, this does not suggest he's lost—rather, it signifies his role as pilgrim on a pilgrimage who knows where he has to go, seeks exact directions, and learns as he goes. Botín's is the perfect place for Jake to give his final summing up of all the things he likes to do (see 246:10).

246:3 **rioja alta:** The Rioja wine district is in the Logroño area in the north of Spain, southwest of Pamplona, and the best wines of the district are the *riojas altas,* from the upper Rioja. The growing conditions are similar to those of Bordeaux, and the wine making follows traditional French methods—"not surprisingly," Alexis Lichine notes, "since French heads and hands did the work . . . [in the early twentieth century after] phylloxera had destroyed the vineyards of Bordeaux but had not yet reached Rioja. The flood of the French into the Rioja in those days has left its mark" (408). Thus *riojas altas* are often said to resemble fine Bordeaux, and Jake's taste in his choice of wine to accompany the roast suckling pig is impeccable.

246:10 **I like to do a lot of things:** In the manuscript version this passage was more extensive; Jake actually listed many things he liked: "I like to eat and I like to drink and I like to lead a quiet life and I like to read books. I like horse races and I like bull fights and I like to fish and I like to eat and drink." When Brett says she likes to sail, Jake says: "I like to sail too" (*Facsimile* 2:613). It's a nice list for the reader to have—especially that reiteration of the "quiet life" Jake likes—but Hemingway must have recognized that he was *telling* what he had already *shown*, probably from a closing recapitulatory impulse common in conventional narrative, and perhaps with overmuch justification of the most outrageous proposition that the novel asks its readers to accept: that a man who cannot have sex can be so happy, can love the world, and can love living in it.

247:1 **I'll finish this:** Everybody remembers Jake's closing words, but few remember this, his next-to-last sentence. He's talking about his glass of wine, of course, but the sentence resonates with the *unfinished* church image a few pages before and perhaps suggests that he'll *finish* his pilgrimage, that he'll *finish* what he's started (see 247:11). Even more, it may suggest, as his last sentence (below) confirms, that he's *finished* with Brett (i.e., as anything more than an old friend).

247:8 **Brett moved close:** Another illustration of the structural principles of Hemingway's fiction, this closing taxi scene echoes two earlier taxi rides. In the first, Georgette the prostitute cuddles against Jake and makes her moves (see 15:19, 15:28). In the second, the motion of the cab jolts Brett and Jake "close together," and they are both "miserable" in a scene informed by frustrated sexual tensions (see 25:12, 25:18). Here Brett moves close to Jake—but no one is "miserable." In all three scenes, Jake puts his arm around the woman next to him, but here, as Jake puts it, "she rested against me comfortably," not miserably.

247:11 **Gran Via:** A major new road, still unfinished in the 1920s. As the last route or street that is named in a novel that has paid close attention to routes and streets (see, e.g., 77:22–31, 78:6–7, and 240:7), it demands special attention, especially given its name. *Vía*, of course, means in Spanish "way," "street," "route"—thus Great Way or Grand Street. But *vía* also means, in other standard Spanish dictionary definitions, "calling" and "spiritual life." And as the *OED* reminds us, "via" has standard meanings in English, too, from a name for one of the great Roman roads to the many uses of "via" to indicate a spiritual way—Via Crucis ("Way of the Cross"), Via Dolorosa (the dolorous or "sad road" that Christ follows to his Crucifixion, generalized as any difficult route or experience), Via Media (the "middle way"), and the Via Negativa (the Christian mystic's "approach to God in which his nature is held so to transcend man's understanding that no positive statements can be made about it; the way to union with God in which the soul leaves behind" the senses and the intellect—see *OED*), associated with San Juan de la Cruz (Saint John of the Cross), the Spanish mystic named by Hemingway as one of his "literary forebears" from whom he "learned the most" (Bruccoli 118). "Via" is also associated with pilgrimage routes, particularly the Santiago de Compostela route, often called the Way of Saint James—or the *Great Way*. The symbolic landscape sketched in miniature in the unfinished-church passage as Jake enters Madrid a few pages earlier (240:4) is extended and resolved here when, having earlier passed through the Puerta del Sol (the Gateway of the Rising Sun), he turns out onto the *unfinished* Gran Vía. (And the last thing he says before making that turn is "I'll finish this"—see 247:1). Jake's difficult yet joyful via includes attributes of several of the spiritual vias mentioned above, and his "great way" here may ultimately turn him northwesterly toward the pilgrim destination of Santiago. And if the reader chooses to translate *Gran Vía* as "Grand Street," that will work, too, if it reminds us of what we learned in the Pamplona cathedral when he was praying and talking about his grand religion and how he hoped to become a better Catholic (see 97:18–20). And he does make his pilgrim's progress—praying, confessing, going to Mass with increasing frequency as his pilgrimage and the novel move along. Cartography is sometimes exact in Hemingway, since the lay of the land and the way of the roads always signifies, but it is more often symbolic, more concerned with *paysage moralisé* than with road maps, more about finding one's way spiritually than taking the best walking or taxi route—from the rue Saint-Jacques to the Gran Vía (see 77:22–31, 78:6–7, and 240:7).

247:12–13 **damned good time together:** Most readers assume, correctly I think, that Brett here means something more than "Oh Jake, we could have had such great sex together if only you weren't wounded." Surely this is not something she would say to Jake. And while her conduct with Cohn, then Romero, might suggest that her life is just the kind of "nymphomaniacs [sic] holiday" that Jake and Montoya discuss when they talk about the Grand Hotel tourists who collect bullfighters and could "wreck" a kid like Romero (see 171:17 and 171:30), the depiction of Jake and Brett's relationship early in the novel suggests a genuine mutual depth and intensity of feeling—call it love—that indicates that she is here saying they would have been a great couple. Jake's response, as slow and deliberate and formal as the uniformed traffic policeman's signals and the decelerated taxi, tells us exactly what he thinks about Brett's statement.

247:14 **mounted policeman:** It is difficult to envision a mounted policeman (i.e., in the usual sense of a policeman on horseback) directing traffic with a baton at a busy intersection. A search of historical archives has turned up no evidence that this would occur, and common sense, horse sense, and historical evidence all suggest that the policeman is mounted on a platform in the middle of the intersection. The obvious sexual imagery of the passage, with the *mounted* cop's *raised baton*, may require no commentary—except to note that the raised baton means "stop" or "slow down," and the slowdown motion of the taxi presses Brett against Jake, as he formulates his response to Brett, which also means "slow down" or "stop."

247:17 **Isn't it pretty:** The first version of this final sentence in the manuscript was "It's nice as hell to think so." Then Hemingway changed that to "Isn't it nice to think so," thus arriving halfway toward the exactly right tone, with the change from "It's" to "Isn't it" (*Facsimile* 2:616). With the final change to the acutely ironic "pretty," Hemingway renders precisely Jake's disagreement with what Brett has just said. It is an ironic distance he did not possess at the beginning of the book, where in spite of his wound he still almost pleads with Brett: "Couldn't we just live together?" She replies that she would just "*tromper*" him "with everybody," that is, cheat, deceive, betray him (55:13–22). The earned vision of the book, for Jake, the knowledge reflected in his tone here—something he could not have said to Brett in the early chapters of the novel—is that even if he had not been wounded things would have been impossible with Brett—love would be impossible. And he has also learned, or confirmed, that we must—in Robert Penn Warren's words—"try to love so well the world that we may believe, in the end, in God" (*Collected Poems* 233). Was there ever another character, another man, with so many reasons not to love, to believe, who believes and loves the world as well as Jake?

What's in a Landscape—Actual and Symbolic

L'Île Saint-Louis

Confusion regarding the walk around l'île Saint-Louis in *The Sun Also Rises* prevails in critical and popular lore—for example, I heard knowledgeable Parisian walking-tour guides say in both the 1970s and 1980s that Hemingway was *lost, confused* about l'île and the river, and that no reader could tell from his text which way Bill and Jake are walking (one guide even read from the text and threw up his hands in Gallic dismay at the impossibility of following the description)—as well as in various scholarly commentaries on this passage. In William Balassi's unpublished commentary we read this:

> The text here is confusing. Quai d'Orleans faces the Left Bank, but Mme. Lecomte's restaurant is 'on the far side of the island,' that is, facing the right bank. It seems likely that Jake and Bill walked east [sic] along Quai d'Anjou past Pont (bridge) Marie [a geographical impossibility] where it becomes Quai de Bourbon, then around the western tip of the island, where the street name changes to Quai d'Orleans, then east to the Pont de la Tournelle, where the street name changes again to the Quai de Béthune. Between 1923 and 1928, the Pont de la Tournelle was being rebuilt, during which time pedestrians crossed the river using a temporary wooden bridge (Fitch 98). It is from this temporary bridge that Jake and Bill look down-river at Notre Dame. (Balassi, "Glossary" 77:4; see explanatory note in preface)

I will address the errors—aside from the obvious error, perhaps a typo in an unfinished manuscript, designating "east" where it should be "west"—in this description in a moment, but for now I want to stress that this description indicates a *counterclockwise half*-circle of the island. I do not know if the unpublished commentary cited above reflects the settled conclusions of James Hinkle, whose voluminous unpublished research materials were the foundation of Balassi's manuscript. I do know that I shared with Hinkle a detailed knowledge of Paris and a deep respect for Hemingway's sense of detail, his exactitude of description. We also tended to practice a similar mode of historical research, stressing precise details regarding location garnered from sources published in the 1920s. And I also know that for years we *shared* the view that this passage was confusing; we debated Jake and Bill's route, drawing maps of l'île on restaurant napkins and Hemingway Conference programs; we sent each other postcards of l'île from Paris with dotted lines and arrows suggesting possible routes for this famous but confusing walk. I also sent, in my capacity as advisory editor to both Hinkle's and Balassi's prospective volumes on *The Sun Also Rises,* some commentary on the île passage that I did not regard as conclusive to both Hinkle and Balassi. Since I am unable to locate copies of that commentary, dating as far back as the 1980s, I am unable to reconstruct exactly my early views of this textual crux. But I do know that before the International Hemingway Conference in Paris in 1994, I was somewhat unsure of Bill and Jake's route, though I had consistently argued (with Jim Hinkle, Mike Reynolds, and others who noticed the apparent textual problem) that Hemingway would not say they *circled* the island if they only *half-circled* it. Then, having agreed to lead a walking tour of l'île for the Hemingway Conference, I spent the better part of a week while *living* on the island walking the island in every possible way, paying such close attention to the text, reading it aloud over and over on the quais, comparing the published text with the manuscript version, that some of my island neighbors were curious about my activity, circling the island again and again with a book and a stopwatch in hand, reading aloud, timing my movements; and one café waiter even decided that I was a "mad scientist"—until I informed him it was just Hemingway research. In short, just before I led that walking tour in 1994 I believe I came up with the answer to this perennially confusing textual crux. But before I explain, the problem should be clarified, first, with a line-by-line, sentence-by-sentence comparison of the published text (passages designated T) with the original manuscript (passages designated M—all from *Facsimile* 1:221–22). Sentences that are the same in both versions will be skipped.

77:2–3
T: "We walked along . . . island."
M: "We walked under the trees along the river on the Quai D'Orlean [sic] side (and then around)." Note: Words in parentheses indicate manuscript cross-outs. Here we note that both text and manuscript place them, immediately after leaving the restaurant, on the far side of the island. Hemingway's cross-out—"and then around"—indicates his concern to be precise and also suggests a clockwise circling of the island.

77:4–5
T: "Across the river . . . torn down."
M: "They were tearing down the old houses across the river." It is still impossible

to tell on which side of the river the house demolition is occurring, although the immediately preceding cross-out ("around") suggests it is the Right Bank (see also following entry).

77:7

T: "'They would,' Bill said."

M: "Damn shame." The disdain and dismay that both Bill and Jake feel over the demolition of historical houses remains the same in text and manuscript, but the addition of the dialogue tag makes it clear that it is Jake who has the local knowledge, who knows what and why they're destroying. Although there was in 1925 some demolition of buildings (but not all old *houses*) *possibly* visible in three directions "across the river" from various points on the island, the most striking destruction was occurring on the Right Bank, looking directly across the river (north) from the western tip of l'île at the neighborhood just south of the church of Saint-Gervais, described in the 1927 Blue Guide as "a picturesque old quarter which is fast disappearing beneath the housebreaker's hammer" (Muirhead and Monmarché, *Paris* 40).

77:8

T: "We walked on and circled the island."

M: "(Then) We walked on up and around the Island and up the other side." The key revision here is the introduction of *circled,* to replace the vague "around" of the manuscript. Also note the imprecise use of "up" in the manuscript version—if they're walking two different directions "around" the island, how can they both be "up"? Hemingway's revisions, both in the manuscript (e.g., cross-outs) and in the process that led to the published text, indicate his concern for precision and his final decision to use "up" and "down" consistently in terms of the river's flow— upstream or downstream.

77:8–10

T: "The river . . . the bridge."

M: "There were lights on the river and a *bateau mouche* went by, all bright, going fast and quiet up and out of sight under the bridge." The substantial revisions to this sentence are revealing. Anyone who has walked along the Seine, especially on l'île, will recognize that sudden sense of illumination that occurs when a quiet but dazzling *bateau-mouche* that you probably didn't even notice until it was right beneath you on the river passes, throwing everything into brilliant relief. This is clearer in the manuscript sentence, but only as *felt, remembered* fact, available only to the reader who has *experienced* it. In the published sentence, Hemingway strives for the "sequence of motion and fact" that makes "the emotion" (*Death in the Afternoon* 2) and renders it more available to the reader who has not physically experienced it. The last part of the sentence remains the same and indicates Hemingway's choice of upstream/downstream denotations of direction. Manuscript and text indicate the same—the only possible—location on the island as the boat passes: they have almost *circled* the island, walking clockwise around the western and the eastern end, and are on the quai de Béthune, alongside the southern channel of the Seine, in which boats move *upstream;* they watch the boat go *up* and disappear under the pont de Sully, and as they continue walking west on the quai de Béthune they see Notre-Dame *downstream* as they approach the bridge they will cross.

77:10–11

T: "Down the river was Notre Dame . . . sky."

M: ("Up the river"—cross-out) "Down the river was Notre Dame squatting ("black"—cross-out) ("dusky"—cross-out) ("dark"—insert and cross-out) ("in the dusky night") against the night sky." We note that this is the most revised sentence in the island passage, a fact that underlines the centrality of Notre-Dame to the scene and Hemingway's elaborate concern to get it right.

77:11–14

T: "We crossed . . . Notre Dame."

M: "We crossed to the left bank by the foot bridge from the Quai de Bethune and looked down the river at Notre Dame." Hemingway adds the notation that the bridge they cross is "wooden" and adds five keywords—"and *stopped* on the bridge" (emphasis added)—to further intensify the prospect, the vision of Notre-Dame; that is, they don't just casually glance at the cathedral as they cross the bridge—they *stop* to take it all in.

77:14–15

T: "Standing on the bridge . . . shadows."

M: "From the bridge the island was dark and ("the houses"—insert) high ("against the sky"—insert) and the trees shadowy." Aside from the changes in rhythm, the sentence is substantially the same, with the added emphasis of "standing" (i.e., stopping on the bridge).

77:16

T: "It's pretty grand . . . back."

M: "It's pretty fine isn't it?" Bill said. "God I love to get back." Hemingway's revision intensifies the emotion contained in Bill's statement by transforming the question into assertion, and replacing "fine" with "grand," thus perhaps elevating the category of appreciation from the aesthetic ("fine") to the spiritual ("grand"). (Later in the novel, Hemingway would add to Jake's prayer scene in Pamplona his view of Catholicism as "a grand religion": see 97:21.)

77:17–18

T: "We leaned . . . big bridges."

M: The first fourteen words of this sentence are exactly the same. Then Hemingway begins a new sentence: "Then across toward the left bank and down to the lights of the big bridges." But there are no "big bridges" downstream; the big bridges, the pont de Sully, the pont d'Austerlitz, and the railroad viaduct are *upstream*. Thus throughout this scene the manuscript version contains directional confusion that is precisely clarified in the published text. In the final version of this sentence it is clear that *after* Bill and Jake look downriver and meditate on the sight of Notre-Dame, they look *upstream* toward the big bridges. All the bridges downstream are small. The next two sentences about the smooth quiet river are substantially the same in manuscript and text, although Hemingway deleted two words, having originally written "Right below us." Finally, he added to the published text the two sentences about the man and the girl on the bridge, thus providing another echo, or paired scene, that resonates with the boy and the girl on the raft during Jake's swimming scene in San Sebastián (235): both scenes introduce the shadow, for Jake, of romance and sexuality into a landscape of natural and spiritual serenity.

In sum, then, we learn from the study of the differences in the manuscript and published versions of the island sequence that Hemingway was concerned, in revision, to make his landscape signals of route and direction more precise and accurate. Two explanations can be offered for the confusion or lack of clarity evident in the manuscript. First, as is well known, Hemingway wrote the manuscript version very quickly, and at least one scholar has convincingly demonstrated, in a detailed study of the day-by-day writing of the manuscript, that Hemingway speeded up and intensified his writing sessions during the composition of this chapter (Balassi, "How It Probably Was," see especially 137–42). Yet another explanation, so obvious it could easily be overlooked, is the fact plainly indicated on the cover of the manuscript notebook ("Book III") in which Hemingway wrote this chapter: it was written in Hendaye, in the south of France, a long way from Paris. This notebook indicates that it was written in Hendaye on 12–17 August (except for later chapters written in Paris on 19–20 August). There is ample evidence, not just in this scene but also in the following paragraphs as Jake and Bill continue their walk, and elsewhere, that Hemingway wrote quickly because he knew that when he got back to Paris in a few days, he would have plenty of time to check his Paris scenes for exactitude, to clarify where necessary, and to fill in whatever omitted details he deemed necessary (see also 78:6–7). Hemingway's symbolic landscape, after all, is built from the ground up, from actual landscape.

Given the clarification provided by the manuscript/text analysis above, it would seem that there is only one problem of location and direction to be accounted for: how do Jake and Bill *circle* the island, coming around the east end from the quai d'Anjou to the quai de Béthune, when immediately after leaving Madame Lecomte's restaurant on the quai d'Anjou, Hemingway's place-and-direction denotations have them walking, apparently west, on the quai d'Orléans. This is what has puzzled every careful reader who has read the novel against a background of local knowledge of place. As I noted above, James Hinkle, long known as an authority (particularly grounded in close reading and place knowledge) on *The Sun Also Rises,* remained puzzled about this passage, so far as I know, until his death in 1990. In spite of decades of research, he had not made exact sense of or resolved what he thought about this passage; not long before his death, in our last conversation on this matter, in my kitchen over several bottles of French wine, he still resisted my tentative conclusions regarding this walk, which were rooted in what I regarded as the key fact—they *circled* the island. Hinkle's massive collection of three-by-five note cards on every detail of *The Sun Also Rises* is legendary in the scholarly circles of Hemingway studies. Some years after his death, when I undertook this project, one small box of his note cards (all of which are eventually bound for the Hemingway Collection at the John F. Kennedy Library) came into my possession. I glanced at these cards at the time then filed them away, for many were written in his miniscule handwriting and nearly illegible; others cited historical sources and Hemingway biographical and critical sources on which I had my own file of notes (but not *note cards*); still other cards, I was pleased to see, cited my essays on Hemingway. Before sending these cards on to the Hemingway Collection, and after writing the above commentary on the island sequence, I tried my best to read (often with a magnifying glass) every word on every three-by-five card and improvised scrap of paper that pertained to the island passage. In an age when the concept of *research* is often misunderstood or confused with a night spent surfing the Web, when Google is thought by many to be a verb synonymous with *research,* it may be difficult to comprehend that Hinkle had made more than *eighty* note cards on this brief island passage—*eighty* cards on less than *one* page of text, compiled over a period of several decades from many obscure historical sources in English and French. These cards support the view that he never resolved the matter, that, at times, he thought Hemingway had made a place-name error in beginning the notation of the walk on quai d'Orléans rather than quai de Bourbon; or he thought that Jake and Bill descended from the street to the actual riverside quai and walked close to the water rather than on the sidewalks of the street-level quais. He seems to have entertained the notion that they walked partly by the river then turned back and walked at street level. His investigations include historical documentation regarding which trees grew, as Hemingway wrote, "out over the river," and on which parts of the island they did so. His most enduring conception of the walk recorded on these cards, which matches my memory of our conversations and communications over the years, is what he wrote on one card dated 1972: "Ref: Quai Bourbon–Quai

D'Orleans. From Mme. Lecomte's, walk about 30–40 yards west past Pont Marie and, at beginning of Quai Bourbon, descend to walk under trees that grow out over river . . . and go around tip . . . on Quai Bourbon until Pont St Louis . . . then it is Quai d'Orleans to Pont de la Tournelle." That is, all his assumptions point to a route that is a counterclockwise half-circle of the island. On none of the eighty-plus note cards does Hinkle entertain the following clockwise route that I finally concluded had to be Jake and Bill's circling of the island, given the signals of the text and the physical realities of the actual place.

To wit: when Jake and Bill come out of Madame Lecomte's restaurant, their intended destination is the Left Bank and Montparnasse via the rue du Cardinal Lemoine and place Contrescarpe. Thus, quite naturally, they would walk a short distance west (left) from the restaurant and turn south (left) on the rue des Deux Ponts, taking the shortest route to the Left Bank, and because it is the least interesting street on the island, no notation is made of this as they walk "along." Then they come, after two short, dull blocks, to the south side of the island, where—reluctant to leave the beauty and serenity of the island—they make the decision that millions must have made over the centuries, that I have made a hundred times over the past thirty-some years: to walk around the island before leaving it. Thus they turn right (west) on the quai d'Orléans and walk to the western tip of the island. It is a route that comes easily and naturally; Madame Lecomte's restaurant was gone before my time, but I have gone often to Au Franc Pinot, which is in the same approximate location on the north side as Lecomte's and has been there since before the French Revolution, when, as island lore tells it, the teenaged daughter of the proprietor tried to kill Robespierre and she and her whole family were executed. After which I have walked the two short blocks to the south side and turned west on quai d'Orléans, walking around the western tip of the island, noting where Hemingway saw the old houses being torn down on the Right Bank and continuing the clockwise circumnavigation of the island as Hemingway's text indicates until on the quai de Béthune I come to the pont de la Tournelle and, having made a full circle, cross the river. It is an almost irresistible walk through one of the most magical landscapes and riverscapes in the world, and once begun, the island circle must be completed. (Has anyone ever sung the old folk-gospel hymn of the unbroken circle as "Will the *Half*-Circle Be Unbroken?") It should be noted that there is no indication in Hemingway's text of a descent down the steep dark stone steps to the actual waterside, and it is (and was) impossible to circle the island at water level, and undesirable to try at night. As for the trees that grow, as Hemingway says, "out over the river," one walks *under* them whether at street level or at water level. It should also be noted that the dazzling illumination from the *bateaux-mouches* is much more sudden (and quiet) when you walk on the street-level quais, and more dramatic too with the play of the light and the shadows of the trees on the facades of the tall old mansions—one of the great evanescent light shows of the world.

My conclusions regarding the route of Jake and Bill's walk, then, are rooted in historical research and close attention to the signals of the text and the manuscript. And they are also based in *felt* reality, in *lived* experience and local knowledge of an island where I have stayed and sometimes lived for extended periods spread over many years. The proper question to ask here is—why does all this matter? How many people have even noticed this textual crux that I have analyzed in such detail? The answer to the latter question is easy: many readers notice, more than we might suppose. Walking-tour guides and their clients would be one group that notices; Hemingway critics and aficionados are another group that notices, since one of the powerful effects of Hemingway's prose is to compel people to go to the actual places of his fiction and take the walks and do the things that his characters do. And, of the thousands of students to whom I have taught this novel, I am aware of about fifty who have gone to l'île and, text in hand, tried to follow the route. They send postcard reports about their island walk. They take pictures, slides, videos—they often report that they are confused about the exact route and have tried several routes but they generally feel the direction to be clockwise, and they know they must make a complete circle of the island—"because Hemingway said they *circled* the island," one student wrote in a postcard, "and Hemingway means what he says about geography."

But there is another important reason why it matters, why we should know the route of the island walk. If we know that, then we can know what is omitted, what is part of the iceberg, what Jake and Bill actually saw if every detail of their twenty-five minute circumambulation (an average measured time for a reasonably paced stroll) of the island were recorded, and thus we are able to comprehend the symbolic landscape, the *paysage moralisé.* Assuming they turn right (west) off the rue des Deux Ponts, the first historic landmark they see is the library and museum honoring the great Polish poet and patriot Adam Mickiewicz (1798–1855), at 6, quai d'Orléans. Long considered one of the greatest Slavonic and eastern European writers, Mickiewicz was also well known for his fervent Catholicism, articulated particularly in two volumes written in Paris in the 1830s: *Book of the Pilgrimage* (sometimes called *Book of Pilgrims*) and *Pan Tadeusz.* In the 1840s his interests became less literary than mystical, and he was fired from his professorship. When the Crimean War broke out, he went to Constantinople to help raise a regiment of Poles to fight the Russians and died there, from cholera, in 1855. Hemingway, who knew the island and its monuments well and knew European literature well, may have seen an omen in Mickiewicz—his Catholicism, his concern with pilgrimage, and his death in the struggle for freedom from the Russian Empire. And Jake, who knows all the statues—even knows about obscure pharmacists and semaphore inventors, as well as Marshal Ney—would know who Mickiewicz was; and even Bill ("Don't try and fool me on Paris"—see 72:18) would know. And if they forgot, the historical marker on the wall of 6, quai d'Orléans would remind them. Next door (#8) to Mickiewicz lived Jean de la Ville de Mirmont (1886–1914), poet and member of the truly "lost" generation of young French writers killed in World War I. Two doors down (#12) they would see the birthplace of the poet Félix Arvers (1806–1850), poet and dramatist remembered primarily for his famous poem of unrequited love—"Un Secret"—from his *Mes heures perdues* (*My Lost Hours*). Lost hours, lost poets, lost causes—these three landmarks alone would give Jake and Bill ample scope for quiet meditation, from Catholic mysticism to unrequited love to young poets killed in the war, as they "walked along" on the quai d'Orléans.

When they came to the tip of the island, they would see on the Right Bank, along with the old houses being torn down in the foreground, the Church of Saint-Gervais (the roof had collapsed, killing seventy-five worshippers, when a German long-range artillery shell struck the church at 3 P.M. on Good Friday, 1918); and in the background beyond the Hôtel de Ville, the Tour Saint-Jacques, the tower that is all that remains of the major pilgrimage church of Saint-Jacques-la-Boucherie—and Jake, and probably Bill, too, would know that the Tour Saint-Jacques contained iconography of Saint James/Santiago/Saint Jacques and marked the Paris beginning of the pilgrimage route of Saint-Jacques-de-Compostelle (Santiago de Compostela). They would probably also note and know the so-called House of the Centaur in its privileged location on the prow of l'île, at 45, quai de Bourbon. Long famous for its literary associations, before the war it had been the site of a literary and arts salon drawing such figures as Guillaume Apollinaire, Jean Giradoux, Max Jacob, and Pablo Picasso.

Around the west end of l'île, on the quai de Bourbon, they would pass even more landmarks. (It would seem an incontestable statement that there is not a single block on l'île that does not have literary, artistic, religious, or historic significance.) At 19, quai de Bourbon, they might have pondered the fate of the sculptor Camille Claudel (1864–1943), who lived here before she was committed to a psychiatric hospital in 1913 and spent the last thirty years of her life in various asylums. Parisians knew well the tragic story of the talented Camille Claudel, who had studied with Rodin as a teenager, becoming his assistant, confidante, lover, and inspiration. For nearly a decade Claudel was Rodin's mistress and muse before she ended their relationship, as the rumors had it, after an undesired abortion in 1892 and Rodin's refusal to sever his ties to his longtime companion Rose Beuret, mother of his son. Increasingly isolated and unstable, Claudel destroyed much of her best work before she was institutionalized. Her younger (and far more famous) brother, Paul Claudel, also lived at 19, quai de Bourbon. For Jake and Bill (and Hemingway)—that is, for *writers*—Paul Claudel (1868–1955) might be the primary association with this address. By the time of *The Sun Also Rises,* Claudel was widely regarded as the greatest living French writer, and acknowledged as a towering presence in twentieth-century French literature. Even more germane to the novel and this scene is the fact that Claudel was widely praised as the greatest Catholic poet since Dante—"c'est le mysticisme qui fait de lui assurément le plus grand poète catholique depuis Dante" (Tilliette 2). American readers and Hemingway aficionados who do not know about Claudel and may be pleased to regard this great Catholic poet as an obscure figure might wish to consider these facts: (1) Not long after *The Sun Also Rises* was published, Claudel was featured on the cover of *Time* magazine (March 1927); (2) He was also a world-renowned diplomat who was, in 1925–1926, the French ambassador to Japan, and then from 1928 to 1933 the French ambassador to the United States; (3) His work was frequently published in the *Nouvelle Revue française,* to which Hemingway alluded when Jake attended the briefing by the *NRF* "diplomat" in chapter 5 (see 36:8–9); (4) In 1925 alone there were literary conferences devoted to his work held in England, France, and Switzerland. All his work—many volumes of poetry and plays as well as his essays—is centered in and profoundly informed by his Catholicism, his orthodox faith, and his lyrical apprehension of Christian mysticism. His mature conversion experience—in the cathedral of Notre-Dame on Christmas Day, when he was eighteen—is probably the most celebrated conversion (certainly of a *writer,* complete with a historical marker inside the church) in the history of the cathedral. Hemingway may well have read with great interest one of Claudel's several essays that describe this famous conversion, since Hemingway dated his own conversion to Catholicism from the moment—also at age eighteen—when he was wounded on an Italian battlefield (see Stoneback, "Nominal Country"). Like Claudel and other well-known Catholic writers he admired (e.g., G. K. Chesterton), Hemingway accepted the orthodox faith and discipline of the Catholic Church, even if he was, as he said, a "very dumb Catholic" (Baker, *Life Story* 185, 333). There were, of course, Catholic writers he did not admire; and Hemingway would resist—as he put it in a manuscript fragment that was most likely written during or soon after his September 1925 sojourn in Chartres when he renamed *The Sun Also Rises* and began his process of revision (see "Title" entry above)—"deadening the glory" with "fancy writing" like "that sloppy brained convert Huysmanns [sic]"; and he would not write "Catholic journalism" like Hilaire Belloc ("On Cathedrals" 2). J. K. Huysmans (1848–1907) was associated, at first, with hyperaestheticism, decadence, and occultism—through such works as the popular *Against the Grain,* the 1922 edition of which was in Hemingway's library (Reynolds, *Hemingway's Reading* 140). Huysmans's later work, after his adult conversion to Catholicism, was profoundly and devoutly Catholic (e.g., *The Cathedral* 1898). Hilaire Belloc (1870–1953), one of the most prolific writers of his time, with more than 140 books to his credit, including poetry, travel writing, children's literature, biographies, and historical and political studies, was probably best known as a writer of Catholic apologetics—or in Hemingway's phrase, "Catholic journalism." An orthodox defender of the faith, his widely known watchword—"Europe is the faith and the faith is Europe"—was repeatedly expressed in such books as *Europe and Faith* (1920). He was so closely involved with Chesterton's Catholic vision and writing that George Bernard Shaw famously christened them as one mythical creature—the "Chesterbelloc." Chesterton, it will be recalled, was alluded to by Hemingway as early as 1924, when in his short story "The Three-Day Blow," Nick Adams and Bill wish Chesterton was there with them in northern Michigan: "We'd take him fishing" (*Complete Short Stories* 88). And Belloc plays a role in the most neglected subtext of *The Sun Also Rises,* concerned not just with Catholicism but also quite specifically with Catholic *writers.* In the original manuscript version, Hemingway tells a three-page anecdote about how Braddocks misidentifies Aleister Crowley as Hilaire Belloc. Braddocks tells Jake that Belloc is "absolutely through" due to his "religious intolerance" (*Facsimile* 1:62). Of course, in a classic values-inversion sequence, the joke is on Braddocks, who gets it all wrong, since the man he identifies as Belloc, probably the most famous Catholic writer of his era, is really Aleister Crowley (1875–1947), probably the most famous satanist, occultist, Christian-baiting, Catholic-hating pseudomystic, sexual revolutionary, and drug addict of his day. Hemingway liked this anecdote so much that, even though he cut it from *The Sun Also Rises,* he used it decades later in *A Moveable Feast* (85–88). Hemingway, then, was well aware of Belloc's Catholic identity and his writing, which is replete with pilgrimage motifs and allusions, evocations of cathedrals, the urgency of belief, and other matters that resonate with *The Sun Also Rises.* That Hemingway probably intended an even more developed Belloc subtext is suggested by the fact that in the manuscript where Jake talks about how San Sebastián is "a good place to get all straightened inside again," the list of books he has with him includes George Borrow's *The Bible in Spain* and "two Mrs. Belloc-Lowndes" (*Facsimile* 2:579). Marie Belloc Lowndes (1868–1947), like her brother Hilaire, was a best-selling writer, whose mystery novels such as *The Lodger* (1913) are still recommended on various lists of "Good Roman Catholic books" written by "Catholic authors." (Although inventories of Hemingway's reading and library list only one book by Hilaire Belloc, ten books by his sister are listed. See Brasch and Sigman 29, 224–25; Reynolds, *Hemingway's Reading* 98, 151.)

To return to the quai de Bourbon, then, Claudel's Catholicism, orthodox and disciplined yet also, as manifest in his writing, suffused with understated mysticism, would be more congenial than the work of a Huysmans or Belloc to a convert (and writer) like Hemingway. In any case, as Jake and Bill walk along the quai, the Claudel residence would resonate with the most famous conversion (certainly of a *writer*) at Notre-Dame; and, as they circle the island, it is the scene-culminating vision of the cathedral toward which they progress. An interesting sidelight, a Claudel-Hemingway connection that might be filed under accidents of history or under the rubric of serendipitous convergence, is this: Hemingway's home address in Paris (1924–1926) was 113, rue Notre-Dame des Champs. It seems very likely that Hemingway would have known that the young Paul Claudel lived *next door* at 111, rue Notre-Dame des Champs in the 1880s, before his conversion at Notre-Dame, before he moved to the quai de Bourbon. And Hemingway probably also knew that Camille Claudel's first atelier was next door (but one) on the other side, at 117, rue Notre-Dame des Champs.

Two doors down the quai, at number 15, lived Émile Bernard (1868–1941)—painter and writer, and friend of Cézanne, Gauguin, van Gogh, Toulouse-Lautrec, and many other painters and writers. Of particular interest to Hemingway, and to Jake and Bill, would be the fact that Bernard was one of the very few confidantes of the older Cézanne, especially in the years after 1891, when, at fifty-two, Cézanne became a devout practicing Catholic, at roughly the same time that he lived on l'île Saint-Louis (see below). Given Hemingway's well-known devotion to Cézanne's work—as he put it in 1924: "He wanted to write like Cézanne painted. . . . He felt almost holy about it" ("On Writing" 239)—it seems likely that he would know Bernard's groundbreaking work on the artist. Although the "first truly notable article about Cézanne" was published by J. K. Huysmans in 1888, when Cézanne was long neglected, the first "long text devoted to Cézanne" was published by Émile Bernard in 1891 (Rishel 27–29). Hemingway must have read some of Bernard's copious work on the artist, including *Souvenirs de Cézanne et lettres,* which was in its fourth edition by 1924. For Bernard, Cézanne is "an artist touched by the divine . . . a saint, a redeemer . . . a painter of mystical temperament" (Rishel 36–38). Bernard's understanding of what Cézanne told him about his landscapes being "incomplete," about omitted details, about transitions from one key to another, or "modulations," may have contributed to Hemingway's ideas about omission and submerged allusiveness as a writing technique, as a writerly mode of painting symbolic landscape that would be as mysteriously *charged* as Cézanne's paintings of mont Sainte-Victoire (Schmitt 91).

As Jake and Bill stroll along the quai de Bourbon, they come to rue le Regrattier, the only side street intersecting the quai between the pont Louis-Philippe and the pont Marie. Here they would no doubt notice one of the most strikingly visible sculptural monuments on the island, a decapitated statue on a pedestal on the corner of the building on the east side of rue le Regrattier, and underneath it these letters in stone: "Femme sans Teste." In Old French, since "teste" means "head," this would translate as "headless woman." Some tour guides, and some guidebooks, regard this caption as a description of the statue above it. However, island lore and early guidebooks maintain that "Femme sans Teste" was the old name of the street, which had nothing to do with the statue that was actually a depiction of Saint Nicholas, patron saint of sailors and river men. During the Revolution, statues of saints did not fare well, and this one was yet another victim of the revolutionary mob. Hemingway would no doubt have heard this bit of island lore repeatedly, and as he walked from his *transatlantic review* office just down the street, turning the corner under the statue to walk down the street of the "Femme sans Teste," sometimes visiting his literary friend Nancy Cunard at 2, rue le Regrattier, he must have considered this statue carefully (as any observant island-walker would). If Jake contemplates this statue as a convoluted pun, a sense of redoubled double entendre may come to mind, as a kind of commentary on his condition. "Sans Teste" sounds and looks to an English speaker all too much like "without testes," or testicles, and although that is not Jake's precise condition, it would suffice to remind him of how he has been unmanned, "womanized." For that matter, "teste" in the sense of "head" also fits the punning text, and if Jake knows the statue is really a man, Saint Nicholas, who seems to be described as a "headless woman," this would amount to a more precise and painful reminder of his wound. Or maybe he knows all about the statue, about its detachment from the words engraved in stone, about the Old French signification of a woman with no head, and it also reminds him of Brett. Standing at the corner of the renamed rue le Regrattier—"street of the huckster"—Jake may think, ruefully, regretfully, of the woman who peddles her wares unthinkingly, the headless huckster.

When Jake and Bill cross the rue des Deux Ponts, they are on the quai d'Anjou, where they pass in rapid succession Madame Lecomte's restaurant at number 33, and Hemingway's *transatlantic review* office at number 29, and the completion of their island-circling walk enters its final phase. At number 17 they come to the most famous mansion on the island, the Hôtel de Lauzun, dating from the 1650s. In the 1840s several French poets lived here, including Théophile Gautier and Charles Baudelaire. While tourists are regaled with tales of the Club of the Hashish Eaters and the "artificial paradise" created here by Baudelaire, Gautier, and other writers (Martineau 106), or echoes of other scandals and legends, writers such as Jake and Bill (and Hemingway) would think of Baudelaire's profoundly influential work, especially *Les Fleurs du mal*—work that is a primary forerunner of twentieth-century modernism, especially the Catholic modernism of such writers (all adult converts to Catholicism) as T. S. Eliot (Anglo-Catholic author of a seminal essay on Baudelaire and sometimes called the "American Baudelaire"), Paul Claudel, Max Jacob, and Ernest Hemingway. It would be hard to overstate the importance of Baudelaire's work for modernists: his revolutionary approach to subject matter, his innovative style, his insistence on a vision of evil (or Original Sin) that leads to the recognition of grace, his paradigms of sin and redemption that hold the promise of new, changed lives. In his relatively brief life (1821–1867) he produced nineteen volumes of poetry, criticism, and translations; and *Les Fleurs du mal* (*Flowers of Evil*, 1867) may well be the single most important and influential nineteenth-century work for the writers (French, English, and American) who came to maturity during World War I and created what has come to be known as modernism. Hemingway's library included seven volumes by Baudelaire, several different editions of *Les Fleurs du mal* (including the 1894 edition introduced by Gautier and another edition illustrated by Rodin), and the *Intimate Journals* (with introduction by T. S. Eliot).

Next door to Baudelaire's abode, at 15, quai de Anjou, was the Paris apartment of Cézanne (1888–1890). Cézanne lived on the island just before he became a devout

Catholic in 1891; at the same time he had an atelier on the rue du Val de Grâce, around the corner from Jake's apartment and on the route that Jake and Bill will follow as they head south from the island and down the pilgrimage route of the rue Saint-Jacques. Perhaps it is not at all far fetched, given Cézanne's devout Catholicism, given the mysticism and redemption that Émile Bernard (living just downriver on the island) found especially in Cézanne's later work, given Hemingway's devotion to Cézanne's work, and given such images as we have of Cézanne chanting the poetry of Baudelaire "in a strange voice like a schoolboy's or a priest's" (Rishel 490), to see Cézanne as a central exemplar in Hemingway's tightly woven historical and aesthetic and Catholic "circle," his île Saint-Louis symbolic landscape that leads to the vision of Notre-Dame.

As Jake and Bill round the upstream east end of the island, they pass the famous Hôtel Lambert, where as tour guides like to point out (on sketchy historical evidence) the Marquise du Châtelet was said to have sheltered Voltaire during one of his flights from the authorities. So perhaps the shadow of the primal ironist, the most famous eighteenth-century mocker of church and state, falls briefly across the island "circle." Now walking west or downstream on the quai de Béthune, Jake and Bill pass the remaining structures of the once magnificent estate of the Hôtel de Bretonvilliers, largely destroyed during and after the Revolution. Baudelaire also had an apartment here. As they walk toward the temporary "wooden foot-bridge" where the quai de Béthune meets the quai d'Orléans (where the pont de la Tournelle was torn down in 1921 and rebuilt in 1921–1927), Jake makes his first notation of Notre-Dame downstream. While it is true that the cathedral would be visible near the beginning of this proposed walking route when Hemingway places them on the quai d'Orléans heading around the island, the angle of vision would not be as direct, or as clear and dramatic through the trees (and if they are on the north side of the street, past the stone abutments or walls along the river) as it would be here, from the quai de Béthune. Finally, it should be noted that the clinching argument for the route here proposed is that Hemingway writes that they approached the bridge from the quai de Béthune. If, in the alternate walking routes that have been proposed, they are walking east or upstream along the quai d'Orléans to get to the bridge, Hemingway would not write that they accessed it "from the Quai de Bethune." Since the bridge is at the rue des Deux Ponts where the quai de Béthune ends (or begins) and across the street is the beginning (or end) of quai d'Orléans, they cannot be walking any other route but in a clockwise circle around the island, approaching the bridge walking west on the quai de Béthune. In any case, the magic circle of the island is completed, and they go out on the bridge, stop, and look downriver at Notre-Dame. All direction aside, all calculations of unimpeded visibility of the cathedral from the quai d'Orléans aside, it is clear that for dramatic reasons, for reasons that have to do with the profound logic of storytelling, Hemingway saves the vision of Notre-Dame for the last thing, after they have *circled* the island.

In that circle, Jake and Bill have seen and felt many things that are not mentioned that nevertheless function as shadow images, oblique signposts for the major concerns of the novel. As Hemingway often observed, what one gets from a text is a measure of the knowledge that one brings to it. The walk around l'île Saint-Louis perfectly illustrates Hemingway's iceberg axiom: "If a writer of prose knows enough about what he is writing about he may omit things that he knows and the reader, if the writer is writing truly enough, will have a feeling of those things as strongly as though the writer had stated them. The dignity of movement of an ice-berg is due to only one-eighth of it being above water" (*Death in the Afternoon* 192). Truly, many things that have not been *stated* in this island circle have been *felt* by many readers. Some years ago, one of my graduate students, an enthusiastic convert to Hemingway's vision and style and especially his trademark brand of symbolic landscape, went to Paris determined to follow exactly in Jake's footsteps. She had little trouble following most of Jake's movements around Paris, but she was mystified by the walk around l'île Saint-Louis. She sent me a postcard saying she'd been trying to follow the walk, guided by textual signals, for three days; she asked if it was possible that Hemingway "screwed up" his directional signals, if he made mistakes in his denotation of the island walk. Then, a few days later another postcard came: "Now I get it! Hemingway does not make landscape mistakes. It's all about the circle [underlined three times], time and motion, timelessness and stillness, how you make the circle and feel and know the unstated things of the iceberg inside the circle, and how you earn the vision of Notre-Dame." I knew then that she was Hemingway's ideal reader—without the benefit of my decades of historical research and *lived* local knowledge on l'île Saint-Louis, she had figured it out and in a few days had come to essentially the same conclusion that it had taken me years to articulate. But of course I had *felt* it all along, from my first reading of the novel, and that was Hemingway's intention, design, genius.

WORKS CITED

Anonymous. "Obituary." *The Princeton Alumni Weekly.* 28 May 1937: 729.

Anonymous. "The Manly Art of Self-Defense." *The Nassau Sovereign.* February 1940: n.p.

Anonymous. "Scopes Is Indicted in Tennessee for Teaching Evolution." *New York Times* 26 May 1925: 1 [front page].

Arrondo, Eusebio Goicoechea. *El Camino de Santiago.* Madrid: Editorial Everest, n.d.

Ayuntamiento de Pamplona, ed. *Pamplona Short Guide.* Pamplona, Spain: Ayuntamiento, 1998.

Baedeker, Karl. *Northern France.* Leipzig, Germany: Karl Baedeker, 1909.

———. *Paris et ses environs.* Leipzig, Germany: Karl Baedeker, 1931.

———. *Southern France.* Leipzig, Germany: Karl Baedeker, 1907.

———. *Spain and Portugal.* Leipzig, Germany: Karl Baedeker, 1913.

Baker, Carlos. *Ernest Hemingway: A Life Story.* New York: Scribner, 1969.

———. *Hemingway: The Writer as Artist.* Princeton, NJ: Princeton University Press, 1952.

Balassi, William V. "How It Probably Was: A Reconstruction of the Day-by-Day Writing of *The Sun Also Rises.*" Diss. University of New Mexico, 1985.

———. "Reading Hemingway: Glossary of *The Sun Also Rises.*" Unpublished manuscript.

———. "The Writing of the Manuscript of *The Sun Also Rises,* with a Chart of Its Session-by-Session Development." *Hemingway Review* 6.1 (1986): 65–78.

Benstock, Shari. *Women of the Left Bank: Paris, 1900–1940.* Austin: University of Texas Press, 1986.

Boreth, Craig. *The Hemingway Cookbook.* Chicago: Chicago Review Press, 1998.

Brasch, James D., and Joseph Sigman. *Hemingway's Library: A Composite Record.* New York: Garland, 1981.

Brault, Gerard J. *The Song of Roland: An Analytical Edition.* University Park: Penn State University Press, 1978.

Bruccoli, Matthew J., ed. *Conversations with Ernest Hemingway.* Jackson: University Press of Mississippi, 1986.

Burgess, Robert F. *Hemingway's Paris and Pamplona, Then, and Now: A Personal Memoir.* San Jose, CA: Writers Club Press, 2001.

Carpenter, Humphrey. *Geniuses Together: American Writers in Paris in the 1920s.* London: Unwin, 1987.

Caswell, Claude. "City of Brothelly Love: The Influence of Paris and Prostitution on Hemingway's Fiction." *French Connections.* Ed. J. Gerald Kennedy and Jackson R. Bryer. New York: St. Martin's Press, 1999. 75–100.

Charters, James, with Morill Cody. *This Must Be the Place—Hemingway's Paris.* New York: Tower, 1965.

Clarey, Christopher. "Holy Week's Rituals Draw in an Outsider." *New York Times* 26 March 2006, sec. 5: 1, 9.

Cross, F. L., ed. *The Oxford Dictionary of the Christian Church.* London: Oxford University Press, 1957.

Darwin, Bernard, ed. *The Oxford Dictionary of Quotations.* New York: Oxford University Press, 1959.

Del Burgo, Maria Antonia. *Roncesvalles.* León, Spain: Editorial Everest, 1984.

Delany, Joseph F. "Distraction." *The Catholic Encyclopedia.* Vol. 5. New York: Robert Appleton, 1909. 16 February 2006. *New Advent.* 2006. www.newadvent.org/cathen/05047b.htm.

Djos, Matts. "Alcoholism in Ernest Hemingway's *The Sun Also Rises:* A Wine and Roses Perspective on the Lost Generation." *Essays on "The Sun Also Rises."* Ed. Linda Wagner-Martin. New York: Cambridge Univeristy Press, 1987. 139–53.

Donaldson, Scott. "Humor in *The Sun Also Rises." New Essays on "The Sun Also Rises."* Ed. Linda Wagner-Martin. New York: Cambridge University Press, 1987. 19–41.

Eliot, T. S. *The Complete Poems and Plays, 1909–1950.* New York: Harcourt, 1952.

Ellmann, Richard. *James Joyce.* New York: Oxford University Press, 1965.

Fain, John Tyree, and Thomas Daniel Young, eds. *The Literary Correspondence of Donald Davidson and Allen Tate.* Athens: University of Georgia Press, 1974.

Farmer, David Hugh. *The Oxford Dictionary of Saints.* New York: Oxford University Press, 1987.

Faulkner, William. *Faulkner in the University.* Ed. Frederick L. Gwynnn and Joseph L. Blotner. New York: Vintage, 1965.

———. *Flags in the Dust.* New York: Random, 1973.

Fitch, Noel Riley. *Walks in Hemingway's Paris.* New York: St. Martin's Press, 1989.

Fitzgerald, F. Scott. *Correspondence of F. Scott Fitzgerald.* Ed. Matthew J. Bruccoli and Margaret M. Duggan. New York: Random, 1980.

———. *The Great Gatsby.* New York: Scribner, 1992.

Gajdusek, Robert E. "Hemingway and Joyce: A Study in Debt and Payment." *Hemingway in His Own Country.* Notre Dame, Ind.: University of Notre Dame Press, 2002. 9–56.

———. *Hemingway in His Own Country.* Notre Dame, Ind.: University of Notre Dame Press, 2002.

Gatewood, Willard B., Jr., ed. *Controversy in the Twenties: Fundamentalism, Modernism and Evolution.* Nashville: Vanderbilt University Press, 1969.

Hemingway, Ernest. *Across the River and into the Trees.* New York: Scribner, 1950.

———. *By-Line: Ernest Hemingway. Selected Articles and Dispatches of Four Decades.* Ed. William White. New York: Scribner, 1967.

———. *The Complete Short Stories of Ernest Hemingway: The Finca Vigia Edition.* New York: Scribner, 1987.

———. *The Dangerous Summer.* New York: Scribner, 1985.

———. *Dateline: Toronto. The Complete "Toronto Star" Dispatches, 1920–1924.* Ed. William White. New York: Scribner, 1985.

———. *Death in the Afternoon.* New York: Scribner, 1932.

———. *Ernest Hemingway: Selected Letters, 1917–1961.* Ed. Carlos Baker. New York: Scribner, 1981.

———. 1929. *A Farewell to Arms.* New York: Scribner, 1957.

———. *The Garden of Eden.* New York: Scribner, 1986.

———. *in our time.* Paris: Three Mountains Press, 1924.

———. *In Our Time.* New York: Scribner, 1925.

———. *A Moveable Feast.* New York: Scribner, 1964.

———. *The Nick Adams Stories.* New York: Scribner, 1972.

———. "Notes on Life and Letters (Or a Manuscript Found in a Bottle)." *Esquire* 3.1 (Jan. 1935): 21, 159.

———. *The Old Man and the Sea.* New York: Scribner, 1952.

———. "On Cathedrals." Unpublished manuscript. Item 630 Hemingway Collection. John F. Kennedy Library.

———. "On Writing." *The Nick Adams Stories.* New York: Scribner, 1972. 233–41.

———. 1926. *The Sun Also Rises.* New York: Scribner, 1954.

———. *The Sun Also Rises: A Facsimile Edition.* 2 vols. Ed. Matthew J. Bruccoli. Detroit: Omnigraphics, 1990.

———. *The Torrents of Spring.* New York: Scribner, 1926.

———. *Under Kilimanjaro.* Kent, OH: Kent State University Press, 2005.

Hinkle, James. "'Dear Mr. Scribner'—About the Published Text of *The Sun Also Rises.*" *Hemingway Review* 6.1 (Fall 1986): 43–64.

———. "What's Funny in *The Sun Also Rises.*" *Ernest Hemingway's "The Sun Also Rises": A Casebook.* Ed. Linda Wagner-Martin. New York: Oxford University Press, 2002. 107–23.

Houvet, Étienne. *The Tourist's Practical Guide Book.* Chartres, France: Durand, 1924.

Josephs, Allen. "*Toreo*: The Moral Axis of *The Sun Also Rises.*" *Hemingway Review* 6.1 (Fall 1986): 88–99.

Kennedy, J. Gerald. *Imagining Paris: Exile, Writing, and American Identity.* New Haven, CT: Yale University Press, 1993.

Killinger, John. *Hemingway and the Dead Gods: A Study in Existentialism.* Lexington: University of Kentucky Press, 1960.

Lamare, Pierre. *The Illustrated Guide-Books: The French and Spanish Basque Country.* Paris: Librairie Hachette, 1928.

Lewis, Robert W. *Hemingway on Love.* Austin: University of Texas Press, 1965.

Lichine, Alexis. *New Encyclopedia of Wines and Spirits.* New York: Knopf, 1977.

Lingeman, Richard. "Review of *A Godly Hero: The Life of William Jennings Bryan.*" *New York Times Book Review* 5 March 2006: 10.

Loeb, Harold. "Hemingway's Bitterness." *Connecticut Review* 1.1 (1967): 7–24.

Lynn, Kenneth S. *Hemingway.* New York: Simon and Schuster, 1987.

Madden, Daniel M. *A Religious Guide to Europe.* New York: Macmillan, 1975.

Mandel, Miriam B. *Hemingway's* Death in the Afternoon*: The Complete Annotations.* Lanham, MD: Scarecrow Press, 2002.

Martineau, Gilbert R., ed. *Les Guides Bleus: Paris.* English Series. Paris: Editions Nagel, 1950.

Metford, J. C. J. *Dictionary of Christian Lore and Legend.* London: Thames and Hudson, 1983.

Milosz, Czeslaw. *To Begin Where I Am: Selected Essays.* New York: Farrar, Straus and Giroux, 2001.

Miñon-Marquina, Matilde, ed. *The Green Guide: Spain.* Watford, UK: Michelin Travel, 2004.

Monmarché, Marcel. *Pyrénées.* Les Guides Bleus. Paris: Librairie Hachette, 1921.

More, Carey, and Julian More. *Impressions of the Seine.* New York: Rizzoli, 1991.

Morton, Brian N. *Americans in Paris.* New York: Morrow, 1986.

Muirhead, Findlay, ed. *Northern Spain with the Balearic Islands.* The Blue Guides. London: Macmillan, 1930.

———. *Southern Spain and Portugal.* The Blue Guides. London: Macmillan, 1929.

Muirhead, Findlay, and Marcel Monmarché, eds. *Paris and Its Environs.* The Blue Guides. London: Macmillan, 1927.

———. *Southern France.* The Blue Guides. London: Macmillan, 1926.

Navarro, Mireya. "Coveting Thy Neighbor's Ex." *New York Times* 4 June 2006, sec. 9: 1–2.

Oliver, Charles M. *Ernest Hemingway A to Z.* New York: Facts on File, 1999.

O'Toole, George. *The Case against Evolution.* New York: Macmillan, 1925.

Perkins, George, and Barbara Perkins, eds. *The American Tradition in Literature.* 10th ed. Vol. 2. New York: McGraw-Hill, 2002.

Putnam, Samuel. *Paris Was Our Mistress: Memoirs of a Lost and Found Generation.* Carbondale: Southern Illinois University Press, 1970.

Reynolds, Michael S. *Hemingway: An Annotated Chronology.* Detroit: Omnigraphics, 1991.

———. *Hemingway: The Paris Years.* New York: Blackwell, 1989.

————. *Hemingway's Reading 1910–1940: An Inventory.* Princeton, NJ: Princeton University Press, 1981.

————. *The Sun Also Rises: A Novel of the Twenties.* Boston: Twayne, 1988.

Rishel, Joseph J., ed. *Cézanne.* Philadelphia: Philadelphia Museum of Art, 1996.

Rodriguez-Hunter, Suzanne. *Found Meals of the Lost Generation.* Boston: Faber and Faber, 1994.

Sarason, Bertram D. *Hemingway and "The Sun" Set.* Washington, DC: Microcard, 1972.

Schmitt, Evmarie. *Cézanne in Provence.* New York: Prestel, 1995.

Slosson, Edwin E. *Great American Universities.* New York: Macmillan, 1910.

Stanton, Edward F. *Hemingway and Spain: A Pursuit.* Seattle: University of Washington Press, 1989.

Stein, Gertrude. *Paris France.* New York: Liveright, 1970.

Stewart, Donald Ogden. *By a Stroke of Luck! An Autobiography.* London: Paddington Press, 1975.

Stoneback, H. R. "Dignity of Movement: Iceberg Variations—Swimming and Diving in the 'Great Strangeness' and Sea Change of Hemingway's Heliophilia." *North Dakota Quarterly* 70.4 (2003): 63–80.

————. "'For Bryan's Sake': The 'Tribute' to the Great Commoner in Hemingway's *The Sun Also Rises.*" *Christianity and Literature* 32.2 (1983): 29–36.

————. "From the Rue Saint-Jacques to the Pass of Roland to the 'Unfinished Church on the Edge of the Cliff.'" *Hemingway Review* 6.1 (1986): 2–29.

————. "Hemingway and Faulkner on the Road to Roncevaux." *Hemingway: A Revaluation.* Ed. Donald R. Noble. Troy, NY: Whitston, 1983. 135–63.

————. "Hemingway and the Camargue: Van Gogh's Bedroom, the 'Gypsy' Pilgrimage, Saint-Louis, the Holy Marys, Mirèio, Mistral, Mithra, and Montherlant." *North Dakota Quarterly* 66 (1999): 164–95.

————. "Hemingway's Other Florida: Symbolic Landscape, *Dépaysement,* and Iceberg Variations in 'The Strange Country.'" *North Dakota Quarterly* 73.1–2 (2006): 103–19.

————. *Hemingway's Paris: Our Paris?* Germantown, NY: Lines, 1990.

————. "'Holy Cross 33–Yale 6': Sport, Ritual, and Religion in Hemingway." *Aethlon* 6.2 (1989): 11–19.

————. "In the Nominal Country of the Bogus: Hemingway's Catholicism and the Biographies." *Hemingway: Essays of Reassessment.* Ed. Frank Scafella. New York: Oxford University Press, 1991. 105–40.

————. "Hemingway on the Road to Roncevaux: The Pilgrimage Theme in *The Sun Also Rises.*" *Proceedings of the VIII Congreso de la Société Rencesvals.* Pamplona, Spain: Institucion de Principe de Viana, 1981. 481–90.

————. "'Very Cheerful and Clean and Sane and Lovely': Hemingway's 'Very

Pleasant Land of France.'" *French Connections*. Ed. Gerald Kennedy and Jackson Bryer. New York: St. Martin's Press, 1999. 33–59.

———. "'You Sure This Thing Has Trout in It?': Fishing and Fabrication, Omission, and 'Vermification' in *The Sun Also Rises*." *Hemingway Repossessed*. Ed. Kenneth Rosen. Westport, CT: Praeger, 1994. 115–28.

Street, Julian. *Where Paris Dines*. Garden City: Doubleday Doran, 1929.

Svoboda, Frederic Joseph. *Hemingway and "The Sun Also Rises": The Crafting of a Style*. Lawrence: University Press of Kansas, 1983.

———. "Who Was That Black Man? A Note on Eugene Bullard and *The Sun Also Rises*." *Hemingway Review* 17.2 (Spring 1998): 1055–10.

Synnott, Marcia Graham. *The Half-Opened Door: Discrimination and Admissions at Harvard, Yale, and Princeton, 1900–1970*. Westport, CT: Greenwood Press, 1979.

Tate, Allen. "Hard-Boiled." *Nation* 15 Dec. 1926: 642–43.

Tate, Brian, and Marcus Tate. *The Pilgrim Route to Santiago*. Oxford: Phaidon, 1987.

Tchamouroff, Steve. "A Short History of the Bal Musette." www.washingtonaccordions.org/balmusette.htm.

Thurston, Herbert. "Sign of the Cross." *The Catholic Encyclopedia*. Vol. 13. *New Advent*. 2006. 6 Feb. 2006 www.newadvent.org/cathen/13785a.htm.

Tilliette, Xavier. "L'Homme de foi." *Paul Claudel*. 28 Jan. 2006 www.paul-claudel. net/homme/foi.html.

Traber, Daniel S. "Whiteness and the Rejected Other in *The Sun Also Rises*." *Ernest Hemingway's "The Sun Also Rises": A Casebook*. Ed. Linda Wagner-Martin. New York: Oxford University Press, 2002. 167–85.

Vanderbilt, Kermit. "*The Sun Also Rises*: Time Uncertain." *Twentieth Century Literature* 15 (October 1969): 153–54.

Vickery, Roy. *The Dictionary of Plant-Lore*. New York: Oxford University Press, 1995.

Wagner-Martin, Linda. ed. *New Essays on "The Sun Also Rises."* New York: Cambridge University Press, 1987.

Waldhorn, Arthur. *A Reader's Guide to Ernest Hemingway*. New York: Noonday, 1972.

Ward, David C. "Poor Sports: Hemingway, Jake Barnes and the Sporting Life in *The Sun Also Rises*." *Aethlon* 6 (Spring 1989): 21–25.

Warren, Robert Penn. *Brother to Dragons*. New York: Random House, 1953.

———. *The Collected Poems of Robert Penn Warren*. Baton Rouge: Louisiana State University Press, 1998.

White, Michael. "Weary at 90, a Musical Warrior Skirmishes On." *New York Times* 12 August 2001, sec. 2: 1, 26.

Williams, Wirt. *The Tragic Art of Ernest Hemingway*. Baton Rouge: Louisiana State University Press, 1981.

Wynne, John J. "Prayer." *The Catholic Encyclopedia*. Vol. 12. New York: Robert Appleton, 1911. 16 February 2006. *New Advent*. 2006. www.newadvent.org/cathen/12345b.htm.

Young, Philip. *Ernest Hemingway.* New York: Rinehart, 1952.

Zaineddin, Mark, and John Gagosian. "Searching for Jack: Two Guys, One Drink, 60 Bars." *Washington Post* 18 June 2003: 18.

ADDITIONAL READINGS

Beegel, Susan F., ed. *Hemingway's Neglected Short Fiction: New Perspectives.* Ann Arbor: UMI Research Press, 1989.

Brooks, Van Wyck. *The Pilgrimage of Henry James.* New York: Dutton, 1925.

Daiker, Donald A. "The Affirmative End of *The Sun Also Rises.*" *McNeese Review* 21 (1974–75):3–21. Reprinted in *Modern American Fiction: Form and Function.* Ed. Thomas Daniel Young. Baton Rouge: Louisiana State University Press, 1989. 39–56.

Fitch, Noel Riley. *Literary Cafés of Paris.* Washington, DC: Starrhill Press, 1989.

———. *Sylvia Beach and the Lost Generation.* New York: Norton, 1983.

Gajdusek, Robert E. *Hemingway's Paris.* New York: Scribner, 1978.

Grimes, Larry E. "Hemingway's Religious Odyssey: The Oak Park Years." *Ernest Hemingway: The Oak Park Legacy.* Ed. James Nagel. Tuscaloosa: University of Alabama Press, 1996. 37–58.

———. *The Religious Design of Hemingway's Early Fiction.* Ann Arbor: UMI Research Press, 1985.

Hays, Peter L. *Ernest Hemingway.* New York: Continuum, 1990.

Huddleston, Sisley. *Paris Salons, Cafés, Studios.* New York: Blue Ribbon Books, 1928.

Hudson, W. H. *The Purple Land.* New York: E. P. Dutton, 1916.

Josephs, Allen. *For Whom the Bell Tolls: Ernest Hemingway's Undiscovered Country.* New York: Twayne, 1994.

———. *Ritual and Sacrifice in the Corrida: The Saga of Cesar Rincon.* Gainesville: University Press of Florida, 2002.

Kennedy, J. Gerald, and Jackson R. Bryer, eds. *French Connections: Hemingway and Fitzgerald Abroad.* New York: St. Martin's Press, 1999.

Loeb, Harold. *The Way It Was.* New York: Criterion, 1959.

Mellow, James R. *Hemingway: A Life Without Consequences.* Boston: Houghton Mifflin, 1992.

Meyers, Jeffrey. *Hemingway: A Biography.* New York: Harper, 1985.

Nagel, James. *Ernest Hemingway: The Oak Park Legacy.* Tuscaloosa: University of Alabama Press, 1996.

North, Michael. *Reading 1922: A Return to the Scene of the Modern.* New York: Oxford University Press, 1999.

Reynolds, Michael S. *The American Homecoming.* New York: Blackwell, 1992.

———. *The Young Hemingway.* New York: Blackwell, 1986.

Root, Waverley. *The Paris Edition, 1927–1934.* San Francisco: North Point, 1987.

Rovit, Earl, and Gerry Brenner. *Ernest Hemingway.* Boston: Twayne, 1986.

Scafella, Frank. *Hemingway: Essays of Reassessment.* New York: Oxford University Press, 1991.

Stokstad, Marilyn. *Santiago de Compostela in the Age of the Great Pilgrimages.* Norman: University of Oklahoma Press, 1978.

Stoneback, H. R. "'Et in Arcadia Ego': Deep Structure, *Paysage Moralisé,* Geomoral and Symbolic Landscape in Hemingway." *North Dakota Quarterly* 65.3 (1998): 186–203.

———. "Freedom and Motion, Place and Placelessness: On the Road in Hemingway's America." *Hemingway and the Natural World.* Ed. Robert E. Fleming. Moscow: University of Idaho Press, 1999. 203–19.

———. "Hemingway's 'Happiest Summer'—'The Wildest, Most Beautiful, Wonderful Time Ever Ever': Or, the Liberation of France and Hemingway." *North Dakota Quarterly* 64.3 (1997): 184–220.

———. "'I Should Have Kissed Him': Hemingway's Last War—Ringing the Changes." *North Dakota Quarterly* 63.3 (1996): 99–114.

———. "'Mais Je Reste Catholique': Communion, Betrayal, and Aridity in 'Wine of Wyoming.'" *Hemingway's Neglected Short Fiction.* Ed. Susan F. Beegel. Ann Arbor: UMI Research Press, 1989. 209–24.

———. "*Poireaux* and *Pétanque:* Or, Games and Crops, Sport and Harvest, Place and Memory, and Hunger and Art in Hemingway's Work." *North Dakota Quarterly* 68.2–3 (2001): 14–27.

Sylvester, Bickford. "Waste Land Parallels Unifying *In Our Time:* Hemingway's Confirmation as a Modernist Writer." *Up in Michigan: Proceedings of the First National Conference of the Hemingway Society.* Ed. Joseph J. Waldmeir and Kenneth Marek. Traverse City, MI: The Hemingway Society, 1983. 11–19.

Wagner-Martin, Linda. ed. *Ernest Hemingway's "The Sun Also Rises": A Casebook.* New York: Oxford University Press, 2002.

INDEX

Adams, Henry, 190

afición, 68, 229–30, 251–52, 266–68. *See also* passion

Alger, Horatio, 22

allusion, strategy of, 12, 15–19, 22, 29, 58, 62, 102

Americans, 105, 149–50, 204–05, 207–08, 230, 243

antiexemplars, 8, 73, 77–78, 89, 93–94, 146, 260

anti-Semitism, 8–9, 25, 171, 250

Apollinaire, Guillaume, 305

Ardennes, 18–19

Arvers, Félix, 305

Ashley, Brett: bathing imagery associated with, 95–97, 122–23; drinking and blindness, 48, 70, 100; first appearance in novel, 46–52; looks and style, 48–50, 140, 235, 245; model for, 49, 147; moral sense of, 289–92; promiscuity, 95, 97–98, 290–92, 295; relationship with Jake, 55–56, 97–98, 111–12, 285–96; renunciation of Romero, 290–92; war victim, 37, 263

Avila (Spain), 286

axiology, 279, 286. *See also* values

Ayuntamiento (Pamplona), 172

Baedeker, 14, 50, 125, 131, 151, 248, 287

Baker, Carlos, 3, 53, 137–38, 176, 191

Balassi, William, 142, 194, 297, 301

bal musette, 41–44

baptismal imagery, 18, 97, 149–50, 273, 280–85

Barnes, Jake: as aficionado, 229–30, 251–53, 266; Catholicism of, 9, 45, 63, 67, 150–51, 173–81, 223–24, 264–65; as exemplar, 66–67, 71–73, 260, 264–65; naming of, 37, 49–50, 138–39, 169, 192; as pilgrim, 37, 138–39, 150–51, 169, 256, 280; pilgrimage routes followed by, 134–39, 158–59, 161–64, 166–68, 188–96, 280; prayer and, 173–81, 264–65; proselytizing and, 257, 265, 292; reading of, 212–13, 236–37, 280–82; as reliable narrator, 11, 76–77, 196, 204, 238–39; religious observances of, 173–81, 223–24, 238–39, 241, 294–95; resolution of relationship with Brett, 111–12, 115, 223–24, 285–86, 288–96; war wound, 34–35, 37, 64–67, 73, 206–07

bars, cafés, and restaurants: Au Rendez-vous des Mariniers, 127–28; Botín, 277, 292–93; Café de la Paix, 79; Café de Versailles, 14; Café du Dôme, 58, 61, 90; Café Iruña 172, 241; Café Marina, 281; Café Suizo, 182, 259; Caves Mura, 25; Closerie des Lilas, 27, 58, 61; Dingo Bar, 77, 146–47; Foyot, 36; Glacier Napolitain, 30; Grand Cerf, 19; La Rotonde, 27, 58, 61; Lavenue, 14; Lavigne's, 36–38, 61; Le Sélect, 58, 61, 90; Madame Lecomte's, 127–28, 277, 302–03, 309; Wetzel's, 77; Zelli's, 70, 107–08, 110

Basque and Navarrese dancing and music, 250, 252, 264

Basque countryside, 160–64

Basque emigration, 186–87

bateau-mouche, 129, 299–300, 303

bathing and water imagery, 18, 95–97, 122–23, 261, 274, 280–85

Baudelaire, Charles, 309–10

Bayonne (France), 156–59, 172–73, 275–79

Beach, Sylvia, 225, 236

short stories and essays: "A Natural History of the Dead," 20; "A Way You'll Never Be," 232; "Big Two-Hearted River," 187, 237; "Black Ass at the Cross Roads," 92, 197; "Che Ti Dice la Patria," 157, 278; "Christmas on the Roof of the World," 131: "Nobel Prize Address," 144, 212, 288; "On Cathedrals" (unpublished essay), 133, 306; "On Writing," 187–88, 237, 308; "Soldier's Home," 79; "The Battler," 73; "The Last Good Country," 184; "The Porter," 155–56; "The Short Happy Life of Francis Macomber," 89, 121; "The Strange Country," 164; "The Three-Day Blow," 307; "Three Shots," 184; "Today is Friday," 92, 110, 144, 219–20, 272; "Wine of Wyoming," 30

Hendaye (France), 146, 194–95

Hergesheimer, Joseph, 87

Hinkle, James, 109, 203, 226, 245–46, 297, 302

Hobin, Georgette, 32–41, 49, 51, 60–61, 68, 294

Holy Cross, 219–20

homosexuals and lesbians, 39–40, 42–43, 45–47, 59, 207–08

hotels: Crillon, 61; Grand Hotel, 253–54, 265; Hostal Burguete, 197–200; Montoya (Quintana), 170; Palace Hotel, 290; du Panier Fleuri (Bayonne), 156–59, 275–76; La Perla, 170; Montana, 275, 288; Ritz, 90, 274

humor, 99, 219–23, 237, 245–46, 288; Jake Barnes and, 22, 39–40, 56, 98, 264, 285; Bill Gorton and, 120–22, 152, 202–08

hunting, 18–19, 25

Huysmans, 306–08

iceberg theory, 22, 37, 67, 107,144, 282, 288, 304, 311; cultural literacy and, 190–92, 196; place and, 45, 51, 133; theory of omission and, 177, 211–12; understatement and, 180

impotence, 64–66, 206–07

insistance poétique, 91

irony and pity, 202–03, 207–08

Jacob, Max, 305

James, Henry, 124, 205–06

Jesuits, 50, 221

Josephs, Allen, 243, 249–50, 258, 266

Joyce, James, 14, 99, 138, 206–07

juxtaposition, 47, 122, 159, 181, 264, 287; juxtapositional minimalism, 79, 142

Kennedy, J. Gerald, 31, 43

key scenes, 99–105, 128–39, 173–81, 187–96, 228–30, 248–51, 264–72, 288–96

Killinger, John, 174

Kipling, Rudyard, 208

Ku Klux Klan, 107, 153–54

Labourd (France), 160

ladder imagery, 184–85, 228, 232–33

Lalanda, Marcial, 268

Landes (France), 155–56

Landscape, actual and symbolic, 3, 19, 34, 43, 61–62, 114, 122–23, 158, 164, 185,187–88; Cézanne and, 187–88; l'île Saint-Louis and, 125–33, 297–311; rue Saint-Jacques and, 134–39; *The Waste Land* and, 52–55, 58–59; writing of, 237, 239, 252, 256, 274–75

La Concha, 97, 114, 280

La Nouvelle Revue française, 75–76

Leblanc, Georgette, 39–40

Lenglen, Suzanne, 89

Les Saintes-Maries-de-la-Mer (France), 42, 51, 110

Lewis, Robert W., 65, 281

Liber Sancti Jacobi, 37, 138–39, 192

L'île Saint-Louis, 120, 125–33, 297–311

little magazines, 12–14

local knowledge, 81–82, 133, 162, 167, 172, 208, 302–04

Loeb, Harold, 7–8, 14, 20, 27, 126

"lost generation" label, 4–5, 62, 81, 175, 205, 208, 305

Lourdes (France), 94–95, 97, 150–51, 153, 158

love, 20, 55–56, 104–07, 111–12, 178, 285–86, 294–96

Lowndes, Marie Belloc, 282, 307

Lynn, Kenneth, 174

MacLeish, Archibald, 220

Madrid, 103, 112, 148, 170, 182, 275–76, 286–96